AMERICAN VISTAS
1877 to the Present

American Vistas

1877 to the Present

Fifth Edition

Edited by

LEONARD DINNERSTEIN
UNIVERSITY OF ARIZONA

and

KENNETH T. JACKSON
COLUMBIA UNIVERSITY

New York   Oxford
OXFORD UNIVERSITY PRESS
1987

OXFORD UNIVERSITY PRESS

Oxford   New York   Toronto
Delhi   Bombay   Calcutta   Madras   Karachi
Petaling Jaya   Singapore   Hong Kong   Tokyo
Nairobi   Dar es Salaam   Cape Town
Melbourne   Auckland
and associated companies in
Beirut   Berlin   Ibadan   Nicosia

Copyright © 1971, 1975, 1979, 1983, 1987
by Oxford University Press, Inc.

Published by Oxford University Press, Inc.
200 Madison Avenue, New York, New York 10016

Oxford is a registered trademark of Oxford University Press

Library of Congress Cataloging-in-Publication Data
American vistas.
    Bibliography: p.
    Contents: [1] 1607-1877—[2] 1877 to the present.
    1. United States—History.   I. Dinnerstein,
Leonard.   II. Jackson, Kenneth T.
E178.6.A426   1987   973   86-8454
ISBN 0-19-504136-4 (pbk. : v. 1 : alk. paper)
ISBN 0-19-504137-2 (pbk. : v. 2 : alk. paper)

10 9 8 7 6 5 4 3 2

Printed in the United States of America
on acid-free paper

For
Myra Dinnerstein
and
Barbara Jackson

PREFACE TO THE FIFTH EDITION

It is now almost two decades since we first embarked on our project of bringing together a series of historical essays that combined interest with readability and which could be used in conjunction with a survey text or a wide variety of other books. We have been gratified by the initial reader response as well as the enthusiasm with which our subsequent editions were received. The testaments that we have read indicate that there are a large number of instructors who find the combination of traditional and off-beat essays on the American past suitable to their own teaching styles. We are particularly pleased that *American Vistas* has been used by a wide diversity of people in every region of the country as well as in Canada and overseas. It reaffirms our belief that the American past can be both enlightening and instructive to all people who are fascinated by the development of societies.

For this revision we have made a searching reexamination of the contents and have kept only those essays that we believe have been particularly successful in the past. Letters from users and comments from other colleagues and scholars clearly indicated which pieces were most suitable for college classes. We have tried to follow this collective advice whenever possible. Many of our selections were so highly praised that we felt it would be an injustice to students and teachers alike if we eliminated them. On the other hand, more recent scholarship and the changing emphasis of societal and classroom interests have resulted in new selections on the "bad guys" in the West, the building of the Brooklyn Bridge, Theodore Roosevelt and Woodrow Wilson, the Scopes trial and the continuing controversy over evolution, women and veterans after World War II, Truman and MacArthur and their differing strategies in the Korean War, reexamination of the impact caused by the end of legal segregation, and the continuing conflict in Soviet-United States relations.

As in the past, the office staff at the University of Arizona History Department facilitated the preparation of the manuscript with its usual aplomb. For this we would like to thank Dawn Polter, Nikki Matz, Dorothy Donnelly, Linda Garcia, Janey Campbell, and Marita Coburn.

Finally, both of us would be grateful for individual comments and suggestions from readers. We also hope that articles included in this edition are as useful for classes as those that were chosen for earlier editions.

L.D.
K.T.J.

June 1986

CONTENTS

I INDUSTRIAL DEMOCRACY, 1877–1920

I

Schooling the Hopi: Federal Indian Policy Writ Small, 1887–1917

DAVID WALLACE ADAMS

• Evidence of Indian existence in what is now North America dates back more than 25,000 years. When Christopher Columbus first sailed to the New World in 1492, there were perhaps two million people already resident on the continent. Europeans called them Indians because of the belief that the Americas were the outer reaches of the East Indies.

Over the course of the next five centuries, the original Americans were pushed slowly westward, where many died in battle or from strange diseases introduced by the new settlers. Ultimately, the white man decided to confine the Indians to reservations, where they could be kept out of the way until they were properly Americanized. Education was of course a favorite method of changing Indian behavioral patterns and of teaching the superiority of Western ways and European culture.

The Hopi were a particularly sedentary farming people who had special skills in pottery, basketry, and textiles. Concentrated in what is now Arizona, they lived peacefully in mesa villages even after Coronado's men visited the area in 1540. After 1820, their primary enemies were the more numerous Navaho, who in 1843 were even given control of most of the Hopi reservation. The following essay by David Wallace Adams focuses on a less violent but equally serious threat— the educational policies adopted by federal officials whose assumptions about "progress" and "savagery" placed little value on tribal traditions.

Although historians have acknowledged the important role of education in late nineteenth-century federal Indian policy, they have failed to examine this subject in much depth. To date, a study of the federal Indian boarding school system does not exist. Yet for many years the "friends of the Indian" looked to the boarding school as an essential ingredient of the government's plan to civilize the "savage." This void in the literature is striking since the boarding school—its organization, formal instruction, and day to day routine—was a major setting for the clash of Native American and white cultures. A deeper understanding of this phase of Indian policy can be gained by examining its application to a single Indian tribe—the Hopi. Several scholars have highlighted various aspects of Hopi-white relations, but none has discussed in great depth the critical role of education in this interaction. This study examines that subject, and in doing so, it integrates tribal and institutional history within the larger context of Indian-white relations.

Late nineteenth-century federal Indian policy was essentially philanthropic in its approach to the Indian question. It was rooted in a series of premises and propositions about what the Indian was and what he ought to become. The pivotal notion was that all cultures could be classified on a scale according to their degree of civilization or savagism. Philanthropists believed that throughout history, which was viewed as a progressive and evolutionary process, only a few societies in the world had reached the upper levels of this scale; the greater proportion of the world's population remained steeped in savagism. American civilization, of course, exemplified the former and Indian culture illustrated the latter.

Those responsible for the formulation of Indian policy were sure of one thing: the Indian could not continue to exist as an Indian. As the Commissioner of Indian Affairs William A. Jones stated in 1903: "As a separate entity he cannot exist encysted, as it were, in the body politic of this great nation." The Indian had to choose, then, between civilization or extinction. Philanthropists were genuinely sincere when they expressed hope that the Indian would choose to learn the ways of the white man rather than become a victim of American progress. By the 1880's the Indian Office had settled upon the means of achieving absorption into white society. The Indian's willingness to accept the gift of the common school was presumed to be his only chance for survival. As Commissioner Jones remarked in 1903: "To educate the Indian in the ways of civilized life . . . is to preserve him from extinction, not as an Indian, but as a human being." Education, then, was the means of moving the Indian along the scale of civilization and ultimately into the mainstream of American culture. Moreover, education was seen as the only way of saving the Indian from extinction, but at a considerable price—by eliminating his Indianness.

In the late 1870's, the Indian Office had found cause for renewed hope in the assimilationist potential of education. The source of this hope lay in the apparent success of Captain Richard Henry Pratt in educating Indians at Carlisle Indian Boarding School. Pratt opened Carlisle in 1879 with the philosophy: "Kill the Indian and save the man." Shortly thereafter, all who visited the institution came away with two key impressions: first, that Indians could be civilized, and second, that education was the way to accomplish it. On the surface, at least, it appeared that, if a young Indian was removed from the savage influence of the reservation and kept for several years in the civilized environment of the boarding school, he might be successfully transformed into a copper-colored white man. Following the Carlisle experiment an elaborate three-tiered system of education was developed in the far West; it was composed of the reservation day school, the reservation boarding school, and, finally the Carlisle-type non-reservation boarding school. In the 1880's the Indian Office began to turn its attention to a remote tribe living on three mesas high above the Arizona desert—the Hopi.

In 1882, Indian agent J. H. Fleming decided to visit the Hopi. With a wagon and mules he followed a very "difficult and circuitous" route and finally reached Oraibi, the largest village of the Hopi. Fleming later recorded that "such an event I am told, had never been known in the history of the town; a span of mules and wagon on the streets of Oribi [*sic*] was indeed a novelty!" Fleming was now part of a continuous stream of Indian agents in the last quarter of the century who formed impressions of this remote people. Those agents who could move beyond their own ethnocentricity—and they were few—noted that the Hopi did not seem to fit the traditional model of savagism. They were not nomadic hunters. The Hopi had achieved instead a high level of agriculture in the almost barren desert. Nor did they live in temporary shelters made of animal skins or brush, but dwelled in well-constructed, stone and plaster houses. Furthermore, they were not warriors, but as the word Hopi implied, a people of peace. Indian agent John H. Sullivan observed in 1881:

> They are a peculiar people, and to me a very interesting branch of the human family, presenting some of the best characteristics known to civilized man, occasionally giving strong proof of the fact of their fathers having once enjoyed the advantages of a high degree of intelligence, the vestiges of which have come to them through a long line of succession from son to son. Their faults as seen by us from our standpoint are the results of their system of education, which being so different from our own, we find cause to complain, and doubtless criticize with unjustifiable severity.

Most agents were not so sensitive to the richness and uniqueness of Hopi culture. In 1890, for instance, agent C. E. Vandever, while admitting that the Hopi had an "unexpected capacity for intelligent reflection," still noted that upon reaching maturity, Hopi children "invariably sink into a state of mental apathy." Leo Crane, one of the most hated of the agents and superintendents during this period, declared in his annual report for 1912 that "the average Hopi has no morals in the white man's sense of morality. They begin as children to live on a moral plane little above their livestock." Crane, who was fond of including snapshots with his reports to Washington to demonstrate "the never-improving moral problem of these people," pointed out on one occasion: "Hopi children of both sexes often go nude in the summer, and in some of the villages boys and girls of twelve and over may be discovered practically nude."

But if nudity bothered Crane's Victorian sensibilities, the cultural characteristic that most offended him was Hopi ceremonialism. "The greatest obstacle to Hopi advancement is the dance," he stated. Crane held a special distaste for one of the most traditional and sacred of Hopi ceremonies, the famous Snake Dance. He noted in 1915 that it showed no signs of "deterioration as a barbaric Indian specticle" [sic]. All agents to the Hopi agreed that while this unique people possessed some enobling characteristics, their religious practices alone condemned them to a lower rung on the ladder of civilization. As one agent noted thirty years prior to Crane's arrival: "The dark superstitions and unhallowed rites of a heathenism still infects them with its insidious poison, which, unless replaced by Christian civilization, must sap their very life blood." In a letter to the Secretary of Interior in 1890, the Commissioner of Indian Affairs Thomas J. Morgan concluded that the solution lay in education: "If their children can be kept in school . . . , they will make very satisfactory progress in the ways of civilization."

The opening of Keams Canyon Boarding School in 1887 signaled the beginning of an uninterrupted effort to educate Hopi youth in the ways of civilization. Initially government officials had every reason for optimism about Hopi responsiveness to education. A boarding school established for the Hopi in 1875 had met with some success before closing a year later. Furthermore, the Hopi agent had written to the Commissioner in 1884 that the Hopi manifested "an earnest desire" for a white education, and he claimed to have received assurances from village leaders that out of a total Hopi population of about two thousand, the government might expect 250 students. It was no surprise, then, that after the Keams Canyon School got under way, Agent James Gallaher reported the venture "a complete success."

Within two years, however, the school was experiencing major difficulties in maintaining enrollments. As a reservation boarding school, students were permitted to return to their village for extended vacation periods. The problem was that many never came back. The Hopi were having second thoughts about turning their children over to the government for education. Thus, just two years after the opening of Keams Canyon, the Commissioner of Indian Affairs received word from agency headquarters that there existed a "disinclination of parents to send children."

At this point five Hopi headmen were invited to Washington for a conference with the Commissioner of Indian Affairs. The government sought to emphasize to the Hopi its determination to enforce school attendance. The trip was also designed to impress this remote people with the wealth and power of white civilization. The journey seems to have had the desired effect. When Chief Lololomai from Oraibi spoke with Commissioner Morgan on June 27, 1890, he began:

> My people are blind. Their ears are closed. I am the only one. I am alone. They don't want to go in the white man's ways, although I am chief . . . I am thankful to see you and I want

your advice as to what to do with my people who are hard headed.

Rather than reply directly to Lololomai's question, Morgan chose to discuss the power of white civilization and the importance of education:

As you see the white people are very much greater in numbers than you are. They are increasing very fast, and are very prosperous. They live in good houses and have good clothes and plenty to eat. Two things make them prosperous, one is that they educate all their children and keep them in school year after year, and they learn about books and how to do all kinds of things. The white people educate the women too, as you see here, and then when they are educated they all work. These are the two things, we educate all our children and we all work.

After a visit to Carlisle, Pennsylvania, where the chiefs witnessed the civilizing power of education in its most developed form, they returned home to proclaim the necessity of cooperating with Washington.

Their appeal went unheeded. Most Hopi remained adamant in their refusal to send their children to the Keams Canyon school. "While the headmen were willing for the children to come," reported the agent, "they had few children of their own, and referred me to the parents, while the fathers said the mothers controlled the children, and the mothers said the children would cry, and hence they would not send them." Finally, at wits end, the Office of Indian Affairs resorted to force. In December 1890 and again in July 1891 federal troops were sent to the village of Oraibi. After this show of force, the Hopi peaceably handed over their children. By the end of 1891, the agent was able to boast of a respectable enrollment of a hundred pupils at Keams Canyon.

Hopi resistance to education did not end, however. In fact, by the turn of the century the Hopi had divided into two factions, the "friendlies" and the "hostiles." As the names imply, the former were more willing than the latter to cooperate with the government's civilization policy. In the main village of Oraibi relations between the two groups degenerated. The village split in 1906, and the hostiles were forced to leave the village. The center of Hopi opposition to government policy thereafter centered in the new hostile village of Hotevilla. Its determined leader was Yukeoma, a traditional Hopi who held an ardent dislike for white ways in general and schools in particular. The persistent refusals of the Hotevilla residents to send their children to school finally brought action in 1911. A troop of cavalry was sent out with orders to force the villagers to give up their children for a white education.

Despite the continued opposition of many Hopi to the government's education policy, a steady stream of Hopi children left the mesas to learn the white man's ways after 1890. While some were eased into the white world by attendance first at one of the village day schools established in the 1890s, many directly entered the reservation boarding school at Keams Canyon. After the turn of the century an increasing number of Hopi attended the nonreservation schools at Phoenix, Arizona, and the Sherman Institute at Riverside, California. It was in the boarding school environment, both reservation and nonreservation, that Hopi pupils received their heaviest dose of civilization.

The Hopi child who came to the boarding school directly from the village received a most abrupt introduction to white society. In the first few days, they were subjected to a process, which for lack of a better term, must be called de-Indianization. The belief was that before Indians could begin to acquire the knowledge, skills, and attitudes of the white world, they must be stripped of all outward signs of their savage heritage. This process involved a threefold attack on their personal appearance and tribal identity. They were forced to abandon traditional dress for a school uniform. For some students, of course, this was a welcome exchange, especially if the Indian clothing was inferior to school apparel in its capacity to keep them warm in winter months. Others objected strongly to the change in dress. Emory Sekaquaptewa, for instance, arrived at Keams Canyon wrapped in a fine new blanket woven for him by his grandfather. At school it was exchanged for the standard issue of blue shirt, mustard-colored pants, and heavy shoes. As for the blanket, he recalled, "I saw it later, in the possession of the wife of the superintendent." After a change of dress, the new recruit was subjected to a haircut. This process, too, many Hopi regarded as an unwelcome assault on their person. Finally, there was the need to change an Indian's name. Where possible the Indian Service preferred that an Indian name be only slightly altered or merely translated into English. Often, however, pupils received a new one altogether; some even acquired names of historical distinction. At Keams Canyon in 1889, for instance, a Ki-Ki-tu was recorded as Albert Gallatin and a Ma-ku-si as Michael Angelo.

De-Indianization was only the beginning stage of an institutional process devoted to totally transforming the subjects. The Hopi received the rudiments of an education; its goal was to teach them to speak and write the English language, provide some knowledge of United States history and constitutional government, and convey an elementary understanding of basic subjects such as science, mathematics, and geography. But if instruction in academic subjects was an important aspect of the Indian's education, it was clearly secondary to instruction in manual and vocational trades. Most male graduates of the boarding school, it was assumed, would return to their western homes and support themselves as farmers or tradesmen. Thus, the average Indian's academic education emphasized reading the local newspaper, writing a short letter, and handling numbers sufficiently well to discover whether the reservation trader was cheating.

The preference for the practical over the theoretical was also rooted in the notion that the Indian's success at agricultural pursuits was the principle measuring rod for indicating his progress toward civilization. This belief found expression in the Phoenix Indian School's weekly newspaper, the *Native American*, which had etched over its masthead the declared purpose of the school: to transform "the man with a gun" into a "man with a hoe." This slogan missed the mark in the case of the Hopi, who were well known for their peaceful nature as well as their capacity to make the desert bloom, but it did serve to emphasize the practical orientation of a boarding school education. Consequently Indian boys at Keams Canyon, Sherman, and Phoenix spent half of their academic day on the school farm or in the shop learning basic carpentry skills. Hopi girls spent an equivalent period learning the skills thought appropriate for their sex in a Victorian age—ironing, sewing, and arranging a table setting consistent with the standards of civilized dining.

The emphasis placed on manual and vocational training had a much deeper purpose than merely teaching skills. It was also a means of instilling in the Indian values and attitudes thought essential to being an "American." Specifically, the Indian had to learn the virtue of work, the principle of private property, and the spirit of acquisitiveness even to the point of selfishness. According to United States Senator Henry L. Dawes, the best solution to the general problem was to take the Indian "by the hand and set him upon his feet, and teach him to stand alone first, then to walk, then to dig, then to plant, then to hoe, then to gather, and then to *keep*." Merrill E. Gates, president of the Lake Mohonk Conference, spoke in similar terms when he told fellow philanthropists that the primary challenge before Indian educators was to awaken "wants" in the Indian child. Only then could the Indian be gotten out "of the blanket and into trousers,—and trousers with a *pocket that aches to be filled with dollars!*" This was to remain an enduring objective of Indian education for years to come, and therefore, it is not surprising that in 1907 Commissioner Francis E. Leupp stressed the same point when speaking to a group of Indian educators in Los Angeles. After noting that a group of Hopi boys from Oraibi had just arrived at Sherman Institute, he pointed to the Sherman flag monogrammed with the letters S.I. and commented that the design came "pretty near being a dollar mark." And then he added: "Sordid as it may sound, it is the dollar that makes the world go around, and we have to teach the Indians at the outset of their careers what a dollar means." This concept was for Leupp "the most important part of their education."

Leupp and other philanthropists were convinced that the Indian's survival hinged on the acceptance of this economic principle. After the Indian had been taught the ways of civilization, including the "value of things," Leupp explained, he must be left alone to "dig out his own future." He admitted that "a considerable number will go to the wall," but "those who survive will be well worth saving." It followed that the message of materialism and rugged individualism must be learned well; so well in fact that it could not be entrusted to any single area of the academic program. It must pervade all aspects of the Indian's education. The *Native American* gave poetic expression to the American ideal of success in a piece entitled "The Man Who Wins."

> The man who wins is the man who works—
> The man who toils while the next man shirks. . . .
> And the man who wins is the man who hears

The curse of the envious in his ears
But who goes his way with head held high
And passes the wrecks of the failures by—
For he is the man who wins.

Another area of Indian education that preoccupied boarding school officials was the student's religious conversion. Because philanthropists had historically perceived an essential relationship between Christianization and civilization, missionaries had always been allowed to assume a prominent role in Indian education. By the turn of the century, Catholic, Mennonite, and other missionaries had had opportunities to convert the Hopi, but with limited success. Undaunted by these failures, the Commissioner of Indian Affairs urged the various religious denominations to exert themselves to the utmost so as not to leave "an inch of pagan territory uncovered." Boarding schools were part of this "pagan territory" in that they housed young Indians, many of whom had never come in contact with Christianity. At Keams Canyon the American Baptist Home Missionary Society was invited to offer Sunday morning services as well as two hours of religious instruction during the week. At the larger nonreservation boarding schools, such as those in Phoenix and Sherman, more than one denomination was permitted to compete for the student's loyalty.

As a result, the Indian student was subjected to religious pressures that struck at the very heart of his tribal heritage. To give in to these pressures was to deny the ways of his ancestors; to reject them was to be condemned to savagery and, if the missionaries were right, to everlasting fire and brimstone. Under these pressures many Hopi, for a time at least, professed conversion to Christianity, if only to please the superintendent. Don Talayesva, a Hopi from Oraibi, rejected the Christian message during his stay at Keams Canyon, but once at Sherman he was moved publicly at one point to declare his intention to return eventually to his village and preach the Scriptures "to my people in darkness." When reflecting on this experience at Sherman, Talayesva later recalled: "At that time I was half-Christian and half-heathen and often wished that there were some magic that could change my skin into that of a white man."

Since the Indian Bureau sought a total transformation of the Indian, every aspect of school life was devoted to this end. The structure and organization of the school environment took on special significance. A careful look at the operation of these schools reveals that they were militaristic in both atmosphere and organization. Literally every aspect of the student's life was regimented and routinized, with each day beginning and closing with the sound of a bugle. Every daily activity—learning, working, sleeping, eating, and playing—was scheduled with the neat precision of a military encampment. The boarding school was not just a place where the Hopi learned the white man's religion, language, and skills; it was also a place where he virtually marched and drilled his way toward civilization. One Hopi who attended Sherman in 1914 later recalled: "When I entered school it was just like entering the school for Army or soldiering. Every morning we were rolled out of bed and the biggest part of the time we would have to line up and put guns in our hands. . . . When a man gave a command we had to stand at attention, another command grab our guns, and then march off at another command."

As this recollection suggests, the emphasis on regimentation was not mandated by the organizational difficulties involved in feeding, housing, and educating several hundred young Indians. The reasons went far deeper and had to do with what anthropologist Bernard L. Fontana has recently called the Indian's sense of "natural time" compared to the European-American's concept of "clock time." Because the notion of clock time was closely associated with such positive virtues as work, money, and progress, school officials assumed that the Indian was hopelessly bound to savagery until he internalized the mechanical and disciplined movements of clockwork and gained an appreciation for the belief that "time" was a valuable resource to be spent on civilized pursuits rather than on savage idleness. The *Sherman Bulletin* reminded its pupils that it was not enough "to do the right thing and in the right way, but it must be done at the right time as well if we would reap the rewards of our labor." Lest students miss the relationship between time and money, they were informed that "many of our most successful businessmen date their success from the time they commenced to practice the virtue of being on time." Indeed, the habit of punctuality was not an end in itself, but rather a habit that, if carried into life, became "one of the main instruments in making real success."

Still another reason for the militaristic organization of the schools was the Indian Office's conviction that the student must be taught the value of obedience. In addition to having close links with punctuality, the emphasis on obedience seems to have been rooted in the philanthropic belief that civilization—especially as it was emerging in the modern context—required the acceptance of rules, regulations, and restraints. Since most believed that the young Indian was the product of a way of life that operated on the principle of wild impulse, the lesson of obedience was seen as an essential element in his elevation. The *Sherman Bulletin,* for example, informed students that the first law of life was the word "obey."

> Obedience is the great foundation law of all life. It is the common fundamental law of all organization, in nature, in military, naval, commercial, political, and domestic circles. Obedience is the great essential to securing the purpose of life. Disobedience means disaster. The first disastrous act of disobedience brought ruin to humanity and that ruin is still going on. "The first duty of a soldier is obedience" is a truth forced upon all soldiers the moment they enter upon the military life. The same applies to school life. The moment a student is instructed to do a certain thing, no matter how small or how great, immediate action on his part is a duty and should be a pleasure. . . . What your teachers tell you to do you should do without question. Obedience means marching right on whether you feel like it or not.

The emphasis on order and regimentation also had a political motivation. A major purpose of the boarding school was to sever forever the ties that bound the Indian to his tribal government and to transfer his loyalty to the nation state. Classroom instruction in American history and government could not be counted upon alone to accomplish this objective. Given the tragic history of Indian-white relations, there were special problems connected with winning the young Indian's allegiance to the federal government. Only by actual participation in patriotic and military rituals, officials thought, could Indians be expected to internalize and then identify with national symbols, institutions, and leaders. The world of flags, uniforms, and parades was devoted to this end. The use of military spectacle, especially when combined with a holiday celebration or the visit of a public figure, was seen as a particularly effective method of forging new political loyalties. One Hopi, for instance, remembered that on Decoration Day at the Keams Canyon school the students were handed small flags and bunches of flowers and then "marched out to the graves of two soldiers who had come out here to fight the Hopi and had died." When President William McKinley visited Phoenix Indian School in May 1901, he watched the entire school population march in rank and assemble before him in perfect military fashion. According to the *Native American* account, "The movement was executed like clockwork, unmarred by a single mistake or bungle. There they stood for an instant, 700 pairs of eyes gazing sharply and intently at the 'great-father.'" And then upon the command of a bugle call, the Indians shouted in unison: "I give my head and my heart to my country; one country, one language, and one flag."

This was what education for civilization was all about: one country, one language, and one flag. This goal combined with de-Indianization, Christianization, and finally, setting the Indian on his feet so that he might "dig out his own future" outfitted in trousers with a "pocket that aches to be filled with dollars" together constituted the multiple purposes of Indian education. These objectives were formulated and universally agreed upon by philanthropic groups and governmental agencies devoted to the noble goal of preserving the red man from extinction in the face of white civilization. The price that the Indian had to pay for his continued existence is revealed in the remarks made by Indian Commissioner Morgan at another boarding school ten years before McKinley visited Phoenix. After listening to some religious songs sung by an Indian choir, Morgan remarked to the students: "As I sat here and listened with closed eyes to your singing, you were not Indians to me. You sing our songs, you speak our language. In the days that are coming there will be nothing save his color to distinguish the Indian from the white man."

To the disappointment of the Indian Office, many students, after returning to their villages, rejected much of their boarding school education and returned to the old Hopi ways. Don Talayesva is a case in point. Talayesva first attended the day school at Oraibi and then spent several years at Keams Canyon. A bright student, he recalled that after one year in boarding school he had learned many English words, could recite part of the Ten Commandments, knew how to pray to Jesus, and could eat with a knife and fork. He also learned that the earth was round, that it was improper to go naked in the presence of girls, and perhaps most important of all "that a person thinks with his head instead of his heart." Talayesva then moved on

to Sherman Institute. When he left Sherman in 1909, he considered
himself a prosperous young man, possessing among other things a
five-dollar watch and a respectable looking suitcase. After a ride on
the Santa Fe Railroad and another by horsedrawn wagon, he was back
in Hopi country again. Like every other returned student, he tried to
fit together the pieces of his life. The first night home he lay on the
roof of a Hopi pueblo, and while gazing at the clear Arizona sky, he
considered the meaning of his education:

> As I lay on my blanket I thought about my school days and all
> that I had learned. I could talk like a gentleman, read, write, and
> cipher. I could name all the states in the Union with their capi-
> tals, repeat the names of all the books in the Bible, quote a
> hundred verses of Scripture, sing more than two dozen Chris-
> tian hymns and patriotic songs, debate, shout football yells,
> swing my partners in square dances, bake bread, sew well enough
> to make a pair of trousers, and tell "dirty" Dutchman stories by
> the hour.

With the exception of the dirty Dutchman stories, the Indian Office would have been pleased with Talayesva's remembrance. About
this returned student's future intentions, however, philanthropic enthusiasm would have been substantially dampened. For after recounting all that he had learned of the white man's world, Talayesva now
"wanted to become a real Hopi again, to sing the good old Katcina
songs, and to feel free to make love without fear of sin or rawhide."

Don Talayesva became part of what the Indian Office commonly
referred to as the "problem of the returned student." The original
faith placed in the boarding school was based on the assumption that
the returned student would not only withstand the pressures to "back-
slide" into savagery, but that he would serve as a progressive example to those Indians amenable to advancement up the scale of civilization. This was the theory. In fact, however, the nonreservation boarding school system had scarcely been created when it came under heavy
criticism for failing to live up to its promise. The problem was not the
inability of the boarding school to bring about a dramatic transformation in the Indian child. Indeed, while under the watchful eye of
school officials and within the regimented atmosphere of institutional
routine, the young Indian appeared to adopt the ways of civilization
rather quickly. The change occurred after the student's return to the

reservation. Agents frequently noted the problem of the "retrograde" student or the "return to the blanket."

In a long letter to the Indian Office in 1917, Superintendent Leo Crane described how the process of relapse affected the Hopi. From the time of birth to the age of seven the Hopi child, Crane reminded officials, "learns Indian legends, attends Indian dances and ceremonies much more colorful and appealing than any later white man's entertainment." At the age of seven he attended a day school located near his village and for the next six years continued his education in the shadow of the pueblo. "Everything learned during the day has been ironed out of him by night, through ridicule and adverse criticism of that fool white teacher, who is obeyed only because behind him is a greater and stronger fool, the Agent." During this period the child was subjected to the competing world views of the white man and the Hopi. One day he "hears of Jesus," and on the next he "attends a dance to propitiate the snake gods." After several years the child was understandably "a little confused."

Later he was sent to the reservation boarding school at Keams Canyon. At this point in his education, the Hopi child was only partly won over to the cause of civilization. While he now understood "that white people have a kindly sympathy for him," and while he genuinely appreciated the clean clothes, regular food, and clean bed that came with boarding school life, once beyond the eyes of the teacher he "still plays Indian games" and "will unconsciously sing Indian chants." He was, in effect, "AN INDIAN under instruction." At the end of his term at Keams Canyon, he might even become an "INDIAN CITIZEN," a phrase Crane never defined, but in the context of his remarks seems to imply a half-civilized status; the student essentially retained his Indian identity and manner of life, while simultaneously he felt a strong sense of political loyalty to the national government and possessed a general understanding of white ways. In any event, this outcome was the best that could be hoped for. After the reservation boarding school, Crane thought the Hopi's education should end.

Crane believed the root of the returned student problem was found in the notion that the student should continue his education at the nonreservation boarding school. Crane felt the nonreservation school was an ill-conceived "white washing process," a doomed endeavor to turn the Indian into an "imitation white man." The education the

Hopi received away from the reservation was tragically irrelevant to the conditions under which the returned student. lived after graduation. Indeed, surrounded by the modern conveniences at Phoenix or Sherman, the Hopi student might reflect on the contrast with his life at home. "He remembers the thirteenth century mesa, insufficient food at home, shortage of fuel in winter, struggle for crops in summer, lack of water, hard work for everything. Perhaps he thinks he is wasting his time, knowing to what he will return." Perhaps, too, he had learned a trade he would probably never be able to practice. Had anyone ever considered, Crane mused, that he would have to apply his modern skills in a thirteenth-century pueblo "located in the heart of the desert one hundred miles from a town or a railroad?" And finally, the student was sent home with a "little pin-money and WITHOUT TOOLS."

Then came the shock of adjustment. "The hand that has been firmly thrusting between his shoulder blades for fifteen years, has suddenly been removed." At first he traveled to the agency seeking employment and an opportunity to apply his newly acquired skills, but in all likelihood this was an impossibility. He was in the ludicrous position of being a blacksmith where there were no forges, a carpenter where lumber was scarce, a tailor where flour-sacks were used for clothes, a shoemaker where moccasins were worn, and a painter where there was nothing to paint. The inevitable process of relapse soon began: "First, the money goes; then the good clothes and the 'Regal' shoes wear out; third, nature is busy on his hair. He binds up his hair with a gaudy handkerchief, as do the others; he begins to make a pair of moccasins." In the meantime, tribal elders, "in strict patriarchal fashion," remind him of the small corn field, a few horses, and some sheep that they have set aside for him. "Gradually he accepts that which he has. He ceases his visits to the Agency asking for a job. The old life is before him. He has, apparently, become an Indian of the Indians."

Despite this depressing scenario, Crane was unwilling to state that the returned student had gone back to the blanket. The educated Hopi was in fact decidedly different from those Hopi who had never been schooled in the white man's ways. While the returned student might soon appear at the agency a trifle unkempt, "he does speak English when not fearful that some stranger will laugh at his grammar, and he has not come as a beggar." Moreover, if he was shown the advantage of a modern convenience or utility, he was more likely to desire it than the Hopi who had never been to school. And perhaps most importantly: "It will be easier to obtain his children for their education, and the hold of the medicine man has been somewhat loosened." Crane felt these were not unimportant consequences of the Hopi's education. He believed the returned student was a failure only to the extent that he was *not what the tax-payer expected him to be.*" Again, Crane remained critical of the nonreservation school. If the Hopi was destined to live a simple life in the vast Arizona desert, then he asked: "Why insert this artificial period in his education?"

Criticism of the nonreservation school caused school officials to search for ways to prepare their graduating students for reservation life. A psychological tactic often used by schools was the "returned student conference." Such conferences not only enabled recent graduates to renew their institutional association with the source of their cultural elevation and to hear again the inspiring message of civilization, it also offered an opportunity to impress upon graduating students just how immense the pressures for conformity were back on the reservation. In 1910, for instance, one school official at Phoenix told members of a conference:

> I most sincerely trust that you who are leaving the school for your homes this year do not underestimate the influence your homes will have to draw you away from what you have learned at this school. . . . I know you feel so well grounded . . . in your hope of doing good . . . on your reservations that you do not realize what you will have to overcome. Remember you are but one against many and among that many . . . are relatives and friends even dearer than any friendships formed in this school. Remember too, they believe themselves just as much in the right in their beliefs as you do in yours. . . . Your lessons of industry, civilization and Christianity have been taught to you but very few years compared with the many years during which customs have been growing in your people.

There was a fatal flaw in how school officials attacked the problem of relapse, and it goes to the very heart of this chapter in Indian-white relations. They assumed that the difficulty was due to the conservative nature of tribal elders and a certain character flaw of the returning students, their inability to withstand ridicule and hardship for the sake of civilized principles. They ignored altogether the charge of superintendent Crane that the nonreservation boarding school was itself to blame because it prepared the Indian student for a life that did not exist on the reservation. They ignored too the possibility that many returning students readopted the old culture out of conscious preference for the Hopi way. Neither the Indian office in Washington nor school officials in the field ever considered the possibility that the real source of the returned student problem lay in the questionable premises that had historically shaped the nation's Indian policy—premises relating to such ethnocentric conceptions as "savagism," "civilization," and "progress." It is not surprising that this last explanation was never considered. To have done so would have required a painful reexamination of the entire rationale by which white Americans had justified the dispossession of the Indian's land and culture. Given all that was at stake, it was simply too much to ask.

2

The Outlaws: The Legend of Jesse James and His Gang

ALBERT CASTEL

• Long before Frederick Jackson Turner gave his famous 1893 address on "The Significance of the Frontier in American History," the idea of the West was important to Americans. In a vast, almost unexplored and unknown land, the men and women who first faced the wilderness and the savages were obvious candidates for hero-worship. Oral legends circulated about a Tennessee backwoodsman named Davy Crockett even before he was dead; when he fell at the Alamo in 1836, his place in folklore was assured. Kit Carson, Wild Bill Hickok, and Buffalo Bill were among other superhuman heroes who shaped a national ideology of self-reliance, energy, and optimism.

Of course the image of the West did not conform to reality; the average frontiersman did not kill wild animals with his bare hands, and the streets of Dodge City did not regularly run with the blood of high noon shootouts. Contrary to the popular Hollywood stereotype, the Plains Indians were not incompetent strategists who rode around in circles until white marksmen could shoot them off their mounts. And at no time in the nineteenth century did the West account for as much as 10 percent of the national population.

Yet the images and the legends live on. The Western outlaw is a popular candidate for mythology, not only because he operated outside the existing legal system, but because he seemed to personify a restless national spirit. The image of the gunfighter is often that of a good and decent man driven to a life of violence and early death by evil and unfortunate circumstances. So it was with Jesse and Frank James and the Younger brothers. They were America's most famous des-

Reproduced through the courtesy of Historical Times, Inc., publisher of *American History Illustrated*.

perados, and there was a high price on their heads. The complexity of their experience is expertly captured by the following essay of Albert Castel.

On August 7, 1863 the Liberty, Missouri *Tribune*, a pro-Union newspaper, carried the following item:

> THREE SOUTHERN GENTLEMEN IN SEARCH OF THEIR RIGHTS—
> On the morning of the 6th of August, Franklin James, with two
> others of the same stripe, stopped David Mitchell, on his road to
> Leavenworth, about 6 miles west of Liberty, and took from him
> $1.25, his pocket knife, and a pass he had from the Provost
> Marshal to cross the plains. This is one of the rights these men
> are fighting for. James sent his compliments to Major Green,
> and said he would like to see him.

Such was the first recorded robbery committed by Frank James.
During the next two decades he, his brother Jesse, and their sidekicks,
the Younger brothers, became America's most famous outlaws. Today,
a century after Jesse's murder and Frank's surrender in 1882, they still
possess that distinction. Here is the story of their rise to fame, along
with the sometimes brutal facts behind it; facts which have been concealed by legend like a bandit's face by a mask.

Alexander Franklin James and Jesse Woodson James were born, respectively, on January 10, 1843, and September 5, 1847, on a farm
near Kearney, Missouri, a town twelve miles northeast of the Clay
County seat at Liberty and twenty-seven miles from downtown Kansas
City to the southwest. Their father, Robert James, was an ordained
minister; their mother, Zerelda Cole, attended school at a Catholic
convent. In 1842, shortly after being married, Robert and Zerelda left
their native Kentucky to settle in Clay County, where Robert became
pastor of a Baptist church, acquired a farm and slaves, and helped
found William Jewell College at Liberty. Thus the family background
of Frank and Jesse seems to have been quite solid and respectable.

But it did not remain so for long. In 1850 Robert joined the rush
to California in quest of gold; instead he found illness and death.
Zerelda remarried twice: first, Benjamin Simms, who soon left her and
then died; next, in 1859, Doctor Reuben Samuel, a quiet, acquiescent
man who devoted himself to working the James' farm. Zerelda bore

him four children, two boys and two girls. How young Frank and Jesse reacted to their father's departure and death, their mother's remarriages, and the influx of half brothers and sisters is unknown, as is any authentic information about their boyhoods.

In the summer of 1861 the Civil War came to Missouri. Most of the population remained loyal to the Union. However, in the hemp-growing and slaveholding counties of western Missouri many people supported the Confederacy. Among them was the James-Samuel family. Frank, now a lanky, callow-looking youth of eighteen, joined the pro-Confederate Missouri forces of Major General Sterling Price and took part in the battle of Wilson's Creek (August 10, 1861) and the siege of Lexington, Missouri (September 12–20, 1861). But when Price retreated into Arkansas early in 1862 Frank, as did many other discouraged Missouri Rebels, deserted and returned home. There he took an oath of allegiance to the United States and posted $1,000 bond for future good behavior.

Meanwhile guerrilla war had broken out in Missouri. Bands of Kansas jayhawkers ravaged the western border, and Unionist militia persecuted and plundered Confederate sympathizers. In defense and retaliation the latter formed gangs of "bushwhackers" who raided into Kansas and terrorized Unionists in Missouri. The most successful and notorious of these gangs was that of William Clarke Quantrill, an Ohio-born renegade. One of Quantrill's followerers was tall, muscular Thomas Coleman Younger. Cole joined Quantrill in January 1862, at the age of eighteen, after jayhawkers burned his father's livery stable at Harrisonville and threatened to kill him. Subsequently they did murder his father, imprisoned his sister, and drove his mother out of the family home, which they burned. Contrary to the assumption of some writers, he in no way was related to the Jameses.

By July 1862 bushwhacking was so rampant that the governor of Missouri ordered every man of military age to enroll in the state militia. Since this had the effect of forcing pro-Confederates to side with enemies against friends, many of them promptly "took to the brush." Among them was Frank James. In time he became a member of a Clay County guerrilla band headed by William "Bloody Bill" Anderson, a ferocious killer who decorated the bridle of his horse with the scalps of Federal soldiers.

On August 21, 1863, Anderson and his gang, Frank included, joined Quantrill in a raid on Lawrence, Kansas, where they helped massacre upwards of 160 helpless men and boys. Six weeks later, on October 6, 1863, they participated in the slaughter of nearly one hundred Union soldiers at Baxter Springs, Kansas. During the winter of 1863–64 the bushwhackers camped near Sherman, Texas, where they robbed and occasionally murdered civilians. Many of them by then were crossing the line, always narrow, between guerrilla war and sheer banditry.

In the spring of 1864 Anderson's band returned to its "stomping grounds" in Missouri. Soon afterward Jesse, now seventeen, joined the group. More than likely he would have done so in any case, but during the past summer Union militia had tortured Dr. Samuel, abused the pregnant Mrs. Samuel, and administered a whipping to Jesse, thereby removing any hesitation he might have felt. Under Anderson, and riding behind Frank, he took part in numerous raids, robberies, ambushes, fights, and massacres. The most gruesome of the latter occurred on September 27, 1864, at Centralia. First Anderson's men stopped a train, robbed all of its passengers, and then murdered nearly thirty of them, mostly unarmed Federal soldiers home on leave. Next they attacked and overwhelmed 147 militiamen, slaughtering 124 of them and mutilating their corpses. If the testimony of Frank is to be credited (a risky thing to do), Jesse distinguished himself in this "battle" by shooting the militia commander, Major A. V. E. Johnston.

A month later Anderson was killed in a fight outside of Richmond, Missouri, by militiamen who subsequently cut off his head and mounted it on a telegraph pole. At the same time the Federals routed Price's army, which had invaded Missouri in a last desperate attempt to secure it for the Confederacy. Most of the bushwhackers, including Jesse, followed Price into Texas, where they spent the winter. However, Frank joined a number of guerrillas who went with Quantrill to Kentucky. There, on July 26, 1865, after the capture and death of Quantrill, Frank and the other survivors of this ill-starred expedition surrendered to the Federal authorities, who released them as soon as they took the oath of allegiance.

Meanwhile, in Missouri most of the remaining Quantrill-Anderson men did likewise upon returning from Texas in the spring and finding that with the collapse of the Confederacy it was pointless to continue their war-within-a-war. Jesse, however, was not one of them. According to his family and friends, he was on the way to Lexington, Missouri, to sign parole papers when a squad of Union soldiers shot and badly wounded him. Possibly this is true; certainly Jesse spent the summer and fall of 1865 at his mother's home recuperating from a wound. In any event he never surrendered.

As was to be expected, Missouri Unionists viewed the ex-guerrillas with resentment and subjected them to varying degrees of harassment, in a few instances driving the more notorious ones from their homes. Even so, the majority of the bushwhackers who wanted to settle down and lead a peaceful, law-abiding life were able to do so. The trouble was that some of them did not want to, or at least did not try very hard. This was especially true of those whose criminal tendencies had been developed and confirmed by bushwhacking. Finding a humdrum, poverty-tinged existence on a farm tedious after the exciting life and easy money of wartime, they could not resist the temptation to make use of the skills acquired under Quantrill and Anderson.

On the afternoon of February 13, 1866, a dozen former bushwhackers looted the Clay County Savings Bank in Liberty of nearly $60,000, in the process murdering a student from William Jewell, the college Frank's and Jesse's father helped establish. It was the first daylight bank robbery in American history, not counting the plundering of two banks in St. Albans, Vermont, in 1864 by Confederate raiders operating out of Canada. It also marked the beginning of a series of bank holdups by gangs of ex-guerrillas: Lexington, Missouri, October 30, 1866; Savannah, Missouri, March 2, 1867; Richmond, Missouri, May 22, 1867; and Russellville, Kentucky, March 20, 1868.

Probably Frank and Jesse participated in at least some of these robberies, although at the time they occurred neither the authorities nor the newspapers accused them of involvement. But then, on December 7, 1869, in Gallatin, Missouri, two men entered the Daviess County Savings Bank, where one of them cold-bloodedly shot the cashier, a former Union militia officer, through the head and heart. As they left the bank carrying several hundred dollars, townsmen opened fire. The bandit who murdered the cashier was unable to mount his excited horse, whereupon he jumped up behind his companion and together they galloped out of the town. Several citizens identified the abandoned horse as a mare belonging to Jesse. A posse pursued the bandits to the James-Samuel farm, only to see Frank and Jesse dash out of a barn on fresh horses and escape.

The James brothers denied responsibility for the Gallatin murder and robbery and even obtained affidavits (of dubious worth) from people in Clay County swearing to their innocence. However, they refused to submit to arrest and stand trial, claiming—with good cause—that they would be lynched like several other former bushwhackers suspected of crimes. Hence they became, if they were not already, professional outlaws.

Little that is reliable is known about the beginning of Cole Younger's bandit career. If we are to believe his own story, which is filled with distortions and exaggerations, following the end of the war he settled down on a farm near Lee's Summit, Missouri (now a Kansas City suburb) and tried to lead a lawful, peaceful life. But vindictive Unionists forced him to go into hiding in order to avoid arrest for an alleged wartime murder; then they falsely blamed him and his brother Jim, also an ex-Quantrillian, for every crime committed in the area. Finally, out of sheer desperation, they decided to live up to their reputations and so teamed up with the Jameses.

Between 1870 and 1876 the James-Younger gang ranged from Kansas to Kentucky and from Iowa to Texas robbing banks, holding up stages, and sticking up trains. The latter especially excited the public imagination, being both novel and dramatic. Although the Reno brothers of Indiana were the first bandits to engage in train robberies, those committed by the Jameses and Youngers received far greater publicity. Furthermore, they did not necessarily get the idea from the Renos; as already noted, Frank and Jesse were with Bloody Bill Anderson when his band waylaid a train at Centralia in 1864.

Soon the "James boys" and "Younger brothers" were household names over America. Newspapers headlined their exploits, often attributing to them deeds they could not possibly have performed unless they had a supernatural knack for being in two widely separated places simultaneously. The *Police Gazette* and similar magazines published vivid accounts, accompanied by garish drawings, of their supposed doings. And hack writers made them the protagonists of highly imaginative stories published in crudely illustrated dime novels which were sold at depots and aboard trains, among them the very trains they robbed!

Sheriffs and police officers throughout the West tried to track down the famed outlaws, as did the Pinkerton Detective Agency. Their efforts were invariably and sometimes absurdly futile. Besides their own bumbling ineptitude, they were handicapped by the fact that thousands of pro-Southern Missourians believed that the Jameses and Youngers were innocent victims of Unionist-Republican persecution and hence were more than willing to help them. Foremost among this element was newspaper editor John N. Edwards, a former Confederate major and the close friend of Frank and Jesse. Not only did he defend them, he glorified them with purple prose in his various writings. Thus, following their robbery of the gate receipts at the Kansas City Fair on September 26, 1872, during which they accidentally shot a little girl in the leg, he published an editorial in the Kansas City *Times* entitled "The Chivalry of Crime" in which he compared them to the Knights of the Round Table.

Missouri sympathy for the bandits peaked early in 1875. On the night of January 26 a group of Pinkerton detectives, three of whose colleagues had been gunned down by the Jameses and Youngers in recent encounters, sneaked up to the James-Samuel home and tossed what they later claimed was a flare lamp through a window. The Samuels shoved the flaming device into the fireplace where it exploded, killing nine-year-old Archie Samuel and mangling Mrs. Samuel's right arm so badly that it had to be amputated below the elbow. Neither Frank nor Jesse was captured, although evidently at least one of them was present.

This tragic event aroused indignation throughout Missouri and led to the introduction of a bill in the legislature which provided for the pardoning of all ex-bushwhackers for their wartime deeds and promised them a fair trial for all alleged postwar crimes. But before the legislature could act Frank and Jesse murdered—or so it was thought— a neighbor whom they suspected of aiding the Pinkertons. As a result the trend of public sentiment turned against them and the bill failed.

So far all of the robberies perpetrated by the Jameses and Youngers had taken place in regions they were familiar with and where friends or relatives could aid escape. Then, late in the summer of 1876, following a July 7 train stickup at Rocky Cut near Otterville, Missouri, a member of the gang known as Bill Chadwell (real name William Stils) persuaded the others that his home state of Minnesota offered rich and easy pickings. As a consequence, on the morning of September 7 eight men, all dressed in long, linen dusters, rode into Northfield, Minnesota. They were Frank and Jesse James, Cole, Bob and Jim Younger, Chadwell, and two ruffians called Clell Miller and Charlie Pitts.

Three of the men dismounted and entered the First National Bank. They ordered cashier Joseph Heywood to open the vault. He refused. One of the bandits, probably either Jesse or Frank, shot him. The teller, A. E. Bunker, ran out the back door, undeterred by a bullet in the shoulder. Meanwhile several townsmen, having perceived that a robbery was in progress, opened fire with rifles and shotguns on the mounted men outside the bank. Two of them—Chadwell and Miller—tumbled dead from their horses. Bullets from the robbers' revolvers in turn killed the sheriff and a Swedish immigrant who understood neither English nor what was happening. The outlaws inside the bank rushed out, remounted, and along with the others galloped away under a hail of bullets. Bob Younger's horse went down; Bob, whose right elbow had been shattered by a rifle bullet, was picked up by a companion, most likely Cole, then continued his flight.

As hundreds of grim-faced possemen scoured western Minnesota, the unsuccessful raiders sought to make their way back to Missouri. But they were slowed down by their ignorance of the countryside, heavy rains, and above all by the badly wounded Bob Younger. According to some accounts, Frank and Jesse proposed abandoning, even killing him. Cole, however, refused to allow it. Eventually the Jameses went off alone and reached home safely.

The Youngers and Pitts were less lucky. On September 21 near Madelia, Minnesota, a posse cornered them in a swamp. A short, one-sided gun battle ensued. Pitts was killed and the Youngers, literally riddled with bullets, surrendered. After recovering sufficiently they stood trial for murder and attempted robbery. They pleaded guilty and were sentenced to life imprisonment in the Minnesota State Penitentiary at Stillwater.

For three years following the Northfield fiasco Frank and Jesse lay low. Contrary to the billboards of certain present-day tourist traps, neither then nor at any other time did they hide out in caves. Instead they lived under assumed names with their wives and children in places like

Nashville, St. Louis, and even Kansas City. As Frank once remarked, "Most people look alike in the city." Given the primitive identification devices and the haphazard police communications of the era, it was not necessary for them to adopt disguises or take elaborate precautions. In fact, law enforcement agencies lacked both photographs and detailed descriptions. All they knew was that they were tall, lanky, and bearded, which was not much to go on.

Then, in spectacular style, the James boys—or at least Jesse—came out of retirement. First, on October 8, 1879, a gang led by Jesse ransacked a safe aboard a train at Glendale, Missouri. Next, on July 15, 1881, they held up a Rock Island train near Winston, Missouri, murdering the conductor and a passenger. And on the night of September 7, 1881 (fifth anniversary of the Northfield raid), the gang robbed both the safe and the passengers on a Chicago & Alton train at Blue Cut, east of Independence. The engineer of the latter stated that the leader of the bandits, before riding off, shook hands with him and said, "You are a brave man . . . here is $2 for you to drink the health of Jesse James with tomorrow morning." In addition, a Jackson County farmer who had been arrested for participating in the Glendale affair testified in court that Jesse had recruited him and provided him with a revolver and shotgun. As a result, only fanatics like Edwards continued to call Frank and Jesse guiltless victims of persecution.

Thomas T. Crittenden, the newly installed Democratic governor of Missouri, decided to put an end to the Jameses once and for all. They had caused Missouri to become known as the "outlaw state," they were bad for business, and they were furnishing political ammunition to the Republicans, who accused the Democrats of not really trying to apprehend them. Accordingly he announced a reward of $10,000 (to be paid by the railroad companies) for information leading to the capture, dead or alive, of either Frank or Jesse.

Crittenden's offer produced results. Among the new members of the James gang were two more brothers—Charles and Robert Ford. On December 4, 1881, Bob Ford and a veteran bandit named Dick Liddil killed Wood Hite, also an outlaw and Frank and Jesse's cousin, in a quarrel over a woman. Fearful that Jesse would slay him in revenge, Liddil arranged to surrender to Sheriff James A. Timberlake of Clay County after first obtaining assurances of leniency from Crittenden if he helped apprehend Jesse. On learning of this, Bob Ford realized that

Jesse surely would suspect him as a friend of Liddel. Hence he too contacted Timberlake and Crittenden, with the result that he and his brother agreed to tip off Timberlake as to the time and place of the gang's next operation. For his part Crittenden promised the Fords immunity from punishment and a share of the reward money.

Late in March 1882, the Fords went to the house in St. Joseph, Missouri, where Jesse, under the alias of Thomas Howard, had been living with his wife and two children since November. Together with Jesse they planned to rob the bank in nearby Platte City on April 4. However, on the morning of April 3, while eating breakfast with the Fords, Jesse read in the Kansas City *Times* that Liddil had surrendered to the authorities. Immediately Bob Ford sensed that Jesse now knew the Fords intended to betray him. So when Jesse removed his pistol belt—something he had never done before—and stood on a chair to dust a picture on the wall, Bob Ford thought two things: first, that Jesse was seeking to throw him off guard by pretending to have complete confidence in him; second, that "Now or never is your chance. If you don't get him now he'll get you tonight." So Bob pulled out the revolver that Jesse had given him the day before and fired. The bullet tore through the back of Jesse's skull behind the right ear and, in Bob Ford's own words, "he fell like a log, dead."

Brought to trial in St. Joseph on a charge of murder, Charles and Bob Ford pleaded guilty, were sentenced to death, and were promptly pardoned by Crittenden. Ten years later, in Creede, Colorado, Bob Ford himself fell victim to a murderer's pistol, having achieved the gloomy notoriety of being "that dirty little coward that shot Mr. Howard." Charles Ford committed suicide in 1896.

By 1882 Frank James was thirty-nine and at least semi-retired from banditry. The murder of Jesse convinced him that if he was going to reach forty, he had better make peace with the law. Therefore, with Edwards serving as his intermediary, he surrendered to Crittenden at Jefferson City on October 5, 1882. Twice, once at Gallatin, Missouri, and again at Muscle Shoals, Alabama, he stood trial for his alleged crimes, and each time a sympathetic jury acquitted him for lack of convincing evidence. It never was proved in a strictly legal sense that the James boys ever committed so much as a single robbery!

During the years that followed his second acquittal, Frank eked out a shabby existence as a shoe store clerk, theater guard in St. Louis, and horse-race starter at county fairs. Meanwhile a group of Missourians sought pardons for the Younger brothers, who in hopes of parole were model prisoners. In 1901 the governor of Minnesota granted conditional paroles to Cole and Jim—Bob had died of tuberculosis in 1889—but required them to remain in the state. Soon after his release Jim, despondent because the parole board refused him permission to marry, committed suicide in a St. Paul hotel room. In 1903 the Minnesota authorities gave Cole a complete pardon, and he returned to his old home at Lee's Summit. He now was a fat, bald, old man. Only his hard, cold eyes bespoke the tough young bushwhacker and bandit of yore.

For a while Frank and Cole traded on their notoriety by touring with the "Cole Younger—Frank James Wild West Show." Then they separated, with Frank spending most of his time at the old James-Samuel farm, where he charged visitors fifty cents apiece for a tour. On February 18, 1915, he died. As for Cole, he gave lectures on "What Life Has Taught Me," published an autobiography in which he claimed that the only robbery he ever took part in was at Northfield, and was the center of attention at the annual reunions of the survivors of Quantrill's band. One year after Frank's death, he too went to his reward.

Thus Frank and Cole ended their long careers as living legends—legends somewhat tarnished, however, by the very fact that they were living and had to make a living. Jesse on the other hand achieved the perfect legend. Even before he died he was more famous than Frank, in part because of the alliterative quality of his name, in part because he had a stronger personality and was more active, at least in the later years. His death and the manner of it wiped away, in the popular mind, the harsh reality of his deeds and transformed him into the classic bandit-hero whose daring and cunning render him invincible until he is brought down by base treachery. In this sense Bob Ford did Jesse a favor: It would not have been the same if he had died in bed, like Cole and brother Frank, from old age.

3

The "Black Codes"

JERRELL H. SHOFNER

• *The surrender terms offered by General Ulysses S. Grant to Robert E. Lee's proud but dwindling Army of Northern Virginia were among the most generous in history, especially in view of the suffering, anguish, and emotion which accompanied the Civil War.* At Appomatox Court House, the commander of the Union Army was both magnanimous and sensitive. All that was required was that Confederate soldiers put down their arms and go home in peace.

But the battlefield result did not immediately make clear what the political future would be for those Southern whites who had led their states out of the Union. According to tradition, and to a considerable segment of Northern sentiment, such men were traitors to the United States. Southern voters understandably took a different view and promptly returned many leaders of the secessionist movement to Washington as members of Congress. Simultaneously, other firebrands of the old Confederacy gained dominance over the various state legislatures and promptly began to limit the social, political, and economic rights of the former slaves.

The result was a series of racist and repressive laws known to history as the "black codes." They were intended both to guarantee the subservience of the entire black population and to assure the continued division of Southern society along strict racial lines. Although they varied from state to state in severity, the black codes generally prevented Negroes from bearing arms or from working at occupations other than farming and domestic service.

As Jerrell H. Shofner makes clear in the following article, these initial inhibitions proved to be only the first set of a long series of measures designed to preserve the "Southern

From *Florida Historical Quarterly*, January 1977.

*way of life." The black codes were followed by the "Jim
Crow" laws between 1890 and 1910. These new restrictions,
which legalized segregation in public facilities and which introduced such concepts as the literacy test, the "grandfather
clause," the white primary, and the poll tax, made it almost
impossible for blacks to rise above the lowest rung of the economic ladder, or indeed even to protest effectively. Thus a
rigidly enforced segregation system came to dominate all aspects of Southern life. Even after two decades of militant civil
rights activity, this legacy has just begun to be erased.*

In October 1956, Dr. Deborah Coggins, health officer for Madison,
Jefferson, and Taylor counties, sat down to lunch in Madison, Florida,
with a public health nurse to discuss a matter of mutual official concern. Because of their busy schedules the lunch hour was the only
mutually available time for the meeting. But since the doctor was white
and the nurse black, the business luncheon led to the dismissal of the
doctor by indignant commissioners of the three counties. Her "breach
of social tradition" had been so serious, according to the commissioners,
that it rendered her unfit to continue in the office to which she had
been appointed about six months earlier. While Governor LeRoy
Collins disagreed, and incensed citizens of South Florida condemned
the commissioners, most white North Floridians nodded approval. As
they saw it, Dr. Coggins had violated one of the strictest taboos of her
community when "she ate with the darkies." As a native of Tampa
married to a descendant of an old Madison County family, she should
have known better.

Social intercourse between whites and blacks was forbidden by both
law and custom in Florida in the 1950s. And it had been that way as
long as most people then living could remember. The one brief period
following the Civil War when things had been different had merely
proved that segregation was the best way for all concerned. This belief
was reinforced by all the myths and folk tales, social institutions, and
statute laws with which Floridians of the 1950s were acquainted.

Those few years following the Civil War had been crucial ones for
white Floridians, most of whom had sympathized with and supported
the Confederate war effort. Defeated, disorganized, and bankrupt in

1865, they had taken heart when President Andrew Johnson announced his plans for reconstructing the nation. Guaranteeing former Confederates retention of all their property except slaves, he appointed William Marvin as provisional governor to oversee the formation of a new government. To gain readmission to the Union, Florida had only to repudiate slavery, secession, and debts incurred in support of the Confederacy, and recognize all laws enacted by Congress while the state was out of the Union. Marvin repeatedly told white audiences that if they would change the laws to provide civil rights to the newly freed blacks that he believed they would not be required to implement Negro suffrage. Retrospectively this implied promise seems to have been an unfortunate one. Radical congressmen had been contending with Abraham Lincoln and later Andrew Johnson for control of Reconstruction policy. What white Floridians regarded as major concessions to former slaves was far less than Radical congressmen believed necessary. The latter watched with growing concern as the southern state governments created by President Johnson enacted their "black codes" which distinguished between black and white citizens. And the final decision on Johnson's Reconstruction program rested with Congress.

The delegates to the 1865 constitutional convention and the members of the 1865–1866 legislature who enacted the Florida black code had spent their lives as members of the dominant white class in a society whose labor system was based on racial chattel slavery. They brought to their law-making sessions all their past experiences gained from a lifetime acquaintance with a comprehensive ideological and legal framework for racial slavery. They believed that blacks were so mentally inferior and incompetent to order their own affairs that subjection to the superior white race was their natural condition. Whites benefited from the labor of blacks, and they were in turn obligated to provide guidance and welfare for their workers. Now that slavery was abolished these men met to comply with Andrew Johnson's requirements, while, at the same time, trying to salvage as much as possible of that system under which whites with their paternalistic responsibilities to blacks, and Negroes with their natural limitations, had lived peacefully.

Florida had a comprehensive slave code regulating almost every activity touching the lives of blacks. Because "free Negroes" had constituted an anomaly in a society where racial slavery was so central, there was also an extensive set of laws regulating their affairs. It was understandable that the lawmakers of 1865–1866 should draw on their past experiences and on the codes regulating slaves and free blacks. But in doing so they invited criticism from suspicious Radicals in Congress who believed that the president had erred in his lenient requirements.

A three-member committee was named by the constitutional convention of 1865 to recommend to the first legislature, scheduled to meet the following year, changes in the old laws necessary to make them conform to the postwar situation. The committee's report did nothing to assuage congressional suspicions. It urged the legislature to preserve, insofar as possible, the beneficial features of that "benign, but much abused and greatly misunderstood institution of slavery." It strenuously asserted the legislature's power to discriminate. Such power had always been executed by all the states of the Union, including those of New England. Slavery had been abolished, but nothing had been done to the status of the "free negro." Certainly, therefore, "Freedmen" could not possibly occupy a higher position in the scale of rights than had the "free negro" before the war.

Provisional Governor William Marvin, who had been appointed by President Johnson in 1865, warned that Congress was likely to intervene unless the state legislature accepted the concept of Negro freedom and extended to freedmen equal protection of the law. Despite this warning, the legislature followed the committee's recommendations. It enacted laws dealing with crime and punishment, vagrancy, apprenticeship, marriages, taxation, labor contracts, and the judicial system which were collectively referred to as the black code. The code clearly established a separate class of citizenship for blacks, making them inferior to whites.

A long list of crimes was enumerated and penalties assigned. The death penalty was imposed for inciting insurrection, raping a white female, or administering poison. Burglary was punishable by death, a fine not exceeding $1,000, or a public whipping and the pillory. Malicious trespass, buying or selling cotton without evidence of ownership, defacement of public or private property, and other crimes of similar nature were punishable by fines, imprisonment, or whipping and the pillory. Whipping or the pillory was also the prescribed punishment for injuring someone else's livestock, hunting with a gun on another's property, or unauthorized use of a horse whether in the employ of the owner or not. According to an antebellum statute continued in force by the 1865–1866 legislature, Negroes were specifically denied the right to carry firearms, bowie knives, dirks, or swords without a license from the probate judge. The punishment was forfeiture of the weapon and a whipping, the pillory, or both. This provision reflected some concern among white Floridians at the time about a rumored Negro insurrection, which had no substantive basis.

"AN ACT to punish Vagrants and Vagabonds" made all persons subject to arrest who could not demonstrate that they were gainfully employed. Aimed at preventing congregation of freedmen in the towns, this law was especially alarming to Radical congressmen. A convicted vagrant could post bond as a guarantee of good behavior for the following year, but if no bond was posted, he could be punished by the pillory, whipping, prison, or by being sold for his labor up to one year to pay his fine and costs. "AN ACT in relation to Apprentices" allowed the courts to apprentice the children of vagrants or paupers to persons who could supervise their activities, provide for them, and teach them a trade. It applied to both races, but in the aftermath of emancipation most of the children affected were black. This was only a slight extension of an antebellum law requiring that all free blacks over twelve years of age have a duly registered white guardian.

For the first time, a statute defined a Negro as any person with one-eighth Negro blood. Although that standard still left much to interpretation, some such ruling was necessary to the enforcement of several acts intended to separate the races. Both blacks and whites were enjoined from attending the meetings of the other race. They were also required to ride only in railroad cars designated for their respective races. Marriages between Negro men and white women were prohibited. White violators of the enactment could be fined $1,000, jailed for three months, or both. In addition to the fine, Negroes could be made to stand in the pillory for one hour, receive thirty-nine lashes, or both.

One of the most controversial enactments was "AN ACT to establish and enforce the Marriage Relation between Persons of Color." Negro couples were given nine months to decide whether they wished to continue living together. After that time they had either to separate or be legally married. This method of correcting a problem arising from slavery and its abolition caused so much criticism in the northern press that the legislature in November 1866 simply passed a law declaring all freedmen living as man and wife to be legally married.

Even the revenue laws seemed discriminatory. There was a provision for a five-mill property tax on real property and a capitation tax of three dollars on every male between twenty-one and fifty-five. The Negroes often did not learn of the tax in time or did not have the money to pay it. If they were delinquent they could be arrested and sold for their labor for a period long enough to liquidate the obligations incurred. Several cases of tax-delinquent blacks being sold for a year's labor soon caught the attention of the northern press. Such an exorbitant punishment for failure to pay a three-dollar tax seemed to some congressmen to be a substitute for the bonded servitude which had just been abolished.

Although the legislators followed closely a system already established by the military commanders, their "ACT in relation to Contracts of Persons of Color" also distinguished between the races. Contracts were to be in writing and witnessed by two white persons. If Negroes broke their agreements, they could be punished as common vagrants by being whipped, put in the pillory, imprisoned, or sold for up to one year's labor. They could also be found in violation of their contract for "willful disobedience," "wanton impudence," "disrespect" to the employer, failure to perform assigned work, or "abandonment of the premises." If the employer broke the contract, the laborer could seek redress in the courts. Although the state attorney general ruled the law unconstitutional, the next legislature rewrote it so as to apply to both races in occupations limited almost entirely to Negroes.

An early crop lien law was intended to keep tenants on the land. A landlord was empowered to seek a writ placing a lien against growing crops on rented land if the rent was not paid within ten days of the due date. If a tenant did not pay out at the end of the year, the lien could be extended to the next year and he could be legally held on the land. Attracting little attention as part of the black code at the time, this statute, with subsequent additions, contributed largely to an agricultural system which kept many tenants in economic bondage for years after the Civil War.

Central features of the black codes were "AN ACT to extend to all the inhabitants of the State the benefits of the Courts of Justice and the processes thereof" and another "prescribing additional penalties for the commission of offenses against the State, and for other purposes." The convention-appointed committee in its recommendations to the legislature had bemoaned the loss of that highly efficient institution which had existed on the plantations for punishing those "minor offenses to which Negroes are addicted." Since those offenses were now under the jurisdiction of the judiciary, the committee declared that circuit courts would be unable to handle the increased volume of litigation. It accordingly proposed that criminal courts be established in each county and the legislative assembly complied. These courts were soon handling cases, but the heritage of slavery days was too much for them. The legislators had permitted Negroes the right to testify only in cases involving blacks, and juries were made up of white men only. These whites had lived in a society where Negro slaves had had no standing in the courts, and they were now unwilling to accept the word of blacks. The courts were abject failures as legal remedies for freedmen accused of crimes or seeking redress of wrongs committed by whites.

The law "prescribing additional penalties" was a response to the special committee's recommendation that "whenever a crime be punishable by fine and imprisonment we add an alternative of the pillory for an hour or whipping up to thirty-nine lashes or both at the discretion of the jury." This discrimination was "founded upon the soundest principles of State policy, growing out of the difference that exists in social and political status of the two races. To degrade a white man by physical punishment is to make a bad member of society and a dangerous political agent. To fine and imprison a colored man . . . is to punish the State instead of the individual."

The Floridians who enacted the "black code" were surprised and angered by the national reaction they caused. Thomas W. Osborn, assistant commissioner of the Freedmen's Bureau in Florida, intervened to prevent the administration of corporal punishment. Radicals in Congress pointed to the discriminatory legislation to show that Negroes could not expect equal treatment as long as the antebellum Florida leaders remained in power. With similar legislation in other former Confederate states, the Florida black code helped the Radicals convince their moderate colleagues that President Johnson's Reconstruction plan had failed to furnish necessary protection to newly-freed persons. In a mammoth executive-legislative struggle which lasted through most of 1866, Congress overturned the Johnson governments in the South and implemented Congressional Reconstruction in 1867–1868.

Based on Negro suffrage—which Provisional Governor Marvin had said would not happen—and military supervision, the congressional plan seemed to Floridians to be a broken bargain. In late 1866 Governor Walker complained that the state had complied with President Johnson's Reconstruction requirements, but that Floridians were still being denied their rights. The subsequent implementation of Negro suffrage, enactment of the 1868 constitution, and the election victory of the newly-founded Florida Republican party were considered by local whites as unwelcome and unwise invasions of the rights of the state.

These developments also embittered them toward their former slaves. When Negro suffrage was first announced, the planters assumed that they could control the freedman's vote. At assemblages throughout the black belt counties former owners competed with "carpetbaggers" for the allegiance of the new voters. When the blacks quite understandably ignored their former masters in favor of the new Republican leaders, the native whites lost most of their paternalistic sentiment toward the freedmen. They determined to resist Negro suffrage and Republican hegemony by every means they could muster.

Landowners and storekeepers applied economic pressures on black voters. Politicians resorted to ingenious political tactics. Conservatives in the legislature blocked action whenever possible by dilatory parliamentary maneuvers. But by far the most visible, and in the long run the costliest, method was violence. With black legislators sitting in the Capitol, black marshals advertising their tax-delinquent property for sale in the county seats, and white Republicans wielding power dependent on black voting majorities, white Floridians believed that destruction of Republican power was a goal which justified any successful means. According to one sympathetic historian who lived in post-Reconstruction Pensacola, "in this contest for a very necessary supremacy many a foul crime was committed by white against black." According to their reasoning, Republican politicians in Washington had overpowered reasonable, well-meaning President Johnson and had implemented, over his vigorous vetoes and in violation of agreements already made with southern leaders, and contrary to sound constitutional theory, a policy of Negro suffrage. Although it was not the fault of the blacks, this policy had subjected an educated, property-owning class to the mismanagement and corruption of ignorant Negroes and their carpetbagger leaders. This wrong had to be corrected regardless of the methods necessary. But in permitting the use of violence for this purpose, the white leaders unleashed a force which was almost impossible to stop.

As soon as the military commander turned over control of the state to Republican Governor Harrison Reed in July 1868 and withdrew his troops to garrison duty, violence began increasing. At first night-riding bands of hooded horsemen attempted to frighten rural Negroes into submission. But partially because many blacks showed more courage than expected and partially because it was easy to commit excesses against helpless people while shrouded in the anonymity of darkness and disguise, the scare tactics soon degenerated into merciless beatings and murder. Threats were delivered and when they went unheeded, recipients were ambushed. Dozens of white Republicans and Negroes were assassinated throughout the Florida black belt from Jackson County on the Apalachicola River to Columbia County on the Suwannee and southward to Gainesville. In Jackson County alone between 1868 and 1871, more than 150 persons were killed.

Congress responded with corrective legislation. A national elections law empowered the United States government to place supervisors at every polling place in Florida and the other southern states. Military guards were also to be deployed during elections to potentially dangerous locations. Two enforcement acts authorized President Grant to declare martial law and employ soldiers where disorder was beyond the ability of state governments to control. Before the 1872 election the worst of the violence had subsided in Florida, as much from the belief among native whites that it had achieved its purpose as from the presence of United States military forces. This episode nurtured the growth of two important aspects of the evolving myth of the Lost Cause: the idea that helpless white Southerners were being mercilessly suppressed by the military power of a hostile central government, and that they were driven to the use of violence to correct an even greater wrong—dominance of the state by an ignorant Negro electorate.

After years of delay due to opposition from Conservative-Democrats and some of the white Republicans, the legislature of 1873 enacted a civil rights law calling for equal accommodations in public places, although it *permitted*, without requiring, integrated schools. Within months of its enactment it was essentially nullified by a Leon County jurist. When several Negroes complained that they had been denied access to a skating rink in Tallahassee, the judge ruled that private owners or commercial establishments had the right to refuse service to anyone they chose. Although it remained on the books for a time, the 1873 civil rights law was a dead letter. Because its principles were opposed by a majority of white Floridians, it did nothing to change social conduct.

During the four years following President Grant's reelection in 1872 the Reconstruction process continued with diminishing velocity. Most southern states were recaptured by native white Conservative-Democratic parties despite the efforts of the Grant administration. A national depression, repeated scandals in the administration, and other matters caused northern interest in the South to wane. As the 1876 presidential election approached, many Northerners were anxious for a settlement of "the southern question." The stage was set for the final episode in the growth of the myth of the Lost Cause. When the campaign of Samuel J. Tilden and Rutherford B. Hayes for president ended in an uncertain election, the nation was subjected to nearly four months of anxiety. Hayes was ultimately inaugurated after tacitly agreeing to withdraw United States soldiers from the South. This resolution of the disputed election became known as the "compromise of 1877." When he withdrew the troops, all remaining Republican administrations in the South collapsed, and Conservative-Democratic regimes took over in their places. The men who headed those new governments came to be called "Redeemers" who had ousted the carpetbaggers and restored "home rule" in the southern states.

Left to their own devices, white and black Republicans were unable to maintain themselves. During the next few years the southern Republican parties became permanent minorities and eventually almost disappeared. The United States Supreme Court's 1883 decision in the *Civil Rights Cases* was regarded as national acceptance of the failure of Reconstruction and restoration of white supremacy in the South. In that decision the court limited the civil rights guarantees of the fourteenth amendment so that they applied only against official discrimination. Thus, while it was unconstitutional for a state to pass a law discriminating on grounds of race, it was legal for private owners of hotels, restaurants, and theaters to refuse service to blacks.

Cautiously at first, but with increasing confidence, white Floridians began rewriting their laws with a view to establishing a society similar to that envisioned in the black codes of 1865–1866. The 1868 constitution was regarded as a carpetbagger document, imposed on the state by outsiders supported by a black electorate and military force. The demand for its replacement swelled in the early 1880s. Attended by a minority of Republicans, only seven of whom were Negroes, an 1885 convention wrote a constitution which prepared the way for disfranchisement of blacks and dissolution of the Republican Party. It authorized a poll tax as a condition for voting and required that all officeholders post bonds before assuming office. The latter was intended to make it difficult for blacks to qualify for office if they were able to win in the northern counties where there were overwhelming majorities of blacks. But the poll tax provision was most important. The 1889 poll tax law required that potential voters pay their tax for two years immediately prior to elections. If the county records did not show the tax paid, then the would-be voter was required to produce receipts to prove that he was eligible to vote. An accompanying statute required separate ballot boxes for each office. These made it necessary that the voter be able to read the names on the boxes in order to place his ballots in the correct places and have them counted. The result was dramatic. Statewide Republican candidates received more than 26,000 votes in 1888; in 1892 they received fewer than 5,000.

The legal changes were accompanied by incessant racist rhetoric from public officials and the state press. School histories taught young children that the "Redeemers" had saved the state from the excesses of "Radical Reconstruction." When white Floridians divided on policy matters, Conservative-Democratic politicians reminded the voters that whites must stand together or risk a return to "Negro rule."

This tactic prevented the sundering of the paramount white man's party, but it also increased the gap between the races. Violence had declined after 1872, but it had never ceased. As the possibility of federal intervention diminished in the 1880s and the doctrine of white supremacy became more firmly entrenched, violence as a means of repressing blacks increased. The brutal Savage-James lynching at Madison in 1882 went without serious investigation. Another in Jefferson

County in 1888 resulted in the arrest of five white men, but all of them were acquitted by all-white juries. Two especially repugnant lynchings in the mid-1890s led Governor William D. Bloxham to deplore the practice in his 1897 inaugural address, but he offered no remedy. The praise of white supremacy and persistent reminders of its alternatives from prominent men perpetuated a climate of tolerance for violence by whites against blacks.

Floridians were reinforced in their views by similar developments in other southern states. Worse yet, racial developments in the South coincided with a growing racial theory throughout the United States. Relying on Joseph Gobineau and other European racist writers, social theorists in the United States were preaching the idea of Anglo-Saxon superiority and the corresponding inferiority of blacks to a receptive audience. At the same time the United States acquired the Philippine Islands, and a little later Theodore Roosevelt added his "corollary" to the Monroe Doctrine. Our decision to uplift our "little brown brothers" in the Philippines and "protect" our Latin American neighbors from European interference by intervening in their internal affairs added powerful impetus to the growing racial theories in our country.

By the turn of the century the Lost Cause myth was virtually beyond question in the South and was gaining adherents elsewhere. It placed little emphasis on the demise of slavery and the failure of secession. Rather it focused on the unsuccessful efforts at postwar Reconstruction. President Johnson had been willing to permit Southerners to reform their society along lines that allowed for the innate inferiority of blacks. But a misguided Radical-controlled Congress had taken direction of Reconstruction away from him. These crusading Northerners had attempted to change natural conditions by legislative fiat, causing immense difficulties for all involved in an experiment which was doomed by nature to failure. Finally seeing the errors of their ways, they had withdrawn from the struggle, leaving Southerners to solve their own racial problems. This was a powerful and satisfying rationale for a caste system which ultimately degraded Negroes to the point where they had absolutely no defense against the worst excesses of the most lawless elements of white society.

Beginning in 1889 a series of Jim Crow laws were passed which gave legal sanction to the segregation which already existed by custom. These laws went far beyond the earlier black codes in separating the races, but they did little more than legalize existing conditions. Racial segregation in Florida was more extensive in 1900 than it had been in 1865.

An 1895 statute prohibited anyone from conducting a school in which whites and Negroes attended either the same classes, separate classes in the same building, or classes taught by the same teachers. Fines and jail sentences were provided for violators. Others soon followed. In 1903 intermarriage was forbidden between white persons and Negroes, including anyone with at least one-eighth Negro blood. Either or both parties to such a marriage could be punished by up to ten years imprisonment or $1,000 fine. A 1905 enactment required separation of the races on street cars and required companies operating them to provide separate facilities. Failure of the company to do so was punishable by a $50 fine with each day constituting a separate offense. Passengers violating the statute were subject to fines of $25 or up to thirty days in jail. Negro nurses travelling with white children or sick persons were exempt. Since slavery days there had been almost unlimited contact between the races where the blacks were in a servant capacity, and this continued. Segregation was a class rather than a physical matter.

In 1905 constables, sheriffs, and others handling prisoners were forbidden to fasten white male or female prisoners to colored prisoners, subject to fines up to $100 or sentences up to six months. The same legislature required terminal and railroad companies to provide separate waiting rooms and ticket windows for whites and Negroes. The penalty for failure was a fine up to $5,000. A 1909 statute required "equal" and "separate" railroad cars or divisions of cars.

These legal reinforcements of existing practices had great significance. Law and custom had been in harmony during antebellum slavery days. The 1865–1866 black code reflected the social experiences of those who enacted them. Then it was overturned by national legislation which ran counter to the beliefs of the dominant groups of Florida society. Because they disagreed with the Reconstruction legislation and the circumstances of its enactment, native white Floridians not only overturned the laws but also developed a rationale—the Lost Cause myth and its corollary of the necessity for white supremacy—which justified and reinforced their actions following the celebrated 1876 election dispute. The Jim Crow laws were the final necessary step. By the early twentieth century white Floridians were living in a society whose customs, ideology, and law code were once more in harmony.

The first third of the twentieth century was the nadir of race relations in Florida and the nation. Although segregation seemed to be permanently entrenched, whites did not let the matter rest. Politicians always referred to it in their campaigns. Newspapers carried editorials dealing with racism and news stories casting obloquy and odium on Negroes. Creative writers dealt with the subject in the same way. There was a widespread movement to solve the race problem by sending the blacks to Africa. A strong advocate of the idea was Frank Clark, an influential Florida congressman who once declared that "Mr. Lincoln said that this nation could not exist 'half slave and half free.' I think it is equally true that this nation can not exist *half white* and *half black*." Likewise, progressive Florida Governor Napoleon B. Broward went so far as to propose mass removal of Negroes from the United States in his 1907 message to the legislature.

Without political rights, economic strength, or legal status, blacks had no defense. Their best hope was to keep away from whites unless they were fortunate enough to identify with someone who would assist them in legal and economic matters. Usually tied to the land by perpetual indebtedness and dependent on the good will of a white man for whatever security they had, blacks in the early twentieth century occupied a social position not significantly different from that of the antebellum "free Negro" who had been obliged by law to have a white guardian. But this unofficial paternalism was not available to all, and it was inadequate to prevent physical abuse on those occasions when blacks came into contact with unruly whites. Insults and petty violence could sometimes be borne in silence. But at other times it was impossible to avoid trouble. With no legal or social restraints, white ruffians and sometimes ordinary citizens angered by some incident assaulted blacks without fear of reprisal.

In 1911 Mark Norris and Jerry Guster of Wadesboro, Leon County, were arrested on a charge of stealing and resisting arrest. B. B. Smith, a sawmill owner who had been deputized especially to arrest them, had struck Norris with a pistol while doing so. In the justice of the peace court in Miccosukee, the two Negroes were acquitted. When they went to Smith's home to talk about the matter, a gun fight ensued, and Smith was killed. A group of blacks gathered to defend the two men against an anticipated mob, but they quietly surrendered when two deputies arrived to arrest them. Ultimately, ten Negroes were arrested, six of whom were charged with murder. A crowd gathered in Tallahassee, and talk of lynching increased. Six of the men were smuggled out of Tallahassee and taken to Lake City for safekeeping. A few evenings later several men drove to Lake City and got the blacks out of jail on a forged release order, took them to the edge of town, and riddled all six with bullets for more than a half hour. No one in Lake City went to investigate the shooting until the assassins were driving away; thus there were no witnesses to the crime. Governor Albert Gilchrist offered a $250 reward for information about the lynching, but a cursory investigation was shortly abandoned without success.

There was almost no provocation for an incident at Monticello in 1913. Sheriff's deputies went into Log Town, a black section, at about eleven o'clock one Saturday evening just "scouting around." Seeing a group of blacks walking down the road, the deputies called on them to stop to be searched. The Negroes ran. The deputies fired and three blacks were wounded; one of them permanently paralyzed by a shot in the back. No weapons were found on any of them. Walking down the road on a Saturday night seemed to be sufficient cause for a presumption of guilt only in the case of blacks.

When J. A. McClellan shot and killed Charlie Perry, a black, in 1918, the coroner's jury found the shooting to have been in self-defense. It was true that an argument between them had been started by Perry. But the reason for the altercation was that McClellan and others had broken into Perry's house and had searched it without either a warrant or the owner's permission. During the 1920 general election, July Perry of Ocoee, Orange County, caused a disturbance when he tried to vote without having paid his poll tax. He even threatened election officials, but it is inconceivable that the aftermath would have been the same had he been white. Whites followed Perry home and ordered him out of his house. He fired on them. When the altercation was over three days later, the entire Negro section of Ocoee had been burned and four innocent people consumed in the fire. The grisly episode ended only after a mutilated July Perry was finally put to death by the mob which had tired of torturing him. Three years later at Rosewood, near Cedar Key, a white mob charged into the black community searching for an alleged rapist, burned six houses and a church, and killed five blacks. This time the blacks fought back and two whites also died.

The lynching of Claude Neal in Jackson County in 1934 was so shocking that it stimulated a renewed effort in Congress to enact anti-lynching legislation. Neal was accused of murdering a white girl with whom it was charged he had had an illicit relationship. Transferred from jail to jail in West Florida and in southern Alabama he was finally overtaken by a mob in the latter state and brought back to Marianna. He was tortured and mutilated, dragged behind a car, and finally displayed on the streets before crowds, including school children, who attacked the then lifeless body. The corpse was hanged on the courthouse square. On the following day mobs threatened blacks on the streets of Marianna, and order was not restored until the militia was called in. The NAACP published a report of the incident which aroused considerable ire across the nation, but nothing was done. The attorney general ruled that the recently enacted federal law against kidnapping across state lines did not apply because a monetary ransom had not been the purpose of the mob. And as always there was no remedy under state law.

Violence was only the extreme and most visible surface of a racially segregated society. Many whites who deplored violence still obeyed the infinite daily reinforcements of their segregated system: separate dining facilities, theaters, restrooms, waiting rooms, railroad cars, and drinking fountains, as well as the customary racial divisions of labor. While blacks and whites often worked at comparable jobs at the lower end of the economic spectrum, nearly all the professional and white collar jobs were limited to whites and the most menial tasks were overwhelmingly filled by blacks. Even where employment of blacks and whites was comparable, compensation was disproportionate. For example, black school teachers in the 1930s in one north Florida county earned from $37.50 to $40 per month, slightly less than half the salaries of their white counterparts. At that time Confederate veterans were drawing pensions of $37.50 per month. Even the New Deal programs of the national government, designed to relieve the poverty of the 1930s, were affected by racism. Relief administration in Jacksonville established a formula which gave forty-five percent of the available funds to Negroes and fifty-five percent to whites, while black relief families outnumbered white by three to one. Florida Negroes were often denied access to the work-relief programs of the Civilian Conservation Corps and the National Youth Administration on the grounds that they were unqualified to meet admission standards.

By the time Claude Neal was lynched in 1934 forces outside the state were already undercutting the racial status quo. Negro migration into northern cities had created potential black political power. Breaking traditional ties with the Republican party, large numbers of urban blacks voted for Franklin D. Roosevelt in 1936, beginning an alliance with the national Democratic party which still exists. The NAACP had gained considerable attention by its publicity of lynching statistics and its lobbying for an antilynch law. It won its first school desegregation case at the graduate level in 1937. In World War II blacks made significant gains in the armed services and in defense jobs at home. Further migrations out of the South occurred. The Truman administration called for fair employment practices and the 1948 Democratic platform endorsed the idea. The military services were integrated in 1949.

Despite all these changes, the 1954 United States Supreme Court decision in *Brown* v. *Board of Education of Topeka* and its 1955 directive to integrate the public schools with "all deliberate speed" fell like a bombshell on Florida and the other southern states. The Florida attorney general sent to the court the results of a study by social scientists showing that attempts to integrate the state's schools would cause violence. On the basis of the report he asked for a stay of execution of the decision. Some public officials said the court decision was too soon; others said it was an invasion of state rights and a usurpation of legislative power by the courts. State Senator John Rawls of Marianna introduced a resolution in the legislature which emphasized that the constitution of Florida added "legal force to the time honored custom and native inclination of the people of Florida, both negro and white, to maintain . . . a segregated public school system . . . integration . . . in the public schools . . . would tend to encourage the . . . unnatural, . . . abhorrent, execrable, and revolting practice of miscegenation."

White Floridians girded themselves to resist. With a full range of laws requiring segregation and the widespread belief in state rights, theirs was a formidable defensive arsenal. Because the segregation laws conformed so closely to the social values of white Floridians, they emphasized the primacy of state legislation and branded the United States Supreme Court an usurper. Opponents of integration eventually destroyed much of the creditability of the national court system by emphasizing the clash of state law with the court. It was at this point that the Jim Crow laws were crucial. Instead of having to face the basic question of how a state could distinguish between its citizens by law, segregationists were able to attack the integrity of the agency which raised the question. It was much more satisfying to defend the right of the state against invasions of the national court than to defend the Jim Crow system on its dubious merits.

Governor LeRoy Collins's unwillingness to defy the court was a setback, but he promised to use all lawful efforts to maintain segregation while at the same time calling on Floridians to obey the law of the land. The legislature went beyond the governor's position, passed a resolution calling on him to interpose the authority of the state to protect Florida citizens from any effort of the national government to enforce the Brown decision, and enacted legislation providing for the closing of the schools if the national government used force to integrate them. Representative Mallory Horne of Leon County led an effort to restrict the authority of the court, and many Floridians prepared to *defend the law by resisting* the Brown decision.

The moderation of Governor Collins made an immense difference in Florida. Despite the attorney general's warnings of incipient violence, and amidst reports of disruptions in other states, Florida passed through this "Second Reconstruction" with markedly little actual violence. Although there was almost no progress toward school integration for years after the Brown decision, the civil rights movement broadened to other areas and accelerated. White Floridians retreated slowly, resisting each attack on their social system by referring to the state laws. Gradually the national court system negated those laws. With constant pressure from the courts, and belatedly from Congress and the president, the legal framework of segregation crumbled.

But the initiative came almost entirely from outside the state. Some Floridians, exasperated at the national government's interference, argued that they had been gradually working out solutions for the racial problem before the Brown decision. Some social scientists argue that as a rural, agricultural society becomes urban and industrialized, racial segregation breaks down because it cannot function in such a society. However that may be, there was little change in the racial caste system in Florida until the nation once more became interested in it. The hideous lynchings of the early twentieth century ceased when Congress started seriously considering antilynching legislation. Education funds went to Negro schools in larger quantity as the NAACP began winning its desegregation cases. New congressional legislation on civil rights, public accommodations, and voting spearheaded changes in these areas.

With assistance from the national courts and marshals, blacks moved from the back of the buses, sat down at public lunch counters, came down out of the theater balconies, attended previously all-white schools at least in small numbers, and moved into the mainstream of Florida society in countless ways which had been denied them by both law and custom in the past. It was still a piecemeal movement, and social approval of segregation was still strong among whites, but the Jim Crow legal system had been nullified by the late 1960s.

Florida society still retains some of its traditional segregation. Negroes still live mostly in the less desirable sections of towns. Many white families have taken their children from the public schools and sent them to "Christian" schools which cropped up rapidly after 1968. But there is a significant difference. Supported by custom *and the law* only a few years ago, segregation and its correlative of white supremacy and black inferiority were taken for granted by most political and other opinion leaders. Some applauded it as beneficial and even necessary for the South. Gubernatorial candidate Bill Hendricks campaigned throughout Florida in the 1950s as the Ku Klux Klan candidate. White supremacists rested confidently and comfortably with their views, knowing that they were supported by the laws of the state.

That has changed. Few Floridians now speak publicly against basic civil rights for blacks. Racial jokes have moved from most drawing rooms into the restrooms. Denial of the legal sanction for segregation has reversed the burden of public approval. It is no longer popular to advocate segregation, at least directly. Those who believe in it are on the defensive. In the 1974 election, Jeff Latham, a candidate for statewide office, ruined his creditability and his chances for election when he admitted appealing for support from a racist organization.

It is difficult to change the values of society by law—or in the jargon of the capitol hallways "You can't legislate morality"—but it is possible to take away the legal basis for repugnant practices. Jim Crow legislation had provided an immense reinforcement of a segregated society and the rationale for it. Its repeal was difficult because it complemented the values of the most powerful groups of Florida society. But once that legislation was nullified, segregationists found themselves on the opposite side of the law. Interposition was a last-ditch effort to justify the system in terms of state sovereignty along lines enunciated by John C. Calhoun more than a century earlier and negated by the Civil War. The state rights defense was gradually discredited in the 1960s by repeated revelations of southern law enforcement officials using the color of law to commit criminal acts in defense of segregation.

Finally forced to the basic question of how to justify segregation on its merits in terms of mid-twentieth century America and without the support of Jim Crow laws—much as their ancestors had had to deal with the problem of converting slaves to freedmen in 1865–1866—white Floridians have exerted remarkable effort to overcome their segregationist views. They have come far from the time when violence was justified on the ground of the necessity for white supremacy. Many people who still prefer a segregated society restrain themselves from open advocacy of it. And most important of all, most Floridians are willing to accept recent changes, albeit sometimes reluctantly, because they are reinforced by the law.

Racial divisions of American society persist and have become a national problem, but they are no longer being dealt with at the level to which they had descended in the early twentieth century. Americans have probably gone as far toward an integrated society as legal changes will take them. Difficulties encountered with the Supreme Court's "busing" decisions reveal the limits on law as a positive force. Legal provisions cannot diverge too far from custom and belief without disruption. But the disparity is not as great in 1977 as in 1867–1868 when the black code was replaced by laws calling for equality. With time—history—and tolerance, custom and the law will once more coincide as they did for white Floridians before 1860.

4

The Great Bridge and the American Imagination

DAVID MCCULLOUGH

• When the Brooklyn Bridge opened on May 24, 1883, it was arguably the grandest structure ever put together by human hands. The pyramids of Egypt were wonders in every regard save usefulness. Rising from the desert they were testimony to foolish attempts to protect booty for the personal use of the departed. In that sense, they pointed toward past greatness, not toward future prosperity and progress. Similarly, the Great Wall of China was both immense and ancient, but that gargantuan structure failed its essential purpose of protecting the country from invaders.

The Brooklyn Bridge was something else entirely, and it was successful in every sense. A triumph of engineering, it was magnificent in conception and in execution, and it is still thought by many to be the world's most beautiful bridge. Skeptics initially argued that the span would collapse of its own weight. Instead, it carried even heavier burdens with grace and elegance, and its delicate features—transposed against the strength and majesty of its great towers—have inspired generations of poets, artists, and photographers. Linking the great metropolis of Manhattan with a former suburb that had grown to become the fourth city of the New World, the huge steel suspension bridge was the product of immigrant labor and American imagination.

David McCullough is one of the most talented and prolific historians in the United States and, as the following essay indicates, he is the preeminent authority on "the Great Bridge."

The day of the grand opening—Thursday, May 24, 1883—it was the President of the United States, Chester A. Arthur, who led the parade over the new Brooklyn Bridge, on foot.

He was one of the nicest touches to the whole show. A towering 6 feet 2, ruddy, impeccably combed and tailored, "Chet" Arthur was the "beau ideal" of the Gilded Age. He loved dressing up and he loved occasions. That breezy spring day, he appeared in a superb black frock coat, white vest and tie, pearl-gray trousers, a top hat that added another seven or eight inches to his height, and a pair of spanking new "Easy Walking" shoes, the gift of a Broadway merchant who would later advertise them as the first shoes in the history of the Republic to carry a President "dry shod" over the East River to Brooklyn.

The day was glorious, warm as summer. Everywhere the Stars and Stripes fluttered in the breeze. The crowds were enormous, packing the rooftops and jamming the waterfront. No fewer than 50,000 people had come into the city by train alone; a Fall River Line steamer docked with 600 on board; a boat from New Haven had 1,000. They were the happiest-looking crowds reporters could remember seeing in a long while.

The newspapers proclaimed the bridge the engineering triumph of the age—the eighth wonder of the world. Angry denunciations of the project were forgotten. Seth Low, "The Boy Mayor of Brooklyn"— who only the year before had tried to dismiss Washington A. Roebling, the chief engineer and son of the bridge's designer, because things were going so slowly—had now prepared a glowing speech in praise of the bridge and everyone involved in it.

A fireworks display scheduled that evening was to be the most spectacular ever seen, with "bouquets of rockets, flights of bombs . . . fountains of colored stars . . . gentle showers of gold and silver rain," all custom-designed for the occasion.

Downstream from the bridge, the river and harbor were solid with ships, almost as far as the eye could see. Bells were ringing, horns tooting, and looming over the private yachts and excursion steamers were the ships of the North Atlantic Squadron—the *Tennessee, Kearsarge, Yantic, Vandalia, Minnesota* and *Saratoga*, which, like the presence of Chester Arthur and the display of red, white and blue everywhere, gave the day the unmistakable air of a national celebration.

The ships were covered with bunting, their crews turned out in dress uniform. A spectator remembered the day being so clear he could see the sun flash on the gold trimmings of the officers.

Once, while going through the great collection of Roebling papers and family memorabilia that had been locked away for years in a storage closet in the old library at Rensselaer Polytechnic Institute in Troy, N.Y., I found among a bundle of letters one of the original invitations engraved by Tiffany for the opening ceremonies; I had an odd urge to dash off a note of acceptance.

But what was the celebration all about? Why such a fuss over the Brooklyn Bridge, then and now? [It was one hundred years old in 1983,] but nothing we've ever built holds quite the same place in our lives. In a sense, the celebration has never stopped.

We have written songs about it, photographed it, etched it on glass, embroidered it on pillows.

It has been sketched and painted as has no other American structure and often with powerful results. A collection of paintings and lithographs of the Brooklyn Bridge [which were] exhibited at the Brooklyn Museum, as part of the centennial celebration, include[d] the works of George Bellows, Childe Hassam, Louis Guglielmi, Georgia O'Keeffe, Joseph Pennell and Joseph Stella, some of whom, like Stella, have painted it several times.

It figures repeatedly in our literature—in novels by John Dos Passos and Thomas Wolfe, poems by Hart Crane and Marianne Moore, an essay on New York by Henry James. It is the setting for the Maxwell Anderson play *Winterset,* and it is the bridge in Arthur Miller's *View from the Bridge.* . . .

It shows up at every level of our culture. It has been taken lightheartedly ("All that trouble just to get to Brooklyn!" was an old vaudeville appraisal) and with a seriousness sometimes verging on the mystical—Hart Crane's epic poem "The Bridge" being a supreme example. For Crane, the bridge was a 'Tall Vision-of-the-Voyage," the "silver-paced" redeeming symbol at the heart of American history.

It has been regarded as a major American work of art from the time it was built. The first serious review of an American structure to appear in a popular American journal was a rave in *Harper's Weekly* by a man named Montgomery Schuyler the week of the grand opening. In the time since, the critic Lewis Mumford has hailed it as a "joy and inspiration." At Yale, [more than thirty-five years] now, Vincent Scully's brilliant lecture on the bridge—part of his course on modern architecture—has been a high point in undergraduate life. To Scully, the bridge is an "incomparable" symbol of the United States: "It is the most majestic embodiment of the American experience of the road— of leaping free." The architect Philip Johnson has said that the bridge and Central Park are his favorite works of architecture in New York.

It has also had a surpassing movie career. In 1899, Thomas Edison made it the subject of one of his earliest experiments in motion pictures. It can be seen in *Tarzan's New York Adventure* and Laurel and Hardy's *Way Out West*. More recently, it has made prominent appearances in *Annie Hall* and *Sophie's Choice*. A documentary on the bridge by Ken Burns—which was made for public television—was a nominee for an Academy Award [in 1982].

The only other New York icons with a screen presence anything like that of the Brooklyn Bridge are the Empire State Building and the Statue of Liberty, and while the Empire State Building's memorable encounter with King Kong remains in a class by itself, there is really no question as to which of these monuments holds first place.

Frank Sinatra sang about the Brooklyn Bridge; Bugs Bunny "sold" it. Its image has been used to peddle everything from sewing machines and cigarettes to Coca-Cola, Kentucky Fried Chicken, fur coats and high-style cowboy boots. It has appeared on post cards, Christmas cards, record jackets. It's been printed, painted or stamped on paperweights, ashtrays, T-shirts, silver spoons. It has done its turn as calendar art, as the symbol for a television channel, as the label for Dr. Brown's Cel-Ray soda.

Nor is the bridge's appeal limited to this country. It is, for example, among the few American works mentioned in "Civilization," the series of filmed lectures by the eminent British art critic Kenneth Clark. Brooklyn Bridge chewing gum happens to be a big seller in Italy. In the Netherlands, a man named Ed Schilders puts out *The Brooklyn Bridge Bulletin*, a small paper devoted exclusively to the subject. "Loving the Brooklyn Bridge is part of being human," wrote one of the bulletin's readers in a recent letters-to-the-editor column.

Part of the explanation has to do with the bridge's place in the history of New York and its prominence as a symbol of old-fashioned nineteenth-century American progress. It was built by a generation that believed wholeheartedly in a shining American future with New York as its vital center—the generation that also built St. Patrick's Cathedral, the American Museum of Natural History, Central Park and the Metropolitan Museum of Art.

To John A. Roebling, who died horribly a few months before construction of the bridge began, there was never a question about the importance of the bridge. In his initial formal proposal of 1867, he declared that the bridge would not only rank as the greatest ever built, and the greatest work of civil engineering in the land and a great work of art, it would also stand the test of time. It would endure as a monument to the people who made it possible.

And so it has, bridging the great divide between our time and theirs as much as it bridges the East River.

It rises out of an age so very different and distant from our own, and yet there it is. We are more accustomed to the "real past" behind glass in a museum case, or gussied up as it is in Williamsburg. But this is the genuine article. And it works, still, when so much else doesn't.

The late nineteenth century is part of our history best remembered for its low politics and the extravagances of the new rich. Yet out of it rises this most magnificent triumph of perseverance and belief in excellence. Only a society of enormous confidence and vitality could have produced such a monument. Today, at a time of diminished expectations and growing national self-doubt, the bridge is a particularly appropriate symbol of affirmation—that America has dared to be great and still can.

It was the first bridge over the East River, a heroic feat in an age that adored the heroic, and it was the biggest, finest bridge in the world just as everybody said. Its size alone would have guaranteed its immediate popularity. When young Theodore Roosevelt of New York declared in a speech in Dakota Territory on July 4, 1886, that "like all Americans, I like big things, big prairies, big forests, and mountains, big wheat fields, railroads—herds of cattle, too—big factories, big steamboats, and everything else," he knew the solid ground he was on with his audience.

From end to end, the bridge measured more than a mile—5,969 feet to be precise. Its four cables were by far the largest of any suspension bridge on earth, each nearly 16 inches in diameter and containing 3,515 miles of wire. Its main span over the river was half again longer than any ever attempted, or thought to be possible back when the work was started. "If there is to be a bridge," said one observer, "it must take one flying leap from shore to shore over the masts of the ships"—which is exactly what this bridge succeeded in doing.

But as thrilling as was its long leap to Brooklyn (or to Manhattan, depending on one's viewpoint), it also reached upward as nothing had before. Its stone towers were taller than anything on either shore. Soaring to the then-dizzy height of 276 feet, they dwarfed even the tallest buildings of the day and could be seen for miles. They carried the cables aloft and, with the cables, they carried the roadway high enough over the river so that the largest of the great clipper ships—still part of the traffic on the river—could pass below with no problem. From street level, the roadway climbed to an elevation of 135 feet over the river, or considerably higher than most people had ever been in their lives.

One of the singular features of the bridge was an elevated boardwalk so that "people of leisure, old and young," might enjoy the sensation of such height and "promenade over the bridge on fine days, in order to enjoy the beautiful views and the pure air," said John Roebling. He had placed the walkway in the center of the bridge and above the other traffic, so anyone going over by foot had a breathtaking uninterrupted panorama of river, harbor and city skyline. It was along this walkway that Chester Arthur and his delegation made their trek on opening day. "The President ran his eye around the horizon with the air of one appreciating the happy combination of the work of God and man," reads one account.

No bridge in the world has ever been designed to provide pedestrians with such a bonus. And it is still the only bridge with such a promenade, which is a major reason why those who walk it regularly, or jog it, or bicycle over it, hold it so dear to their hearts.

To build it took 14 years, chiefly because almost every step was pioneering. It was begun in 1869, the year of the opening of the Suez Canal and the Transcontinental Railroad. Ulysses S. Grant was in the White House. There were no telephones as yet, no electric lights, no typewriters, no explanation for most diseases, including one called the bends.

Materials were brought to the site by horse and wagon. Stones for the towers were hoisted into place by derricks with wooden masts and wooden booms, not unlike those used in the Middle Ages to build cathedrals. The summer the towers were finished was the summer of Custer's last stand.

In the time it took to build the bridge, Tolstoy wrote *Anna Karenina*, Monet introduced Impressionism, Chicago burned and Chicago was rebuilt.

"Perhaps if they had known, they never would have built it," Gov. Alfred E. Smith recalled his mother's saying when he was a boy growing up on South Street, a stone's throw from the bridge tower on the Manhattan side. His father was a watchman on the project. His mother told chilling tales of the work under the river, inside the caissons.

The project was at first financed by the New York Bridge Company, a private corporation authorized by the New York legislature in 1867 to build and operate an East River toll bridge; its initial capital stock was fixed at $5 million. In 1874, when the company ran into severe financial difficulties, the bridge project became the responsibility of the cities of Brooklyn and New York (for they were separate cities then). The final sum spent was nearly $16 million, a colossal figure at the time and more than twice what John Roebling had estimated. It also cost Roebling his life, made a cripple and recluse of his son Washington and took the lives of another 26 men, by rough count, which was the only kind of count anyone bothered with.

Though John Roebling had no part in the building of the bridge, he was its "mastermind," according to his son. He was brilliant, imperious, a man of wintry eyes, humorless, tireless, demanding, a German-born, German-trained architect and mathematician, a practicing spiritualist and the leading civil engineer of his time. He was a virtuoso and a pioneer. His earlier bridges at Niagara Falls, Pittsburgh and Cincinnati had brought him world renown.

On a summer's day in Brooklyn, while some preliminary surveys were being made by his son, he stood watching from a pier beside the Fulton Street ferry slip. When one of the boats docked, it slammed against the pier, his right foot was caught in something sticking out from one of the nearby piles and his toes were crushed. He was taken at once to a doctor's office, where his toes were amputated—without benefit of anesthetic, at his own request. A confirmed believer in hydropathy (the water cure), he also insisted that nothing be administered to the wound except water. A few weeks later, on July 22, 1869, he died of lockjaw. He was 63.

So it was his son, Col. Washington A. Roebling, who took charge at the age of 32. He is the story's hero, the builder of the bridge. It was he who designed the caissons—the pneumatic foundations for the towers. He is the one who was struck down by the bends and who withdrew to a house on Brooklyn Heights overlooking the river, from which, year by year, never seen but always watching, he directed everything, aided by his wife, Emily Warren Roebling. He is Brooklyn's legendary "man in the window." Only when the bridge was finished, 10 years after he was stricken, did he re-emerge and then quietly, privately, once the public fanfare was done with.

He had trained in engineering at Rensselaer and, later, as his father's apprentice. For four years he had fought in the Union Army, from the second battle of Bull Run to the siege of Petersburg. At the battle of Gettysburg, he had been the first man on Little Round Top. He had a marked capacity, his whole life, for being on the spot when needed.

Of medium height, with brown hair and full beard, he looked out on the world, as a friend said, as if it were all an empty show. He had little of the senior Roebling's vanity or sense of playing a great part in history. He had humor and humility and an iron will as formidable as his father's.

The other engineers he assembled about him were as young as or younger than he. The average age of the staff was all of 31. With few exceptions, no one's prior experience applied to the problems at hand. But the caissons were the worst of all. They were the most novel, uncertain and dangerous element in the whole scheme. They were Colonel Roebling's own creation, his great contribution to the design, and they were what nearly killed him. The towers stand on them to this day.

There were two, each a gigantic, bottomless wooden box big enough inside to have provided space for four tennis courts and room to spare. Each box was filled with compressed air (to keep the water out) and forced to the bottom of the river by the tremendous weight of the tower being built on top. Crews of men went down inside each box to dig away at the riverbed with picks and shovels. As the tons of stone overhead increased steadily, each box would be driven deeper and deeper into the riverbed, until both boxes rested on rock; when this was done, the interior of the caissons would be filled with concrete. On the Brooklyn side, a solid foundation was reached at a depth of 44 feet.

Newspapers ran vivid accounts of the scene below and expressed amazement that anyone could endure such conditions. The only illumination was from candles, or later, calcium lamps (old-fashioned limelight). The compressed air was uncomfortably heavy, with a temperature hovering around 80 degrees; visitors who had only to stand and watch soon found themselves drenched in perspiration. Voices had a thin, eerie sound, again because of the compressed air. Walls, tools, everything and everybody were splattered with river muck and slime.

The deeper the caissons went, the more the pressure of the air within had to be increased. In December 1870, a fire broke out that was nearly disastrous—the compressed air drove the flames deep into the overhead timbers. The story created a sensation. "I don't believe any man now living will cross that bridge," wrote the noted New York diarist George Templeton Strong after perusing his morning paper.

Washington Roebling was in the caisson all night, fighting the blaze. The battle over, he collapsed and on being carried out into the fresh air, he was stricken suddenly with excruciating pains and paralysis. It was his first attack of the bends, or caisson disease, which, as we now know, is caused by coming out of compression too rapidly. For relief, he was dosed with morphine and rubbed all over with a solution of salt and whisky. When a report reached him that the fire had broken out again, he dressed and went back.

His agony had only begun. On the Manhattan side, there was no rock at 40 feet or even 60 feet. The crucial time came when they were down to a depth of 70 feet. That was in the spring of 1872. Hardly any man who worked in the caisson had escaped an attack of the bends by this time. Three men had died. Roebling himself was working 14 to 16 hours a day.

He made an extraordinary decision. He called a halt. The caisson would stand where it was, on sand—extremely hard-packed sand, to be sure, but sand all the same. The depth was 78 feet 6 inches. Had he proceeded down to rock, it might have been at a cost of 100 lives. That, at least, was his estimate.

He had examined the geological strata and determined to his own satisfaction that there had been no shift or disturbance at that level for several million years and so, in all likelihood, it would remain stable. The bridge, and his career, depended on his being right. He was.

It was almost immediately after this that he went into seclusion, having again collapsed from the bends and from total exhaustion. His wife, Emily, became his nurse, companion, protector, confidante and private secretary. She was the intermediary between him and the engineering staff. She was also his emissary first to the directors of the Bridge Company and then to the trustees of the New York and Brooklyn Bridge.

She was as indispensable to him as he was to the bridge. He was never to set foot on the bridge until well after it was completed, but for 10 years nothing was done without his say. Every detail was worked out in his mind. He was like a blindfolded man playing—and winning—several games of chess at once.

She went to the bridge with his directives almost daily. While increasing mystery surrounded him, her role grew more conspicuous. It was rumored he had lost his mind, that a woman was building this monument to nineteenth-century daring. *The New York Times* stated categorically that she was the chief engineer.

He was unable to tolerate more than one or two visitors at a time and only those he trusted implicitly. The briefest conversation exhausted him. From what I have been able to determine, it seems possible that he had become addicted to drugs—to the morphine that was used to save him from the agony of the bends, or to laudanum, which he depended on in later years when his physical suffering was not as serious.

Yet, his intellectual faculties were not impaired in the slightest. He was the chief engineer. He never gave up. Nor did she. It is a love story, in the sense the writer Antoine de Saint-Exupéry had in mind when he wrote that "life has taught us that love does not consist in gazing at each other but in looking outward together in the same direction."

It should be added that not one member of Washington Roebling's engineering staff quit in the 14 years, however difficult and dangerous things became.

All told, thousands of men worked on the bridge—masons, carpenters, riggers, machinists, blacksmiths and common laborers. The majority were Irish immigrants, though there were many Germans and English, some Italians, a few Chinese, and a good number of native-born Americans, both white and black. The workday was eight hours. Everybody worked a six-day week. Wages varied according to the job. For the most miserable work, in the caissons, the men got $2 a day.

After the Bridge Company was dissolved, financing came from the two cities, with Brooklyn putting up twice what New York did. Private stockholders in the Bridge Company were reimbursed, with interest. At one time, though, it had appeared that some stockholders stood to profit more than was proper.

Besides vision and civic pride and technical virtuosity, plain old greed had entered in.

A quantity of political "grease" had been necessary. New York aldermen saw the virtue of the project only after being bribed rather handsomely. The approval of William Marcy Tweed, head of Tammany Hall, was essential. Without it, there would have been no bridge. Tweed preferred stock to cash and the political boss would have made a small fortune, as he later testified, had his ring not collapsed when the bridge was only just begun.

Vestiges of corruption were even built permanently into the bridge itself—in the cables. A crooked manufacturer, J. Lloyd Haigh of Brooklyn, managed to get a quantity of substandard wire past Roebling's inspectors and was not found out until a lot of it had been used in the cables. It is still there, because Roebling, anticipating something of the sort, had designed the cables with a more than sufficient safety factor.

"Spinning" the cables (twisting the individual strands of steel wire to form the cables) took a little more than a year, from the spring of 1877 to October 1878. The sight of workers scrambling about high up among the wires and cables was a spectacle daily commuters on the Brooklyn ferries would never forget. Vertical wire ropes, or suspenders, were strung like harp strings from the cables to the beams of the roadway. Diagonal stays were added—these are the wire ropes that radiate from the towers and produce the fishnet effect so characteristic of the bridge and so beloved by photographers.

With the roadway completed in the spring of 1883—a few weeks before the official opening—Emily Roebling took the first carriage across, to test the effect of a trotting horse. She carried a rooster with her, as a symbol of victory.

Fifty years before, arriving in Delaware Bay by sailing ship from Germany, the young immigrant John A. Roebling had marveled at a country in which such splendid steamboats as he saw, such handsome highways, railways, canals, public buildings had "sprung up" in so little time. He was sure that only an enlightened, self-governing people could attain such things. The same theme was struck by those who spoke at the opening of the bridge; only joined now with the ideal of freedom was the "wonder of science"—technology.

The suspension-bridge form, which John Roebling, more than any other engineer, had perfected, was technology at its most elegant. The catenary curve of the bridge's cables—the curve made by flexible cables suspended between two fixed points—made tremendous strength and long spans possible with a minimum of material and thus a minimum of weight. This had been accomplished even in the days of his earlier bridges, when the wires had all been of iron, not steel.

The Brooklyn Bridge was beautiful in large part because of the contrast of its materials—stone and steel—and because those materials did exactly what they were best suited for. Several speakers on opening day saw the bridge as an "incentive" to the bigger and better things Americans were capable of. It "shall revive the confidence of the people in their own power," said Representative Abram S. Hewitt, one of the trustees. Hewitt was particularly fascinated by the idea that the bridge was designed to adjust itself to the seasons, that its roadway was built with big expansion joints to allow for the expansion and contraction caused by temperature changes. (The vertical rise and fall at the center of the main span, for example, could be nearly three feet.) Only by thus working with nature, rather than against it, could the bridge survive.

There was really no limit to what the country might attain, said Richard S. Storrs, a Brooklyn preacher, "as we see what skill and will can do to overleap obstacles. . . ."

The bridge was the essence of "the modern spirit."

From the time it opened, people came by the tens of thousands to see the Great Bridge and walk or ride over it. P. T. Barnum took a herd of 21 elephants across and declared afterward that now he, too, was satisfied with the solidity of the masterpiece.

For millions of new Americans arriving by ship, it was the first thing to be seen of the New World, its twin towers rising like triumphant gateways.

"You see great ships passing beneath it and this indisputable evidence of its height confuses the mind," wrote a man from France. "But walk over it . . . and you will feel that the engineer is the great artist of our epoch, and you will own that these people have a right to plume themselves in their audacity."

A proud Brooklyn shopkeeper put a sign in his window: "Babylon had her hanging gardens, Egypt her Pyramid, Athens her Acropolis, Rome her Athenaeum; so Brooklyn has her Bridge."

But, of course, it wasn't just Brooklyn's bridge. Ironically—inevitably—the bridge that was supposed to put Brooklyn on the map became at once New York's most popular and readily identifiable landmark.

When the project began, a common belief—especially in Brooklyn— was that the bridge would make Brooklyn the first city in the country. Brooklyn was bound to surpass the small island that was then the City of New York in population and importance. Manhattan Island, unlike Brooklyn, had little space in which to grow (it wasn't until 1874 that sections of what is now the Bronx became part of the City of New York). The bridge, by providing a more convenient and reliable alternative to the East River ferries, would lure New Yorkers away from their crowded and crime-ridden island to Brooklyn, and property values would skyrocket. Manufacturers, Long Island farmers and Brooklyn brewers would have easier access to their New York market.

But, in fact, the bridge was a harbinger of a New York no one could yet imagine, one that would grow up instead of out, and that upward climb may be dated from the summer of 1876, when the bridge towers were completed. Besides, the vertical city of the future was to be built of steel, and the first use of steel in a major way in New York was the bridge. "All modern New York, heroic New York, started with Brooklyn Bridge," says Kenneth Clark.

For Brooklyn, the bridge marked the beginning of the end of a fierce old sense of individuality. By being physically connected to New York, Brooklyn became an appendage. Even before the century was out, Brooklyn would relinquish all independence and become a borough of New York.

Indeed, the very fact that the bridge was in New York had much to do with its prestige and how people responded to it, just as it does today. "There's really no place like New York," Chester Arthur was heard to exclaim to a friend at the height of the opening ceremonies.

The bridge stopped being the only East River bridge long ago—in 1903, when the Williamsburg Bridge was completed. The George Washington Bridge, built over the Hudson in 1931, had a span more than twice that of the Brooklyn Bridge. Like Lindbergh's flight, the Brooklyn Bridge doesn't seem so astonishing compared with what has happened since. Its towers are all but lost against present-day downtown New York.

Still, the gentle arc of its center span gives it a nobility like that of no other bridge. When sunlight plays on the network of wires, it has a magic quite its own. In a time of headlong impermanence in a city of frenetic change, its stone towers do not, will not move or change.

"Everything was built to endure," said one of Washington Roebling's assistant engineers. The engineers who look after it now say it could last forever. It needs only to be properly cared for. When one of the diagonal stays snapped [in 1981], killing a Japanese photographer, it was because of improper care. Soon after the accident the city's Transportation Department announced plans to spend more than $100 million, over a period of 10 years, to overhaul the bridge.

. . . .

The bridge has different meanings for each of us, of course. Many, and I am one, are moved most by the realization that human beings have it in them to build something so fine. "Nothing is easy and nothing does itself," Washington Roebling once said in a letter to his son. "Character and action are everything."

Perhaps at this juncture in the life of our country the Brooklyn Bridge and its story can serve as a symbol of rededication. For those who built the bridge, it meant not only the chance to work on a project of grand scale and importance, but a chance to be judged by their work. The bridge is a measure of their tremendous courage, constructive energy and huge determination, but it is also, perhaps above all, a measure of their self-respect. They would build exceedingly well because it was expected of them. They could and would, in the old expression, rise to the occasion, and seldom had an occasion been larger or more conspicuous.

But they also worked and built so well because they felt beholden as self-respecting Americans to be out ahead of the rest of the world, to do the job better than it could be done anywhere else by anyone else. They believed implicitly that tomorrow would be an improvement on today because they would make it so. Wasn't the bridge itself proof of that? For the many immigrants among them, the bridge was a first big chance to take hold in American life, and being judged by the way you took hold of your job was part of being American.

May 24 could be a day of national celebration no less than it was over 100 years ago. Maybe what we should be celebrating—honoring— is the fact that it was made here, made in America. Implicit in every line of it is a truth we cannot be reminded of too often: that what we do with our energies, our material wealth, our ingenuity need not be ugly or destructive or short-lived—or anything other than the best.

5

The East European Jewish Migration

LEONARD DINNERSTEIN

• *Jews have been in the United States since 1654. By 1790 they numbered perhaps 1,200 and sixty years later about 15,000. Spread thinly throughout the land they had little difficulty finding a place for themselves in the greater society and were accepted as individuals or in small groups. During the middle of the nineteenth century Jews from the German states of Europe entered the United States along with Protestant and Catholic Germans and they, too, were absorbed easily. By the 1880s, however, East European Jews started coming in the hundreds of thousands. A changing industrial society, Pan-Slavism, and continual pogroms proved too difficult a combination to combat, especially while opportunities existed in the United States.*

The colonial Jews—mostly Sephardim from the Iberian Peninsula and Brazil—settled mainly in the port cities of Newport, New York, Philadelphia, Charleston, and Savannah and engaged in shopkeeping and mercantile activities. Many chose to assimilate into the dominant community, married gentiles, and raised their children as Christians. The Jews who were a part of the mid-nineteenth-century influx also gravitated toward cities but they did not remain exclusively in the East. Many a Jew put a pack on his back, traveled in different sections of the country, and finally settled down in places as different as Greenville, Mississippi; Boise, Idaho; Columbus, New Mexico; Cleveland; Atlanta; Dallas; and Los Angeles. Other Jews, however, went directly to New York, Cincinnati, Chicago, Philadelphia, and Detroit, and immediately set down roots. As a result, the families of the mid-nineteenth-century Jewish migration were spread throughout

From *Uncertain Americans: Readings in Ethnic History* by Leonard Dinnerstein and Frederic Cople Jaher. Copyright © 1977 by Oxford University Press, Inc. Reprinted by permission.

the United States. They, too, engaged in the traditional commercial activities usually associated with Jews, but they also had children who were trained for the professions. The German Jews achieved a level of prosperity well above those of other ethnic groups. In 1890, when the majority of American Jews were still of Sephardic or German extraction, the Hebrew community was considerably more prosperous than the national average. Two thirds of all Jewish families in the United States had at least one servant, while over ninety percent of the American population failed to earn enough money to maintain a family in moderate circumstances. But the massive influx of Eastern European Jews, most of them poor, was already operating to lower the aggregate wealth of American Jewry to the point where this ethnic minority became collectively an underprivileged group.

The new migrants differed in several ways from their predecessors. They came in the hundreds of thousands and could not disappear into the American population with relatively little notice. They were also more Orthodox in religion, bizarre in dress, and determined to settle in Jewish enclaves and perpetuate Orthodox customs. They also tended to concentrate in a few localities. More than seventy percent remained in New York City and the surrounding area. They threatened the security of the Americanized Jews who had already moved into the middle class and who feared, correctly, that the newcomers might stimulate waves of overt anti-Semitism in the United States which would victimize all of the Jews.

Most knew how to read and write Hebrew or Yiddish, and the men had some urban and vocational skills. But the opportunities originally available to them were as unskilled or semiskilled laborers, and for years they were plagued with poverty and occupied cheap tenements on New York's Lower East Side.

The story of their experiences, and ultimate accomplishments, is discussed in the following selection.

INTRODUCTION

Jewish migration to the United States in the nineteenth and twentieth centuries may be divided into three groups: the German, the East European, and the Central European. During the first period of heavy Jewish immigration to the United States, mainly during the pre-Civil War years but roughly from the 1840s through the 1870s, about 50,000 Jews arrived from the German states. They engaged almost exclusively in trade and commerce, many starting off as peddlers and some moving up quickly into banking and department stores. The second and most important wave, from the 1870s through 1924, came primarily from Eastern Europe. Responding to the economic uprooting of society and the frequent pogroms of the late nineteenth and early twentieth centuries, more than 2,000,000 Jews left Russia, Galicia, Rumania, and Hungary for the great trek to the United States. These people included artisans, skilled workers, small merchants, and shopkeepers. They and their descendants have made the greatest impact of all the Jews in the United States and are the subject of this essay. The third group, from Central Europe, numbering about 365,000, came to America between 1925 and 1953, with approximately 132,000 in the years between 1948 and 1953. Some of these people emigrated for economic reasons, but the overwhelming majority were victims of Hitler's rise to power in Germany. In the 1930s Nazi persecutions and brutalities forced many German Jews to leave the country, and after the Second World War some concentration camp victims and the displaced refugees were granted opportunities to resettle in the United States. This third group quickly moved into the Jewish mainstream in the United States. They made major impacts in the American scientific and intellectual communities.

Before the Second World War these Jewish groups were quite different and easily identifiable: by income, education, jobs, residence, and organized associations. In the past thirty-five years, however, the differences have diminished considerably because of a vast leap in both educational and income levels of American-born Jews. It would be quite difficult, if not impossible, today to distinguish among the descendants of the previous generations of Jewish immigrants. In terms of life style, occupation, and income the overwhelming majority of

Jewish families are in the middle and upper middle class and their breadwinners occupy professional, technical, and managerial positions.

CAUSES FOR EMIGRATION

The Jews left Eastern Europe for much the same reason that most other peoples left their states—grinding poverty at home made them yearn for a decent life elsewhere. In Russia 94 percent of the Jews lived in the "pale of settlement," a huge belt of land in Western and Southwestern Russia and the Ukraine stretching from the Baltic to the Black Sea. Jews could live outside of this area only by special permission. Within the pale their population increased from 1,000,000 in 1800 to 4,000,000 in 1880 and this expansion constricted the possibilities of economic opportunities. In Rumania they were regarded as aliens, while in Galicia Jews suffered from economic boycotts and other manifestations of hostility.

During the 1870s the industrial revolution began to make a significant impact in Russia. That impact was greatest within the pale, where industrialization took place most rapidly. The Russian government, which had earlier set numerous restrictions on Jews, feared their influence, especially after industrialization began. Jews actively engaged in trade and commerce, which attracted many of the gentiles once they were forced off the land. Competition for positions in a tight economy heightened Christian-Jewish tensions. Industrialization also stimulated the movements of Jews and gentiles from rural to urban areas to seek employment. The city of Lodz, which had eleven Jews in 1797, counted 98,677 one hundred years later and 166,628 in 1910. Warsaw's Jewish population leaped from 3,521 in 1781, to 219,141 in 1891. Industrial expansion also led to a major flight of people to the west. Many Jews went to Germany, France, and England in Europe, and to Argentina, Canada, South Africa, and Palestine. More than 90 percent of the Jewish migrants, however, wound up in the United States.

Other factors also propelled the Jewish exodus. As in the case of emigrants from other nations, flight was impelled by specific items like the unsuccessful Polish uprising of 1863, the Lithuanian famine of 1867–69, the Polish cholera epidemic of 1869, and by the predisposition of young people to try their fortunes in a new world, and the developing political ideologies of Zionism and socialism which made traditional modes of thought and behavior too confining. Many Jews were outspoken socialists. They envisioned a new democratic social order with a more equitable distribution of the nation's wealth and resources. Anti-Semitism, which rose in intensity as Pan-Slavism gripped the Eastern Europeans, however, provided a unique reason for the Jewish migration. Jews were not Slavs and therefore stood as an impediment toward nationalistic unity. The assassination of Tsar Alexander II of Russia in 1881 by a group of socialists spawned a wave of pogroms against the Jews which continued intermittently until the First World War. Major pogroms occurred in 1881, 1882, 1903, and 1906, and hundreds of others have been recorded. These pogroms, often inspired by government officials, resulted in wanton and brutal assaults upon Jews and their property. Russia also codified and curtailed Jewish rights after Tsar Alexander's assassination. The May Laws of 1882 restricted the numbers of Jews that might attend Russian universities and the kinds of occupations Jews might pursue. They could not rent or own land outside of the towns and cities nor could they keep their shops open on the Christian sabbath or on Christian holidays.

American letters and money sent by earlier immigrants, along with the advertisements from railroad and steamship lines anxious to transport emigrants, further stimulated migration from Eastern Europe to the New World. Promising economic conditions in the United States, combined with increased persecutions and deprivations in Russia, Galicia, and Rumania, expanded the exodus to the West, as revealed in the following figures:

1870s: 40,000
1880s: 200,000+
1890s: 300,000+
1900-14: 1,500,000+

PATTERNS OF SETTLEMENT

Over 90 percent of the more than 2,000,000 Jews who left Eastern Europe between 1870 and 1924 went to the United States. Unlike many other immigrant groups, the Jews mostly traveled with their families. During the years 1899 to 1910, females made up 43.4 percent of the total number of Jewish immigrants and children 24.7 percent, the highest figure for any arriving peoples. During the same period males constituted 95.1 percent of the Greek immigrants and 78.6 percent of the southern Italians. Only the Irish had a larger percentage of females than the Jews (52.1 percent), but it is believed that many of them came alone to work as domestics. Statistical estimates indicate that 71.6 percent of the Jews came from the Russian empire, including Latvia, Lithuania, and Poland; 17.6 percent from Galicia in the Polish area of the Austro-Hungarian empire; and 4.3 percent from Rumania.

Most of these people landed, and remained, in New York City. In 1870 the city's Jewish population had been estimated at 80,000; in 1915 almost 1,400,000 Jews lived there. The newcomers found friends, relatives, jobs, and educational opportunities in New York City, and, in any case, few had the money to travel elsewhere. Moreover, the Orthodox knew that they could find kosher butchers which would allow them to maintain Jewish dietary laws, and jobs where they would not have to work on the sabbath. To be sure, those who landed in Boston, Philadelphia, or Baltimore, or even those who made their way to Chicago and other cities, found small Jewish communities in which they could settle. Chicago, in fact, had 200,000 Jews by 1912. But the major center, by far, for East European Jews was New York.

Most of the immigrants who chose to live in New York City settled originally in a small section of Manhattan Island known as the Lower East Side. The boundaries of this ghetto lay roughly within the blocks bordered by Fourteenth Street, Third Avenue and the Bowery, Canal Street, and the East River. The heart of the district, the tenth ward, housed 523.6 people per acre at the beginning of the twentieth century. In the 1890s Jacob Riis, an enterprising reporter, observed that "nowhere in the world are so many people crowded together on a square mile" as in the Jewish quarter. Within the Lower East Side numerous subdivisions could be identified as streets housing primarily Russian, Galician, Rumanian, or Hungarian Jews. The area contained 75 percent of New York City's Jews in 1892, 50 percent in 1903, and 23 percent in 1916.

The tenements where the Jews lived can best be described as dark, dank, and unhealthful. One magazine described the dwellings in 1888 as great prison-like structures of brick, with narrow doors and windows, cramped passages and steep rickety stairs. They are built through from one street to the other with a somewhat narrower building connecting them. . . . The narrow courtyard . . . in the middle is a damp foul-smelling place, supposed to do duty as an airshaft; had the foul fiend designed these great barracks they could not have been more villainously arranged to avoid any chance of ventilation. . . . In case of fire they would be perfect death-traps, for it would be impossible for the occupants of the crowded rooms to escape by the narrow stairways, and the flimsy fire-escapes which the owners of the tenements were compelled to put up a few years ago are so laden with broken furniture, bales and boxes that they would be worse than useless. In the hot summer months . . . these fire-escape balconies are used as sleeping-rooms by the poor wretches who are fortunate enough to have windows opening upon them. The drainage is horrible, and even the Croton as it flows from the tap in the noisome courtyard, seemed to be contaminated by its surroundings and have a fetid smell.

Two families on each tenement floor shared a toilet. In the summer months the heat and stench in these places were unbearable and the stagnant air outside provided little relief.

The first Jewish immigrants, despite their toil, earned barely enough to subsist on. As a result it was not uncommon to find parents, children, other relatives, and some boarders in a two-, three-, or four-room apartment. The boarder may have paid three dollars a month for his room and free coffee, but that came to 30 percent of the family's ten-dollars-a-month rent. Looking back, the prices of four cents for a quart of milk, two cents for a loaf of bread, and twelve cents for a pound of *kosher* meat may look ridiculously cheap, but when one reckons this on an average weekly income of less than eight dollars, the picture is quite different.

Fortunately for the Jews, their earnings increased sufficiently after a few years in this country so that they did not have to rot in the slums for an interminable period. "It was judged to be a ten-year trek," Moses Rischin tells us, from Hester Street, on the Lower East Side, to Lexington Avenue, in the more fashionable uptown area. The tenements, of course, did not disappear, but their inhabitants continually changed.

Most of the immigrant Jews from Eastern Europe resided first on the Lower East Side and the Hebrew population in that area of the city peaked at more than half a million in 1910; by the 1920s fewer than ten percent of New York's Jews still lived there. The completion of the subways in the early part of the century opened up vast tracts for settlement in upper Manhattan, Brooklyn, and the Bronx (other boroughs of New York City), and the Jewish working class, anxious and able to take up residence in better neighborhoods, moved away.

Jewish immigrants in Boston, Chicago, and other large cities had initial experiences similar to those who remained in New York. In most other places where Jews went, the tenement areas were smaller or nonexistent, the neighborhoods less congested, and the opportunities to live in more healthful surroundings considerably better. East European Jews who went south or west had experiences considerably different from their brethren who went to the urban areas of the Northeast and Chicago, but they constituted fewer than five percent of the entire migration.

Over the years the children and grandchildren of the newcomers moved out of these cities to surrounding suburban areas or flourishing new communities where economic opportunities beckoned. Most of the subsequent growth in the American Jewish population took place in the states closest to New York: Pennsylvania, New Jersey, and Connecticut, with two major and a few minor exceptions. After World War II job opportunities and a pleasant year-round climate drew hundreds of thousands of Jews to California, especially the Los Angeles area, and many older people first visited and then retired in Miami Beach, Florida. The growth of the Jewish population in California and Florida is primarily a phenomenon of the past thirty years.

LABOR AND BUSINESS

East European Jewish immigrants differed from most of the other foreign-born arrivals in the late nineteenth and early twentieth centuries in that 95 percent of them came from urban rather than rural areas. Their urban origins resulted in the development of skills and talents which would aid them greatly in the United States. An 1898 survey of the Russian pale of settlement found that Jews owned one third of all the factories in the area and that Jewish workers concentrated in the clothing (254,384), metal-working (43,499), wood-working

(42,525), building (39,019), textile (34,612), and tobacco (7,856) industries. The skills they acquired there were also in demand when they reached the United States.

An American survey of the occupations of immigrants entering the United States between 1899 and 1910 listed 67.1 percent of the Jewish workers as skilled compared with a general figure of 20.2 percent for all newcomers. In his study *The Promised City*, Moses Rischin indicates that

> Jews ranked first in 26 out of 47 trades tabulated by the Immigration Commission, comprising an absolute majority in 8. They constituted 80 per cent of the hat and cap makers, 75 per cent of the furriers, 68 per cent of the watchmakers and milliners and 55 per cent of the cigarmakers and tinsmiths. They totaled 30 to 50 per cent of the immigrants classified as tanners, turners, undergarment makers, jewelers, painters, glaziers, dressmakers, photographers, saddle-makers, locksmiths, butchers, and metal workers in other than iron and steel. They ranked first among immigrant printers, bakers, carpenters, cigar-packers, blacksmiths, and building trades workmen.

In the United States the Jewish immigrants found jobs in distilleries or printing, tobacco, and building trades, while significant numbers of others started out as butchers, grocers, newspaper dealers, or candy store operators.

The majority of the Jewish immigrants, however, found work in the needle trades, which were—because of the increasingly efficient methods of mass production and the existence of a mass market—undergoing rapid expansion. The arrival of the East Europeans with their particular talents coincided with this vast growth. By the end of the nineteenth century Jews had just about displaced the Germans and Irish from the industry. In New York City the development of the clothing industry transformed the economy. In 1880 major clothing manufacturers numbered only 1,081, or 10 percent of the city's factories, and employed 64,669 people, or 28 percent of the city's work force. By 1910 the borough of Manhattan (which before the consolidation of the five boroughs in 1898 had been New York City) had 11,172 clothing establishments, which constituted 47 percent of the city's factories. The industry employed 214,428 people, slightly more than 46 percent of Manhattan's workers. In 1890, 60 percent of the employed immigrant Jews worked in the garment industry and on the eve of the First World War more than half of all Jewish workers, and two thirds of Jewish wage earners, were still to be found in the industry. The Jewish influence was so great that the manufacturing of wearing apparel in the United States came to be regarded as a Jewish endeavor. Hebrews not only labored in the garment factories; they also worked their way up to supervisory positions and the bolder ones opened their own establishments. Before the Second World War it was estimated that Jews controlled 95 percent of the women's dress industry, 85 percent of the manufacturing of men's clothing, and 75 percent of the fur industry.

Initially, the owners were German Jews who at first looked down on their East European coreligionists and exploited their labor. Many of the early twentieth-century factories were nothing more than reconverted lofts and tenements or else small areas of workers' apartments. Many garments were actually finished in home sweatshops. Workdays lasting from 4:00 a.m. to 10:00 p.m. in these hovels were not uncommon, and wages averaged $6.00 to $10.00 a week for men and $3.00 to $5.00 for women. (Children also worked on these garments and in other industrial areas as well. Naturally, they earned lower wages than adults.) Because of the seasonal nature of the work, few had a steady yearly income. The annual wage of the average garment worker came to $376.23 in 1900, $1,222 in 1921, and $873.85 in 1930.

Low wages, appalling working conditions, and the insecurity of workers' positions prompted many to think about union organization. Among the Jewish immigrants were many socialists and members of the Russian Jewish Bund who had tried to improve social conditions in Europe. Many of these men also provided the backbone for unionization in the garment trades in the United States. The International Ladies' Garment Workers Union was founded in 1900 but not until the major strikes of clothing workers in 1909 and 1910 were significant victories won and the union firmly established. In Chicago 40,000 garment workers struck in 1910 and in New York 20,000 waist and dressmakers went out from November 1909 through February 1910. In July 1910 as many as 60,000 cloakmakers struck. The strikes attracted wide attention in the press, among social workers, and throughout the Jewish community. The workers won a victory when in July 1910 a

"Protocols of Peace" set up a Board of Arbitration, a Board of Grievances, and a Board of Sanitary Control. Four years later the cloakmakers formed the core of the new Amalgamated Clothing Workers of America, a union which had its origins in Chicago with a less effective group, the United Garment Workers of America.

The International Ladies' Garment Workers and the Amalgamated were the two major Jewish unions in the United States. Because of the socialist heritage of so many of their participants, the two unions were concerned not only with improving labor conditions but with a vast program for improving the living conditions of all of their members. The unions were responsible for ending sweatshops, raising wages, and improving working conditions. They also pioneered in the development of a large number of auxiliary services for members. They built housing developments, established educational programs, maintained health centers, provided pensions, set up vacation resorts, developed a system of unemployment insurance benefits long before the state and federal governments assumed this responsibility, and opened banks giving services at significantly lower cost than other financial institutions. The Jewish unions, in sum, initiated social reforms which other labor organizations adopted. Aside from the ILGWU and the Amalgamated, the only other powerful labor union made up primarily of Jewish workers and leaders was the United Federation of Teachers (now the American Federation of Teachers) which galvanized New York City's schoolteachers in the 1960s and propelled its president, Albert Shanker, to the forefront of labor leadership in America.

EDUCATION AND SOCIAL MOBILITY

Despite the benefits obtained by and from the labor unions, Jews had no desire to remain in the working class. Their ambition to "get ahead" knew no bounds and as soon as possible they, and/or their children, strove to move up to more lucrative and prestigious occupations. As early as 1900, American-born sons of Russian Jews constituted six times as many lawyers and seven times as many accountants as were to be found in their parents' generation but only one third the number of garment workers. As the years passed, this tendency became even more pronounced. Jewish workers also tried to become manufacturers. Many of those who started out as peddlers eventually moved into small retail outlets and some of the latter then expanded into larger emporiums. It was the rare community, in fact, that did not have some Jewish storekeepers. Random samplings in different decades through the 1940s showed anywhere from 31 to 63 percent of the Jews engaged in trade. In one study of the South the author noted, "It is said, 'If there is a Jewish holiday, you cannot buy a pair of socks in this whole country,' a remark which illustrates how complete the control of the retail dry-goods trade by Jews is supposed to be."

The entertainment industry also provided an avenue of advancement for some immigrant Jews. In 1905 it was estimated that half of the actors, popular songwriters, and song publishers in New York City were Jewish. Within a few years Jews also pioneered in the motion picture industry.

The Jews made great economic and social advances because educational and business opportunities were available to the more enterprising and because the masses of East European Jewish immigrants considered it necessary to "Americanize" their children and have them learn the language and customs of the new country as quickly as possible. From their beginnings in this country, the East European Jews also showed a passion for education and professional advancement unique in American history. Members of other immigrant groups, before or since, have not been as zealous in their quest for knowledge. The newcomers themselves were forced to do manual work, but whenever possible they encouraged their children to remain in school, attain an education, and move up in the world. As Samuel Gompers, leader of the American Federation of Labor, observed, "The Jews were fairly ravenous for education and eager for personal development. . . . All industrial work was merely a steppingstone to professional and managerial positions." Jewish parents wanted their children in high-status positions where they could operate on their own and not be subject to the bigotry of employers. Jewish boys strove to become doctors, lawyers, dentists, accountants, and teachers. They also opened pharmacies and other retail businesses. In these occupations Jewish parents felt their children would be both prosperous and independent at the same time. In 1903 it was estimated that Jews comprised about half of New York City's 5,000 to 6,000 physicians and thirty-four years later 65.7 percent of the city's lawyers and judges, 55.7 percent of its physicians, and 64 percent of its dentists. In the 1960s Jews still made up a majority of these professions in New York City.

Statistics of Jewish occupational categories for other cities are similar. By the 1930s only one third of all Jewish workers were still engaged in manual jobs while two thirds were in white-collar positions. The figures for non-Jews were just the reverse: two thirds in manual occupations, one third in white-collar jobs. Jews also moved into professional positions at a much faster rate and in much higher percentages than non-Jews. In the 1930s eighteen out of every 1,000 Jews in San Francisco were lawyers and judges, while sixteen were physicians. For every 1,000 gentiles the figures were five and five, respectively. Similarly, in Pittsburgh fourteen of every 1,000 Jews were lawyers and judges, thirteen were physicians, while the corresponding figures for non-Jews were five and four, respectively.

The tendency for Jews to seek and obtain the highest status positions in American society has not diminished in recent decades. In 1955, some 55 percent of all gainfully employed Jews, compared with 23 percent of non-Jews, had professional, technical, managerial, executive, or proprietary positions while in 1967, 51 percent of the Jews, compared to 23 percent of the Catholics and 21 percent of the Protestants in the United States were classified as professionals. Among younger Jewish adults the figures for professional occupations were even higher. With higher status occupations came higher incomes. In 1967 the Gallup Poll found that 69 percent of the Jews had incomes over $7,000 a year but only 47 percent of the Catholics and 38 percent of the Protestants claimed earnings of that level or higher. By 1971, 60 percent of the Jewish families where the head of the household was between thirty and fifty-nine years old had annual incomes exceeding $16,000.

But money alone does not tell the whole story. Since the end of World War II not only has there been an almost complete disappearance of Jewish young men in blue-collar jobs, but Jews in increasingly larger numbers have shunned retail businesses—frequently owned by their fathers—to seek careers and greater personal satisfaction as journalists, writers, scientists, architects, engineers, and academics, as well as the traditional favorites of the Jewish immigrants: lawyers and physicians. Discouraged earlier by family preferences and gentile bigotry from seeking careers where they would have to be employed by others, the enormous expansion of opportunities in the 1950s and '60s made previously unheralded vocations or fields formerly difficult to enter more attractive and more accessible.

CULTURAL AND RELIGIOUS LIFE

The East European Jews, despite their poverty, arrived in this country with certain advantages. They had a strong commitment to a religion which rigidly dictated much of their daily behavior and gave their lives a structure and continuity which helped them to overcome problems of displacement in a new society. Moreover, unlike other immigrants to the United States who may have been poor at home but who otherwise "belonged," the Jews had been minorities wherever they had dwelled in Europe. As a result they had acquired a knowledge of how to move deftly among the dominant groups who, at best, tolerated them or, at worst, despised them. They had learned how to survive under a variety of hostile conditions and this experience served them well in the United States where they also had to struggle with adversity. Another important advantage that the Jews had brought with them can best be described as a middle-class view of life. They were ambitious, self-disciplined, and intellectually curious. A number of them had been socialists and participants in the revolutionary movement in Russia and Poland. Most had lived in small towns and villages and were attuned to what might now be considered the urban style of life.

The culture that the Jews brought with them to the United States survived in New York City. In recent decades attempts have been made to transplant it, as well, to Miami Beach and Los Angeles. In Boston, Chicago, and other cities where the Jews initially dwelled, they composed too small a percentage of the population to make much impact on the community. They may have had their own food stores and shared an affinity for literature, music, art, and religious observances, and perhaps even were more socialistically inclined than their neighbors, but in time their tastes and views blended with the dominant values of their respective communities, and today outside of the strongholds of the remnants of East European Jewish orthodoxy in New York, Chicago, Cleveland, Pittsburgh, Los Angeles, and Miami Beach, about the only thing left to distinguish Jews from everyone else in the United States is the Reform Temple.

In New York City, however, an East European Jewish culture flowered for decades and still lends a distinctive tone to the life in this vast metropolis. Cafés abounded where Jews would sit around and *shmooze* (talk) for hours over cups of coffee or glasses of hot tea. "For immigrant Jews," one chronicler reminds us, "talk was the breath of life itself." Discussions during these get-togethers ranged over a wide spectrum of topics and no one ever felt the necessity to refrain from participation because of a limited knowledge of the topic under consideration. The cafés gave the Jewish East Side a flavor—"a Yiddish Bohemia, poor and picturesque"—and their patrons included the most intellectual and articulate Jewish actors, poets, playwrights, journalists, and politicians of the day.

Jews also relaxed in the theater. The coming of the East European Jews not only spawned a Yiddish theater in the ghetto but also stimulated vaudeville and the Broadway stage. They also pioneered in the radio industry and virtually founded the motion picture industry.

Jews throughout the United States have been known for their patronage of the arts and their interest in literary endeavors. Between 1885 and 1914, for example, over 150 Yiddish daily, weekly, monthly, quarterly, and festival journals and yearbooks appeared in New York City, including the daily *Forward* which is still published today. Cultural centers were established wherever sufficient numbers of Jews congregated. Typically, the Cleveland Jewish Center had a gym, a roof garden, a library, classes in Hebrew language and literature, a scouting program, art classes, political forums, sewing and baking clubs, etc.

Owners of art galleries and concert halls (about one third of whom in New York City are Jewish) know that the larger a community's Jewish population the more likely it will be that their showings and musicales will be rewarded with large audiences. Jews are also heavily represented in every aspect of radio and television production. They purchase more books and attend more poetry readings than non-Jews and have also been among the major book publishers in New York City.

For the recent arrivals, however, the single most important cultural institution was the synagogue. Unlike the German Jews who came before them and worshiped, for the most part, in Reform temples barely distinguishable from Unitarian churches, the overwhelming proportion of the East Europeans maintained a devout orthodoxy during their first years in the United States. The numbers of synagogues proliferated in geometric proportion. In 1870 there were 189 Jewish congregations in the United States, the majority peopled by German Jews. By 1906 there were 1,769 and twenty years after that 3,118. In New York City alone the number of synagogues increased from 300 at the turn of the century to 1,200 in 1942. Usually these places of worship were no more than converted store fronts or private homes which came into being because one group of men had an argument with another group and then stormed out to find someplace else to pray. Since the end of World War II Americanized Jews have tended to worship in distinguished and substantial edifices but, aside from New York, Miami, and the four or five other cities in the country with large Jewish populations, it would be rare to find a community with even half a dozen Jewish temples or synagogues.

In the Jewish ghettos early in the twentieth century, shops closed on the Sabbath and the men and women, separated by curtains, prayed in the neighborhood synagogues. On the most holy days of the Jewish year, generally in September, 95 percent of the East European Jewish families went to the synagogue. As the Jewish immigrants and their children assimilated and Americanized, this percentage dwindled considerably. Although no statistics on high holy day attendance are available, it would be a safe guess to say that today the figure is at best 50 percent. All we can assert with accuracy, however, is that "all surveys of religious commitment, belief, and practice in the United States indicate that Jews are much less involved in religious activities than Protestants, who are in turn less active than Catholics." Nevertheless, it is still true today that the New York City public schools are closed for the major Jewish holidays because Jews constitute a majority of the teachers and their absence would create severe administrative headaches. Furthermore, on the Jewish holidays many of the city's businesses are closed, restaurants in commercial areas are nearly empty, and the mass transportation system has no more than half, if that many, of its usual patrons.

GERMAN VS. EAST EUROPEAN JEWS

The East European Jews who arrived in the United States in the late nineteenth and early twentieth centuries encountered an unreceptive American Jewry. The American Jews, descended mostly from the German migrations of the middle of the nineteenth century, had achieved a secure middle-class position in the United States. They were doctors, lawyers, bankers, manufacturers, and merchants. They had established or developed some of the leading department stores in the country like Macy's and Sears Roebuck. In addition, they had made every effort to appear indistinguishable from the more prosperous gentile Americans.

The coming of the East European Jews threatened the security of the German Jews. One of them wrote, in 1893, that the experience of the United Jewish Charities in Rochester, New York, "teaches that organized immigration from Russia, Rumania, and other semibarbarous countries is a mistake and has proved a failure. It is no relief to the Jews of Russia, Poland, etc., and it jeopardizes the well being of American Jews." The Americanized Jews felt little kinship with the newcomers and also feared that their presence would constitute a burden on society and stimulate an outburst of anti-Semitism. When the *Hebrew Standard* declared, on June 15, 1894, that "the thoroughly acclimated American Jew . . . is closer to the Christian sentiment around him than to the Judaism of these miserable darkened Hebrews," it probably expressed the dominant sentiment of American Jewry at the time.

Despite their antipathy, the Americanized Jews realized that the gentiles in the United States lumped all Jews together and that the behavior of the Orthodox would reflect on everyone. As Louis D. Brandeis later phrased it,

> a single though inconspicuous instance of dishonorable conduct on the part of a Jew in any trade or profession has far-reaching evil effects extending to the many innocent members of the race. Large as this country is, no Jew can behave badly without injuring each of us in the end. . . . Since the act of each becomes thus the concern of all, we are perforce our brothers' keepers.

One should not minimize, however, the fact that the American Jews
also had a paternalistic sympathy for their East European brethren
and therefore, since they could not contain the stampede from Russia, Galicia, and Rumania, they set about, after an initial display of
coldness, to improve the "moral, mental and physical conditions" of
the immigrants.

Once they decided to facilitate assimilation by assisting the newcomers, the American Jews spared no efforts and "few human needs
were overlooked." Of all immigrant groups none proved so generous
to "their own kind" as did the Jews. Money and organizational talent
combined to provide hospitals, orphan asylums, recreational facilities,
and homes for unwed mothers as well as for the deaf, the blind, the
old, and the crippled. Educational institutions were also established
and the "zeal to Americanize underlay all educational endeavor." Part
of this Americanizing process also resulted in the building up of the
Jewish Theological Seminary in New York City to train Conservative
rabbis. The American Jewish establishment could not tolerate orthodoxy but recognized that the East European immigrants would not
come around to Reform Judaism. Conservatism provided an acceptable compromise since it preached American values while retaining the
most important orthodox traditions.

Another of the projects resulted in an attempt to disperse the immigrants throughout the United States. The Americanized Jews did
not want the newcomers to congregate in one massive ghetto. Between 1901 and 1917 the Industrial Removal Office dispatched 72,482
East European Jews to 1,670 communities in forty-eight states. Nevertheless, many of those transplanted eventually returned to New York.
In fact, of the 1,334, 627 Jews who did arrive in New York City between 1881 and 1911, 73.5 percent remained there.

The most important and lasting agency set up by the Americanized
Jews to help—and lead—their brethren was the American Jewish Com-
mittee. Ostensibly formed as a result of the outrageous pogroms in
Russia between 1903 and 1905 and dedicated to protecting the civil
rights of Jews wherever they were threatened, the American Jewish
Committee came into being in 1906 primarily because the established
Jewish community in the United States wanted "to assert some con-
trol over existing Jewish institutions and mass movements." As Louis

Marshall, one of the American Jewish Committee's leading members and its president from 1912 to 1929, put it in 1908, the purpose of those who formed the organization was "to devise a simple and efficient instrument which might deal quickly, and at the same time deliberately, and with an understanding based on experience, with the problems that might present themselves from time to time."

The American Jewish Committee, composed of wealthy Jews, exercised great influence politically "through private contacts with men in power." Since Jacob Schiff, Cyrus Adler, Louis Marshall, Felix Warburg, Oscar Strauss, Julius Rosenwald, Mayer Sulzberger, and others of their stature dealt regularly with the most prominent Americans of their generation, the Committee "on the whole, acted effectively in the interests of American Jewry." The American Jewish Committee, as one scholar has pointed out, "offered American Jewry a vigorous, disciplined and highly paternalistic leadership as well as a program of Americanization," but its members looked down upon the East Europeans and expected them to follow its leadership. This did not occur. Perhaps if the Committee had been more democratically organized it might have served as a bridge to the newcomers and won them over. But as one of the group said, "let us get away from the idea that the American Jewish Committee must be representative and that its members must be chosen in some way by the vote of the Jews in this country. No great moral movement has been undertaken and carried through except in just such a manner in which we are doing our work."

The enormous assistance provided by the Americanized Jews to the immigrants was accepted with reservations. The established Jews showed disdain for the East Europeans and their culture and the recipients of their largesse felt like beggars and poor relations. The charity may have been given out of a sense of obligation but it did not come with warmth and kindness. And the leadership provided by the American Jewish Committee definitely smacked of elitism which the immigrants would not tolerate. As soon as the East Europeans could provide their own network of charitable and welfare organizations they did so. It would be a long time before they would look upon their "benefactors" without a jaundiced eye.

ANTI-SEMITISM

The German and East European Jews in the United States recognized
the vast gulf that separated them socially, economically, and culturally
but gentiles did not. The coming of the new Jews intensified latent
anti-Semitic feelings among gentile Americans and, as the German
Jews had originally feared, this hostility erupted in public. The German Jews felt the sting first. In 1877 a prominent Jewish banker was
barred as a guest from a resort hotel that had previously accepted his
patronage. As the nineteenth century came to a close, German Jews
also found themselves excluded from private schools, prominent social
clubs, and other resorts. In 1890 the editors of *The American Hebrew*
sent around a questionnaire to prominent Americans inquiring why
gentiles were so hostile to Jews and one university president responded
that "All intelligent Christians deplore the fact that the historical evi-
dences for Christianity have so little weight with your people."

The East European Jews were not affected at first by social anti-
Semitism but in the early years of the twentieth century the bigotry
became acute. In rapid succession crude slurs, journalistic reports, and
supposedly learned commentaries lambasted the Jews. A letter to the
editor of the *New York Herald* complained that "these United States
are becoming rapidly so Jew ridden . . . ," while a faculty member at
Teacher's College in New York wrote to a colleague and asked him to
"please do me the favor of not coming to the banquet tomorrow night,
as I have invited a friend who does not like Jews." A magazine writer
asked of the Russian Jew, "is he assimilable? Has he in himself the
stuff of which Americans are made?" University of Wisconsin sociologist E. A. Ross claimed that "the lower class of Hebrews of eastern
Europe reach here moral cripples, their souls warped and dwarfed by
iron circumstance . . . many of them have developed a monstrous
and repulsive love of gain." Finally, University of Berlin Professor
Werner Sombart's prediction "that in another hundred years the
United States will be peopled chiefly by Slavs, negroes and Jews," was
prominently featured in one of the leading American periodicals of
the day.

In view of these prejudices it is no wonder that outside of the garment district and other Jewish-owned establishments Jews had little

chance for obtaining decent jobs. Many help-wanted advertisements specified "Christian only," and real estate agents preferred gentile clients. To combat this discrimination one of the older American Jewish fraternal organizations, B'nai B'rith, which had been founded in 1843, established its Anti-Defamation League in 1913. The League over the years has proved quite successful in combating anti-Semitism.

Despite the efforts of the Anti-Defamation League, schools and employers continued discriminating against Jews. Quotas in higher education began in the 1920s and became more rigid during the depression years of the 1930s. As late as 1945 the president of Dartmouth College defended regulations which kept Jewish students out of his school, but he was probably the last outspoken advocate of an already waning policy. Beginning with World War II more opportunities opened to practically all skilled white people and the growth of the economy, the passage of state laws forbidding discrimination in employment and entry into universities, and a generally more tolerant spirit in the land led to widened economic and occupational opportunities for Jews. Law firms, scientific organizations, universities, and businesses needing the very best talent available hired goodly numbers of Jews who were among their few qualified applicants.

Bigotry did not disappear completely. The executive suites of America's largest corporations contain relatively few Jews and one still reads of prominent Jews being denied admission to country clubs. On December 14, 1973, *The Wall Street Journal* ran a story on Irving Shapiro, the new chairman and chief executive of Du Pont and Company, the world's largest chemical concern. Well into the article the author noted that being a lawyer, a Jew, and a Democrat were not helpful to Mr. Shapiro in his rise to prominence within the firm (although his talents, of course, overrode these "handicaps") and then tellingly, "Mr. Shapiro's official biography is noticeably lacking in the kind of club affiliations that adorn those of his colleagues."

LEGISLATION AND POLITICS

There were never any specific laws in the United States regarding East European Jews, but their arrival contributed to the movement for immigration restriction. The major American laws keeping out aliens passed Congress in 1921 and 1924 and these set quotas for groups based on a percentage of their population in the United States in 1910 and 1890, respectively. Such laws were designed to drastically curtail southern and eastern European migration to this country. The Jews, being the second largest immigrant group in the early twentieth century, were obviously one of the major targets of this legislation. As early as 1906 an Italian American had been told by a member of President Theodore Roosevelt's immigration commission that the "movement toward restriction in all of its phases is directed against Jewish immigration. . . ." The Irish, the English, and the Germans who constituted the majority of nineteenth-century immigrants to the United States received the largest quotas. No religious test was allowed by this legislation. Consequently, Jews born in Germany were counted under the German quota and Jews born in England came in under the English quota even though their parents might have come from Russia or Rumania. Subsequent legislation affecting the East European Jews came in 1948 and 1950 when some of the persons displaced by the German policies of the 1930s and the Second World War were allowed to come into the United States under special provisions. Current immigration regulations in the United States make no statement about religion and have done away with quotas based on national origins. Present legislation gives preference to immigrants with close relatives in the United States and to those who have occupational skills in demand in this country.

Jews in the United States have never been legally restrained from pursuing any social or economic interests that struck their fancy. Many states originally restricted voting rights to adult males who believed in the divinity of Jesus Christ, but these were abolished in all but a few states by the beginning of the nineteenth century.

The East Europeans, like other whites, voted after becoming citizens (which took only five years after entering the United States), but they registered and voted in much higher proportion to their numbers than did members of other ethnic groups. They took stands on political issues of concern to them and supported candidates for office who appeared to be in harmony with their own views. A number of Jews have been elected to high political office, such as governor of a state or United States senator, but before the Second World War almost all of these people were of German background. In the past score of years, however, Jews of East European background have achieved similar prominence. The best known of these are former United States Senators Jacob Javits of New York and Abraham Ribicoff of Connecticut, and former Governors Milton J. Schapp and Marvin Mandel of Pennsylvania and Maryland, respectively. Numerous Jews who were born, or whose parents were born, in Russia, Rumania, and Poland have been elected to the United States House of Representatives and the various state legislatures.

Although Jews have supported Republicans, Democrats, and socialists, since the New Deal era the vast majority have been loyal Democrats both with their votes and their financial contributions. In fact, their contributions are so lavish and their votes so important that policies affecting American Jews—and especially Israel—have to be taken into account by the leading Democratic politicos. So devoted to the Democrats are the Jews that in Richard Nixon's overwhelming re-election victory in 1972 they were the only white ethnic group in the nation that gave a majority of its votes to the Democratic nominee for President, George S. McGovern, although not by the overwhelming support usually accorded Democratic candidates. A few Jews, notably Max Fisher of Detroit, also lubricated Republican coffers. As a result, an anti-Israel policy simply would not be politically acceptable to most of the elected officials in Washington.

SUMMARY AND CONCLUSION

The East European Jews have accomplished great things for themselves in the United States. Most of them arrived on the brink of poverty around the turn of the century and their descendants have risen to comfortable and secure middle-class positions in American society. They can live where they like, work almost any place where they have the necessary skills, and worship—or not—in any manner that pleases them. This almost total freedom has resulted in a good deal of interfaith marriage and a slackening of religious and ethnic ties. During the past decade one out of every three Jewish marriages has been with a non-Jew.

Overt anti-Semitism, with the exception of the controversy between blacks and Jews arising out of the 1967 and 1968 schoolteachers' strikes in New York City, has subsided considerably during the past few decades, and recent laws have forbidden discrimination on the basis of race, creed, or national origins in employment and housing. These laws are not always observed, but they do indicate that the state and federal governments are putting up formal barriers against wanton bigotry. Ironically, diminished discrimination loosens the ties that bind ethnic minorities. The educational system, especially at the college and university levels, inculcates a national culture and a national way of thinking and it is the rare individual who, after being subject to such exposure, can be completely comfortable again in a strictly ethnic setting. With each succeeding generation of educated Jews, therefore, the ties to the traditional culture are weakened. Most American Jews today are products of the American education system and work and live in areas with people of varying ethnic backgrounds. Only some of the Jewish immigrants and their children can still be found in ghettos. And with each passing year their numbers fade.

Also on the wane is Orthodox Jewry. The attachment to the traditional faith was strong among the immigrants and their children but later generations found it a burden. Only a tiny fraction of American Jews keep the Sabbath and only a few more observe the dietary restrictions. Outside of New York, Los Angeles, Chicago, and Miami Beach, the Conservative and Reform branches of Judaism hold sway in temple memberships while the way-of-life practiced by practically all American Jews is in the Reform tradition. Thus attendance at religious services is sparse except at the beginning of the Jewish New Year and the Day of Atonement, and a middle-class life style, almost totally devoid of ethnic flavor, is vigorously pursued.

In the early 1960s one American rabbi said, "Today there is little that marks the Jew as a Jew except Jewish self-consciousness and association with fellow Jews." It is difficult to assess the strength and significance of this self-consciousness. It one "feels" Jewish and seeks out other Jews for companionship, the ties are still there. Jewish identity has also been reinforced by the emergence and travails of the State of Israel. It is impossible, of course, to predict for how many generations such sentiments will sustain American Jewry.

As the Jews become Americanized, strains and dissimilarities between the German and Russian elements have disappeared. When Hitler began persecuting Jews in Germany, and especially in the past score of years, when differences in income and life styles have narrowed considerably, there have been few if any clashes between Jews of German and East European ancestry in the United States. In fact, one might say that with each succeeding generation there is less and less difference among all American Jews regardless of their grand-fathers' native lands. Class, geographical location, education, occupation, and income would be more appropriate categories for demarcation than German-Russian or Orthodox-Reform background. The only exception to this generalization would be the American Council for Judaism, whose members are primarily of German-Jewish ancestry. It is supported by only a fraction of 1 percent of the American Jews and it differs considerably from other Jewish organizations in its regard of Israel as just another foreign country with which American Jews should have no special relationships.

Still another aspect of the migration and its subsequent impact in the United States is the fantastic influence that East European Jews have had on the academic, intellectual, medical, political, and cultural life in the country, especially since the end of the Second World War. Whereas in the 1930s it was rare to find Jews, let alone those of East European descent, on the faculties of American colleges, in more recent times Jews whose parents or grandparents came from Russia, Poland, and Rumania adorn the most prestigious American universities. It would be difficult to name them all, but even a cursory cataloging would include sociologists Daniel Bell, Nathan Glazer, and Seymour Martin Lipset (all, by the way, graduates of New York City's City College); Harvard historian Oscar Handlin; and the former Dean of the Yale Law School, Abraham Goldstein. Nobel Prize winner Simon Kuznets; economist Herbert Stein; former United States Supreme Court Justice and Ambassador to the United Nations, Arthur Goldberg; the discoverer of the vaccine to prevent polio, Jonas E. Salk; film-maker Stanley Kubrick; musician Leonard Bernstein; violinist Yehudi Menuhin; playwrights Arthur Miller and Neil Simon; and artist Ben Shahn are only a few of the others of East European Jewish descent who have made their mark in the United States. In fact, the East European Jews and their descendants have made a much greater impact, and in a wider range of activities, than people from any of the other contemporary groups of immigrants.

And yet, despite their absorption into American society, it is still true, as Jacob Neusner wrote in 1973, that "to be a Jew in America is to be in some measure different, alien, a minority." The dominant culture in the United States is still intolerant of differences among groups of people and of non-Christians loyal to a foreign state or a different faith. This, of course, presents great difficulties to the various ethnic minorities in the United States. On the one hand "cultural pluralism" is celebrated in song and spirit from every official podium while deviation is regarded as a sign of subversion and inferiority. This schizophrenic conflict affects all American minorities and to be a non-WASP is to be somehow marginal and alien. For most Jews who are prosperous, employed, and ensconced in comfortable homes, these feelings are rarely discussed, but the fierce American-Jewish devotion to the State of Israel suggests that even in the United States Jews do not feel absolutely secure. Somehow they feel that loyalty to a Jewish state is necessary. Whether it is because of an attachment to the heritage and traditions of Jewry or because of a sense of being part of the same group, or even because they fear that someday they or their descendants might have to flee the United States and take refuge in Israel is impossible to say. But we do know that the sense of identification with Israel is strong and this, in a very specific way, differentiates Jews from other Americans.

6

Here Come the Wobblies!

BERNARD A. WEISBERGER

• Throughout the nineteenth century organized labor in the
United States never embraced a majority of the industrial
working people. In 1901, only one out of every fourteen non-
agricultural workers belonged to any union, about half the
proportion in Great Britain. The pattern of organizing only
specialized craftsmen resulted partly from the exclusionary
policy of the American Federation of Labor and partly from
public antipathy for the aspirations and organizations of the
unskilled working class. The Knights of Labor championed
industrial unionism in the 1870s and attempted to unite
the nation into one big cooperative enterprise. But it dwindled in effectiveness after the public's false association of it
with the Haymarket Riot and anarchism in 1886.

An even more spectacular effort to broaden the base of
organized labor was the formation in Chicago, in 1905, of the
Industrial Workers of the World. Led by "Big Bill" Haywood of the Western Federation of Miners, the "Wobblies"
wanted to abolish the wage system. They hoped to gain
their objectives by violent abolition of the state and the formation of a nationwide industrial syndicate governed by the
workers themselves. The Wobblies were strongest among
unskilled migratory workers in the West, but they had a
hand in a number of strikes in the East. During World
War I the Wobblies suffered from the patriotic fervor of
the government and several vigilante groups, and they waned
as a force in the labor movement. Bernard A. Weisberger's
essay catches the tragedy and the persecution of the Industrial Workers of the World as they sought to protect the
welfare of the American worker.

Reprinted by permission from *American Heritage* (June 1967). © 1967 American Heritage Publishing Co., Inc.

On a hot June day in 1905 William D. Haywood, a thirty-six-year-old miner, homesteader, horsebreaker, surveyor, union organizer, and Socialist, out of Salt Lake City, stood up before a large crowd in a Chicago auditorium. He gazed down at the audience with his one good eye and, taking up a loose board from the platform, impatiently banged for silence.

"Fellow workers," he shouted, "this is the continental congress of the working class. We are here to confederate the workers of this country into a working-class movement that shall have for its purpose the emancipation of the working class from the slave bondage of capitalism."

Thus, in manifesto, the working-class crusade known as Industrial Workers of the World came to birth. It grew amid storms of dissent, lived always in the blast furnace of conflict, and was battered into helplessness over forty years ago. It is still alive, but as a "church of old men" in one author's words, old men still muttering "No" to the status quo. The *Industrial Worker*, the official newspaper of the "One Big Union," still appears, still carries as its masthead motto "An injury to one is an injury to all," still valiantly runs on its editorial page the uncompromising preamble to the constitution adopted at that Chicago convention in 1905:

> The working class and the employing class have nothing in common. There can be no peace so long as hunger and want are found among millions of working people and the few, who make up the employing class, have all the good things of life. . . .
> It is the historic mission of the working class to do away with capitalism. The army of production must be organized, not only for the everyday struggle with capitalists, but also to carry on production when capitalism shall have been overthrown. By organizing industrially we are forming the structure of the new society within the shell of the old.

But the old society is still here, thriving more vigorously than ever; the workers have late-model cars, and the struggle of the I.W.W.'s young radicals to burst its bonds is history now—good history, full of poets and tramps, bloodshed and cruelty, and roads not taken by American labor. The history not merely of an organization but of an impulse that stirred men from the lower depths of the economy—vagrants, lumberjacks, harvest hands, immigrant millworkers—and set them to marching in step with Greenwich Village literary radicals to the tune of gospel hymns and innocent ballads fitted with new, class-conscious verses.

But it was not all ballads and broadsides. The I.W.W. was radical in the word's truest sense. When it denied that the working and employing classes had anything in common, it meant precisely what it said. The I.W.W. put no faith in the promises of bourgeois politicians or in the fairness of bourgeois courts. It made no contracts with employers, and it spurned other unions—like those enrolled in the American Federation of Labor—that did. It was composed of hard, hard-working men, little known to respectability. As a result, it badly frightened millions of middle-class Americans, and it meant to.

Yet it must be understood that the I.W.W. did not grow in a vacuum. It arose out of an industrial situation for which the adjective "grim" is pallid. In the America that moved to productive maturity between 1880 and 1920, there was little room or time to care about the worker at the base of it all. It was an America in which children of ten to fourteen could and did work sixty-hour weeks in mine and factory; in which safety and sanitation regulations for those in dangerous trades were virtually unknown—and in which industrial accidents took a horrible toll each year; in which wages were set by "the market place" and some grown men with families worked ten to twelve hours for a dollar and stayed alive only by cramming their families into sickening tenements or company-town shacks; in which such things as pensions or paid holidays were unknown; lastly, it was an America in which those who did protest were often locked out, replaced by scabs, and prevented from picketing by injunction and by naked force. At Homestead, Pullman, Coeur d'Alene, Cripple Creek, Ludlow, and other places where strikers clashed with troops or police between 1892 and 1914, the record of labor's frustrations was marked with bloody palm prints. And at the bottom of the scale was the vast army of migrant workers who beat their way by rail from job to job—not only unskilled, unprotected, and underpaid but unnoticed and unremembered.

Out of such a situation grew the I.W.W. It gained much not only from the horror of its surroundings, but from the spirit of an infant century when the emancipation of almost everyone—women, workers, artists, children—from the dragons of the past seemed to be a live possibility, and "new" was a catchword on every tongue.

The opening years of the organization's life were not promising. Its founding fathers were numerous and diverse—discontented trade unionists, Socialists like Eugene V. Debs and the whiskered, professorial Daniel De Leon, and veterans of almost every other left-wing crusade of the preceding twenty years. There was among them all, a recent I.W.W. historian has written, "such a warfare as can be found only between competing radicals." They were, however, united in objecting to the craft-union principles of A.F.L. chieftain Samuel Gompers, whom Haywood described as "a squat specimen of humanity" with "small snapping eyes, a hard cruel mouth," and "a personality vain, conceited, petulant and vindictive."

Gompers' plan of organizing only skilled craftsmen and negotiating contracts aimed only at securing a better life from day to day struck the I.W.W.'s founders not only as a damper upon whatever militancy the labor movement might generate to challenge capitalism, but also as a betrayal of the unskilled laborers, who would be left to shift for themselves. The new leaders therefore created a "single industrial union," as far removed from craft divisions as possible.

All industrial labor was to be divided into thirteen great, centrally administered divisions—building, manufacturing, mining, transportation, public service, etc. Within each of these would be subgroups. But each such group would take in all employees contributing to that industry's product or service. On the steam railroads, as an instance, clerks, telegraphers, and trackwalkers would share power and glory with engineers, brakemen, and conductors. A grievance of one lowly set of workers in a single shop could bring on a strike that would paralyze a whole industry. And some day, on signal from the One Big Union, all workers in all industries would throw the "Off" switch, and the wage system would come tumbling down.

Much of the scheme came from the brain and pen of a priest, Father Thomas Hagerty, who while serving mining parishes in the Rockies had come to believe in Marx as well as Christ. He had the scheme of industrial unionism all worked out in a wheel-shaped chart, with the rim divided into the major industries and the hub labelled "General Administration." Gompers looked at a copy of it in a magazine and snarled: "Father Hagerty's Wheel of Fortune!" He did not expect it to spin very long.

Nor, during the I.W.W.'s first three years of existence, did it seem likely to. Factional quarrels wracked national headquarters and the

Western Federation of Miners, the biggest single block in the entire
I.W.W. structure, pulled out. By spring of 1908 the organization,
whose paper strength was perhaps 5,000 but whose actual roster was
probably much thinner, was broke and apparently heading toward the
graveyard that seems to await all clique-ridden American radical bodies.

But the death notices were premature. The headquarters brawls were
among and between trade unionists and Socialists, and the I.W.W.'s
future was, as it turned out, linked to neither group. It belonged to a
rank-and-file membership that was already formulating surprise tactics
and showing plenty of vigor. In Schenectady, New York, for example,
I.W.W.-led strikers in a General Electric plant protested the firing of
three draftsmen by staying at their machines for sixty-five hours, a use
of the sit-down strike thirty years before it was introduced by the auto
workers as a radical measure during the Great Depression. In Goldfield,
Nevada, the I.W.W. under thirty-one-year-old Vincent St. John organized the town's hotel and restaurant workers into a unit with the
local silver and gold miners. This unlikely combination of hash-slingers
and miners, an extreme example of industrial unionism, forced the
town's employers to boost wage scales, temporarily at least, to levels of
five dollars per eight-hour day for skilled underground workers, down
to three dollars and board for eight hours of dishwashing by the lowly
"pearl divers." It seemed to be clear proof that "revolutionary industrial unionism" could work. The fiery St. John was even able to close
down the mines one January day in 1907 for a protest parade—on
behalf of Haywood, Charles Moyer, and George Pettibone, three officers of the miners' union who had been arrested (they were later acquitted) in the bomb-killing of former Governor Frank Steunenberg of
Idaho. St. John's parade brought three thousand unionists into the
small-town streets "all wearing tiny red flags."

The real turning point came at the organization's fourth convention, in 1908. The believers in "direct action at the point of production" forced a change in the I.W.W.'s holy writ, the preamble. It had
originally contained the sentence: "A struggle must go on until all the
toilers come together *on the political, as well as the industrial field*, and
take and hold that which they produce" (italics added). Now this "political clause" was scuttled, over the violent protests of Socialist De
Leon, who helplessly denounced the change as an exaltation of "physical force." The shock troops of the direct-action group were twenty

lumber workers known as the Overalls Brigade. Gathered in Portland by an organizer named Jack Walsh, they had bummed their way to Chicago in boxcars, raising grubstakes along the way at street meetings in which they sang, harangued, peddled pamphlets, and passed the hat. One of their favorite tunes, with which they regaled the convention, was "Hallelujah, I'm a Bum," set to the old hymn tune "Revive Us Again":

> O, why don't you work
> Like other men do?
> How in hell can I work
> When there's no work to do?
>
> Hallelujah, I'm a bum,
> Hallelujah, bum again,
> Hallelujah, give us a handout—
> To revive us again.

Sourly, De Leon dubbed Walsh's men The Bummery, but the day was theirs. The veteran Socialist leader retreated and organized a splinter I.W.W., which dwindled away in seven years.

It was the I.W.W.'s second split in a short history, but its most important. It gave the organization over to soapbox singers and bums, brothers in idealism who were poor in all things save "long experience in the struggle with the employer." They were to break from past labor practices and give the I.W.W. its true inwardness and dynamism; to fit it with its unique costume and role in history.

They gave it, first, a musical voice. Walsh's crusaders sang because when they sought the workers' attention on street corners they were challenged by those competing sidewalk hot-gospellers, the Salvation Army. By 1909, the press of the organization's newspaper, the *Industrial Worker*, was able to put out the first edition of *Songs of the Workers to Fan the Flames of Discontent*. More succinctly known as the "Little Red Songbook," it has gone through over thirty subsequent editions—all scarlet-covered and fitted to the size of an overalls pocket. The songbook and the preamble were to the I.W.W. membership what the hymnbook and the *Discipline of the Methodist Church* had been to frontier preachers—the sum and touchstone of faith, the pearl of revelation, the coal of fire touching their lips with eloquence. Most of the songs were the work of men like Richard Brazier, an English-born construction worker who joined up in Spokane in 1908; or Ralph Chaplin, a struggling young Chicago commercial artist who wanted to chant "hymns of hope and hatred" at the shrine of rebellion; or Joe Hill, born Joel Haaglund in Sweden, who wrote not parodies alone but also original compositions, which Chaplin described as "coarse as home-spun and as fine as silk"; or bards known simply as T-Bone Slim or Dublin Dan. The I.W.W. members soared on those songs, enjoying them as much for their mockery as anything.

To the patriotic cadences of "The Battle Hymn of the Republic" they sang "Solidarity forever, for the Union makes us strong" (a version which Ralph Chaplin had given them and which the entire labor movement took over without credit). To the sentimental notes that enfolded Darling Nelly Gray they sang of "the Commonwealth of Toil that is to be," and to the strains that had taken pretty Red Wing through ribald adventures in every barroom in the country, they roared that "the earth of right belongs to toilers, and not to spoilers of liberty." They raided the hymnbook of Moody-and-Sankey revivalism for "Hold the fort for we are coming, union men be strong," and for "There is power, there is power, in a working band" (instead of "in the blood of the Lamb"). They laughed in sharps and flats at Casey Jones, of the craft-proud Brotherhood of Railway Engineers, as a union scab who "kept his junk pile running" and "got a wooden medal for being good and faithful on the S.P. line." They sang in the hobo jungles, on the picket line, and in the jailhouse, and it was their singing especially that separated them from the A.F.L. by an abyss of spirit.

The "new" I.W.W. soon had a nickname, as derisive and defiant as its songs: the Wobblies. It is not certain how the name was born, though a popular legend declares that a Chinese restaurant owner in the Northwest was persuaded to grubstake I.W.W. members drifting through his town. His identification test was a simple question, "Are you I.W.W.?" but it emerged in Cantonese-flavored English as "Ah loo eye wobble wobble?" Whatever its origin, the name was a badge of pride.

The I.W.W.'s new leadership provided halls in the towns where a wandering Wobbly could find a warm stove, a pot of coffee, a corner in which to spread a blanket for the night, and literature: the *Industrial Worker* and *Solidarity*, leaflets by St. John or Haywood, and books like Jack London's *The Iron Heel*, Edward Bellamy's *Looking Back-ward*, Laurence Gronlund's *Co-operative Commonwealth*. All of them furnished material for arguments with the unorganized, and also such stuff as dreams were made on.

In 1909 the I.W.W. attracted national attention through the first of its spectacular clashes with civic authority. In Spokane a campaign was launched urging loggers to boycott the "job sharks," employment agents who hired men for work in lumber and construction camps deep in the woods, charging them a fee for the "service." Many a lumberjack who "bought a job" in this way was swindled—sent to a nonexistent camp or quickly fired by a foreman in cahoots with the shark to provide fast turnover and larger shared profits. At street meetings, the Wobblies preached direct hiring by the lumber companies. Spokane's thirty-one agencies retaliated by getting the city council to ban such meetings. The *Industrial Worker* promptly declared November 2, 1909, Free Speech Day and urged every man in the vicinity to "fill the jails of Spokane."

From hundreds of miles around, Wobblies poured in by boxcar, mounted soapboxes, and were immediately wrestled into patrol wagons. In a matter of weeks, the jail and a quickly converted schoolhouse were overflowing with five or six hundred prisoners. They came into court bloody from beatings; they were put to hard labor on bread and water, jammed into cells like sardines, and in the name of sanitation hosed with ice water and returned to unheated confinement. Three died of pneumonia. Among the prisoners was a dark-haired Irish girl from New York, Elizabeth Gurley Flynn. Eighteen years old and pregnant, she complicated her arrest by chaining herself to a lamp post. "Gurley," a proletarian Joan of Arc, was lodged with a woman cellmate who kept receiving mysterious calls to the front office. It turned out that she was a prostitute, serving customers provided by the sheriff "for good and valuable consideration." This fact was trumpeted by the I.W.W. as soon as Gurley figured it out.

Fresh trainloads of Wobblies poured relentlessly into town, while those already in jail kept the night alive with selections from the Little Red Songbook roared at full volume, staged hunger strikes, refused to touch their hammers on the rock pile, and generally discomfited their captors. In March of 1910 the taxpayers of Spokane threw in the towel, released the prisoners, and restored the right of free speech to the I.W.W. Other free-speech fights in the next few years carried the Wobbly message throughout the Far West and helped in organizing new locals among the militant.

Two years after the end of the Spokane campaign, the I.W.W. made headlines in the East. In the textile-manufacturing town of Lawrence, Massachusetts, on January 11, 1912, more than 20,000 workers struck against a wage cut that took thirty cents—the price of three loaves of bread—out of pay envelopes averaging only six to eight dollars for a fifty-four-hour week. It was an unskilled work force that hit the bitter-cold streets, and a polyglot one, too. Some twenty-five nationalities, speaking forty-five languages or dialects, were represented, including French Canadians, Belgians, Poles, Italians, Syrians, Lithuanians, Greeks, Russians, and Turks.

There was only a small I.W.W. local in Lawrence, but the tactics of One Big Union under the slogan "An injury to one is an injury to all" had never been more appropriate. I.W.W. pamphlets and newspapers in several languages had already appeared. Now the leadership deployed its best veterans in the field—Haywood, William Trautmann, Elizabeth Gurley Flynn—and in addition a big, jovial-looking Italian organizer of steelworkers, Joe Ettor, whose usual costume was a black shirt and a red tie.

For over two months, something akin to social revolution went on in Lawrence. A strike committee of fifty-six members, representing all nationalities, filled days and nights with meetings and parades. Haywood stood out like a giant. He hurdled the linguistic barrier by speeches partly in sign language (waving fingers to show the weakness of separate craft unions; balled-up fist to demonstrate solidarity), visited workers' homes, and won the women's hearts by joshing the children or smacking his lips over shashlik or spaghetti. He also shrewdly exploited the publicity that bathed Lawrence, which was near the nation's journalistic capitals. Demonstrations were called with an eye not only to working-class morale but to public opinion. It was an education for many Americans to read about "ignorant, foreign" mill girls carrying signs that said: "We Want Bread and Roses, Too."

The employers played into Haywood's hands. National Guardsmen were called out. Police arrested more than three hundred workers and, in a climax of stupidity, clubbed a group of mothers and children preparing to leave town by railroad for foster homes. In defiance of the evidence, Ettor and Arturo Giovannitti, another Italian organizer, were arrested as accessories in the shooting of a woman striker. Authorities held them for seven months before a trial. When it came, it not only let the two men go free but gave Giovannitti a chance to spellbind jury and reporters with an oration on behalf of "this mighty army of the working class of the world, which . . . is striving towards the destined goal, which is the emancipation of human kind, which is the establishment of love and brotherhood and justice for every man and every woman in this earth."

Long before that speech, in March of 1912, the bosses had given up and agreed to the strikers' terms. It was the I.W.W.'s finest hour up to then. Flushed with success, the One Big Union next answered the call of silk workers at Paterson, New Jersey, to lead them in a strike that began in February, 1913. The pattern of Lawrence seemed at first to be repeating. There were nearly fifteen hundred arrests, and in addition police and private detectives killed two workers by random gunfire. One of these, Valentino Modesto, was given a funeral at which twenty thousand workers filed by to drop red carnations on the coffin. But after five months even relief funds and singing rallies could not prevail over hunger. The strike was broken.

Not, however, before it produced a unique project and a strange alliance. One of the reporters who came to Paterson on an April day was John Reed—talented, charming, Harvard '10—who was enjoying life to the hilt in the Bohemian surroundings of Greenwich Village, then in its heyday. When Reed stopped to talk to a striker, a Paterson policeman on the lookout for "agitators" hustled him off to jail. There he stayed for four days, sharing smokes and food with the strikers and amiably teaching them college fight songs and French ballads in return for instruction in the arts of survival in prison. On his release he became an enthusiastic supporter of the embattled workers and brought such friends as Mabel Dodge, Hutchins Hapgood, Walter Lippmann, Lincoln Steffens, and others to hear Haywood and other Wobbly leaders speak.

Between the individualistic rebelliousness of the young artists and writers escaping their bourgeois backgrounds and the hard-shelled but dream-drenched radicalism of the I.W.W. leaders, there was instinctive connection. Reed conceived the idea of a giant fund-raising pageant to present the strikers' case. On June 7, thousands of silk workers came into New York by special train and ferry and marched to Madison Square Garden. There they watched hundreds of fellow strikers reenact the walkout, the shooting of Modesto, his funeral, and the mass meetings that followed. Staged by Reed's Harvard friend Robert Edmund Jones against a backdrop created by the artist John Sloan, the pageant was described by *Outlook* as having "a directness, an intensity, and a power seldom seen on the professional stage." Since it ran for only one night, it failed to earn any money beyond expenses, despite a full house. Yet as a moment of convergence in the currents of radicalism vitalizing American life and letters in the last days of prewar innocence, it has a historic place of its own.

The Lawrence and Paterson affairs were only forays, however. The I.W.W. ran strikes and kept footholds in the East—the dockworkers of Philadelphia were firmly organized in the I.W.W.-affiliated Marine Transport Workers Union, for example—but it lacked staying power in the settled industrial areas. As it moved into its peak years, the future of the One Big Union was in the West, where its message and tactics were suited to the style of migrant workers, and to the violent tempo of what Elizabeth Flynn recalled as "a wild and rugged country where both nature and greed snuffed out human life."

Here, in the mountains and forests, were men who needed protection even more than the unskilled rubber, textile, steel, and clothing workers receiving I.W.W. attention—men like the "timber beasts," who worked in the freezing woods from dawn to dusk and then "retired" to vermin-ridden bunkhouses, without washing facilities, where they were stacked in double tiers like their own logs. The companies did not even furnish bedding, and a lumberjack between jobs was recognizable by his roll of blankets—his "bundle," "bindle," or "balloon" —slung on his back. The bindle stiff who "played the woods," however, was only one member of an army of migrant workers, as many as a half million strong, who as the cycle of each year turned followed the harvests, the construction jobs, the logging operations, and the opening of new mines. Sometimes they got a spell of sea life in the forecastle of a merchant ship; often they wintered in the flophouses of

Chicago or San Francisco; and not infrequently they spent the out-of-season months in jail on charges of vagrancy. The public mind blurred them together, and made no distinction among hoboes, bums, and tramps, assuming them all to be thieves, drunkards, and pan-handlers. But the true migrant was none of these. He was a "working stiff," emphasis on the first word, and thus ripe for the tidings of class war.

The I.W.W. reached him where he lived: in the hobo "jungles" out-side the rail junction points, where he boiled stew in empty tin cans, slept on the ground come wind, come weather, and waited to hop a freight bound in any direction where jobs were rumored to be. The Wobblies sent in full-time organizers, dressed in the same caps and windbreakers, but with pockets full of red membership cards, dues books and stamps, subscription blanks, song sheets, pamphlets. These job delegates signed up their men around the campfires or in the box-cars ("side-door Pullmans" the migrants called them), mailed the money to headquarters, and then followed their recruits to the woods, or to the tents in the open fields where the harvest stiffs unrolled *their* bindles after twelve hours of work in hundred-degree heat without water, shade, or toilets. But there were some whom the organizers could not reach, and the I.W.W. sent them messages in the form of "stickerettes." These "silent agitators" were illustrated slogans on label-sized pieces of gummed paper, many of them drawn by Ralph Chaplin. They sold for as little as a dollar a thousand, and Chaplin believed that in a few weeks a good "Wob" on the road could plaster them on "every son-of-a-bitch of a boxcar, watertank, pick handle and pitchfork" within a radius of hundreds of miles.

The stickers were simple and caught the eye. "What Time Is It? Time to Organize!" shouted a clock. "Solidarity Takes the Whole Works" explained a Bunyan-sized workingman with an armload of trains and factories. The three stars of the One Big Union (Organiza-tion, Education, Emancipation) winked bright red over a black and yellow earth. A "scissorbill"—a workingman without class loyalty—knelt on bony knees and snuffled to the sky, "Now I get me up to work, I pray the Lord I may not shirk." But the most fateful stickers to appear between 1915 and 1917, as the nation moved toward war, were those that urged: "SLOW DOWN. The hours are long, the pay is small, so take your time and buck 'em all"; and those on which appeared two portentous symbols: the wooden shoe of sabotage, and the black cat, which, as everybody knew, meant trouble.

A tough problem for the I.W.W. was how to achieve "direct action" in the migrant workers' spread-eagle world. A factory or a mine could be struck. But how could the I.W.W.'s farmhands' union, the Agricultural Workers' Organization, "strike" a thousand square miles of wheatfield divided among hundreds of farmer-employers? How could the Forest and Lumber Workers' Industrial Union tie up a logging operation spread among dozens of camps separated by lonely miles?

The answer was, as the Wobblies put it, "to bring the strike to the job," or, more bluntly, sabotage. To the average American, sabotage conjured up nightmares of violence to property: barns blazing in the night, crowbars twisting the steel and wire guts out of a machine. The word itself suggested a European tradition of radical workers' dropping their *sabots*, or wooden shoes, into the works. But the I.W.W. leaders insisted that they had something less destructive in mind—merely the slowdown, the "conscientious withdrawal of efficiency," or, in working-stiff terms, "poor pay, poor work." To "put on the wooden shoe," or to "turn loose the black kitty" or "sab-cat," meant only to misplace and misfile order slips, to "forget" to oil motors, to "accidentally" let furnaces go out. Or simply to dawdle on the job and let fruit rot on the ground or let threshing or logging machinery with steam up stand idle while farmers and foremen fumed.

I.W.W. headquarters was vague about where the limits to direct action lay. Nor did it help matters when it printed dim, oracular pronouncements like Bill Haywood's "Sabotage means to push back, pull out or break off the fangs of Capitalism." Such phrases were enough to frighten not only the capitalists, but the Socialists, who in their 1912 convention denied the red sacraments to any who advocated "crime, sabotage or other methods of violence as a weapon of the working class to aid in its emancipation." (The next year, the Socialists fired Haywood from the party's executive board, completing the divorce between the Wobblies and politics.) Still the I.W.W. leaders in the field pushed ahead with their tactics. The Agricultural Workers, to strengthen the threat of mass quittings by harvest hands, organized a "thousand-mile picket line" of tough Wobblies who worked their way through freight trains in the farm belt, signing up new members and unceremoniously dumping off any "scissorbills" or "wicks" who refused a red card. The Lumber Workers forced the camp owners to furnish clean bedding by encouraging thousands of lumberjacks to celebrate May Day, 1918, by soaking their bindles with kerosene and making huge bonfires of them.

Potentially such tactics were loaded with danger, but from 1913 to 1919 they worked. Ralph Chaplin estimated that in early spring of 1917, when the A.W.O. was signing up members at the rate of 5,000 a month, the going wage in the grain belt had jumped from two dollars for a twelve-to-sixteen-hour day to five dollars for a ten-hour day. Two years later northwestern loggers were averaging twenty-five to fifty dollars a month plus board. These facts meant more to the average reader of *Solidarity* and the *Industrial Worker* than I.W.W. theories about the overthrow of capitalism. If he thought about the shape of society after the final general strike, it was only in the vague way of a church deacon who knew there was a celestial crown reserved for him, but did not trouble his mind about it from day to day. Yet the very success of the organization anywhere stirred not only the anger of its enemies but the fears of unsophisticated Americans who were ready to believe that the Wobblies were already putting the torch to the foundations of government and justice. With war hysteria actively feeding the fires of public hostility, the I.W.W. became the victim of new and spectacular persecutions.

Perhaps it was inevitable that the blood of martyrs would splash the pages of the I.W.W.'s book of chronicles. The mine owners, lumber-camp operators, and ranchers whom the Wobblies fought were themselves hard, resourceful men who had mastered a demanding environment. They knew a challenge when they saw one, and the West, in 1915, was not too far past Indian, stagecoach, and vigilante days. Sheriffs and their deputies were ready to use any method to rid their communities of "agitators"—especially those described in the press as "America's cancer sore." The Los Angeles *Times*, for example, said that

A vast number of I.W.W.'s are non-producers. I.W.W. stands for I won't work, and I want whisky. . . . The average Wobbly, it must be remembered, is a sort of half wild animal. He lives on the road, cooks his food in rusty tin cans . . . and sleeps in "jungles," barns, outhouses, freight cars. . . . They are all in all a lot of homeless men wandering about the country without fixed destination or purpose, other than destruction.

"When a Wobbly comes to town," one sheriff told a visitor, "I just knock him over the head with a night stick and throw him in the river. When he comes up he beats it out of town." Lawmen furnished similar treatment to any hobo or "undesirable" stranger, particularly if he showed a tendency to complain about local working conditions or if, after April 6, 1917, he did not glow with the proper enthusiasm for the war to end wars. Hundreds of suspected and genuine Wobblies were jailed, beaten, shot, and tortured between 1914 and 1919, but some names and episodes earned, by excess of horror or myth-creating power, a special framing among dark memories.

There was the case of Joe Hill. He was the most prolific of the Wobbly bards; the dozens of numbers he composed while drifting from job to job after his emigration from Sweden to America (where his name transformed itself from Haaglund into Hillstrom and then into plain Hill) had done much to make the I.W.W. a singing movement. His songs had, a recent Wobbly folklorist has written, "tough, humorous, skeptical words which raked American morality over the coals." They were known and sung wherever Wobblies fought cops and bosses.

In January, 1914, Salt Lake City police arrested Hill on the charge of murdering a grocer and his son in a holdup. Circumstantial evidence was strongly against him, but Hill went through trial and conviction stoutly insisting that he had been framed. Though a popular ballad written many years afterward intones, "The copper bosses killed you, Joe," Hill was not definitely linked to any strike activity in Utah, and had been in the I.W.W. for only four years. But his songs had made him a hero to the entire radical labor movement, and he had a sure sense of drama. Through months of appeals and protest demonstrations he played—or lived—the role of Pilate's victim magnificently. On November 18, 1915, the day before a five-man firing squad shot him dead, he sent to Bill Haywood, in Chicago, a classic telegram: "Goodbye, Bill. I die like a true blue rebel. Don't waste any time mourning. Organize!" Thirty thousand people wept at his funeral. At his own request, his ashes were put in small envelopes and distributed to be scattered, the following May Day, in every state of the Union.

And there was the "Everett massacre." On October 30, 1916, forty-one Wobblies had travelled from Seattle to Everett, Washington, some forty miles away, to speak on behalf of striking sawmill workers. Vigilantes under Sheriff Donald McRae arrested them, took them to the edge of town, and forced them to run the gantlet between rows of deputies armed with clubs, pick handles, and bats. Next morning the grass was stiff with dried blood. Five days later, two steamer loads of I.W.W. members sailed up Puget Sound from Seattle for a meeting of protest. As they approached the Everett docks singing "Hold the Fort for We Are Coming," the sheriff and his men were waiting. They opened up with a hail of gunfire, and five Wobblies were killed, thirty-one wounded; in the confused firing, two vigilantes were also killed. Seventy-four Wobblies were arrested and tried for these two deaths but were acquitted. No one was tried for killing the I.W.W. men.

The following summer Frank Little, a member of the I.W.W. executive board, died violently in Butte, Montana. Little was a dark-haired man, with only one good eye and a crooked grin. He was part Indian, and liked to josh friends like Elizabeth Gurley Flynn and Bill Haywood by saying: "I am a real Red. The rest of you are immigrants." In June, with his leg in a cast from a recent auto accident, he left Chicago headquarters for Butte to take command of the copper miners' strike, denounced by the mine owners as a pro-German uprising. On the night of August 1, 1917, six armed and masked men broke into his hotel room and dragged him at a rope's end behind an automobile to a railroad trestle, from which he was hanged, cast and all. No arrests were made by Butte police.

As a final gruesome example, there was what happened in Centralia, Washington, on Armistice Day, 1919. An American Legion parade halted before the town's I.W.W. hall, long denounced as a center of seditious efforts to stir lumberjacks to wartime strikes and already once raided and wrecked by townsmen. Now, again, a group of men broke from the line of march and swarmed toward the building. The Wobblies inside were waiting. Simultaneous shots from several directions shattered the air; three legionnaires fell dead. The marchers broke in, seized five men, and pursued a sixth. He was Wesley Everest, a young logger and war veteran. He killed another legionnaire before they captured him and dragged him, with his teeth knocked out, to jail. That night a mob broke in and took Everest to a bridge over the Chehalis

River. There he allegedly was castrated with a razor and then hanged from the bridge in the glare of automobile headlights.

The hand of history struck the I.W.W. its hardest blow, however, in September of 1917. The United States government moved to cripple the One Big Union, not because it was a threat to capitalism (the government insisted, without convincing the Wobblies) but because it was impeding the prosecution of the war. Whereas Samuel Gompers had moved skillfully to entrench the A.F.L. deeper in the hearts of the middle class by pledging it fully to Wilson's crusade, the I.W.W. remained hostile. In its eyes, the only war that meant anything to a working stiff was that foretold in the preamble, between the millions who toiled and the few who had the good things of life. Wobblies had seen too many strikes broken by troops to warm to the sight of uniforms. "Don't be a soldier," said one popular stickerette, "be a man."

The General Executive Board knew the dangers of that position once war was declared. The members hedged on expressing any formal attitude toward America's entry, and when the draft was enacted, the board advised them to register as "I.W.W. opposed to war" and thereafter to consult their own consciences. (Wesley Everest had been one of many Wobblies who chose uniformed service.) But the militant I.W.W. campaigns were frank challenges to the official drive for production. Five months after the declaration of war, federal agents, under emergency legislation, suddenly descended on I.W.W. offices all over the country. They confiscated tons of books, newspapers, letters, and pamphlets—as well as wall decorations, mimeograph machines, and spittoons—as evidence, then returned to remove Wobbly officials handcuffed in pairs.

The biggest trial of Wobblies on various counts of obstructing the war effort took place in federal district court in Chicago in the summer of 1918. Relentlessly the prosecutors drew around one hundred defendants a net of rumors and accusations charging them with conspiring to burn crops, drive spikes in logs, derail trains, dynamite factories. Judge Kenesaw Mountain Landis (later to be famous as professional baseball's "czar") presided in shirt-sleeved informality over the hot courtroom as, day after day, government attorneys read into the record every savory piece of I.W.W. prose or verse from which such phrases as "direct action" and "class war" could be speared and

held up for horrified scrutiny. The jury took less than an hour to consider thousands of pages of evidence and hundreds of separate alleged
offenses, and returned against all but a handful of the defendants a
predictable wartime verdict of "guilty" on all counts. The white-
thatched Judge Landis handed out sentences running as high as twenty
years, as if he were in magistrate's court consigning the morning quota
of drunks to thirty days each.

The 1918 federal trials (which were followed by similar episodes in
a number of states that hastily enacted laws against "criminal syndi-
calism") were a downward turning point for the I.W.W. In theory,
the One Big Union was wholly responsive to its rank and file, and in-
vulnerable to the destruction of its bureaucracy.[1] But democratic enthusiasm could not override the fact that the veteran officers and keen-
est minds of the I.W.W. were behind bars, and their replacements
were almost totally absorbed in legal maneuvers to get them out. A
pathetic Wobbly fund-raising poster compressed the truth into a single
line under a picture of a face behind bars: "We are in here for you;
you are out there for us." In 1920 there might still have been fifty thousand on the I.W.W. rolls, but they were riding a rudderless craft.

Other troubles beset the One Big Union. The Communist party
rose on the scene and sucked into its orbit some respected veterans, including Elizabeth Gurley Flynn (though she had left the I.W.W. in
1916) and William D. Haywood himself. Released from Leavenworth
while his case was on appeal, Big Bill jumped bail and early in 1921
fled to the Soviet Union. Forgivably and understandably, perhaps, his
courage had at last been shaken. He was fifty-one years old, seriously
ill, and certain that he would die—with profit to no cause—if he had
to spend any more time in jail. He was briefly publicized in Russia as
a refugee from capitalism. He married a Russian woman, and for a
time held a job as one of the managers of an industrial colony in the
Kuznetsk Basin. But soon there was silence, and rumors of disillusionment. In May of 1928 he died. Half his ashes were sent to Chicago for
burial. The other half lie under the Kremlin wall—like those of his old
friend of Paterson days, John Reed. By and large, however, Bolshevik

---

1. The fact was that it made valorous efforts to keep its officialdom humble.
As general secretary-treasurer, Bill Haywood received thirty-five dollars a week—
just twice what a field organizer took home.

politicians had as little appeal for old-time Wobblies as any other kind. (Yet in 1948 the leadership of what was left of the organization refused to sign Taft-Hartley non-Communist affidavits. No contract, and no deals with bourgeois governments. Principle was principle still.) More cracks crisscrossed the surface of solidarity. Some of the more successful I.W.W. unions experienced a yearning for larger initiation fees, and for just a taste of the financial stability of the A.F.L. internationals—the stability which had never been a Wobbly strong point. They quarrelled with the General Executive Board. A few locals chafed under what they thought was too much centralization. And finally, in 1924, there was an open split and a secession of part of the organization, taking precious funds and property with it. The last great schism, in 1908, had freed the I.W.W. for vigorous growth. Now it was sixteen years later, and time and chance were playing cruel games.

Middle age was overtaking the young lions, dulling their teeth—especially those who, one by one, accepted individual offers of clemency and emerged from prison, blinking, to find a changed world. The harvest stiff no longer took the side-door Pullman. He was a "gas tramp" now, or a "flivver hobo," riding his battered Model T to the job, and beyond the reach of the thousand-mile picket line. The logger, too, was apt to be a "home-guard," living with his family and driving through the dawn hours to where the saws whined and the big ones toppled. The children of the sweated immigrants of Paterson and Lawrence were clutching their high school diplomas, forgetting their working-class background, becoming salesmen and stenographers. Even the worker who stayed in the mill or the mine was sometimes lulled into passivity by the squealing crystal set or the weekly dream-feast of the picture-show. The ferment in the unskilled labor pool was hissing out. A new society *was* being built; but Ford and the installment plan had more to do with it than the visionaries who had hotly conceived and lustily adopted the I.W.W. preamble of 1905.

There was some fight left in the old outfit. It could run a free-speech fight in San Pedro in 1923, a coal strike in Colorado in 1927–28. But it was dwindling and aging. When the Depression came, labor's dynamism was reawakened by hardship. The C.I.O. was created, and fought its battles under the pennons of "industrial unionism," the heart of the Wobbly plan for organizing the army of production. The C.I.O. used singing picket lines, too, and sit-down strikes—techniques pioneered by such men as Haywood and Vincent St. John when labor's new leaders were in knickers. The old-timers who had known Big Bill and The Saint could only look on from the sidelines as the younger generation took over. Moreover, the success of organizing drives in the thirties, and the programs of the New Deal, vastly improved the lot of millions of working people. The agony that had nourished the I.W.W.'s revolutionary temper was now abating. Ironically, the very success of labor in uplifting itself through collective bargaining and politics drove one more nail into the I.W.W.'s coffin.

But "coffin" is perhaps the wrong word. Like Joe Hill, the I.W.W. never died. In its offices scattered across the country, old-timers still sit and smoke under pictures of Frank Little and Wesley Everest, or leaf through copies of the *Industrial Worker* like the great readers they always were. They do not give up; they expect that history will knock some sense into the workers soon, and that then the cry of "One Union, One Label, One Enemy" will rise again from thousands of throats. But meanwhile, their offices are, in the words of a recent observer, haunted halls, "full of memories and empty of men."

By contrast, the steel and glass office buildings of the bigtime A.F.L.-C.I.O. unions are alive with the ring of telephones, the hum of presses, the clatter of typewriters, and the clicking of secretaries' heels hurrying through the doors behind which sit organized labor's well-dressed statisticians, economists, lawyers, accountants, editors, co-ordinators, and educators. They have given much to their workers, these unions— good wages, decent hours, vacations, benefits, pensions, insurance. But they may be incapable of duplicating two gifts that the I.W.W. gave its apostles, its knights, its lovers—gifts that shine through a pair of stories. One is of the sheriff who shouted to a group of Wobblies, "Who's yer leader?" and got back a bellowed answer, "We don't got no leader, we're all leaders." The other is a recollection by an unidentified witness at the Chicago trial:

> Well, they grabbed us. And the deputy says, "Are you a member of the I.W.W.?" I says, "Yes," so he asked me for my card, and I gave it to him, and he tore it up. He tore up the other cards that the fellow members along with me had. So this fellow member says, "There is no use tearing that card up. We can get duplicates." "Well," the deputy says, "We can tear the duplicates too." And this fellow worker says, he says, "Yes, but you can't tear it out of my heart."

7

"The Warrior and the Priest":
Theodore Roosevelt and Woodrow Wilson

JOHN MILTON COOPER, JR.

• Theodore Roosevelt and Woodrow Wilson were the two
dominant American political personalities of the first quarter
of the twentieth century. They each became President of the
United States, they each accepted diplomatic responsibilities
around the world, and they each left a strong personal stamp
upon the nation at a critical point in its history. But they
were also frequent political enemies whose methods, ideals,
and policies diverged sharply. Theodore Roosevelt was a fer-
vent nationalist and a rank imperialist who sought to project
the image of a strong and decisive man throughout his adult
life. He accepted uncritically the views of Alfred Thayer
Mahan, and he fought consistently for a powerful Navy and
for a greater American role in international affairs. And partially because of his experience in overcoming a sickly childhood, Theodore Roosevelt wanted to be at the center of the
fray. During the Spanish-American War, for example, he
resigned his post as assistant secretary of the Navy in order
to organize the "Rough Riders." Subsequently, he covered
himself and them with glory as their colonel in the battle for
San Juan.

Woodrow Wilson had many careers: first as a scholar of
the first rank, then as a college administrator, then as a reform governor of New Jersey, and finally as President of the
United States. But unlike Roosevelt, he vigorously associated
himself with the peace movement, and during his first term
as the nation's chief executive he made much of the fact that
he kept America's sons out of the trenches in France. He
later succumbed to the pressures of intervention, but he
always saw himself as an advocate of nonviolence, and he

Reprinted by permission of the author from "The Warrior and the Priest,"
South Atlantic Quarterly, 80 (Autumn 1981).

made strenuous efforts to persuade the American people to
accept the League of Nations.

Roosevelt and Wilson were adversaries even before they
opposed each other in the Presidential election of 1912.
During World War I, TR actively supported the Anglo-
French cause, and he was sharply critical of Wilson's neu-
trality policies. In 1917, President Wilson rejected Roose-
velt's offer to raise and lead an American division into combat
against the German Army, and thereafter, the two men con-
tinued to differ on both domestic and international issues.
Professor John Milton Cooper of the University of Wiscon-
sin has won an enviable reputation as the leading authority
on the divergent careers of these two towering public figures,
and his essay on "The Warrior and the Priest" sums up his
highly respected judgment.

The biggest difference between views of twentieth century American
political history and those of the earlier period lies in the attention
devoted to ideological conflict before 1900. Whereas eighteenth- or
nineteenth-century political history has seldom strayed far from awareness and analysis of doctrines based upon divergent social, economic,
and sectional interests, twentieth century political history rarely shows
such preoccupation. The most striking manifestation of this difference
comes in the way that the conflict between the Federalism of Alexander Hamilton and the Republicanism of Thomas Jefferson has
formed the basic perspective from which nearly all subsequent political
history has been viewed. Thirty years ago, Samuel Eliot Morison noted
the competition between what he termed the "Federalist-Whig" and
the "Jefferson-Jackson" views. Morison lamented that the triumph
of the second view had created "a sort of neoliberal stereotype," and
he called for "history written from a sanely conservative point of
view. . . ." Whether or not they have heeded Morison's call, a number of historians of the revolutionary period, the conflict over slavery,
the Civil War and Reconstruction, and the Populist revolt have produced sophisticated, penetrating inquiries into the ideological dimension of those events. Yet the twentieth century remains largely innocent of that kind of investigation.

One partial exception has relieved this contrast. Appropriately, in view of the major changes that have occurred in the twentieth century, that exception involves foreign policy. Many historians, political scientists, and other writers have explored the doctrines and interests surrounding American conduct in the world since the turn of the century, and some of these interpreters have discerned a conflict between two significant schools of thought inspired and articulated by quasi-prophetic leaders, somewhat after the manner of Hamilton's Federalism and Jefferson's Republicanism. The two schools of foreign policy have received various labels, but generally they have been divided into regard for national self-interest on one side and pursuit of transcendent values on the other. Adherents of the first school have graced it with the name "realism," while both friends and enemies have dubbed the second school "idealism." Devotees of both schools have also usually agreed in choosing as their respective champions Theodore Roosevelt for realism and Woodrow Wilson for idealism.

Unlike ideological interpretations in earlier American history, however, treatments of Rooseveltian realism and Wilsonian idealism have concentrated less on either the ideas the men espoused or the interests they represented than on investigations of their psychological underpinnings. The best description of both the conflicting schools of foreign policy and the psychological dimensions has come, fittingly, in Robert E. Osgood's *Ideals and Self-Interest in America's Foreign Relations*, which after nearly thirty years is still the fullest and most penetrating twentieth-century study of realism and idealism. On Roosevelt's attitude toward Wilson, Osgood has written, ". . . there was something elemental in his antipathy for that good gentleman. One is reminded of [Friedrich] Nietzsche's distinction between the Warrior and the Priest. The Warrior with all his natural strength and virility exults in the free and unabashed exercise of the will-to-power." The Warrior hates the Priest because "the will of the Priest is not the frank, straightforward will of the Warrior but rather the devious influence of a crafty intellect, which compensates the Priest for his physical weakness by investing cowardice with the semblance of morality, by embellishing weakness with the holy glow of enlightenment, self-denial and the gentle Christian virtues." Osgood acknowledges that the comparison is imperfect, since Roosevelt had his own idealistic streak and Wilson could become a fierce fighter, but he concludes that as World War I unfolded in Europe, "the differences between these two men grew sharper and more strident, and their mutual antipathy came to symbolize a profound temperamental and idealogical split in the nation as a whole. . . ."

The comparison of Roosevelt and Wilson with Nietzsche's Warrior and Priest furnishes a comparative perspective which offers three important insights in viewing them and their approaches to politics. The first insight is the revelation of a common political identity which linked the two men. Invocation of Nietzsche's concepts of the will-to-power and philosophical stances in relating to it underscores the way in which Roosevelt and Wilson were not ordinary politicians but men who reflected on the exercise of power and went to lengths to justify their pursuit and wielding of power. Both men were intellectuals. They were the only two genuine intellectuals to become presidents since John Quincy Adams, and as intellectuals in power they were fit companions with Adams, his father John Adams, Thomas Jefferson, and James Madison. As such, Roosevelt and Wilson present illuminating contrary examples to the widely assumed and much discussed alienation between modern intellectuals and political power. Further, the comparison with Nietzsche's Warrior and Priest suggests a distinction which can be drawn between types of intellectuals in power. As commonly used, the term *intellectual* embraces two different and not necessarily compatible kinds of figures—the artist and the scholar or philosopher. By that distinction Roosevelt could be seen as an artist whose medium was power, and for whom ideas entered his activity secondarily, to refine and inform his artistic expression. Likewise, Wilson could be viewed as the scholar or philosopher, for whom ideas and ideals were primary and for whom power entered secondarily, to realize those ideals.

The second insight afforded by Nietzche's categories comes in stress on the psychological dimension of Roosevelt's and Wilson's attitudes toward power. Clearly, both men sought political careers because of personal characteristics which stemmed from childhood, and their justifications of both domestic and foreign policies projected beliefs about themselves and their individual conduct. With Roosevelt it has become almost a truism to relate his approval of all forms of power, particularly military power, with his youthful self-transformation from a sickly, puny child into a virile, masterful man. Later, when as president he adjured his countrymen to avoid class conflicts at home and pursue strong, honorable policies abroad and when he scorned Wilson's diplomacy during World War I as weak and cowardly, Roosevelt was obviously projecting himself onto the mass of Americans and onto the role of the United States in the world. Similarly, with Wilson, three generations of interpreters have sought to relate his childhood experiences and his behavior in his academic career with his conduct as president. Most psychological interpretations of Wilson have been controversial, and usually rightly so, but one of the most fruitful of these is Edwin Weinstein's speculation on the probable effects of congenital dyslexia—difficulty in learning to read—on his solitariness and self-reliance. It seems equally obvious that when Wilson urged Americans to remain "neutral in thought" at the outbreak of the world war and asked them to be "too proud to fight" after the sinking of the *Lusitania,* he was projecting his beliefs in self-control and self-mastery onto his countrymen and his nation.

The final insight offered by Osgood's use of the Warrior and the Priest lies in its suggestion of the major part played by foreign policy in the conflict between Roosevelt and Wilson and, by extension, in twentieth-century American politics. Roosevelt stood almost alone among politicians of his time in giving equal concern to foreign and domestic affairs and in joining them in a single political vision. In both the great personal conflicts of Roosevelt's career, foreign policy entered at a critical stage. Opposition to William Howard Taft's arbitration treaty with Great Britain in 1911 furnished the first occasion for public criticism of his successor and moved Roosevelt closer to the contest that he made in 1912 inside and outside the Republican party. It is interesting to speculate what might have happened between Roosevelt and Wilson if World War I had not broken out. Their mutual criticisms in the 1912 campaign, together with Roosevelt's denunciations of Wilson's Mexican policies and his anger at the treaty of "apology" with Colombia over the Panama incident, suggest that their conflict was unavoidable and that foreign policy considerations would have separated them anyway. But the world war gave special edge and moment to their clash. On the psychological side, much of Roosevelt's ire at Wilson plainly stemmed from jealousy at seeing someone else president at such an unquestionably crucial time in history. On the ideological side, the war had the effect of bringing Roosevelt back to basics in his beliefs. "When root questions such as national self-preservation, and the upholding of national honor, and the performance of duty in international affairs are concerned," he wrote to Henry Cabot Lodge in March 1917, "the ordinary matters that divide conservative and progressive must be brushed aside."

These are three valuable insights which Osgood's comparison with the Warrior and the Priest provides. Yet each of these insights has a corresponding drawback which deflects its thrust, and, when added together, their drawbacks undermine the value of invoking those Nietzschean categories. The first insight, about Roosevelt and Wilson as political intellectuals, is useful only insofar as it points to their common identity. It does not offer a valid distinction between them. Although Roosevelt does seem to have been Nietzsche's Warrior in his artistic exercise of power, Wilson never fitted the role of Priest by believing that power must be repressed or thwarted in the realization of ideals. Even a cursory examination of the early volumes of *The Papers of Woodrow Wilson*, which deal with the development of his political thought and personality, shows that Wilson also regarded power and political life as the primary reality and viewed theorists and ideologues with suspicion and skepticism. Wilson's expressions of contempt for impractical visionaries, prissy reformers, and "mugwumps" in the eighties and nineties are virtually interchangeable with Roosevelt's. His attraction to Edmund Burke in the early 1890s sprang from a grasp of "organic," antitheoretical politics that foreshadowed the proclamations of the "end of ideology" in the 1940s and 1950s. The difference between Roosevelt and Wilson as political intellectuals was between two kinds of artists in power. The difference involved both personal style and the relative balance between emotional and rational elements. Roosevelt was the more emotional, or "Dyonisiac" in the art historians' distinction, and Wilson the more rationale, or "Apollinian." But the difference was one of emphasis within a common commitment and approach.

The second insight, into the psychological dimensions of Roosevelt's and Wilson's conflict, likewise introduces a serious distortion. Osgood's labeling one man the Warrior and the other the Priest and, thereby, realist and idealist, implied a judgment on each one's adjustment to reality and mental health. That judgment typified the drift of most psychological interpretations of the two men, which have passed

Roosevelt silently by and therefore implicitly given him a clean bill of health, while concentrating on Wilson's supposed maladjustment and pathology. This drift is in one way ironic and in another way perverse. The irony lies in having missed an opportunity for psychological interpretation that cries out to be seized. Perhaps because the psychological roots of Roosevelt's attitude toward power have seemed so obvious, there has appeared little need to probe them. Yet even a slight acquaintance with his family background and his views of war and personal struggle raises questions about whether more was involved than physical zest born of youthful bodybuilding and outdoor pastimes. In particular, his father's not having fought in the Civil War and the trail of revealing remarks that Roosevelt left behind about the fact indicated that some kind of guilt probably entered into his militarism and his near obsession with personal combat. If one believes that psychological interpretations of historical figures should serve some therapeutic or exemplary purpose, then Roosevelt is a patient who has a long overdue appointment on the analyst's couch.

Wilson presents the reverse problem regarding the psychological implications of the Nietzschean category to which he is assigned. Nearly all the earlier interpretations of his political personality have reflected a desire to diagnose his pathology. Fortunately, more recent work by Edwin Weinstein and John Mulder has restored much needed perspectives to inquiries into Wilson's childhood, his relations with his parents, and his conflicts with academic colleagues before he entered politics. Here, too, minimal reading in the first volumes of the *Wilson Papers* provides a ready appreciation of the complexity and the advantages which he derived from his early life and prepolitical career. Not only has it become increasingly difficult, perhaps impossible, to pin the psychological connotations of a repressive, maladjusted Nietzschean Priest on Wilson, but questions also arise about whether Wilson may not have been a more admirable figure than Roosevelt by Nietzsche's lights. As Walter Kaufmann pointed out, for Nietzsche the highest exemplar of the will-to-power was not the Warrior, who directed it outward and sought mastery over others, but the "Superman" in the sense of superior human being, who sublimated his will-to-power and sought self-mastery. In his exhortations to national self-control during World War I and in his call to be "too proud to fight," Wilson seems to have come close to embodying Nietzsche's ideal, and his stress on

calm and restraint made a favorable psychological contrast to Roosevelt's fulminations and fury.

The final insight in the Warrior-Priest comparison, about the significance of foreign policy to the conflict between Roosevelt and Wilson,
contains two misleading connotations. The first is the impression that
as a realist and an idealist they differed fundamentally from the outset
and that their differences widened. That view is wrong. Before Wilson
became president, few differences over foreign policy separated him
from Roosevelt. A startling revelation of the earlier volumes of the
Wilson Papers has been what an enthusiastic, committed imperialist
Wilson was at the turn of the century. An equally striking revelation
of the first volumes dealing with his presidency has been how concerned, informed, and assertive Wilson was in foreign affairs as soon
as he entered the White House. Likewise, as Edward Wagenknecht
has observed, during the two-and-a-half years between the outbreak of
World War I and American intervention, Roosevelt did not pursue a
consistently interventionist line, and his attacks on Wilson often pur-
veyed more heat than substance. Finally, in the postwar conflict over
the League of Nations, Roosevelt was sympathetic to collective security before his death in January 1919, and assuming that Henry Cabot
Lodge acted as his ideological heir and surrogate, the affair turned out
tragically in part because some measure of common ground existed on
which a compromise might have been built. These observations do not
mean that deep, substantial differences did not separate Roosevelt and
Wilson over foreign policy, but they do mean that those differences
were neither stark nor simple.

The second misleading connotation of the stress on foreign policy in
their conflict is to downgrade their domestic differences. Such an assessment agrees with the judgment of nearly everyone who has studied
Roosevelt's and Wilson's domestic policies. Another disclosure of the
Wilson Papers is that before 1905 an uncanny similarity joined their
views on virtually all important issues, domestic as well as foreign.
Also, the two men admired each other until Wilson engaged in his
brief flirtation with conservatism from 1905 to 1908. Thereafter,
rivalry replaced former friendship, but on most domestic questions
their positions once more converged. During the 1912 presidential
race, despite an apparently sharp conflict over regulation of the trusts,
few historians have been able to discover much practical difference in

their policies. As Arthur Link has shown, by the end of the first term Wilson had enacted most of Roosevelt's 1912 platform. After the United States entered World War I, the Wilson Administration went still further in pursuit of the kind of centralized direction of the economy and governmental promotion of public welfare that Roosevelt had previously advocated.

Yet behind those similarities lay a basic divergence of political viewpoint that partook of the distinction between realism and idealism, if not the Nietzschean categories. Roosevelt and Wilson did not diverge on the main domestic issues of their time because they were both reflective, adaptable politicians who shared a belief in the importance of politics and government and therefore usually responded in similar ways to the major public sentiments of the day, which ran toward reform of political processes in a more democratic direction and efforts to curb the power of big business. Their divergence came over basic purposes of politics and visions of the good society. This divergence reflected not only their personal characters but also their social and political backgrounds. As president and as a reform leader afterward, Roosevelt's basic message consisted of tireless exhortations to people to rise above material interests and reject class conflict in pursuit of exalted national ideals. In one way, Roosevelt was projecting himself onto his nation, urging Americans to emulate his self-transformation and career of public service. But he was also preaching an antimaterialist brand of conservatism that derived from his aristocratic background, and in urging flexibility and mutual understanding he was admittedly striving to preserve the power of the Republican party, which represented the groups and regions that were better off economically. In the breadth of his political sympathies and the cultivation of his historical and social perspectives, Roosevelt represented American conservatism of the last century at its most enlightened, but his ideas and attitudes sprang from his class and his party as well as his psyche.

Coming to politics after a long academic career, Wilson began with a belief in continuous, evolutionary adaptation of institutions to people's pursuit of their interests. His devotion to Burke may have made him a sort of philosophical conservative, but his conviction that politics and government must be organic outgrowths of the nation's economic and social life and must not be derived from detached theories and visions meant that he was hardly an idealist. Philosophically, Wilson was the realist. Instead of exhorting people to rise above material interests, he urged them to pursue those interests, with government helping them in that pursuit, tempered by morals and laws but freed from unfair restraints imposed by privilege and chicanery. Wilson believed that public good would result from such free, unfettered, moral pursuit of private ends. Therein lay the basic divergence between Roosevelt and Wilson. Roosevelt belonged to the ancient conservative tradition that held public good to be superior to and apart from individual, selfish interests. That belief, as Cecilia Kenyon has pointed out, had separated Hamilton and Jefferson, with Hamilton standing as the idealist and Jefferson the realist. Roosevelt was an idealist in the mold of Hamilton, who was one of his greatest heroes, and Wilson was a realist of the stripe of Jefferson, whom Roosevelt fittingly despised but whom Wilson did not greatly admire, either.

In an ideological sense, Roosevelt and Wilson were the twentieth-century inheritors and analogues of Hamilton and Jefferson. The parallel also ran further on Wilson's side than his mind and personality. Despite intellectual detachment and living most of his adult life in the Northeast, Wilson remained a southerner by background and a Democrat by allegiance. Although his family had suffered comparatively little in the Civil War and its aftermath, Wilson had had to make his own living and his own way in the world. Nor did his long association with Princeton ever wean him from identification with hardworking, upwardly striving people. Once he emerged on the national political scene, Wilson hastened to identify himself with the progressive wing of the Democrats, who sought to reopen opportunities for disadvantaged interests and sections. When they ran against each other for president in 1912, Roosevelt and Wilson engaged in a debate about the best way to achieve the good society. Roosevelt's program of the "New Nationalism" 'embodied a vision of disinterested leadership that would arouse the citizenry to pursue a transcendent national purpose. Wilson's program of the "New Freedom" embodied a vision of the citizenry unharnessed to pursue individual aspirations and in the process producing leaders through debate and competition. Both visions were democratic, but they reflected their authors' social and political backgrounds. Roosevelt's New Nationalism represented a democratic aristocracy, in which disinterested service would guide and restrain selfish, potentially antisocial passions. Wilson's New Freedom represented a democratic elitism, in which talent would rise from below to insure energy and growth in society. Despite public images and interpretations to the contrary, it was Wilson who had the more dynamic view of society and was more tolerant of social conflict. In the Nietzschean comparison, domestically at least, Wilson was more of the Warrior and Roosevelt more of the Priest.

But that comparison is not the best perspective to use in viewing the two men and their impact on twentieth-century American politics. The Jefferson-Hamilton comparison is much more fruitful because it shifts the center of attention away from primarily psychological differences and toward broader ideological considerations which involved the two men's thought, social identities, and party followings. That comparison, moreover, recaptures the full range of their differences, which encompassed not only foreign policy but also convictions that lay at the heart of their whole politics. Roosevelt and Wilson were far more interesting and important figures than American incarnations of Nietzshe's Warrior and Priest. Their influence on the subsequent history of American politics proved profound and lasting, though not always simple or easy to classify. But neither was the influence of Jefferson and Hamilton on the previous period. Beginning to appreciate the significance of Theodore Roosevelt and Woodrow Wilson and their conflict can open a new and richer understanding of American political history, particularly its ideological dimension, in the twentieth century.

II MATURE NATION, 1920 TO PRESENT

8

Al Capone: "I Give the Public What the Public Wants"

JOHN G. MITCHELL

• Long before the Civil War, temperance enthusiasts had
sought to make the country safe from demon rum. In 1880,
Neil Dow labeled the liquor traffic "the most important political question facing the nation," and thereafter two generations of religious fundamentalists, Anti-Saloon Leaguers,
and Women's Christian Temperance Union members carried
on the fight. Enthusiasm for prohibition swept across the
United States in the early years of the twentieth century, and
it became law finally in 1919 by riding the patriotic fervor of
World War I. As Frederick Lewis Allen wrote: "If a sober
soldier was a good soldier and a sober factory hand was a productive factory hand, then the argument for prohibition was
for the moment unanswerable."

At best, the moral amendment to the Constitution was a
mixed blessing. In part it represented the attempt of the
middle class to impose its values upon inner-city residents
who found that drinking eased the drabness of their daily
lives. The strong desire for spirits felt by many people was not
quenched by legislation. Some legitimate businesses folded
and alcoholism may have declined, but much of the liquor
trade simply went underground. Speakeasies replaced saloons,
and underworld entrepreneurs built illegal empires out of the
liquor trade.

No city was more troubled by gangster violence than Chicago, and no underworld figure was more notorious than
"Scarface" Al Capone. Born in a tough neighborhood near
the Brooklyn Navy Yard, Capone gained a reputation as a
fighter as a youth and moved to Chicago to escape a possible

From "Said Chicago's Al Capone," *American Heritage* (February/March
1979). Reprinted by permission of International Creative Management. Copyright © 1979 by American Heritage.

New York murder indictment. Gaining the confidence and support of the famous Johnny Torrio, Capone operated initially on Chicago's South Side before gradually expanding his influence, usually via the gun, throughout the metropolitan area. As John G. Mitchell notes in the following essay, Capone simply gave the public what it wanted, thus demonstrating the difficulty of altering standards of personal morality by constitutional dictums.

The newspapers called him Scarface, but the sobriquet did not safely bear repeating in his presence. It was *Mister* Capone instead, or Big Al; or, among trusted lieutenants of his palace guard, "Snorky," a street word connoting a certain princely elegance. The elegance was mostly in cloth, in expensive suits from Marshall Field, silk pajamas from Sulka, the upholstery of the custom Cadillac that was said to have cost more than twenty grand in 1920's dollars. In his pockets, it was rumored, he carried cash enough to buy two such limousines; he tipped lavishly, and showered his friends with gold-plate gifts. To hide the furrows of the scars on his left cheek, he powdered his face with talcum and explained that the wounds were inflicted by shrapnel while he was fighting in France with the "Lost Battalion." He believed in the sanctity of the American family. "A woman's home and her children are her real happiness," he once told a reporter. "If she would stay there, the world would have less to worry about."

For a time, a good part of the world worried about Alphonse Capone of Chicago, Illinois. He was a prince, all right. Beneath the elegant veneer he was prince of the bootleggers, baron of the brothels, and vicar of assorted vices that for more than a decade scrambled the innards of the Second City, its labor, its industry, its law enforcement, its municipal officialdom. He ruled an empire of corruption the likes of which had never before and have not since been witnessed by any American city. He commanded an army of emissaries and assassins whose numbers at peak approached one thousand. He sat at the pinnacle of a society so grotesque the newspapers felt obliged to give both its principals and its understudies nicknames: Mike de Pike, Bathhouse John, Greasy Thumb Guzik, Hinky Dink Kenna, Two-

Gun Alterie, and Bloody Angelo; Ecola the Eagle and Izzy the Rat and Lupo the Wolf and Duffy the Goat; Hop Toad Giunta and Blubber Bob, among dozens of others.

In Capone's supreme snorkiness there was always some wrinkle. Though the tailoring was splendid, it never quite seemed to conceal the bulge in his jacket beneath the left armpit. The Cadillac was custom-made not just for the plush upholstery but for a half a ton of armor plate, the steel visor over the gas tank, the thick, bulletproof glass, the removable rear window that converted the back seat into a machine-gun emplacement. The generous tipping was not limited to newsboys and hatcheck girls; he also tipped the eccentric William Hale Thompson a quarter-million dollars to help elect him mayor of Chicago, and Thompson later rewarded his benefactor by dismissing the city's official obeisance to gangsters as "newspaper talk." For Capone, a quarter-million was merely a fractional gratuity. His syndicate's net profits in the late 1920's were estimated by the Chicago Crime Commission at sixty million dollars a year.

There was even a wrinkle in his story about the scars, for he had never been to France in military uniform, had never felt shrapnel. He had felt instead the cutting edge of a pocketknife in a Brooklyn saloon, his reward for insulting a woman. Of which, in Capone's view of the species, there were two distinct kinds—the ones who stayed home, and the ones who didn't. "When a guy don't fall for a broad," said Big Al years later, "he's through." There was a bit of self-fulfilling prophecy in the remark. In his time, Capone no doubt dodged—and dispensed in kind—more flying metal than any doughboy who served in France. Yet it was to be his fate to die not with his spats on but in his silk pajamas, *through* at the age of forty-eight, from neurosyphilitic complications.

He was of an era that today seems more romantic than grotesque, more imagined than real. He brought to the third decade of this century much of its celebrated roar; and for that, in the minds of many Americans born too late to have heard the harsh authentic decibels, he looms as something of a folk hero, a Robin Hood of the Loop, a grand desperado much closer in style to the flamboyant two-gun type of the Old West than to today's furtive *capo* who, in stressful moments, is more likely to reach for a pocket calculator than a snubnosed Smith & Wesson. In a society vicariously fascinated with crime and violence, it is not surprising that Alphonse Capone should be accorded such retrospective honors. He was the last of the Great American Gunslingers.

After Big Al—notwithstanding the subsequent rise of Lucky Luciano and Vito Genovese and Frank Costello and other latter-day godfathers—everything changed. To be sure, the violence did not end with Capone; it simply became more sophisticated—ice picks through the eardrum instead of baseball bats about the head and shoulders, corpses consolidated with scrap metal rather than abandoned in the gutter. After Capone, the rackets diversified, dope preempted illicit booze, the crime families intermarried, and the profits proliferated. But no one ever quite managed to fill Snorky's shoes. And no other name again became synonymous with Chicago.

According to all accounts, Chicago had always been special, the distinctively American town. It was the Queen of the Lake, the Wonder of the Wonderful West. Sarah Bernhardt found in it "the pulse of America." Carl Sandburg praised it as hog butcher for the world. For a time, however, part of the city's distinction was its capacity to inspire the pejorative phrase. Strangers turned away appalled by its open display of raw vice and spectacular mayhem. "It is inhabited by savages," wrote Rudyard Kipling. "A grotesque nightmare," said Don Marquis. One of its own, the alderman Robert Merriam, observed that Chicago was unique because it "is the only completely corrupt city in America." The English writer Kenneth Allsop noted in his book *The Bootleggers and Their Era* that Chicago during the 1920's "was effectively a city without a police force, for [the police] operated partially as a private army for the gangs." And in his informal history of the city's underworld, *Gem of the Prairie*, Herbert Asbury described the decade as a time when "banks all over Chicago were robbed in broad daylight by bandits who scorned to wear masks. . . . Burglars marked out sections of the city as their own. . . . Fences accompanied thieves into stores and appraised stocks of merchandise before they were stolen."

After one especially noisy series of intergang bombings, a newspaper pundit wryly remarked that "the rockets' red glare, the bombs bursting in air / Gave proof through the night that Chicago's still there." In the United States Congress, a Midwestern senator suggested that President Calvin Coolidge recall the Marine expeditionary force then in Nicaragua and dispatch it to a place more worthy of armed intervention—Chicago.

The city's pernicious reputation was well established long before the arrival of Al Capone. By the turn of the century the Queen of the Lake had become the hussy of America. Its red-light district—outshining even those of New York, New Orleans, and San Francisco—sprawled for block after block across the seamy South Side. The district, according to one chronicler, swarmed with "harlots, footpads, pimps, and pickpockets" operating in and out of "brothels, saloons, and dives of every description." Within the area were a number of subdistricts affectionately known as the Bad Lands, Coon Hollow, Satan's Mile, Hell's Half-Acre, and Dead Man's Alley; later these quaint neighborhoods became known collectively as the "Levee."

Among the city's most notorious whoremasters was one James Colosimo. Son of an immigrant from Calabria, Italy, Big Jim Colosimo had learned all the ropes that the Levee had to offer. He had been a bootblack, pickpocket, pimp, and bagman for the aldermen who controlled the district's votes and vices. In 1902 he met and married the brothelkeeper Victoria Moresco. Soon Big Jim was managing scores of bordellos and ancillary saloons; and from every dollar earned by a prostitute, more than half went to Colosimo. Colosimo's Café, on South Wabash Avenue, had green velvet walls and crystal chandeliers. It had the best entertainers, the most beautiful chorus girls, the largest selection of imported wines in Chicago. It established Colosimo as a man of considerable means. Inevitably, too, it marked him as a target for extortion.

Extortion was then the specialty of the Black Hand, the secret Sicilian underworld society. Colosimo, being Calabrian, was fair game. If he could afford to pay off the South Side aldermen and the police, surely he could afford some modest tribute to the society. Say, for starters, about five thousand dollars? Colosimo agreed. Then the Black Handers upped the ante. On the second scheduled payoff, Colosimo contrived to ambush the extortionists and left three of them dead under a South Side bridge. But the threats and demands continued. Colosimo needed help. He sent for his nephew in New York, Johnny Torrio, a veteran of the notorious Five Points gang. Several years later Johnny Torrio in turn would send for Al Capone.

He was the fourth of nine children born to Gabriel and Teresa Capone, who in 1893 had emigrated from Naples to the slums of the Brooklyn Navy Yard district. Gabriel was a barber. The family lived in a dingy flat heated by a potbellied stove. Dodging vegetable carts and ice wagons, the children played stickball in the streets. Nearby, according to Capone's most definitive biographer, John Kobler, were the fleshpots of Sands Street where "sailors piled ashore, clamoring for liquor and women." Alphonse attended P.S. 7 on Adams Street. One of his closest friends was a boy named Salvatore Luciana, later known as Lucky Luciano. When Al was eight, the family moved a mile south to Garfield Place. There was a new social club in the neighborhood. Gilt letters in a window identified it as the John Torrio Association.

To what extent Torrio figured in the early underworld education of Al Capone is not altogether clear. Kobler quotes Capone as having said, from the perspective of middle age, that he "looked on Johnny like my adviser and father and the party who made it possible for me to get my start." No doubt it was Torrio who steered both Capone and Luciano to apprenticeship with the Five Points gang while they were still in their mid-teens. Torrio was a man of eclectic connections and alliances. He commanded the respect of Frankie Uale (alias Yale), who specialized in murder contracts and who for ten years was national boss of the *Unione Siciliane*, a sort of institutional missing link between the Black Hand of the Old World and the Mafioso of the New. Yale hired Capone as a bouncer-bartender at his Harvard Inn at Coney Island. There, according to Kobler, young Al's "huge fists, unarmed or clutching a club, struck [obstreperous carousers] with the impact of a pile driver." In 1918 Capone married Mae Coughlin of Brooklyn. The following year, facing a murder indictment should a man he had pile-driven in a barroom brawl die, he received word from Torrio that his huge fists were needed in Chicago. Though the brawl victim survived, Big Al was already a murder suspect in two other New York cases. To Chicago he went.

It was a good time to be going to Chicago. His mentor, Torrio, was beginning to eclipse Colosimo for control of the South Side rackets. William Hale Thompson, the laissez-faire mayor, was soon to be reelected. And Congress was preparing to make the nation dry with passage of the Volstead Act. One hour after Prohibition became the law, at midnight January 17, 1920, a whisky shipment stamped "for medicinal purposes" was hijacked on Chicago's South Side. The Anti-Saloon League had promised "an era of clear thinking and clean living." But it had misjudged the prodigious thirst of the American people. By 1929 the bootleg liquor industry was reaping an annual income of three billion dollars—a sum more than three times greater than the amount paid that year by individual taxpayers to the Internal Revenue Service. By 1930 Chicago had ten thousand speak-easies. Each speak-easy, on a weekly average, purchased two cases of liquor (at ninety dollars the case) and six barrels of beer (at fifty-five dollars the barrel). Estimated bootleg revenues each week came to $5,300,000. And sooner than later every dollar passed through the hands of one or another of Chicago's multitudinous gangs. Increasingly each year, the largest share found its way to the gang that was headed by Johnny Torrio and Scarface Al Capone.

Torrio had seized control of the South Side as early as 1920. On May 11 he had arranged for a shipment of whisky to be delivered to Colosimo's Café, and Colosimo himself was to be there to receive it. The whisky never arrived. Waiting in the café vestibule, Colosimo instead received a fatal bullet in the back of his head. Police suspected, but could never prove, that the assassin was Frankie Yale, imported from New York under contract to Johnny Torrio.

With Colosimo gone, Torrio promoted Capone to the unofficial rank of chief field general, installed him as manager of Torrio headquarters at the Four Deuces on South Wabash Avenue, cut him in for 25 percent of all brothel profits, and promised him half the net from bootleg operations. As Kobler reconstructs it: "They complemented each other, the slight older man, cool, taciturn, reserved, condoning violence only when guile failed; the beefy younger one, gregarious, pleasure-loving, physically fearless, hot-tempered. By the second year they no longer stood in the relationship of boss and hireling; they were partners."

Among Torrio's many schemes for extending his operations beyond the South Side was a dream of ruling the nearby suburb of Cicero. Cicero traditionally had been the turf of the O'Donnell brothers and their West Side gang; but Torrio, a master of crafty diplomacy, had managed to secure a beachhead in the community and soon installed Capone in new headquarters there at the Hawthorne Inn.

The final siege of Cicero began in the spring of 1924. It was election time. Joseph Klenha, the corrupt incumbent president of the village board, was facing a challenge from a slate of Democratic reformers. To counter the threat of a reform victory, the Klenha machine made an offer that Torrio and Capone could hardly afford to refuse: Ensure a Klenha landslide, the gangsters were told, and Cicero is yours. It was a task tailor-made for Al Capone.

In his detailed account of crime and politics, *Barbarians in Our Midst*, Virgil W. Peterson, director of the Chicago Crime Commission, described the Cicero election as "one of the most disgraceful episodes in American municipal history." Armed with machine guns, Capone mobsters (some two hundred by Kobler's count) "manned the polls. Automobiles filled with gunmen patrolled the streets. Polling places were raided and ballots stolen at gunpoint. Voters were kidnapped and transported to Chicago where they were held captive until after the polls closed." Apprised of the reign of terror, a Cook County judge dispatched over a hundred patrolmen and detectives from Chicago to Cicero, and gun battles between gangsters and police raged through the afternoon. Among the several fatal casualties was Big Al's brother, Frank Capone. President Klenha was handily reelected. "And Cicero," observed Virgil Peterson, "became known throughout the nation as one of the toughest places in America, a reputation it was to retain for many years."

Capone's stunning conquest of Cicero left little doubt in the minds of rival mobsters that a new and formidable leader had arrived in their midst. From Torrio he had acquired the organizational skills to put together a tightly disciplined army of thugs, hit men, and specialists in assorted vices; and with them—after the retirement of Torrio in 1925—he proceeded to wrest from his rivals a large piece of virtually any racket he fancied.

Directly under Capone on the organizational flow chart was his good friend and business manager, Jake "Greasy Thumb" Guzik. For liaison with the *Unione Siciliane*, there was Frank "The Enforcer" Nitti. His departmental chieftains included, for bootlegging operations, Capone's brother Ralph (nicknamed "Bottles") and his cousin, Charlie Fischetti; for brothels, Mike de Pike Heitler; and for gambling, Frank Pope. Farther down on the chart were Capone's musclemen: Jim Belcastro, the bomber of breweries; Phil D'Andrea, the sharpshooting bodyguard; and Samuel Hunt, alias "Golf Bag," so-called for the luggage in which he preferred to carry his shotgun. (Golf Bag's first intended victim survived the buckshot, Kobler notes, and was thereafter known as "Hunt's hole in one.") Other torpedoes of importance included Anthony Accardo (alias Joe Batters), Sam Giancana, Paul "The Waiter" Ricca, Murray "The Camel" Humphreys, and Jack "Machine Gun" McGurn, whose real name was De-Mora and to whom police over the years attributed no fewer than twenty-two murders.

For the most part, Capone's lieutenants enjoyed an *esprit de corps* unlike that of any other mob in Chicago. There was no place in the organization for men who would not adhere to a code of unfaltering loyalty and rigid discipline. Despite the predilection of some associates for booze and cigars, Capone insisted on keeping his troops in fine fighting shape. In one headquarters spread, at the Hotel Metropole, two rooms were set aside as a gymnasium and equipped with punching bags and rowing machines.

A subsequent command post was established in the Lexington Hotel. Capone occupied a corner suite, presiding at the head of a long mahogany conference table. Framed on the wall behind him were portraits of George Washington, Abraham Lincoln, and Mayor William Hale Thompson. Two floors below, in a maids' changing room, a hinged full-length mirror concealed a secret door leading to an adjacent office building. Capone used it frequently to frustrate those who tried to pry into the pattern of his daily itinerary.

He lived constantly within a shield of armed guards. When he dined in public, the bar of the chosen restaurant would be crowded—in advance—by his trusted henchmen. When he went to the theater, twelve seats were reserved for him and his entourage in the rear of the house, where vigilance was easy. In transit, the custom-built Cadillac was always preceded by a scout car, and followed by a touring car filled with his most proficient marksmen. His headquarters swivel chair had an armor-plate back. He crossed sidewalks and hotel lobbies in a huddle of bodies three deep. Yet for all these precautions, no life insur-

ance company would write him a policy. Capone and his kind had
been going to too many funerals, and too many rivals were planning
a funeral for Capone.

On the North Side, for example, there was Dion O'Banion, the choir-
boy-turned-safecracker, and now ostensibly a florist, who had supplied
twenty thousand dollars in wreaths and arrangements for the funeral
of the slain Frank Capone. "A most unusual florist," observed Virgil
Peterson, for O'Banion "not only furnished flowers . . . but also provided the corpses." Chicago police said he was responsible for twenty-
five murders. O'Banion detested Capone. Among the choirboy's chief
lieutenants was George "Bugs" Moran, whom history remembers not
only as the inspiration for a memorable Valentine's greeting from Al
Capone, but as the man who first produced and directed murder-by-
motorcade, a system whereby, if all went well, the victim was rapidly
riddled from a slow procession of passing cars.

Swinging counterclockwise from O'Banion's North Side, one pres-
ently arrived on the turf of Roger "The Terrible" Touhy, whose headquarters were in Des Plaines and who had little traffic—or trouble, for
that matter—with the mob of Capone. At nine o'clock—west lay the
precincts of the aforementioned O'Donnell gang, perennial foes of
the South Side Italians. At eight o'clock, in the valley between Cicero
and Chicago's own Little Italy, one entered the fiefdom of Terry
Druggan and Frankie Lake, pious Irishmen both. Once, hijacking a
beer truck parked in front of a Catholic church, Druggan was said to
have ordered the bootleggers out of the cab of the truck at gunpoint.
"Hats off when you're passing the House of God," said Druggan, "or
I'll shoot 'em off."

On the Southwest Side, at seven o'clock, near the site of today's
Midway Airport, yet another gang skulked under the leadership of
Joe Saltis and Frank McErlane, the latter being regarded by the Illinois Association for Criminal Justice as "the most brutal gunman who
ever pulled a trigger in Chicago." Like Bugs Moran, McErlane was an
innovator, the first gangster in America to demonstrate the superior
firepower of the Thompson submachine gun.

Virtually all these mobs, at one time or another in the 1920's, were
aligned against the army of Capone. In fact, there was only one independent organization with which Capone had any strong ties what-

soever, and that was the Sicilian community ruled by the six Genna brothers. Through political connections, the Gennas had obtained a license to process industrial alcohol. They processed it, all right—into bootleg whisky; and soon, under their direction, alky cooking (as Kobler recounts it) "became the cottage industry of Little Italy." The mash was powerful, the denaturing process resulted in a product capable of blinding the consumer, and in a single lot of one hundred confiscated barrels of the liquor, police were said to have found dead rats in every one. For hit men, the Gennas relied on John Scalise and Albert Anselmi, who, in the mistaken belief that garlic in the bloodstream could cause gangrene, anointed all their bullets against the possibility of a slightly misplaced shot.

Thus were the territories staked out and the players positioned when the great Chicago beer wars broke out in the fall of 1924. Sometimes the action was difficult to follow. As Virgil Peterson perceived it, "The lines of battle were constantly shifting." No matter. The florists and undertakers had never had it so good.

O'Banion was the first to go. There had been a confrontation with Torrio over sharing profits from saloons. There had been much bad blood between North Siders and the Gennas. O'Banion had ordered the hijacking of one of the Gennas' alky trucks. He had told the Sicilians to go to hell, and had boasted of outwitting Johnny Torrio. At noon on November 10, 1924, three men (two later identified as Scalise and Anselmi) called at O'Banion's flower shop while the Irishman was clipping chrysanthemum stems. Six shots were fired. None were misplaced.

On January 12, outside a restaurant at State and Fifty-fifth streets, a limousine with Hymie Weiss and Bugs Moran at the curbside windows pulled abreast of a parked vehicle. A moment earlier, Al Capone had stepped from that vehicle into the restaurant. Weiss and Moran raked the car with buckshot, wounding Al's chauffeur. The unscathed Capone later surveyed the damage, then put in a call to General Motors with specifications for a bulletproof Cadillac.

It was Torrio's turn twelve days later. Standing on the sidewalk near his apartment, he was hit in the jaw, the right arm, and the groin by buckshot and bullets from a passing limousine. At Jackson Park Hospital, Capone came and sat at his bedside, weeping. But

Torrio was tough. He survived, and eagerly accepted a sentence of nine months in the Lake County Jail. It was safe there. Having served his time, he announced that he would retire and leave everything to Capone. Then he departed for Italy.

Meanwhile, in May of 1925, the O'Banionites had resumed their reprisals. They struck down Angelo Genna. He was buried in unconsecrated ground at Mt. Carmel Cemetery, within shotgun range of the grave of Dion O'Banion. Capone may have sent flowers, but he shed no tears. The lines had been shifting. He wanted control of the Gennas' alky industry. Within six weeks, two more Gennas, Michael and Anthony, were ambushed and killed. Scalise and Anselmi defected to Capone's camp. Both were captured by the police and charged with murder. There were many suspects, but no convictions.

Then the lines shifted again, to Cicero and the West Side. In the first four months of 1926, police recorded twenty-nine gangland slayings. Among the last of that group to die was the assistant state's attorney, William McSwiggin. He was cut down by gunfire in front of the Red Pony Inn, not far from Capone's Cicero command post. Capone went into hiding for three months.

It was a relatively quiet summer—a few desultory killings here and there, a gun battle on Michigan Avenue. Capone reappeared in his old haunts. On September 20 he lunched at a restaurant next door to the Hawthorne Inn. Suddenly there was a burst of machine-gun fire. Capone dove for the floor. Outside, on Twenty-second Street, an eleven-car motorcade slowly passed in review. Guns protruded from every window. The inn, the restaurant, storefronts on either side were raked by tommy guns, shotguns, and revolvers. Slugs ripped through twenty-five autos parked at the curb, and the sidewalk glittered with shards of broken glass. As the eleventh car sped away, up from the floor rose Capone, unhurt, but paler than the talc on his otherwise ruddy jowls. There is no record of what he was thinking then, but very possibly he was thinking only—and darkly—of Hymie Weiss and Bugs Moran.

And within a month, Weiss was dead, shot down from ambush in the shadow of Holy Name Cathedral, near the flower shop where O'Banion had died barely two years before. "It's a real goddamn crazy place," New Yorker Lucky Luciano was reported to have said of Chicago after a visit. "Nobody's safe in the streets."

Throughout all the vicious years, Al Capone no doubt held himself in high personal esteem. After all, he was merely providing services, the supply of which, like his brothel whores, could never quite meet the demand. "I give the public what the public wants," he told a reporter during one of his many "frank" interviews. "I've given people the light pleasures . . . and all I get is abuse."

Surprisingly, a large segment of the public seemed to share Capone's view of himself as the pleasurable benefactor. Though on one day Chicagoans might read with horror of the latest atrocity linked to his mob, on the next they might cheer his waving arrival at Charlestown Racetrack. In Evanston once, during a Northwestern University football game, an entire troop of Boy Scouts startled the crowd with the rousing cry "Yea, Al!" (He had bought them their tickets.) His fan mail was heavy. By some accounts, he was Chicago's greatest philanthropist. At the pit of the Depression, he was said to have financed a South Side soup kitchen dispensing 20,000 free meals a week. People liked to remember things like that—and liked to forget just exactly what it was the big fellow did to afford such beneficence.

But not everyone was impressed by the good-guy image. On a visit with his wife to Los Angeles, his presence came to the attention of the police; they gave him twenty-four hours to clear out of town. In Miami he was *persona nongrata* until he discovered that the mayor was a realtor. So Capone bought a house, a fourteen-room villa on Palm Island in Biscayne Bay. He promptly improved it with an encircling wall of concrete blocks and a thick, oaken portcullis. Capone liked to swim and fish and bask in the sun; the sun helped him forget all the troubles of Chicago. In fact, he was doing just that on Februray 14, 1929. It was Valentine's Day.

The infamous massacre of seven Bugs Moran associates in a warehouse on Chicago's North Clark Street bears no detailed recounting here (having been the focus of numerous books and movies), except to note that quite by accident Moran was not among the machine-gunned victims, and that the triggermen were the garlic anointers, Scalise and Anselmi. For these two thugs, it should further be noted, there was a strange reward. On May 7, at the Hawthorne Inn, Capone assembled a roomful of mobsters ostensibly to honor Scalise and Anselmi for their recent deeds. It was a jovial occasion until, shortly after midnight, Capone announced to the guests of honor that he was privy to their part in a budding conspiracy to dethrone him. Having passed sentence on the Sicilians, Capone signaled his bodyguards to bind and gag them; and then, according to witnesses, the good guy who gave people so many simple pleasures proceeded to club his lieutenants to death with a baseball bat.

The following week Capone was in Atlantic City, attending a business convention. Guzik and Nitti flanked him at the conference table. Joe Saltis was there, and Frankie McErlane. There was "Boo Boo" Hoff from Philadelphia. From New York there were Lucky Luciano, Frank Costello, and Dutch Schultz. Torrio had returned from Italy to preside as the elder statesman. The purpose of the conference was peace. There was to be an end to the killing. The nation henceforth was to be redistricted; the *Unione Siciliane* was to be reorganized, and the Chicagoans were to stop this petty quarreling among themselves and merge under the leadership of Capone. Big Al was delighted, except for one catch: Bugs Moran had declined an invitation to the meeting. Back in Chicago, Moran would still be after him. Back in Chicago, a dozen Sicilian gunmen were awaiting their chance to avenge the clubbing of Scalise and Anselmi.

And the risks were by no means limited to Chicago. According to crime reporter Edward Dean Sullivan, who wrote the following in 1930, "The effort to 'get' Capone became virtually nationwide. Killers in every town that Capone might reach were assigned to the job. . . . When he got to Philadelphia from Atlantic City, having failed to arrange a peace with the Moran outfit on any terms, Capone, charged with having a concealed weapon, was soon in prison and untroubled."

Released from Eastern Penitentiary in March, 1930, Capone returned to Chicago with a bodyguard, wrote Sullivan, "the size of which indicated his state of mind." But the climate of the windy city was such that "he left for Florida within ten days and as this is written, six months later, he has just returned to Chicago. Twenty of his enemies died in his absence."

Sullivan further noted that Capone's most frequently repeated statement was: "We don't want no trouble." As it turned out, he was about to get a large measure of trouble. By 1931 the troubles had piled up on two fronts. There were frequent raids against the Capone breweries and distilleries; G-men with sledgehammers were wrecking the old alky stills and pouring the contraband booze into the gutters. Meanwhile, as if this were not enough for Capone to contend with, agents of the Internal Revenue Service began making discreet inquiries about town as to why, after so many extravagant years of big spending, he had never once filed a tax return. In a kind of dress rehearsal for their biggest act, the IRS agents won tax-evasion indictments against Ralph Capone and Frank Nitti. Then Big Al himself was charged with twenty-two counts of failing to render unto Uncle Sam what was Uncle Sam's; and in October, 1931, in federal court, he was found guilty by jury trial, fined fifty thousand dollars, and sentenced to eleven years in prison. Capone was stunned. It would never have turned out like this in the good old days.

But the good old days were long gone. Pending an appeal, Capone was held in the Cook County Jail, where the amenable warden David Moneypenny provided his celebrated prisoner with all the comforts of home, including unlimited visitations by the likes of Jake Guzik and Murray Humphreys and Lucky Luciano and Dutch Schultz. For all such audiences, Capone insisted on absolute privacy; and Moneypenny obliged by allowing Big Al to use the most secure suite in the entire jail—the death chamber.

The appeal was denied. In the spring of 1932, handcuffed to a fellow prisoner, Capone was transferred to the federal penitentiary at Atlanta, Georgia. There he was given the identifying number 40,822 and assigned to work eight hours daily cobbling shoes. For the most part he stayed out of trouble; but his old reputation belied to authorities his new good behavior. In the retributive penal spirit of the times, he was considered an "incorrigible." And by 1934 the government had a special place for people like that. They called it Alcatraz.

Capone was among the first of the incorrigibles confined on the skullcap rock in San Francisco Bay. His new number was 85. He was assigned to Cellblock B and the laundry-room detail. He was conceded no favors. Feisty young inmates, looking for ways to enhance their own reputations for toughness, insulted Capone to his face. They called him "wop with the mop." A thug from Texas shoved a pair of barber's scissors into his back. He was jumped in a hallway and almost strangled before he managed to flatten his assailant. Capone somehow endured. But his health was failing. The syphilis which had gone so long untreated was beginning to erode his central nervous system. There were periods when lucidity escaped him. He could respond to treatment, but the disease was too advanced to hope for a cure.

In January, 1939 (with time off the original sentence for good behavior and working credits), Capone left Alcatraz for the less dismal precincts of a federal correctional institution near Los Angeles; and in November, at Lewisburg, Pennsylvania, he was released into the custody of his wife Mae and brother Ralph. In Chicago, according to Kobler, "reporters asked Jake Guzik if Capone was likely to return and take command again." Whereupon Guzik "replied in language harsher than he intended, for his loyalty had never wavered." Al, said Guzik, was "nutty as a fruitcake."

Capone lingered on in Miami, his mind confused, his sleep haunted by dreams of assassins. Finally, in January, 1947, he suffered a brain hemorrhage. The hemorrhage was soon followed by pneumonia. The body was taken to Chicago for burial. The funeral was modest; the Church had forbidden a requiem mass.

There are those who say that Scarface Al Capone bequeathed to America a legacy of corruption that prevails to this day. In 1963 Senator John L. McClellan's Subcommittee on Investigations elicited from Chicago police superintendent Orlando Wilson a remarkable statistic. Since 1919, Wilson reported, there had been 976 gangland murders in his city, but only two of the killers had ever been convicted. Wilson's choice of 1919, not being round numbered, may have seemed arbitrary to most of his listeners; but to seasoned observers of organized crime it was clearly Chicago's watershed year. For in 1919 a young man from New York had come to Chicago—an unsingular happenstance at the time, yet one that seems to have made all the difference ever since.

9

From Scopes to Creation Science: The Decline
and Revival of the Evolution Controversy

WILLARD B. GATEWOOD, JR.

• In March 1925, the state of Tennessee passed a law that prohibited the teaching in public schools of biological theories of evolution which contradicted the biblical account of divine creation. The argument seemed clear cut: Did man descend from monkeys, as Charles Darwin suggested in his influential study, The Origin of the Species, or did God create Adam and Eve as recounted in the Book of Genesis? The people of Tennessee, and no doubt most of the other residents of the United States in 1925, chose to side with the angels rather than with the scientists on this issue.

In a case of world importance, John T. Scopes, a biology teacher, was tried in July 1925 for the crime of teaching the Darwinian theory in a Dayton, Tennessee, classroom. Clarence Darrow, the most famous defense attorney in the nation, represented the young teacher, while William Jennings Bryan, the "Great Commoner" and perhaps the most renowned orator the United States has ever produced, aided the state prosecutor.

The "monkey trial" was dramatic, with Darrow arguing that evolutionary theory was consistent with certain interpretations of the Bible, and with Bryan countering that the only acceptable interpretation of God's word was one that accepted the Scriptures exactly as they were written. Scopes was convicted and then quickly released on a technicality, but the trial itself captured the imagination and the attention of the entire country.

Willard B. Gatewood's essay on the persistence of the evolution controversy points out that the disagreement between

Willard B. Gatewood, "From Scopes to Creation Science: The Decline and Revival of the Evolution Controversy," *South Atlantic Quarterly* 83:4, 363-383. Copyright © 1984 Duke University Press.

*the fundamentalists and the modernists did not come to an
end in 1925 or indeed in 1985. Instead, he shows how the
legacy of a dramatic courtroom confrontation remains with
us today.*

An incongruous assortment of people converged on Dayton, Tennessee, in July 1925, to witness the trial of John Thomas Scopes, the local
high-school football coach and science teacher, accused of violating the
state's anti-evolution statute. The town, in fact, assumed the appearance of a crowded carnival. Leather-lunged vendors of hot dogs and
lemonade competed with hawkers of Bibles, biological treatises, and
stuffed monkeys. Gaunt, godly hill people mingled with internationally
famous scientists on hand to testify for the defense and with journalists from all parts of the world vying for news stories about the
"strange happenings" in what one described as a pleasant little country
town "forty miles from the nearest city and a million miles away from
anything urban, sophisticated and exciting."

Following eight days of unprecedented courtroom drama, the jury
deliberated less than ten minutes before finding Scopes guilty. An
appeal to the Tennessee Supreme Court resulted in a decision early in
1927 which upheld the constitutionality of the state's anti-evolution
law but reversed the judgment against Scopes on technical grounds
and directed the attorney general to *nol-pros* all proceedings in what
was termed this "bizarre" case. Although the Scopes trial represented
the climactic event in the post-World War I struggle over evolution,
it by no means marked the end of opposition to Darwin's theory or of
efforts to eliminate it from public schools. Following the Dayton
affair, Mississippi, in 1926, and Arkansas, in 1929, enacted anti-evolution statutes that remained in effect for almost forty years.

The controversy over Darwin in the 1920s represented only the
most publicized aspect of a larger and more complex conflict within
American Protestant culture between contending forces popularly
known as liberals and fundamentalists. Northern and urban in origin, fundamentalism emerged in the late nineteenth century as a distinct version of the highly respectable evangelical protestantism—a version committed to a supernatural, biblically based, traditional faith
militantly opposed to liberal theology and the cultural changes that

such a theology accommodated. Essentials of the fundamentalists' faith appeared from time to time in doctrinal statements known as the "fundamentals." But whether stated in five or fifteen points, the most important doctrine was the belief in a divinely inspired, errorless Bible. Those who formulated the "fundamentals" and subscribed to the doctrine of an inerrant scripture, including the account of creation in Genesis, were neither uneducated nor hostile to science. The problem was that their perception of science rested on the Baconian model, which meant that the role of scientists was not to impose theories but to confine themselves to "knowledge gained and verified by exact observation and correct thinking." Fundamentalists, says Professor George Marsden, resisted Darwin and his theory, not because they were opposed to science but because they "were judging the standards of the later scientific revolution [of Darwin] by the standards of the first—the revolution of Bacon and Newton. In their view, science depended on fact and demonstration. Darwinism, so far as they could see, was based on neither."

The emergence of a more aggressive theological liberalism, coupled with the cultural crisis accelerated by World War I and with the absence of a Dwight Moody to restrain the more militant wing of conservative Christianity, galvanized the diverse elements of a usually quiescent fundamentalism into a potent coalition dedicated to reviving the evangelical consensus of a previous generation. Their battle for the Bible became a battle for civilization, and, through the mysterious processes by which complex phenomena become simplified into symbolic issues, their defense of the faith—and of civilization—came to focus on opposition to the theory of evolution and the mind it represented.

In the 1920s, as they would a half century later, anti-evolutionists indicted Darwin's theory on both theological and scientific grounds. Evolution, they maintained, directly challenged the authority of the Bible by contradicting the divinely inspired account of creation. As if by a single stroke, the argument ran, evolution shattered the theory of an inerrant Bible, invalidated the whole premise of original sin, and eliminated the hope of salvation. No less disturbing was the Darwinian emphasis on chance variations which, operating independently of a creator, produced not man, but man as an animal, a concept incompatible with the idea of a creature in God's own image. Darwin's theory, then, robbed man of his dignity, relieved him of moral responsibility, and encouraged him to exalt the attributes of his brutish ancestors—precisely the same assertions made by creationists in the 1970s and 1980s.

Although objections to evolution in the 1920s tended to be primarily theological in nature, its opponents also challenged the theory's scientific validity. They repeatedly emphasized that evolution was a "mere guess," "unproved and unprovable." Insistent that true science must adhere to the model of Lord Bacon in which "an ounce of fact is worth a ton of theory," a leading anti-evolutionist in 1922 observed that unfortunately the prevailing drift of the scientific world was "back toward the pre-Bacon period." Opponents of the Darwinian theory cited the works of nineteenth-century scientific authorities hostile to evolution as well as differences regarding the evolutionary process within contemporary scientific circles as evidence of its invalidity. But anti-evolutionists in the 1920s were not without their own "true scientists." Of these the most widely quoted was George McCready Price, a Seventh-Day Adventist, a geology teacher, and a prolific author, who subscribed to what he called the New Catastrophism that claimed to confirm a literal interpretation of the biblical account of creation. In Price's view evolutionists made a mockery of "true scientific methods" and were "the real obscurantists," guilty of the most "intolerant dogmatism" in an effort to thwart the rapid accumulation of evidence against Darwin's theory.

By the mid-1920s evolution had become a code word used to symbolize the totality of error in modern America. It came to be identified with everything Americans in the postwar decade found reprehensible, from "godless education" and "creeping secularism" to sexual immorality and communism. The campaigns to exclude by law the "pernicious" theory from schools and colleges prompted a succession of noisy, highly emotional debates, deepened denominational divisions, and confronted policymakers with a host of sensitive and complex issues. Between 1921 and 1929 thirty-seven anti-evolution bills were introduced in twenty legislatures. Just as the anti-evolutionists seemed on the brink of success, the death of their best-known spokesman, William Jennings Bryan, shortly after the Scopes trial and the liberals' effective appeal to the American tradition of tolerance disrupted the fundamentalist coalition. In the absence of a leader of Bryan's stature and prestige, the direction of the movement became diffused among rival organizations and individuals whose penchant for sensationalism and factional fighting alienated those elements of the population that might otherwise have provided significant support for the anti-evolution cause.

By 1930 the furor over Darwin's theory no longer made good copy. But neither side in the struggle could claim a clear-cut victory. To assert, as the liberal *Christian Century* did, that fundamentalism was a "vanishing" phenomenon was as naive as the widely held view that anti-evolution sentiment somehow dissipated in the wake of the Scopes trial. Tangible legacies of the fundamentalist crusade persisted not only in the laws of three states, but also in the policies of local school boards and in the proliferation of Bible-reading statutes which in many cases served as less controversial substitutes for evolution laws. By 1931, thirty-five states either required or permitted Bible reading in public schools. That half of all American high school biology teachers shied away from teaching evolution as late as 1942 attested to the enduring impact of the anti-evolution crusade.

Throughout the period from 1930 to 1960 repeated efforts to repeal the so-called monkey laws in Tennessee and Arkansas were abysmal failures, but the publicity that attended these efforts reminded teachers that such laws existed and could presumably be enforced. Watson Davis of the *Science Newsletter*, who covered the Scopes trial in 1925, returned to the scene in 1960 and reported that "no teacher who wants to hold his job teaches evolution." Nor were such conditions peculiar to the three states with anti-evolution laws. Elsewhere, local school boards periodically disciplined teachers, eliminated textbooks, and cancelled school theatrical productions that offended anti-evolution sentiment. In 1947 the board of education in Wall, South Dakota, eliminated from schools "all books or pages of books which contain . . . atheistic evolution." Such actions seemed to validate the warning in 1930 by Maynard Shipley of the Science League who urged scientists and academicians to disabuse themselves of any notion that "the fight is over and science has won."

Textbook publishers, for obvious reasons, were acutely sensitive to the large body of anti-evolution opinion. As a result, between 1925 and 1960 high-school biology textbooks de-emphasized discussions of evolution, treated it under different terminology, or dropped references to it and Darwin altogether. Some books incorporated religious quotations into the text. At best the treatment of evolution was fragmentary and incomplete. Because the professional scientific community remained ignorant of, or indifferent to, such developments, no group exerted pressure on publishers to present "a biologically respectable treatment of evolution." Most scientists appeared to assume that science and the theory of evolution had somehow won a great victory in the Scopes trial. But as a study in 1974 indicated, "as far as the teaching of biology in the high schools was concerned, they had not won; they had lost. Not only did they lose, but they did not know they had lost." The study concluded that the major reason was the failure of scientists to comprehend, sympathetically or otherwise, the strength of the opposition to evolution. This lack of comprehension was not, of course, confined to scientists.

For those who equated American religious life exclusively with the major or mainline denominations, it was easy to assume that fundamentalism somehow fell apart in the wake of the Scopes trial. To be sure, it failed to capture control of a single major denomination, largely disappeared from the headlines by the early 1930s, and emerged from the struggle of the previous decade stereotyped as a cranky, marginal movement existing on the fringe of modern culture. Viewing themselves as the faithful remnant surrounded by apostates, fundamentalists in the 1930s regrouped, put down roots largely outside the mainline denominations, and ultimately developed into a subculture or "a second wing of Protestantism." No more reconciled to evolution than their theological forebears, fundamentalist groups such as the National Association of Evangelists, in 1939, and the Word of Life Fellowship, in 1945, periodically appealed for a renewal of a nationwide antievolution crusade.

Despite their hostility to evolution, the numerous and often competing groups within fundamentalism devoted their energies to what they considered at the time more pressing concerns. Among these were efforts to organize alternative institutions such as independent churches, Bible institutes, mission programs, radio ministries, and colleges. During the depression decade alone, when many older educational institutions struggled to survive, more than twenty-five Bible colleges and schools were established. They joined older nondenominational institutions such as Moody, Wheaton, and the Northwestern Bible School in Minneapolis in "standing firm for Genesis" and in teaching that evolution was unsupported by scientific evidence and contrary to Bible Christianity. Between 1930 and 1960 the number of institutions with similar orientations dramatically increased. Their graduates, counted in the thousands, came to constitute a significant component of the nation's upwardly mobile professions, so that by the time evolution and creation again became public issues in the 1970s, they were citizens of means and influence in local communities.

In the four decades following the Scopes trial the institutional base of fundamentalism came to include a variety of publishing, broadcasting, and film enterprises. Presses affiliated with sects, emerging denominations, and evangelical associations, as well as those operated by individual evangelists, turned out literally millions of pieces of literature, no small portion of which, like that produced by the Seventh Day Adventists, Jehovah's Witnesses, and others, focused on an anti-evolution theme. In addition to their publications, fundamentalists found radio and later television invaluable in the dissemination of antimodernist theology hostile to Darwin's theory.

In 1945 the Moody Institute created a film studio for the production of specialized scientific films in Santa Monica, California, known as the Moody Institute of Science. The founder was Irwin A. Moon who, in 1937, began a nationwide evangelical lecture-demonstration tour that he called "Sermons from Science." Concerned that the rising prestige of science would "lead the world into a materialistic philosophy" which left no room for the omnipotent God he loved and convinced that scientific experiments could be used to demonstrate the reliability of the scriptures, Moon persuaded the officials of Moody Institute to underwrite a motion picture studio so that his "Sermons from Science" could be put on film. He discovered that he could bring thousands "to a saving knowledge of Christ" by giving his evangelical efforts "a scientific slant." Such a discovery was scarcely lost upon other anti-evolutionists who were well aware that theological arguments alone would no longer suffice. The use of "a scientific slant" offered the possibility of legitimatizing their position.

Individuals conspicuous in the anti-evolution crusade of the 1920s who continued to oppose Darwin's theory throughout the generation after the Scopes trial not only kept the issue alive but also served as intellectual links between the anti-evolutionists and the scientific creationists a half century later. One of these, J. Frank Norris of Texas,

"the epitome of an independent fundamental Baptist" and a staunch
opponent of Darwin's theory, exerted a powerful influence within fundamentalist circles until his death in 1952. In fact, a whole generation
of preachers and evangelists were "inspired by his example." Another
individual of more limited influence was Gerald Winrod of Kansas,
founder of the Defenders of the Faith, who promoted the anti-evolution
cause throughout the decade of the thirties. Winrod represented the
tendency among anti-evolutionists to identify Darwin's theory and
communism as two important and closely related menaces confronting
modern America. All the while a steady stream of anti-evolutionist literature flowed from the pen of Arthur I. Brown, a physician born in
Michigan and educated in Canada and Europe, who abandoned medicine to become an evangelist and achieved prominence in the 1920s
first as a leader in the Anti-Evolution League and later as the "National Scientist" of the Bible Crusaders of America. His anti-evolutionist
works published in the 1930s and 1940s were curious blends of biology, physiology, and scripture, couched in language that the layman
could easily interpret as that of authoritative science.

   One of the most vocal opponents of evolution during the decades
following the Scopes trial was Harry Rimmer, a Presbyterian evangelist, skilled debater, and the author of more than two dozen books, including *The Theory of Evolution and the Facts of Science* and *Modern Science and the Genesis Record*. In 1920 he organized and headed
until his death in 1952 the Research Science Bureau, "an organization
whose objective was to study scientific evidence in support of the authenticity of the Holy Scriptures" and to document his claims regarding the scientific accuracy of the Bible and the absurdity of evolution.
But for all his labors, Rimmer was not a professionally trained scientist; in fact, his exposure to formal scientific education was slight.
While the most prominent group of scientific creationists in the 1970s
acknowledged Rimmer's contribution, their appreciation of him was
less than enthusiastic because he did not subscribe to their notions of
a young earth and universal flood and adhered to the so-called "gap
theory" in interpreting verses one and two in the first chapter of
Genesis.

   The pivotal figure in the era between the Scopes trial and the emergence of scientific creationism was George McCready Price, whose in-

fluence was as pervasive as it was profound. A man of limited scientific training, Price served as professor of geology in various Seventh Day Adventist colleges in the West and Midwest, where his anti-evolutionist views influenced hundreds of students during a long educational career. Between the publication, in 1906, of his *Illogical Geology: The Weakest Point in the Evolution Theory*, and his death almost sixty years later he wrote more than two dozen volumes in which he propounded the tenets of his so-called New Catastrophism, i.e., a universal flood, a young earth that was six- to ten-thousand years old, and a fossil record that contradicted uniformitarianism and evolution. An armchair geologist lacking field experience, Price nonetheless read widely in contemporary geological literature and produced works that, to the uninitiated at least, appeared as solid scientific treatises replete with charts, graphs, and technical vocabulary. For the few orthodox geologists even aware of Price and his New Catastrophism, his works constituted "a geological nightmare." Nevertheless, Price functioned for more than a half century as the principal scientific apologist of the anti-evolution cause. Religious opponents of Darwin's theory readily embraced the "scientific slant" of his arguments even if they rejected the eccentricities of his Adventist theology.

What might be termed the Adventist connection in the intellectual background to contemporary scientific creationism received substantial reinforcement in the works of Price's students. One of these was Harold W. Clark, who earned a master's degree in biology at the University of California at Berkeley and taught in an Adventist college. Espousing what he termed Neo-Creationism, Clark published a lengthy volume in 1946 entitled *The New Diluvialism*, which accepted "the Genesis record and the Flood at face value as an inspired historical record." While Clark did not deny "the possibility of variation, isolation, natural selection, and such factors producing new species," he maintained that "the world and its life originally came into existence in 6 days through the direct intervention of the power of God." In his view theories of evolutionary progress lacked sufficient scientific evidence to make them conclusive. Although Clark admitted that he could not prove by scientific methods that creation took place by direct command of God, he was convinced that "the facts of the natural world support rather than oppose the viewpoint of creationism." Outraged by what he considered Clark's unwarranted capitulation to evolution, Price launched a campaign against his former student that reverberated throughout Adventist circles.

More influential and viewed with greater favor by Price were the works of another of his students, Frank Lewis Marsh, who possessed a master's degree from Northwestern and a Ph.D. in plant ecology from Nebraska. In addition to a variety of technical papers, Marsh in 1944 published the first edition of his *Evolution, Creation and Science,* which was generally considered one of the most sophisticated antievolutionist works in existence. By his own admission, Price envied his former student's "ability to generate light without heat." Marsh appears to have been one of the earliest popularizers of the term *creationism,* and his book included a twelve-point "creationist creed" that emphasized belief that "about six thousand years ago, on the third, fifth and sixth days of a literal week . . . the Creator . . . made to appear upon this earth a richly diversified flora and fauna consisting in many instances of individuals just as complex as any of our present day forms." His emphasis on "the fixity of the species" later became a fundamental tenet of scientific creationism. Marsh preferred to designate the original creations as "Genesis kinds" rather than species. "Variation is the law of nature," he wrote, "but each organism can never produce a variant which is sufficiently different from itself to constitute a new kind." Even though Theodosius Dobzhansky, the famed geneticist who reviewed Marsh's book, was critical of its contents and baffled that such a work could be written by a person with bona fide scientific credentials in the mid-twentieth century, he nonetheless admitted that it was the work of "a reasonable and well-informed person."

The Seventh Day Adventist role in providing an intellectual connection between the anti-evolutionism of the 1920s and contemporary scientific creationism received support from and occasionally blended with what may be termed a Lutheran connection, especially involving Lutherans of the Missouri Synod variety. Byron C. Nelson, a Lutheran minister and seminary professor who had been active in the anti-evolution campaign of the 1920s relied heavily upon Price's New Catastrophism in his *The Deluge Story in Stone: A History of the Flood Theory of Geology,* published first in 1931 and reissued eighteen years later. *The Deluge Story* was Nelson's effort to disprove one of the main supports of the evolution theory, namely "the supposed progression of life shown by the fossils." Another Lutheran seminary professor whose approach resembled that of Nelson was Alfred M. Rehwinkle. His major work, *The Flood in the Light of the Bible, Geology and Archeology,* published in 1951 and in its eighth printing a decade later, also owed much to the influence of Price, whom Rehwinkle described as "a noted geologist" and "brilliant champion of Biblical truths." By the 1960s Lutheran ministers and writers as well as faculty members in several colleges sponsored by the Missouri Synod assumed places of leadership in what was then known as the creationist movement. A specific instance of Adventist-Lutheran cooperation in battling evolution occurred in 1945 when Frank Lewis Marsh, an Adventist, prepared a publication entitled *Genesis: Fact or Fable?* for the Missouri Synod's Student Service Commission. The work went through numerous printings and was widely distributed on college campuses.

Ignored by the orthodox scientific community and existing outside its organizational framework, creationists formed societies and sponsored their own journals. Inspired by the Evolution Protest Movement in Britain, founded by prominent professional and amateur scientists in 1932, Dr. Arthur P. Kelley organized the Creationist Society to carry on the anti-evolutionist campaign in the United States. More important was the Society for the Study of Deluge Geology and Related Sciences organized in 1938. Centered in California and largely the work of George McCready Price, the Society sponsored secret geological investigations to disprove the theory of evolution and published a bulletin, which appeared regularly for a few years. Because of the dominance of Seventh Day Adventists, who gave it the appearance of a denominational subgroup, and disagreements over the age of the earth, the Society disbanded in 1945, but re-emerged briefly under the name Society for the Study of Natural Science. Plagued by internal discord over competing theories of creation and by theological differences, the early creation science organizations also suffered from what has been termed the "lack of a critical mass of scientifically trained creationists."

Of greater and more enduring significance was the American Scientific Affiliation organized in 1941. Sponsored largely by officials of Moody Bible Institute, particularly Irwin A. Moon, who later headed the Moody Science Institute, the ASA had as its primary aim the "correlation of the facts of science with the tenets of the Christian faith." Many creationists joined the ASA whose journal, in its early years, served as an outlet for their views. But increasingly in the late 1940s the organization's membership came to include more evangelical Christians from the science faculties of Columbia, Stanford, Harvard, and similar institutions who were little inclined to accept a strict creationist viewpoint. The split that developed within the ASA during the late 1940s and early 1950s paralleled the polarization taking place within the ranks of conservative Protestantism between those who became known as evangelicals or neo-evangelicals and those who continued to be labelled fundamentalists. Within the ASA strict creationists complained that as the organization came to include more members with secular scientific training its "thrust against evolution was lessened."

Smoldering differences over creation within the ASA flared into the open in 1949 at the annual meeting in Los Angeles when George McCready Price, in his seventy-ninth year, presented his ideas on deluge geology, the young earth, and the fallacy of evolution. J. Lawrence Kulp, a Wheaton alumnus, Princeton Ph.D., and member of the Columbia University geology faculty, not only responded with a devastating critique but also continued his assault on Price's geological argument againt evolution in articles in the ASA journal. The defense of Price's views by a young engineer, Henry M. Morris, did little to repair the damage done by Kulp. Although Morris and other Price disciples who later became leaders in the creation science movement remained for a time identified with the ASA, its new constitutions adopted in 1950 and 1959 and the rising prominence within its ranks of evangelical scientists of Kulp's persuasion reduced them to a minority.

The decade beginning in 1959 witnessed a series of events that focused attention on the Darwinian theory and transformed the relatively quiet minority of strict creationists in the ASA into activists prepared to do battle against evolution. Among these events were the numerous publications, conferences, and symposia in 1959 commemorating the centennial of Darwin's *The Origin of Species*. Of these none attracted more attention than the five-day convocation at the University of Chicago where discussions by an international assemblage of famous scientists indicated general agreement that evolution was a demonstrable fact and that Darwin's theory was essential to the interpretation of nature's processes. The climactic event of the Chicago celebration was an address, on Thanksgiving Day, 1959, by Sir Julian Huxley, entitled "The Evolutionary Vision." "In the evolutionary pattern of thought," declared the grandson of Darwin's original defender, "there is no longer need or room for the supernatural." Nor, he emphasized, was it possible for man any longer to take refuge "in the arms of a divinized father figure, whom he himself has created." Huxley's address merely confirmed for anti-evolutionists the validity of their contention, at least since the 1920s, that evolution led inescapably to atheism.

Outraged and aroused by the "evolutionary vision" of Huxley and others in 1959, anti-evolutionists were prodded into action the following year by the appearance of the first in a series of textbooks prepared by the Biological Sciences Curriculum Study and funded by the National Science Foundation. The launching of Sputnik by the Soviet Union in 1957 prompted a frenzied effort to reform the science curriculum in American schools. Professional scientists who had previously devoted little attention to high-school science education suddenly discovered during their investigations in the wake of Sputnik that Darwin and evolution were taboo subjects in secondary schools. Their discovery prompted them to applaud the geneticist H. J. Muller in 1959 when he proclaimed that "one hundred years without Darwinism are enough." The new textbooks in science, issued early in the 1960s, as well as those in the social sciences, also underwritten by the federal government and published in 1963, possessed a forthright evolutionary orientation. With the introduction of these books into high schools, local and state boards of education from West Virginia to California found themselves under siege. The appearance of the textbooks spawned a network of self-appointed textbook-watchers and galvanized veteran opponents of evolution into action. The result was the eruption of an acrimonious and prolonged dispute.

Nowhere was the anti-evolutionist assault more persistent or effective than in California. The campaign originated in 1962 with two San Diego housewives, Nell Segraves, a Baptist, and Jean Sumrall, a Missouri Synod Lutheran, who enlisted the support of a remarkable group of engineers, scientists, and diverse technicians from the aerospace industry. Their tactic was first to insist upon the use of textbooks that taught evolution not as a fact, but only as a theory. Winning this concession, the Segraves group returned to the California State Board of Education three years later demanding the textbooks "teach creationism along with evolution as an equally viable theory." "At present," Nell Segraves argued, "the evolutionists own the system and they are crying because they may have to give it up. That's the way it is. We're not asking for our position to be the only position. We're asking for 50 percent of the education system back. At one time we owned it all." While the creationists fell short of their ultimate goals in California, their proposals elicited considerable support even from members of the State Board who, not especially friendly to creationism, deeply resented what one referred to as the "unrelenting dogmatism" of the scientists appearing in opposition to Segraves' demands. After witnessing the struggle in California, Calvin Trillin of *The New Yorker* concluded that, regardless of other factors involved in creationism, it was basically "a class issue." "What divided evolutionists and creationists," he observed, "was not the number of degrees they held but the width of their lapels and the flatness of their accents."

The struggle that began in California and that was re-enacted elsewhere pointed up the ambivalent public attitude toward science, which an eminent zoologist characterized as a complex love-hate relationship. On the one hand, Americans revered the practical benefits bestowed by science; on the other, some resented what they perceived as a threat posed to their deeply held religious values by science and its "too cocksure" elite of practitioners. As Dorothy Nelkin has amply demonstrated in her study, the textbook controversies revealed a deepening mistrust of and disillusionment with science; a profound resentment of what was interpreted as the arrogance and dogmatism of scientists; and a fear that the structured meritocratic processes operating within science threatened the more egalitarian, pluralistic values in society. Nor could the critics of the new textbooks and opponents of evolution in the 1960s be classified as representatives of the uneducated, culturally deprived sector of the population; rather they, or at least many of their leaders, were middle-class citizens, whose response to the uncertainties of a technological society was not the rejection of technology but a return to traditional values and beliefs. In fact, some observers have noted that much of the initial thrust of the creation science movement occurred in "high technology" areas and involved those associated with technological enterprises.

Frustrated by a war in Vietnam and confronted by a succession of cultural and social traumas, including a sexual revolution, a counterculture, and a "now generation" scornful of the past and its values, many Americans in the mid 1960s searched frantically for certainties and islands of safety to relieve their anxieties. Those who sought refuge in the values of the "historic faith" viewed with especial alarm the proliferation of exotic cults, the emergence of a radical theology that spoke in terms of the "death of God," and the Supreme Court decisions in 1962 and 1963 that banned prayer and Bible reading in the public schools. Such developments seemed to many to clear the way for the final triumph of "decadent scientism" and secularism, which the religiously orthodox anti-evolutionists interpreted as the inevitable products of Darwin's theory.

Just the renewal of a campaign to outlaw evolution appeared appropriate, the Supreme Court in 1968 struck down as unconstitutional the forty-year-old Arkansas anti-evolution law. The court's decision forced a change in the tactics of those inclined to combat evolution in the legislative arena. Rather than advocating legislation to ban the teaching of evolution, they concentrated instead on securing "equal time" for creationism—an approach pioneered by Segraves in her textbook struggles earlier. Such an approach had broad appeal as an expression of fair play and democratic values. Creationists bent upon legislative remedies extended the "equal time" doctrine to the teaching of science in the belief that their struggle against scientific conformity paralleled the struggles of other groups against cultural conformity.

When the war on evolution reopened in the 1960s, a new generation of leaders, many of whom possessed advanced degrees in the sciences from reputable universities, assumed direction of what became known as the creation science movement. Their approach and the contours of their argument were already evident, especially in the works of Henry M. Morris, an engineer and Southern Baptist, who, at least since 1946, had been publishing books on creationism. Morris's *The Genesis Flood*, co-authored with a Grace Brethren theologian and published in 1961, has remained one of the most authoritative sources in creation science. So obvious was the influence of George McCready Price, who read and criticized *The Genesis Flood* in manuscript, that one reviewer characterized it as merely a "reissue" of Price's work.

At the annual meeting of the American Scientific Affiliation in 1963—the year of Price's death—Morris and a group of evangelical scientists disenchanted with the ASA because of its lack of attention to creationism organized the Creation Research Society. The "team of ten" who founded the society also included Frank L. Marsh, Price's former student, Walter Lammerts, an associate of Segraves in her California crusades and a plant geneticist who developed the Queen Elizabeth rose, and Duane Gish, a biochemist with a Ph.D. from Berkeley. Viewed as the scholarly arm of the creation science movement, the society eschewed involvement in political lobbying efforts and, in fact, took the position that "the legal and political arena" was not "the proper place" for creationism to wage its battle. Although its primary purpose was to publish a scientific quarterly, the society in time also produced several anthologies and a high-school biology textbook written from the creationist viewpoint. An independent, unaffiliated organization, incorporated in Michigan, the Creation Research Society required its voting members to possess advanced degrees in science and all members to subscribe to a four-point "statement of belief" which embodied the basic tenets of the literal-historical theory of creation. While the organization was nondenominational and its leadership included the Baptist Morris and the Seventh Day Adventist Marsh, Missouri Synod Lutherans were dominant during its early years.

The organization of other creationist groups quickly followed the establishment of the Creation Research Society. Among the most notable of these was the Bible Science Association, also founded in 1963 by Walter Lang, a Lutheran minister in Idaho. More inclined to political activism than the Creation Research Society, the Bible Science Association published a monthly *Newsletter* that regularly featured articles on DNA, fossils, and other favorite creationist topics and that served as an information clearinghouse regarding the activities of creationist groups throughout the United States and the world.

In 1970 Nell Segraves organized the Creation Research Center in San Diego as an affiliate of Christian Heritage College, an institution sponsored by Tim Lahaye's Scott Memorial Baptist Church. Henry

Morris resigned his engineering professorship at Virginia Polytechnic Institute to become associated with the college and the Creation Research Center which primarily focused on a curriculum reform program and the production of creationist literature for schools. In 1972, owing to internal conflicts and doctrinal differences, Segraves separated the Center from the college, and its place was taken by the Institute for Creation Research with Morris as director, Duane Gish as associate director, and a staff of scientists engaged in graduate education and creation research, including projects to recover Noah's Ark. Described as a "trans-denominational agency," the Institute produced a steady flow of books, monographs, and pamphlets and included a corps of articulate lecturers and skilled debaters ready to defend the particular theory of creation that it represented.

The arguments of the Institute's creationists clearly indicated their debt to George McCready Price. To demonstrate that evolution was impossible and absurd, for example, they emphasized gaps in the fossil record and devoted extraordinary attention to the Noahian flood and the Second Law of Thermodynamics. Dismissing radiometric dating procedures as of dubious validity, they insisted that the geological record, properly interpreted, indicated "a young age for the earth" and did not support "the general theory of evolution." Price had invoked the Second Law of Thermodynamics on occasion, but his intellectual descendants gave it a central place in the creationist argument. Like Price, they also made much of disagreements among scientists over the details of evolution. "Any negative evidence against evolution," Director Morris explained, "is the same as positive evidence for creation." Quotations from evolutionists themselves provided a substantial portion of this negative evidence. By citing the science philosopher Sir Karl Popper, who argued that a theory must be testable in order to be scientifically valid, strict creationists claimed that evolution was clearly unscientific. To support their contention that their "creation model" deserved equality with the "evolution model," they invoked the name of Thomas Kuhn, another philosopher of science, who explained scientific progress in terms of competing models or paradigms rather than the accumulation of objective knowledge. The "creation model," in sharp contrast to the "evolution model," embodied the concept of a providential, purposive design in nature.

"Within the framework . . . of the three great events of history—
the Creation, the Fall and the Flood," Morris declared, "can be explained all the data of true science and history."

Like Price and the anti-evolutionists of the 1920s, the creation scientists associated with the Institute by no means limited their discussion to the scientific aspects of Darwin's theory but devoted much
attention to its moral and philosophical implications. Director Morris,
for example, claimed that evolution was "responsible for most of the
world's modern problems," including pollution, abortion, energy de-
pletion, racism, educational decline, and communism. Since Darwin's
theory was viewed as the root of "secular humanism," a catchall term
signifying an infinite variety of what was perceived as evidence of
moral decay, such as pornography, homosexuality, and alternate life
styles, the "need of the hour" was clear; an effort to neutralize if not
to eliminate the theory was an essential first step in readjusting the
nation's moral values.

By 1980 the Institute for Creation Research had become the best-
known and most influential organization dedicated to strict creationism, that is to a special creation theory that incorporated the salient
features and "scientific slant" of George McCready Price's argument
against evolution. Both the Institute and its ally, the Creation Research Society, adhered rigidly to the literal-historical theory of creation, which was only one of at least a half dozen creation theories
espoused by diverse groups. Others emphasized an old earth and went
far toward accommodating evolution. Even though the creation movement may have acquired "a critical mass of scientifically trained creationists," rival theories of creation continued to be sources of disunity
and discord. Creationism, like anti-evolution in the 1920s, possessed
multiple meanings. As a result, the arguments advanced by the Institute of Creation Research have been condemned as both unscientific
and unbiblical by creationists who do not subscribe to the literal-
historical theory.

While the Institute for Creation Research and the Creation Research Society provided the leadership for the creation science movement, dozens of local, state, and national organizations initiated grass-
roots campaigns to secure the enactment of "equal time" or "balanced
treatment" legislation. That their campaigns coincided with a growing
dissatisfaction with public schools undoubtedly helped in rallying sup-

port to their cause. Appearing under a variety of names that implied fairness and equality, these organizations by 1975 had secured the introduction of such measures in legislatures of more than half the states and the adoption of favorable policies by numerous local boards of education. Despite strenuous efforts in Washington, Colorado, Michigan, and elsewhere, creationists were only successful in securing "equal time" legislation in 1973 in Tennessee, which had repealed its old anti-evolution law six years earlier after a science teacher was dismissed for violating it. In 1975 as a result of a suit brought by the National Association of Biology Teachers a federal court declared the "equal time" statute "unconstitutional on its face." Undaunted by this decision or by other legal setbacks, creationist organizations perfected their lobbying techniques and strived to formulate foolproof "equal time" or "balanced treatment" legislation. By 1979 Paul Ellwanger, a Roman Catholic and a respiration therapist who headed the creationist organization in South Carolina known as Citizens for Fairness in Education, announced that such a measure had been drafted and samples could be secured for one dollar. "This law," Ellwanger wrote, "contains no references to the Bible but stresses a two-model scientific approach." The Arkansas legislature enacted this two-model statute in 1981.

In many respects the creation science movement that took shape early in the 1960s resembled the crusade against evolution waged a half century earlier. Both viewed the theory of evolution as scientifically invalid and theologically unacceptable and held it responsible for a host of social and cultural trends considered objectionable. No less than in the 1920s, creationists in the 1970s proved to be skilled in public debates in which they described evolution as a "mere theory" no more provable and less plausible than the theory of creation. As their predecessors fifty years earlier did, the opponents of evolution in the 1970s also accused those who subscribed to the theory of displaying a spirit of intolerance incompatible with American concepts of democracy and fair play.

Despite such similarities, however, the creation science movement differed in some important respects from the crusade of the 1920s. The change in terminology indicated a shift in emphasis that attempted to give primacy to scientific rather than religious objections to evolution. Although theological considerations obviously figured prominently in the creation science movements, overtly at the popular level, its intellectual leaders, unlike those in the 1920s, were university-trained scientists and engineers rather than professional evangelists and clergymen. That officials of major, mainline denominations opposed Arkansas' "balanced treatment" law of 1981 and spearheaded the legal contest that declared it unconstitutional suggests the extent to which the situation differed from that in the 1920s when evolution prompted tumultuous battles and sharp divisions in such denominations. But to say that creationism failed to become a disruptive issue in mainline denominational circles is not to say that religious forces played an inconsequential role in the more recent movement. Just the opposite, of course, has been the case. The point is that much of the vocal popular support for creationism within the religious community has come from those sources outside what is called mainline protestantism, that is from those theologically conservative groups whose numbers and influence dramatically increased in the decades since the Scopes trial, a period that witnessed a relative decline in the strength of major Protestant denominations.

The creation science movement also differed from the earlier anti-evolution crusade in terms of its popular leadership, rhetorical tone, and sectional focus. First, no one has yet emerged to do for creationists what William Jennings Bryan did for the anti-evolutionists. A man with immense prestige and a large, loyal following, Bryan unified the disparate opponents of Darwin's theory and transformed their cause into a popular crusade. Second, the rhetoric of the creationist movement has been more restrained, in part because of its effort to oppose evolution within a scientific context. It would be difficult to imagine the mild-mannered, professorial Henry M. Morris, the gentle, gracious Frank Marsh, or even the feisty Duane Gish employing the flamboyant langauge that characterized the verbal combat of Billy Sunday, Jasper Massee, Baxter F. ("Cyclone") McLendon, and other warriors against Darwin's theory in the 1920s. Third, even though some insist that creationists, no less than their predecessors in the 1920s, are products of "southern and southwestern populism," the contemporary movement can scarcely be explained as a phenomenon of the hinterlands of the rural South. To be sure, only the legislatures of Tennessee, Arkansas, and Louisiana have enacted "equal time" and "balanced treatment" statutes, but much of the creationist struggle has occurred outside the South, and most of the leadership of the movement has been based elsewhere, notably in California and Michigan. If indeed the descendants of the Arkies and Okies and other transplanted heirs of southern populist culture are responsible for the creationist offensive, the southernization of America may well be more complete than most have been willing to admit.

In the highly polarized atmosphere created by the debate over creation/evolution, the voice of those willing to separate the "how" of creation from the "who" and the "why" has been drowned out by the passionate rhetoric of combatants on both sides who are equally adept in the use of proof-texts. Their charges and counter-charges, aside from generating more heat than light, tend to obscure what the dispute is all about. At issue, as Richard Berry has observed, are two profoundly important stories of ultimate meaning. For creationists this ultimate meaning involves the role of God as Creator. Their fear is that a theory which threatens the biblical steps of creation threatens the existence of God as well. For conventional scientists, the ultimate meaning concerns the scientific method and scientific objectivity which they preceive as being subtly but potently undermined by an idea or "model" put forward as "true science" that they consider at best as no more than pseudo-science.

So long as there are those who insist that the "how" of creation is inseparable from the "who" and "why" the theory of evolution is likely to continue to arouse opposition. To issue another obituary for the creation/evolution conflict in the wake of recent court decisions would be to duplicate the error of those who, following the Scopes trial, believed the matter had been permanently laid to rest. Resolution of the controversy will require, as a minimum, that combatants on both sides heed the warning of Vernon Kellogg in 1926 about the perils of assuming a stance of "all mightiness and all-knowingness." A re-reading of Darwin might also be helpful. "There is," reads the last sentence in *The Origin of Species*, "a grandeur in this [evolutionary] view of life, with its several powers, having been originally breathed by the Creator into a few forms or into one. . . ."

IO

Race, Ethnicity, and Real Estate Appraisal

KENNETH T. JACKSON

● *Relentlessly, almost unconsciously, the United States has become the world's first suburban nation. Since 1950, millions of acres of brush, shrub oak, pine, and prairie have given way to crabgrass and concrete, and the suburban total of 85 million now represents the largest single element of the national population. Indeed, suburbia has become the most quintessential aesthetic achievement of the United States and has come to symbolize the fullest, most unadulterated embodiment of the American present, a manifestation of some of the most fundamental characteristics of modern society, among them conspicuous consumption, a reliance upon the private automobile, upward mobility, the breakdown of the extended family into nuclear units, the widening division between work and leisure, and a tendency toward racial and economic exclusiveness.*

Despite certain common human attitudes about "home," any residential comparison of the United States with the rest of the world will reveal that America is unusual in terms of its preference for the free-standing house on its own plot, its high degree of home ownership (about 66 percent of all households in 1981), its use of wood as the predominant building

Reprinted from *Journal of Urban History,* August 1980, © Sage Publications, Beverly Hills, by permission of the publisher.

AUTHOR'S NOTE: I wish to express my appreciation to Herbert J. Gans, Robert Kolodny, Peter Marcuse, William E. Leuchtenburg, and John A. Garraty of Columbia University; to Joseph B. Howerton, Jerry N. Hess, and Jerome Finster of the National Archives; to Frederick J. Eggers, Mary A. Grey, and William A. Rolfe of the Department of Housing and Urban Development; to Joel A. Tarr of Carnegie-Mellon University; to John Modell of the University of Minnesota; to Mark Gelfand of Boston College; to Joan Gilbert of Yale University; and to Margaret Kurth Weinberg of the Connecticut Governor's Office.

material, and its pattern of wealthy suburbs and poor inner-city neighborhoods.

Why have the metropolitan areas of the United States suburbanized so quickly? One might think of the plentiful land around most cities, of the relative wealth of the nation, of the heterogeneity of the American people, of the cheap energy and its inducement to decentralization, of the attractiveness of the domestic ideal, and of rapid technological advances like streetcars and automobiles which made long-distance commuting feasible. But government has not been an impartial observer in the contest between cities and their suburbs. Federally financed interstate highways have undermined the locational advantages of inner-city neighborhoods, while income-tax deductions have encouraged families to buy houses rather than rent apartments. In the following essay, Professor Kenneth T. Jackson focuses on the much-praised mortgage policies of Uncle Sam and points out the extraordinarily flagrant discrimination that was built into them from the beginning.

If a healthy race is to be reared, it can be reared only in healthy homes; if infant mortality is to be reduced and tuberculosis to be stamped out, the first essential is the improvement of housing conditions; if drink and crime are to be successfully combated, decent sanitary houses must be provided. If "unrest" is to be converted into contentment, the provision of good houses may prove one of the most potent agents in that conversion.

King George V, 1919

A nation of homeowners, of people who own a real share in their own land, is unconquerable.

President Franklin D. Roosevelt, 1933

The appeal of low-density living for more than a century in the United States and across regional, class, and ethnic lines has led some observers to regard it as natural and inevitable, a trend "that no amount of government interference can reverse." Or, as a senior Federal Housing Administration (FHA) official told the 1939 convention of the American Institute of Planners: "Decentralization is taking place. It is not a policy, it is a reality—and it is as impossible for us to change this trend as it is to change the desire of birds to migrate to a more suitable location."

Despite such protestations, there are many ways in which government largesse can affect where people live. For example, the federal tax code encourages businesses to abandon old structures before their useful life is at an end by permitting greater tax benefits for new construction than for the improvement of existing buildings. Thus, the government subsidizes an acceleration in the rate at which economic activity is dispersed to new locations. Similarly, Roger Lotchin has recently begun important research on the importance of defense spending to the growth of Sunbelt cities since 1920. Military expenditures have meanwhile worked to the detriment of other areas. Estimates were common in the late 1970s that Washington was annually collecting between $6 billion and $11 billion more than it was returning to the New York metropolitan area.

On the urban-suburban level, the potential for federal influence is also enormous. For example, the Federal Highway Act of 1916 and the Interstate Highway Act of 1956 moved the government toward a transportation policy emphasizing and benefiting the road, the truck, and the private motor car. In conjunction with cheap fuel and mass-produced automobiles, the urban expressways led to lower marginal transport costs and greatly stimulated deconcentration. Equally important to most families is the incentive to detached-home living provided by the deduction of mortgage interest and real estate taxes from their gross income. Even the reimbursement formulas for water line and sewer construction have had an impact on the spatial patterns of metropolitan areas.

The purpose of this article, which is part of a much larger analysis of the process of suburbanization in the United States between 1815 and 1980, is to examine the impact of two innovations of the New Deal on the older, industrial cities of the nation.

THE HOME OWNERS LOAN CORPORATION

On April 13, 1933, President Roosevelt urged the House and the Senate to pass a law that would (1) protect small homeowners from foreclosure, (2) relieve them of part of the burden of excessive interest and principal payments incurred during a period of higher values and higher earning power, and (3) declare that it was national policy to protect home ownership. The measure received bipartisan support. As Republican Congressman Rich of Pennsylvania, a banker himself, remarked during the floor debate:

> I am opposed to the Government in business, but here is where I am going to do a little talking for the Government in business, because if aid is going to be extended to these owners of small homes, the Government will have to get into this business of trying to save their homes. The banker dares not loan for fear the depositor will draw out his deposit; then he must close his bank or the Comptroller of the Currency will close it for him.

The resulting Home Owners Loan Corporation (HOLC), signed into law by the President on June 13, 1933, was designed to serve urban needs; the Emergency Farm Mortgage Act, passed almost a month earlier, was intended to reduce rural foreclosure.

The HOLC replaced the unworkable direct loan provisions of the Hoover administration's Federal Home Loan Bank Act and refinanced tens of thousands of mortgages in danger of default or foreclosure. It even granted loans at low interest rates to permit owners to recover homes lost through forced sale. Between July 1933 and June 1935 alone, the HOLC supplied more than $3 billion for over a million mortgages, or loans for one-tenth of all owner-occupied, nonfarm residences in the United States. Although applications varied widely by state—in Mississippi, 99 percent of the eligible owner-occupants applied for loans while in Maine only 18 percent did so—nationally about 40 percent of eligible Americans sought HOLC assistance.

The HOLC is important to housing history because it introduced, perfected, and proved in practice the feasibility of the long-term, self-amortizing mortgage with uniform payments spread over the whole life of the debt. Prior to the 1930s, the typical length of a mortgage was between 5 and 10 years, and the loan itself was not paid off when the final settlement was due. Thus, the homeowner was periodically at the mercy of the arbitrary and unpredictable forces in the money market. When money was easy, renewal every five or seven years was no problem. But if a mortgage expired at a time when money was tight, it might be impossible for the homeowner to secure a renewal, and foreclosure would ensue. Under the HOLC program, the loans were fully amortized, and the repayment period was extended to about 20 years.

Aside from the large number of mortgages which it helped to refinance on a long-term, low-interest basis, the HOLC systematized appraisal methods across the nation. Because it was dealing with problem mortgages—in some states over 40 percent of all HOLC loans were foreclosed even after refinancing—the HOLC had to make predictions and assumptions regarding the useful or productive life of housing it financed. Unlike refrigerators or shoes, dwellings were expected to be durable—how durable was the purpose of the investigation.

With care and extraordinary attention to detail, HOLC appraisers divided cities into neighborhoods and developed elaborate questionnaires relating to the occupation, income, and ethnicity of the inhabitants and the age, type of construction, price range, sales demand, and general state of repair of the housing stock. The element of novelty did not lie in the appraisal requirement itself—that had long been standard real estate practice. Rather, it lay in the creation of a formal and uniform system of appraisal, reduced to writing, structured in defined procedures, and implemented by individuals only after intensive training. The ultimate aim was that one appraiser's judgment of value would have meaning to an investor located somewhere else. In evaluating such efforts, the distinguished economist C. Lowell Harriss has credited the HOLC training and evaluation procedures "with having helped raise the general level of American real estate appraisal methods." A less favorable judgment would be that the HOLC initiated the practice of "redlining."

This occurred because HOLC devised a rating system which undervalued neighborhoods that were dense, mixed, or aging. Four categories of quality—imaginatively entitled First, Second, Third, and Fourth, with corresponding code letters of A, B, C, and D and colors of green, blue, yellow, and red—were established. The First grade (also A and green) areas were described as new, homogeneous, and "in demand as residential locations in good times and bad." Homogeneous meant "American business and professional men"; Jewish neighborhoods or even those with an "infiltration of Jews" could not possibly be considered "Best."

The Second security grade (blue) went to "still desirable" areas that had "reached their peak," but were expected to remain stable for many years. The Third grade (yellow) or "C" neighborhoods were usually described as "definitely declining," while the Fourth grade (red) or "D" neighborhoods were defined as areas "in which things taking place in C areas have already happened."

The HOLC's assumptions about urban neighborhoods were based on both an ecological conception of change and a socioeconomic one. Adopting a dynamic view of the city and assuming that change was inevitable, its appraisers accepted as given the proposition that the natural tendency of any area was to decline—in part because of the increasing age and obsolescence of the physical structures and in part because of the filtering down of the housing stock to families of lower income and different ethnicity. Thus physical deterioration was both a cause and an effect of population change, and HOLC officials made no real attempt to sort them out. They were part and parcel of the same process. Thus, black neighborhoods were invariably rated as Fourth grade, but so were any areas characterized by poor maintenance or vandalism. Similarly, those "definitely declining" sections that were marked Third grade or yellow received such a low rating in part because of age and in part because they were "within such a low price or rent range as to attract an undesirable element."

The HOLC did not initiate the idea of considering race and ethnicity in real estate appraising. As Calvin Bradford has demonstrated, models developed at the University of Chicago in the 1920s and early 1930s by Homer Hoyt and Robert Park became the dominant explanation of neighborhood change. They suggested that different groups of people "infiltrated" or "invaded" territory held by others through a process of competition. These interpretations were then adopted by prominent appraising texts, such as Frederick Babcock's *The Valuation of Real Estate* (1932) and *McMichael's Appraising Manual* (1931). Both advised appraisers to pay particular attention to "undesirable" or "least desirable" elements and suggested that the influx of certain ethnic groups was likely to precipitate price declines.

The HOLC simply applied these notions of ethnic and racial worth to real estate appraising on an unprecedented scale. With the assistance of local realtors and banks, it assigned one of its four ratings to every block in every city. The resulting information was then translated into the appropriate color and duly recorded on secret "Residential Security Maps" in local HOLC offices. The maps themselves were placed in elaborate "City Survey Files," which consisted of reports, questionnaires, and workpapers relating to current and future values of real estate.

Because the two federal agencies under analysis here did not normally report data on anything other than a county basis, the St. Louis area was selected as a case study. There, the city and county were legally separated in 1876 so that there was no alternative to individual reporting. In addition, an even older industrial city, Newark, New Jersey, was selected because of the availability of an unusual FHA study.

The residential security map for the St. Louis area in 1937 gave the highest ratings to the newer, affluent suburbs that were strung out along curvilinear streets well away from the problems of the city. Three years later, in 1940, the advantage of the periphery over the center was even more marked. In both evaluations, the top of the scale was dominated by Ladue, a largely undeveloped section of high, rolling land, heavily wooded estates, and dozens of houses in the $20,000 to $50,000 range. In 1940, HOLC appraisers noted approvingly that the area was "highly restricted" and occupied by "capitalists and other wealthy families." Reportedly not the home of "a single foreigner or Negro," Ladue received an "A" rating. Other affluent suburbs like Clayton and University City were also marked with green and blue on the 1937 and 1940 maps, indicating that they, too, were characterized by attractive homes on well-maintained plots and that the appraisers felt confident about mortgages insured there. And well they might have been; in University City almost 40 percent of the homes had been valued at more than $15,000 in 1930, while in Clayton the comparable figure was an astounding 72.3 percent (see Table 1).

At the other end of the scale in St. Louis County were the rare Fourth grade areas. A few such neighborhoods were occupied by white laborers, such as "Ridgeview" in Kirkwood, where the garagelike shacks typically cost less than $1,500. But the "D" regions in the county were usually black. One such place in 1937 was Lincoln Terrace, a small enclave of four- and five-room bungalows built about

TABLE 1

Home Values, HOLC Ratings, and Population Growth in Selected St. Louis Area Communities

Community	Percentage of Homes Owner-Occupied in 1930	Value of Owned Homes, 1930 (in thousands of dollars)				Predominant HOLC Rating in 1940	Population in 1940	Population in 1970
		Below 3	3-7½	7½-15	Above 15			
St. Louis City	31.6%	11.6%	49.6%	30.1%	7.7%	C	816,048	622,236
University City	50.1	4.8	19.9	23.2	37.5	A	33,023	46,309
Webster Groves	78.5	7.3	29.5	39.2	23.2	A	18,394	27,455
Maplewood	56.3	7.0	60.9	28.2	12.0	C	12,875	12,785
Kirkwood	68.3	13.0	41.9	32.1	11.2	—	12,132	31,769
Richmond Heights	57.2	6.5	28.3	50.6	13.8	B	12,802	13,802
Clayton	49.8	2.5	7.5	17.4	72.3	A	13,069	16,222
Ferguson	72.7	9.7	52.2	29.6	7.4	B	5,724	28,759
Brentwood	66.3	14.6	70.5	13.2	1.5	C	4,383	11,248
Ladue	84.6	1.2	4.8	14.9	79.1	A	3,981	10,591

SOURCE: 1930 United States Census Tracts for St. Louis; HOLC City Survey Files in National Archives, and National Resources Committee, *Regional Planning, Part II—St. Louis Region* (Washington: Government Printing Office, 1936), p. 52.

1927. Originally intended for middle-class white families, the venture was unsuccessful, and the district quickly developed into a black neighborhood. But even though the homes were relatively new and of good quality, the HOLC gave the section (D-12 in 1937, D-8 in 1940) the lowest possible grade, asserting that the houses had "little or no value today, having suffered a tremendous decline in values due to the colored element now controlling the district."

In contrast to the gently rolling terrain and sparse settlement of St. Louis County, the city had proportionately many more Third and Fourth grade neighborhoods, and more than twice as many renters as homeowners. Virtually all the residential sections along the Mississippi River or adjacent to the central business district received the lowest two ratings. This harsh judgment was in part a reflection of their badly deteriorated physical character. Just a few years earlier, the City Plan Commission of St. Louis had made a survey of 44 acres surrounding the business section. Only about 40 percent of the 8,447 living units had indoor toilets, and the tuberculosis morbidity rate was three times that of the city as a whole. As the St. Louis Regional Planning report pessimistically concluded in 1936:

> The older residential districts which are depreciating in value and in character constitute one of the most serious problems in this region. They can never be absorbed by commercial and industrial uses. Even if owners wished to build new homes within them, it would be inadvisable because of the present character of the districts.

But the HOLC appraisers marked other inner-city areas down not because of the true slum conditions but because of negative attitudes toward city living in general. The evaluation of a white, working-class neighborhood near Fairgrounds Park was typical. According to the description, "Lots are small, houses are only slightly set back from the sidewalks, and there is a general appearance of congestion." Although an urban individual might have found this collection of cottages and abundant shade trees rather charming, the HOLC thought otherwise: "Age of properties, general mixture of type, proximity to industrial section on northeast and much less desirable areas to the south make this a good fourth grade area."

As was the case in every city, any Afro-American presence was a source of substantial concern to the HOLC. In a confidential and generally pessimistic 1941 survey of the economic and real estate prospects of the St. Louis metropolitan area, the Federal Home Loan Bank Board (the parent agency of HOLC) repeatedly commented on the "rapidly increasing Negro population" and the resulting "problem in the maintenance of real estate values." The officials evinced a keen interest in the movement of black families and included maps of the density of Negro settlement with every analysis. Not surprisingly, even those neighborhoods with small proportions of black inhabitants were typically rated "D," or hazardous.

Like St. Louis, Newark has long symbolized the most extreme features of the urban crisis. In that troubled city, federal appraisers took note in the 1930s of the high tax rate, the heavy relief load, the per-capita bonded debt, and the "strong tendency for years for people of larger incomes to move their homes outside the city." The 1939 Newark area residential security map did not designate a single neighborhood in that city of more than 400,000 as worthy of an "A" rating. "High class Jewish" sections like Weequahic and Clinton Hill, as well as Gentile areas like Vailsburg and Forest Hill all received "B" or the Second grade. Typical Newark neighborhoods were rated even lower. The well-maintained and attractive working class sections of Roseville, Woodside, and East Vailsburg were given Third grade or "C" ratings; the remainder of the city, including immigrant Ironbound and every black neighborhood, was written off as "hazardous."

Immediately adjacent to Newark is New Jersey's Hudson County, which is among the half-dozen most densely settled and ethnically diverse political jurisdictions in the United States. Predictably, HOLC appraisers had decided by 1940 that Hudson County was a lost cause. In the communities of Bayonne, Hoboken, Secaucus, Kearny, Union City, Weehawken, Harrison, and Jersey City, taken together, they designated only two very small "B" areas and no "A" sections.

The HOLC insisted that "there is no implication that good mortgages do not exist or cannot be made in Third and Fourth grade areas." And, there is some evidence to indicate that HOLC did in fact make the majority of its obligations in "definitely declining" or "hazardous" neighborhoods. This seeming liberality was actually good business because the residents of poorer sections generally maintained a better pay back record than did their more affluent cousins. As the Federal Home Loan Bank Board explained:

> The rate of foreclosure per 1000 non-farm dwellings during 1939 was greater in St. Louis County than in St. Louis City by about 2½ to 1. A partial explanation or causation of this situation is the fact that County properties consist of a greater proportion of units in the higher priced brackets.

The damage caused by the HOLC came not through its own actions, but through the influence of its appraisal system on the financial decision of other institutions. During the late 1930s, the Federal Home Loan Bank Board circulated questionnaires to banks asking about their mortgage practices. Those returned by savings and loan associations and banks in Essex County (Newark), New Jersey, indicated a clear relationship between public and private redlining practices. One specific question asked: "What are the most desirable lending areas?" The answers were often "A and B" or "Blue" or "FHA only." Similarly, to the inquiry, "Are there any areas in which loans will not be made?" the responses included, "Red and most yellow," "C and D," "Newark," "Not in red," and "D areas." Obviously, private banking institutions were privy to and influenced by the government's Residential Security Maps.

THE FEDERAL HOUSING ADMINISTRATION

Direct, large-scale Washington intervention in the American housing market dates from the adoption of the National Housing Act on June 27, 1934. Although intended "to encourage improvement in housing standards and conditions, to facilitate sound home financing on reasonable terms, and to exert a stabilizing influence on the mortgage market," the primary purpose of the legislation was the alleviation of unemployment in the construction industry. As the Federal Emergency Relief Administrator testified before the House Banking and Currency Committee on May 18, 1934:

> The building trades in America represent by all odds the largest single unit of our unemployment. Probably more than one-third of all the unemployed are identified, directly and indirectly, with the building trades. . . . Now, a purpose of this bill, a fundamental purpose of this bill, is an effort to get the people back to work.

Between 1934 and 1968, the FHA had a remarkable record of accomplishment. Essentially, it insured long-term mortgage loans made by private lenders for home construction and sale. To this end, it collected premiums, set up reserves for losses, and in the event of a default on a mortgage, indemnified the lender. It did not build houses or lend money. Instead, it induced leaders who had money to invest it in residential mortgages by insuring them against loss on such investments, with the full weight of the U.S. Treasury behind the contract. And it revolutionized the home finance industry in the following ways.

First, before FHA began operations, first mortgages typically were limited to one-half or two-thirds of the appraised value of the property. During the 1920s, for example, savings and loan associations held one-half of America's outstanding mortgage debt. Those mortgages averaged 58 percent of estimated property value. Thus, prospective home-buyers needed a down payment of at least 30 percent to close a deal. By contrast, the fraction of the collateral that the lender was able to lend for a FHA-secured loan was about 93 percent. Thus, large down payments were unnecessary.

Second, continuing a trend begun by the HOLC, the FHA extended the repayment period for its guaranteed mortgages to 25 or 30 years and insisted that all loans be fully amortized. The effect was to reduce both the average monthly payment and the national rate of mortgage foreclosure. The latter declined from 250,000 nonfarm units in 1932 to only 18,000 in 1951.

Third, FHA established minimum standards for home construction that became almost universal in the industry. These regulations were not intended to make any particular structure fault-free, or even to assure the owner's satisfaction with the purchase. But they were designed to assure with at least statistical accuracy that the dwelling would be free of gross structural or mechanical deficiencies. Although there was nothing innovative in considering the quality of a house in relation to the debt placed against it, two features of the system were new; first, that the standards were objective, uniform, and in writing; second, that they were to be enforced by actual, on-site inspection—prior to insurance commitment in the case of an existing property and at various fixed stages in the course of construction in the case of new housing. Since World War II, the largest private contractors have built all their new houses to meet FHA standards, even though financing has often been arranged without FHA aid. This has occurred because many potential purchasers will not consider a home that cannot get FHA approval.

Fourth, in the 1920s, the interest rate for first mortgages averaged between 6 and 8 percent. If a second mortgage was necessary, as it usually was for families of moderate incomes, the purchaser could obtain one by paying a discount to the lender, a higher interest rate on the loan, and perhaps a commission to a broker. Together, these charges added about 15 percent to the purchase price. Under the FHA and Veterans Administration (VA) programs, by contrast, there was very little risk to the banker if a loan turned sour. Reflecting this government guarantee, interest rates fell by two or three percentage points.

These four changes substantially increased the number of American families who could reasonably expect to purchase homes. By the end of 1972, FHA had helped nearly 11 million families to own houses and another 22 million families to improve their properties. It had also insured 1.8 million dwellings in multiunit projects. And in those same years between 1934 and 1972, the percentage of American families living in owner-occupied dwellings rose from 44 percent to 63 percent.

Quite simply, it often became cheaper to buy than to rent. Long Island builder Martin Winter recently recalled that in the early 1950s, families living in the Kew Gardens section of Queens were paying almost $100 per month for small two-bedroom apartments. For less money they could, and often did, move to the new Levittown-type developments springing up along the highways from the city. Even the working classes could aspire to home ownership. As one person who left New York for suburban Dumont, New Jersey, remembered: "We had been paying $50 a month rent, and here we come up and live for $29 a month. That paid everything—taxes, principal, insurance on your mortgage, and interest." Not surprisingly, the middle-class suburban family with the new house and the long-term, fixed-rate FHA-insured mortgage became a symbol, and perhaps a stereotype, of "the American way of life."

Unfortunately, the corrollary to this achievement was the fact that

FHA programs hastened the decay of inner-city neighborhoods by stripping them of much of the middle-class constituency. This occurred for two reasons. First, although the legislation nowhere mentioned an antiurban bias, it favored the construction of single-family and discouraged construction of multifamily projects through unpopular terms. Historically, single-family housing programs have been the heart of FHA's insured loan activities. Between 1941 and 1950, FHA-insured single-family starts exceeded FHA multifamily starts by a ratio of almost four to one (see Table 2). In the next decade, the margin exceeded seven to one. Even in 1971, when FHA insured the largest number of multifamily units in its history, single-family houses were more numerous by 27 percent.

Similarly, loans for the repair of existing structures were small and for short duration, which meant that a family could more easily purchase a new home than modernize an old one. Finally, the only part of the 1934 act relating to low-income families was the embryonic authorization for mortgage insurance with respect to rental housing in regulated projects of public bodies or limited dividend corporations. Almost nothing was insured until 1938, and even thereafter, the total insurance for rental housing exceeded $1 billion only once between 1934 and 1962.

The second and more important variety of suburban, middle-class favoritism had to do with the so-called unbiased professional estimate that was a prerequisite for any loan guarantee. This mandatory appraisal included a rating of the property itself, a rating of the mortgagor or borrower, and a rating of the neighborhood. The lower the valuation placed on properties, the less government risk and the less generous the aid to the potential buyers (and sellers). The purpose of the neighborhood evaluation was "to determine the degree of mortgage risk introduced in a mortgage insurance transaction because of the location of the property at a specific site." And unlike the HOLC, which used an essentially similar procedure, the FHA allowed personal and agency bias in favor of all-white subdivisions in the suburbs to affect the kinds of loans it guaranteed—or, equally important, refused to guarantee. In this way the bureaucracy influenced the character of housing at least as much as the 1934 enabling legislation did.

The FHA was quite precise in teaching its underwriters how to

TABLE 2

New Housing Starts in the United States, 1935–1968
(in thousands)

Year	Total Starts	FHA Starts	VA Starts	Public Housing
1935	216	14	0	5
1936	304	49	0	15
1937	332	60	0	4
1938	399	119	0	7
1939	458	158	0	57
1940	530	180	0	73
1941	619	220	0	87
1942	301	166	0	55
1943	184	146	0	7
1944	139	93	NA	3
1945	325	41	9	1
1946	1015	69	92	8
1947	1265	229	160	3
1948	1344	294	71	18
1949	1430	364	91	36
1950	1408	487	191	44
1951	1420	264	149	71
1952	1446	280	141	59
1953	1402	252	157	36
1954	1532	276	307	19
1955	1627	277	393	20
1956	1325	192	271	24
1957	1175	168	128	49
1958	1314	295	102	68
1959	1495	332	109	37
1960	1230	261	75	44
1961	1285	244	83	52
1962	1439	259	78	30
1963	1582	221	71	32
1964	1502	205	59	32
1965	1451	196	49	37
1966	1142	158	37	31
1967	1268	180	52	30
1968	1484	220	56	38

SOURCE: U.S. Bureau of the Census, *Housing Construction Statistics, 1889–1964* (Washington: GPO, 1966), TABLE A-2; and U.S. Department of Housing and Urban Development, *HUD Trends: Annual Summary* (Washington: HUD, 1970).

measure the quality of residential area. Eight criteria were established (the numbers in parentheses reflect the percentage weight given to each):

- (1) relative economic stability (40 percent)
- (2) protection from adverse influences (20 percent)
- (3) freedom from special hazards (5 percent)
- (4) adequacy of civic, social, and commercial centers (5 percent)
- (5) adequacy of transportation (10 percent)
- (6) sufficiency of utilities and conveniences (5 percent)
- (7) level of taxes and special assessments (5 percent)
- (8) appeal (10 percent).

Although FHA directives insisted that no project should be insured that involved a high degree of risk with regard to any of the eight categories, "economic stability" and "protection from adverse influences" together counted for more than the other six combined. Both were interpreted in ways that were prejudicial against heterogeneous environments. The 1939 *Underwriting Manual* taught that "crowded neighborhoods lessen desirability" and "older properties in a neighborhood have a tendency to accelerate the transition to lower class occupancy." Smoke and odor were considered "adverse influences," and appraisers were told to look carefully for any "inferior and nonproductive characteristics of the areas surrounding the site."

Obviously, prospective buyers could avoid many of these so-called undesirable features by locating in peripheral sections. In 1939, the Washington headquarters asked each of the 50-odd regional FHA offices to send in the plans for six "typical American houses." The photographs and dimensions were then used for a National Archives exhibit. An analysis of the submissions clearly indicates that the ideal home was a bungalow or a colonial on an ample lot with a driveway and a garage.

In an attempt to standardize such ideal homes, FHA set up minimum requirements for lot size, for setback from the street, for separation from adjacent structures, and even for the width of the house itself. While such requirements did provide air and light for new structures, they effectively eliminated whole sections of cities, such as the traditional 16-foot-wide row houses of Baltimore, Philadelphia, and New York from eligibility for loan guarantees. Even apartment

owners were encouraged to look to suburbia: "Under the best of conditions a rental development under the FHA program is a project set
in what amounts to a privately owned and privately controlled park
area."

Reflecting the broad segregationist attitudes of a majority of the
American people, the FHA was extraordinarily concerned with "inharmonious racial or nationality groups." Homeowners and financial
institutions alike feared that an entire area could lose its investment
value if rigid white-black separation was not maintained. Bluntly
warning, "If a neighborhood is to retain stability, it is necessary that
properties shall continue to be occupied by the same social and racial
classes," the *Underwriting Manual* openly recommended "enforced
zoning, subdivision regulations, and suitable restrictive covenants"
that would be "superior to any mortgage." Such covenants were a
common method of prohibiting black occupancy until the U.S.
Supreme Court ruled in 1948 (*Shelley v. Kraemer*) that they were
"unenforceable as law and contrary to public policy." Even then, it
was not until late 1949 that FHA announced that as of February 15,
1950, it would not insure mortgages on real estate subject to covenants. Although the press treated the FHA announcement as a major
advancement in the field of racial justice, former housing official
Nathan Straus noted that "the new policy in fact served only to warn
speculative builders who had not filed covenants of their rights to do
so, and it gave them a convenient respite in which to file."

In addition to recommending covenants. FHA compiled detailed
reports and maps charting the present and most likely future residential locations of black families. In a March 1939 map of Brooklyn,
for example, the presence of a single, nonwhite family on any block
was sufficient to mark that entire block as black. Similarly, very extensive maps of the District of Columbia depicted the spread of the
black population and the percentage of dwelling units occupied by
persons other than white. As late as November 19, 1948, Assistant
FHA Commissioner W. J. Lockwood could write that FHA "has
never insured a housing project of mixed occupancy" because of the
expectation that "such projects would probably in a short period of
time become all-Negro or all-white."

Occasionally, FHA racial decisions were particularly bizarre and
capricious. In the late 1930s, for example, as Detroit grew outward,

white families began to settle near a black enclave near Eight Mile Road. By 1940, the blacks were surrounded, but neither they nor the whites could get FHA insurance because of the presence of an adjacent "inharmonious" racial group. So in 1941, an enterprising white developer built a concrete wall between the white and black areas. The FHA then took another look and approved mortgages on the white properties.

One of the first persons to point a finger at FHA for discriminatory practices was Professor Charles Abrams. Writing in 1955, he said:

> A government offering such bounty to builders and lenders could have required compliance with a nondiscrimination policy. Or the agency could at least have pursued a course of evasion, or hidden behind the screen of local autonomy. Instead, FHA adopted a racial policy that could well have been culled from the Nuremberg laws. From its inception FHA set itself up as the protector of the all white neighborhood. It sent its agents into the field to keep Negroes and other minorities from buying houses in white neighborhoods.

The precise extent to which the agency discriminated against blacks and other minority groups is difficult to determine. Although the FHA has always collected reams of data regarding the price, floor area, lot size, number of bathrooms, type of roof, and structural characteristics of the single-family homes it has insured, it has been quite secretive about the spatial distribution of these loans. For the period between 1942 and 1968, the most detailed FHA statistics cannot be disaggregated below the county level.

Such data as are available indicate that neighborhood appraisals were very influential in determining for FHA "where it would be reasonably safe to insure mortgages." Indeed, the Preliminary Examiner was specifically instructed to refer to the Residential Security Maps in order "to segregate for rejection many of the applications involving locations not suitable for amortized mortgages." The result was a degree of suburban favoritism even greater than documentary analysis would have indicated. Of a sample of 241 new homes insured by FHA throughout metropolitan St. Louis between 1935 and 1939 a full 220 or 91 percent were located in the suburbs. Moreover, more than half of these home buyers (135 of 241) had lived in the city immediately prior to their new home purchase. Clearly, the FHA was helping to denude St. Louis of its middle-class residents. As might be expected, the new suburbanites were not being drawn from the slums or from rural areas, but from the "B" areas of the central city. A detailed analysis of two individual subdivisions in St. Louis County—Normandy and Affton—confirms the same point. Located just northwest of the city limits, Normandy was made up in 1937 of new five- and six-room houses costing between $4,000 and $7,500. In 1937 and 1938, exactly 127 of these houses were sold under FHA-guaranteed mortgages. Of the purchasers, 100 (78 percent) moved out from the city, mostly from the solid, well-established blocks between West Florrissant and Easton Streets.

On the opposite, or southwest, edge of St. Louis, Affton was also the scene of considerable residential construction in 1938 and 1939. Of 62 families purchasing FHA-insured homes in Affton during these years, 55 were from the city of St. Louis. Most of them simply came out the four-lane Gravois Road from the southern part of the city to their new plots in the suburbs.

For the period since 1942, detailed analyses of FHA spatial patterns are difficult. But a reconstruction of FHA unpublished statistics for the St. Louis area over the course of a third of a century reveals the broad patterns of city-suburban activity. As Table 3 indicates, in the first 27 years of FHA operation (through Decmber 31, 1960), when tens of thousands of tract homes were built west of the city limits, the county of St. Louis was the beneficiary of more than five times as much mortgage insurance as the city of St. Louis, whether measured in number of mortgages, amount of mortgage insurance, or per capita assistance.

One possible explanation for the city-county disparities in these figures is that the city had very little room for development, that the populace wanted to move to the suburbs, and that the periphery was where new housing could be most easily built. But in the 1930s, many more single-family homes were constructed in the city than in the county. Moreover, more than half of the FHA policies traditionally went to *existing* rather than *new* homes, and the city of course had a much larger inventory of existing housing than did the county in the period before 1960. Even in terms of home improvement loans, a category in which the aging city was obviously more

TABLE 3

Cumulative Total of FHA Home Mortgage Activities and Per Capita
Figures for Ten Selected United States Counties, 1934–1960

Jurisdiction	Cumulative Number of Home Mortgages, 1934–1960	Cumulative Amount of Home Mortgages, 1934–1960	Per Capita Amount of Home Mortgages, as of January 1961
St. Louis County, Mo.	62,772	$558,913,633	$794
Fairfax County, Va.	14,687	190,718,799	730
Nassau County, N.Y.	87,183	781,378,559	601
Montgomery County, Md.	14,702	159,246,550	467
Prince Georges County, Md.	15,043	144,481,817	404
St. Louis City	12,166	94,173,422	126
District of Columbia	8,038	66,144,612	87
Kings County (Brooklyn), N.Y.	15,438	140,330,137	53
Hudson County, N.J.	1,056	7,263,320	12
Bronx County, N.Y.	1,641	14,279,243	10

SOURCE: These calculations are based upon unpublished statistics available
in the Single Family Insured Branch of the Management Information Systems
Division of the Federal Housing Administration.
a. The per capita amount was derived by dividing the cumulative amount of
home mortgages by the 1960 population.

needy, only $43,844,500 went to the city, while about three times
that much, or $112,315,798, went to the county through 1960. In
the late 1960s and early 1970s, when the federal government attempted to redirect moneys to the central cities, the previous imbalance was not corrected. Figures available through 1976 show a
total of well over $1.1 billion for the county and only $314 million
for the city. Thus, the suburbs have continued their dominance.

Although St. Louis County apparently has done very well in terms
of per capita mortgage insurance in comparison with other areas of
the nation, the Mississippi River was not an isolated case of FHA
suburban favoritism. In Essex County, New Jersey, FHA commitments went in overwhelming proportion to Newark's suburbs. And

in neighboring Hudson County, residents received only $12 of mort-
gage insurance per capita through 1960, the second lowest county
total in the nation after the Bronx (Table 3).

The New Jersey data reveal that the most favored areas for FHA
mortgage insurance were not the wealthiest towns. Rather, the most
likely areas for FHA activity were those rated "B" on the Residential
Security Maps. In 1936, 65 percent of new housing units in suburban
Livingston were accepted for insurance; for Caldwell and Irvington,
also solidly middle-class, the percentages were 59 and 42, respectively.
In elite districts like South Orange, Glen Ridge, Milburn, and Maple-
wood, however, the FHA assistance rates were about as low as they
were for Newark, or less than 25 percent. Presumably this occurred
because the housing available in the so-called "Best" sections was
beyond the allowable price limits for FHA mortgage insurance, and
also because persons who could afford to live in such posh neighborhoods did not require government financing.

Even in the nation's capital, the outlying areas were considered
more appropriate for federal assistance than older neighborhoods. FHA
commitments at the beginning of 1937 in the District of Columbia
were heavily concentrated in two peripheral areas: (1) between the
U.S. Soldiers Home and Walter Reed Hospital in white and prosperous Northwest Washington and (2) between Rock Creek Park
and Connecticut Avenue, also in Northwest Washington. Very few
mortgage guarantees were issued in the predominantly black central
and southeastern sections of the district. More important, at least
two-thirds of the FHA commitments in the metropolitan area were
located in the suburbs—especially in Arlington and Alexandria in
Virginia and in Silver Spring, Takoma Park, Bethesda, Chevy Chase,
University Park, Westmoreland Hills, and West Haven in Maryland.
Perhaps this was but a reflection of the 1939 FHA prediction that:

> It should be noted in this connection that the "filtering-up"
> process, and the tendency of Negroes to congregate in the Dis-
> trict, taken together, logically point to a situation where eventu-
> ally the District will be populated by Negroes and the suburban
> areas in Maryland and Virginia by white families.

Following a segregationist policy for at least the next 20 years, the
FHA did its part to see that the prophecy came true; through the

end of 1960, as Table 3 indicates, the suburban counties had received more than seven times as much mortgage insurance as the District of Columbia.

For its part, the FHA usually responded that it was not created to help cities, but to revive homebuilding and to stimulate homeownership. And it concentrated on convincing both Congress and the public that it was, as its first Administrator, James Moffett, remarked, "a conservative business operation." The agency emphasized its concern over sound loans, no higher than the value of the assets and the repayment ability of the borrower would support, and its ability to make a small profit for the federal government.

But FHA also helped to turn the building industry against the minority and inner-city housing market, and its policies supported the income and racial segregation of most suburbs. Whole areas of cities were declared ineligible for loan guarantees; as late as 1966, for example, FHA did not have a mortgage on a single home in Camden, New Jersey, a declining industrial city.

Despite the fact that the government's leading housing agency was openly exhorting segregation, throughout the first 30 years of its operation, very few voices were raised against FHA's redlining practices. Between 1943 and 1945, Harland Bartholomew and Associates prepared a series of reports as a master plan for Dallas. The firm criticized FHA for building "nearly all housing" in the suburbs and argued that "this policy has hastened the process of urban decentralization immeasurably." And Columbia Professor Charles Abrams wrote in 1955 against FHA policies that had "succeeded in modifying legal practice so that the common form of deed included the racial covenant."

Not until the civil rights movement of the 1960s did community groups and scholars become convinced that redlining and disinvestment were a major cause of neighborhood decline and that home improvement loans were the "lifeblood of housing." In 1967, Martin Nolan summed up the indictment against FHA by asserting, "The imbalance against poor people and in favor of middle-income homeowners is so staggering that it makes all inquiries into the pathology of slums seem redundant." In the following year, Senator Paul Douglas of Illinois reported for the National Commission on Urban Problems on the role of the federal government in home finance:

The poor and those on the fringes of poverty have been almost completely excluded. These and the lower middle class, together constituting the 40 per cent of the population whose housing needs are greatest, received only 11 per cent of the FHA mortgages. . . . Even middle-class residential districts in the central cities were suspect, since there was always the prospect that they, too, might turn as Negroes and poor whites continued to pour into the cities, and as middle and upper-middle-income whites continued to move out.

Moreover, as Jane Jacobs has said, "Credit blacklisting maps are accurate prophecies because they are self-fulfilling prophecies."

The main beneficiary of the $119 billion in FHA mortgage insurance issued in the first four decades of FHA operation was suburbia, where approximately half of all housing could claim FHA or VA financing in the 1950s and 1960s. In the process, the American suburb was transformed from a rich person's preserve into the normal expectation of the middle class.

CONCLUSION

The HOLC was created in the midst of the Great Depression to refinance mortgages in danger of default or foreclosure. In the course of accomplishing its mission, the HOLC developed real estate appraisal systems that discriminated against racial and ethnic minorities and against older, industrial cities. But HOLC apparently extended aid without regard for its own ratings and evaluations and met the needs of a variety of families and neighborhoods.

The FHA cooperated with HOLC and followed HOLC appraisal practices. But unlike the HOLC, the FHA acted on the information in its files and clearly favored suburban areas over industrial cities. It is conceivable that the heavy disparity demonstrated in this article was the result not of prejudicial intent, but of other factors, such as family size, attitudes toward child rearing, or stages in the life cycle. In my judgment, however, the evidence is clear; both FHA guidelines and actual FHA assistance favored new construction over existing dwellings, open land over developed areas, businessmen over blue-collar workers, whites over blacks, and native-born Americans over immigrants.

II

A Klansman Joins the Court:
The Appointment of Hugo L. Black

WILLIAM E. LEUCHTENBURG

• *Fear of blacks and foreigners was largely responsible for the enormous popularity of the Ku Klux Klan in the early 1920s. The secret order got its start in 1915 when "Colonel" (the title was honorary in the "Woodmen of the World") William Joseph Simmons, a tall, clean-shaven, two-hundred-pound fraternal organizer, persuaded fifteen fellow Atlantans to motor out to nearby Stone Mountain to burn a cross, raise an American flag, and read a few biblical verses. The small group swore allegiance to the Invisible Empire, Knights of the Ku Klux Klan.*

For almost five years, the Invisible Empire remained confined to the Peachtree State and neighboring Alabama, and could best be described as just another indolent Southern fraternal group. In the spring of 1920, however, two enterprising promoters took a long, interested look at the Klan, recognizing its financial, as well as patriotic, possibilities. Edward Young Clarke, an unimposing dark-haired man in his early thirties, and Mrs. Elizabeth Tyler, a crafty, voluptuous divorcee, noticed the secret order's floundering condition and reasoned correctly that it could greatly broaden its appeal by exploiting the fears and prejudices of uncritical minds against the Catholic, the Jew, the Negro, the Oriental, and the recent immigrant. They formed the Southern Publicity Association and entered into negotiations with Simmons, who despite his title as Imperial Wizard, was richly endowed with neither character nor ability. According to the contract, Clarke would be appointed Imperial Kleagle and receive two dollars and fifty cents for each new recruit. It was a tidy arrangement

From the *University of Chicago Law Review.* © 1973 by the University of Chicago. Reprinted by permission of the author and the journal.

and would occasionally yield him thirty thousand dollars per week.

Once free to put their booster techniques into practice, Clarke and Tyler quickly transformed the little society into the militant, uncompromising instrument that soon scourged the nation. By 1925 about two million persons had paid the ten-dollar initiation fee to become a citizen of the Invisible Empire, which by that time was being described by Stanley Frost as "the most vigorous, active and effective organization in American life outside business." Strongest in Indiana, Ohio, Texas, and in such big cities as Chicago, Portland, Denver, Indianapolis, and Dallas, the Klan was particularly successful in the political arena and for a time claimed a half dozen governorships, including those of Oregon, Indiana, and Colorado. It had only a minor impact upon presidential politics, but its divisiveness as a national issue was well illustrated by the appointment of Hugo L. Black to the United States Supreme Court. Soon after President Franklin D. Roosevelt announced the nomination, Black's involvement with the Birmingham chapter of the Invisible Empire became known. In the article below, one of the nation's most eminent historians, William E. Leuchtenburg of University of North Carolina, Chapel Hill, discusses the ironies involved in the selection of a Klansman who was to become one of the country's leading exponents of civil liberties.

I. THE NOMINATION

On August 12, 1937, Franklin Delano Roosevelt, rebounding from the worst setback of his long Presidency, took the first of a series of steps toward creating what historians would one day call "the Roosevelt Court." Galling defeat had come less than a month before when the Senate had killed his scheme to add a Justice to the Supreme Court for every member aged seventy or over who did not resign or retire. The original plan would have allowed the President to name as many as six new Justices, but after a bitter 168-day fight, the measure was buried, amid loud rejoicing from FDR's opponents. Roosevelt was not finished yet, however, for one legacy of the protracted struggle was the creation of a vacancy on the Supreme Court, and it was the President's prerogative to nominate a successor. The choice he finally made would trigger an acrimonious controversy and would have a momentous impact on the disposition of the Court.

The vacancy resulted, at least indirectly, from Roosevelt's "Court-packing" plan. The President had advanced his bold proposal in February because he was frustrated by the performance of the Supreme Court, particularly the conservative "Four Horsemen"—Willis Van Devanter, Pierce Butler, James McReynolds, and George Sutherland. In May, during the congressional battle, Van Devanter announced his retirement in what some thought was a well-timed move to dispose of the plan. Roosevelt was urged to drop the Court bill, since replacing Van Devanter with a liberal would give the Administration a decisive margin in most cases. As soon as Van Devanter's communication was made known on the Senate floor, however, the senators crowded around their colleague, Joseph T. Robinson, to congratulate him on his impending nomination for Van Devanter's seat. They all but usurped the power of appointment from Roosevelt, who knew that he could not avoid honoring the Majority Leader without inciting an uprising. Unfortunately for the New Dealers, Robinson was a 65-year-old conservative who had close connections to private utility interests. So the fight went on into June and July with tempers growing short in the brutal Washington heat. In July, at a critical point in the Great Debate, Robinson died. His death doomed the President's Court-packing scheme, but it left Roosevelt with an opportunity that his opponents had hoped to deny him—naming the first Justice of his own choosing to the Supreme Court.

The battle over the Court plan, Joseph Alsop and Turner Catledge have written, "conferred a strange, almost a lurid importance on the President's choice for the Supeme Court vacancy." As he had done in February while preparing his Court-packing message, Roosevelt moved in a covert manner that put Washington on edge. Each day it was expected that he would send a name to the Senate, but July ran its course without a decision and Congress, which had hoped to go home in June, found itself in the sultry capital in August with adjournment near and still no word from the White House.

In early August, a *New York Times* correspondent noted that "an

unusually fierce attack of nervous irritability has seized the 529 legislators." "You have to see the shaking hands and the quivering facial
muscles, hear the rage-quavers of the voices" of Congressmen as they
spoke to appreciate "the violence of the nerve tension." They "snap at
each other over trifles in floor debates" and were biting the heads off
secretaries, prompting the correspondent to report "a new high in
headless . . . secretaries." One secretary remarked, "Yesterday morning I had to phone six Senators, all of them my friends, and remind
them of a subcommittee meeting. Five of them bawled me out for it,
and the sixth hung up on me." Another secretary said: "The boss
came back from a subcommittee row over a technicality the other day
so ill that I had to nurse him and dose him for an hour and then call
a doctor. It's the first time I've ever known him to be sick without a
hangover for eleven years."

Roosevelt had added to this anxiety when, at a press conference on
July 27, he said that he was exploring the possibility of making the
appointment after the Senate had adjourned. Mutinous legislators
were incensed at the prospect of not having a chance to act on Roosevelt's selection until after the nominee had donned the black robes of
a Justice and taken part in the Court's decisions. The President's declaration also indicated that he might be contemplating a particularly
offensive nomination, making it desirable for him to bypass the Senate.
Attorney General Homer Cummings assured Roosevelt that he could
fill a vacancy at any time, even when the Senate was not in session, although, of course, any designee would ultimately have to be confirmed. The historical record on this point, however, did not give the
President as much comfort as he wanted, and the Senate was kicking
up a storm. By early August he had resolved to settle on a nominee
before the Senate adjourned.

Although Roosevelt may have been needling the senators with his
talk of a recess appointment, he did have a valid reason for his inquiry.
On August 4 Stephen Early, the White House press secretary, reviewed the situation for a Scripps-Howard columnist, Raymond Clapper. Early explained that the President did not know how long Congress would remain in session, and he needed two to four more weeks
to make up his mind. It had not been clear until the Senate killed the
Court bill in late July that he would have only one seat to fill. It
might be supposed, Early said, that Roosevelt could easily come up

with one name since he had originally sought to choose six, but in fact it was harder to pick one, because he could not submit a balanced group and had to "make it a bull's eye." Clapper summarized the President's position in his diary: "been sixty to 75 names recommended since Robinson died. All have to be carefully investigated. Is serious matter and Rvt [Roosevelt] would be in bad spot if he sent up a name and then the opposition dug out some dumb chapter in his record. . . . Opposition which has been complaining that Rvt is slapdash would leap on him and say this is the kind of dumb[b]ell or bad actor he would have given us six of."

As the tension mounted, congressmen and reporters made book on whom the President would pick, but they had little to go on. Although it was expected that Roosevelt would try to heal the breaches within his party and the Senate by making an especially judicious choice, he gave no sign of where his favor might light. Even veteran Administration senators like James F. Byrnes remained in the dark. "I haven't the slightest idea who will be appointed to the Supreme Court, nor has anybody in Washington other than the President," Byrnes wrote a South Carolina friend on August 10. "The President certainly has not consulted anybody in the Senate about it. The only information we have is that contained in the Press; namely, that Sam Bratton of New Mexico, now a Judge of the Circuit Court of Appeals and formerly a member of the Senate, is receiving serious consideration. It may be that it is because the Senators have such a high opinion of Bratton that they think he has a good chance."

When Roosevelt finally made his decision, he moved in the same furtive manner he had used in preparing the Court plan. On the night of August 11 the President startled the man he had finally chosen by summoning him to the White House after dinner and, upon informing him of the honor in store for him, pledged him to silence. Not even the White House staff knew what had transpired. The next morning Stephen Early indicated that Roosevelt was still considering a list of sixty or seventy names and that a selection might not be made during the current congressional session. Two hours later the President sent a courier to Capitol Hill with a notice of appointment that Roosevelt had written in his own hand. The President kept the secret almost to the very end, but it had become too much for him. Like "a small boy waiting for his surprise to be revealed," as Virginia

Hamilton has written, he had to blurt out the news to someone. Before the messenger reached the door of the Senate chamber, Roosevelt told Early the name of the nominee. "Jesus Christ!" Early exploded. FDR grinned.

II. THE SENATE CONSENTS

The words "I nominate Hugo L. Black . . . ." sent the Senate into a state of shock. Senator Black, who had not let on at any point that he knew what the message contained, now slumped in his seat, white-faced and wordless, and nervously shredded a sheaf of papers. A few liberal colleagues came over to congratulate the Alabama senator, but other legislators did not try to hide their unhappiness. The House of Representatives responded more volubly. One reporter noted, "From the House press gallery it was quite a show to watch the reactions of the Congressmen as the news swept across the floor. A great buzzing as the name of Black was passed from lip to lip."

If Roosevelt anticipated immediate acquiescence from the Senate, he was reckoning without the diehards. Henry Fountain Ashurst, the eloquent chairman of the Judiciary Committee, rose on behalf of the administration and asked the senators to confirm instantly the appointment of this "lawyer of transcendent ability, great, industrious and courteous in debate, young, vigorous, of splendid character and attainments." Ashurst contended that there was "an immemorial rule of the Senate that whenever the Executive honors this body by nominating a member thereof, that nomination by immemorial usage is confirmed without reference to a committee for the obvious reason that no amount of investigation or consideration by a committee could disclose any new light on the character or attainments and ability of the nominee, because if we do not know him after long service with the nominee no one will ever know him." When Hiram Johnson of California and Edward Burke of Nebraska objected, however, Ashurst was compelled to name a subcommittee to consider the nomination. Not since 1888, when President Grover Cleveland nominated Lucius Quintus Cincinnatus Lamar to the Supreme Court, had a proposed appointment of a senator or former senator been sent to committee.

Roosevelt could hardly have made a choice that would have discomforted his opponents more. Black was an ardent New Dealer and had been a strong supporter of Court-packing; indeed, it was said that he was one of the few senators who actually believed in the plan. Most people had expected that Roosevelt would take pains to name someone like a federal judge, but Black's only judicial experience consisted of eighteen months as a police court judge in Birmingham. Little about him suggested the judicial temperament, and he had especially incensed conservatives by his performance as an exceptionally vigorous prosecutor on Senate committees. As one biographer described it, "The paths of his investigations had been lurid with charges and countercharges, *subpoenas duces tecum*, searches and seizures, and contempt proceedings," and the political scientist Earl Latham has noted that "Senator Black in 1936 was the kind of legislator Justice Black had no use for twenty years later."

A year before the nomination Newton D. Baker, a onetime progressive leader who had become a prominent corporation attorney, had written a friend: "I heard last week that the incredible Senator Black with his eavesdropping, peeping-Tom committee had secured from the Western Union Telegraph Company all the telegrams sent out of my office in a year. As I run a law office and not a criminal conspiracy, I am entirely indifferent as to what he discovered from the telegrams, but the oftener I permit myself to reflect on this outrage, the more violent I become. Man of peace as I am, I am quite sure I could not keep my hand off the rope if I accidentally happened to stumble upon a party bent on hanging him."

Conservatives outdid themselves in expressions of indignation. "If the President had searched the country for the worst man to appoint, he couldn't possibly have found anyone to fill the bill so well," grumbled one senator. "Mr. Roosevelt could not have made a worse appointment if he had named John L. Lewis," wrote the columnist David Lawrence, and Herbert Hoover protested that the court was now "one-ninth packed." The most devastating critique appeared on the editorial page of the *Washington Post:*

> Men deficient in the necessary professional qualifications have occasionally been named for the Supreme Court. And qualified men have sometimes been put forward primarily because they were also politically agreeable to a President. But until yesterday students of American history would have found it difficult to refer to any Supreme Court nomination which combined lack of train-

ing on the one hand and extreme partisanship. In this one
respect the choice of Senator Black must be called outstanding.

.   .   .   .

If Senator Black has given any study or thought to any aspect
of constitutional law in a way which would entitle him to this
preferment, his labors in that direction have been skillfully concealed. If he has ever shown himself exceptionally qualified in
either the knowledge or the temperament essential for exercise
of the highest judicial function, the occasion escapes recollection.

Although Black came from Alabama, no group was unhappier about
his nomination than the Southern congressmen. A sharp-tongued, unrelenting partisan who kept too much to himself, Black had never
been a member of "the club." More important, he was a Southern
liberal, and his selection signaled Roosevelt's determination to back
those who were attempting to transform the conservative structure of
Southern politics, an inclination that was later manifested in the 1938
purge. A Georgia congressman called the nomination of Black "the
worst insult that has yet been given to the nation"; a Texas congressman said, "I wouldn't appeal a case with him there." Black had particularly antagonized Southern conservatives by sponsoring the wages
and hours bill, which they claimed was denying their constituencies a
competitive advantage granted by God. When reporters asked the
veteran Virginia Senator Carter Glass for a comment on Black, he replied, "Don't start me off again."

Yet Roosevelt knew very well that there was not a thing they could,
or would, do about it. Black was a senator, and the sense of collegiality
was so strong that it was inconceivable that the Senate would fail to
confirm one of its members. As the President told Democratic Chairman James A. Farley, "They'll have to take him."

The Senate proved unwilling to entertain the real objections many
felt to Black's nomination. It would not consider the assertion that
Black was too liberal, because ideological differences were not regarded as proper grounds for refusing to confirm a fellow senator; nor
was Black's lack of judicial background explored, since it could not
be conceded that any member of the Senate might be unqualified to
sit on the Supreme Court. The little consideration given the appointment therefore focused on technical matters. Senator William E. Borah
of Idaho claimed that since Van Devanter had taken advantage of

legislation passed earlier in the session allowing retirement rather than resignation, he was still a member of the Court, and there was no vacancy for Black to fill. Ashurst retorted that if all nine Justices retired or went mad, according to Borah's reasoning, there would be no Court; even Van Devanter thought the argument was nonsense, since he had no intention of ever returning to the bench. Others speculated that Black was ineligible for another reason: since the retirement legislation also guaranteed the pensions of retiring Justices, Congress had increased their emoluments, and the Constitution forbade any member of Congress to accept a post under such circumstances. Few people thought much of that argument either.

Two days after the nomination, a more explosive consideration arose—it was said that Black, at the outset of his career, had been associated with the Ku Klux Klan. The National Association for the Advancement of Colored People and the Socialist Party each urged the Senate to explore Black's racial attitudes. The Socialist leader Norman Thomas also asked the Judiciary Committee to investigate Black's opposition during the Hoover administration to proposals to equalize relief between Whites and Negroes, his hostility to antilynching legislation, and his silence about the "Scottsboro boys," a group of Negroes convicted in Alabama in what appeared to be an outrageous miscarriage of justice. "We fully appreciate Senator Black's championship of labor legislation," Thomas said, but "no other excellence can fit a man for the Supreme Court whose record is marred by race prejudice."

Despite these reservations the nomination moved quickly through committee, but not without occasioning some animosity. Matthew Neely of West Virginia, an Administration stalwart, allotted the matter only two hours in a meeting of his subcommittee on Friday, August 13, the day after the nomination; the subcommittee then reported the recommendation by a vote of 5–1, with only Warren Austin of Vermont dissenting on constitutional grounds. On the following Monday, as the Judiciary Committee convened behind closed doors, William Dieterich of Illinois accused certain committee members of trying to "besmirch" their colleague by linking him to the Ku Klux Klan. Dieterich's tirade nearly resulted in a fist fight with a fellow Democrat when Senator Burke charged at him. Although "tempers flared to white heat," the committee approved the nomination 13–4.

When the full Senate took up the Black appointment on August

17, Senator Royal S. Copeland of New York opened the debate by asserting that his Alabama colleague's first election to the Senate in 1926 had been supported by the Klan. Before crowded public galleries, Copeland read a *New York Times* report on Black's exploitation of anti-Catholic sentiment in attacking the Presidential ambitions of Alfred E. Smith. Copeland asserted, "We are free because we are guarded by the Supreme Court. Catholics, Protestants, Negroes, Jews, Gentiles, all of us, are guarded by the Supreme Court. But what will happen if a half dozen men of the mental bias of the nominee should be seated on the bench? . . . Does the leopard change his spots? Will Mr. Justice Black be any different from Candidate Black? . . . Naturally we wonder what Mr. Justice Black would do were another Scottsboro case appealed to the Supreme Court."

Copeland made no headway with his charges, because they were regarded as blatantly political and because the Senate received reassurances. Many believed that Copeland, an anti-New Deal Democrat who was running for Mayor of New York City, was exploiting the Klan issue to curry ethnic voters. Although Black left the question unresolved when cornered by some of his supporters during the debate, the unpredictable Borah came to his aid. The Idaho maverick, who eventually voted against confirmation on the technical ground of ineligibility, conceded that senators had received thousands of telegrams about Black and the Klan, but insisted, "There has never been at any time one iota of evidence that Senator Black was a member of the Klan. . . . We know that Senator Black has said in private conversation, not since this matter came up but at other times, that he was not a member of the Klan." When Copeland asked Borah how he would vote if he knew that Black was or had been a Klansman, the Idaho senator replied, "If I knew that a man was a member of a secret association organized to spread racial antipathies and religious intolerance through the country, I should certainly vote against him for any position."

Late in the afternoon of August 17, just five days after the Black nomination was made and after only six hours of debate, the Senate confirmed the appointment by the lopsided margin of sixty-three to sixteen. Of the Republicans present all but three voted "nay," as did six Democrats, including Burke and Copeland. However, some of the most reactionary Southern Democrats, who had bitterly fought the Court plan, ended up supporting the administration. Ickes recorded,

"Even 'Cotton Ed' Smith, of South Carolina, who 'God-damned' the nomination all over the place when it was first announced, didn't have the courage to stand up and vote against a fellow Senator from the Deep South." The Klan issue had fizzled, but it left some uneasiness. In Washington, a one-liner went from mouth to mouth: "Hugo won't have to buy a robe; he can dye his white one black." Despite the rumbling about the KKK, Roosevelt and the New Dealers had apparently won a stunning victory, less than a month after the opposition thought FDR was on the ropes. Ickes concluded: "So Hugo Black becomes a member of the Supreme Court of the United States, while the economic royalists fume and squirm, and the President rolls his tongue around in his cheek."

The outcome left conservatives disconsolate. When Carter Glass heard the nomination called a triumph for the common man, he snapped, "They must be Goddam common!" Senator Peter Gerry of Rhode Island explained to Canada's prime minister, "His legal experience was not considered sufficient and he hasn't a judicial attitude of mind. He is a prosecutor and not a judge." An Oregon editor went even further: "His appointment of Black was the grossest insult to the Supreme Court and the American people that we have ever been called upon to accept." Roosevelt's former adviser Raymond Moley commented, "There have been worse appointments to high judicial offices; but . . . I can't remember where or when."

After Congress adjourned, Hiram Johnson wrote a confidant in California: "This was a most unsatisfactory session. We wound up by confirming Black, who is unfit to be a Supreme Court Justice. . . . Had it not been for me, Black's nomination would have gone through with a 'Hurrah!' . . . Borah and other distinguished patriots wished it so, but I had 'guts' enough to stop it. I accomplished nothing —save that sixteen men in the Senate showed their feeling of his unfitness. I understand he was a member of the Ku Klux Klan when first elected to the Senate. He never dared say anything about it subsequently, and Borah and his other friends, saw to it that he was not called as a witness."

Once Black was confirmed, the hubbub died down. Congressmen left the capital, and Black sailed with his wife to Europe for a vacation. His name soon disappeared from the newspapers, and the controversy appeared to be at an end.

III. THE REVELATION

On September 13 the Pittsburgh *Post-Gazette* detonated a bombshell. It published the first of six articles by Ray Sprigle, an enterprising reporter who had dug up original materials, including the transcript of a Klan meeting, conclusively connecting Hugo Black to the Ku Klux Klan. The series grabbed front page headlines in newspapers throughout the country.

Sprigle began, "Hugo Lafayette Black, Associate Justice of the United States Supreme Court, is a member of the hooded brotherhood that for ten long blood-drenched years ruled the Southland with lash and noose and torch, the Invisible Empire, Knights of the Ku Klux Klan." Since it was generally suspected that Black had once had a KKK relationship, that allegation hardly constituted news. Sprigle developed three points in his series, however, that were very damaging. First, he demonstrated that Black had not merely run with Klan backing, but had actually been a member of the organization. He gave an account of the night of September 11, 1923, when Black pledged that he would never divulge, even under threat of death, the secrets of the Klan; surrounded by white-robed members of the Robert E. Lee Klan No. 1 in Birmingham, Black had vowed, "I swear that I will most zealously and valiantly shield and preserve by any and all justifiable means and methods . . . white supremacy."

Second, Sprigle recounted vivid examples of the views held by the Klansmen with whom Black had associated. In a meeting on September 2, 1926, the Imperial Wizard Hiram Wesley Evans said, "We find that America up to now has done all that has been worthwhile under the leadership of native-born, white, gentile, Protestant men. . . . There isn't a Negro in Alabama that dares open his mouth and says he believes in social equality of the black man. . . . I mean to tell you any time they propose to produce equality between me and a certain said Negro they are simply going to have to hold a funeral for the Negro." The Imperial Wizard added that Northern Negroes "will be murdered by the Yankees that have gotten all the sass from the Negroes that they want." On that same occasion the KKK's Imperial Legal Adviser in Washington observed, "To come down here now and find that you have given us a man named Black who wears 'white'—do you get that boys—to occupy a seat in the Senate of the United States is like getting an inspiration before baptism." Turning to Bibb Graves, who had just won the Democratic nomination for Governor, tantamount to election, he added, "I am so glad that you have a man, all but elected Governor, who comes from a town that, prior to his advent as Exalted Cyclops of the local Klan, I am told was owned by the Jews, controlled by the Catholics and loved by Negroes [Laughter and applause]. Now he tells me that the Jews have a foreclosure sale at bankruptcy, selling out, the Catholics are on the run, and the Negroes are in hiding [Applause]."

Most of Black's own remarks that afternoon were unexceptionable. In fact he spoke of the "principles of liberty which were written in the Constitution of this country" and the ideal of loving one's enemies. But he also assured the assembled Klansmen, "I realize that I was elected by men who believe in the principles that I have sought to advocate and which are the principles of this organization," and said to them and to the Grand Dragon, "I thank you from the bottom of a heart that is yours."

Finally, Sprigle made a third and critical contribution—he established that, on the same afternoon in 1926, Black, who had resigned from the Klan in the summer of 1925 for reasons of political expediency, had been awarded a special life membership, a gold "grand passport." Black had thanked the Klan for this honor, which only a half dozen men in the United States had received. Most important, the card was presumably still valid because there was no evidence in the Klan archives that it had been returned. In short, Sprigle was saying not merely that Black had been elected with Klan backing, not merely that Black had thanked the Klan leaders for their aid, but that Black was *still* a member of the Ku Klux Klan.

Sprigle's articles prompted denunciations of Black and Roosevelt that far exceeded, in both volume and vehemence, the protests that had greeted the nomination. Cartoonists had a field day depicting the members of the Supreme Court assembled in their silk, eight in black and the ninth in the white robe and hood of the KKK. In the pages of the *American Mercury* the mordant critic Albert Jay Nock called Black "a vulgar dog" and wrote that Roosevelt's appointment "was the act of a man who conceives himself challenged to do his very filthiest."

Several senators who had voted to confirm Black hastened to declare that if they had known of his Klan connection they would have opposed his elevation to the Court. Some thought they had been duped, since Black had temporized when the KKK rumors surfaced in August, and others had given assurances that there was no foundation to the allegations. Democratic senators from New Jersey and South Dakota charged that John Bankhead of Alabama had deliberately misled them by stating that Black had not been a member of the Klan. "I feel that not only I but the rest of the Senators were deceived and imposed upon," complained Clyde Herring, and his Iowa colleague, Guy Gillette, added, "I hope something is done to keep Black from the high court bench."

The issue hit directly at the core of Roosevelt's urban coalition since the main targets of the KKK had been Catholics and Negroes. The revelations also embarrassed Northern Democratic senators with large ethnic constituencies who had voted for Black. Groups like the Ancient Order of Hibernians demanded that Black resign or be removed; the Catholic Club of the City of New York deemed the appointment "a direct affront to the more than 20,000,000 Catholic citizens of the United States as well as to countless numbers of other citizens." In New Hampshire the Knights of Columbus adopted resolutions castigating Senator Fred Brown for supporting confirmation, and a member of the staff of Senator Theodore Green of Rhode Island noted, "At a very large meeting of the Hibernian County Convention last night a great many Democrats were denouncing Roosevelt. Very severe criticism among the Democrats."

Irish Catholic politicians played a numerically disproportionate role in the campaign to get rid of Black. Representative John J. O'Connor, chairman of the House Rules Committee, reported he had been canvassing congressmen about instituting impeachment proceedings and had found no one opposed to such a move. "If Mr. Justice Black was a member of the Klan when nominated and confirmed, his silence constituted a moral fraud upon the American people," said Representative Edward L. O'Neill, a New Jersey Democrat. Lieutenant Governor Francis E. Kelly of Massachusetts drafted a resolution asking the President to insist upon Black's resignation, and Senator David I. Walsh, who favored the same course, declared, "There are two counts against him, one that Black, for political advantage joined the Klan and took the oath of a Klansman and subscribed to its creeds; two, that Black obtained his nomination and confirmation by concealment and thereby deceived the President and his fellow-Senators, especially the latter."

Sprigle's articles appeared just as the campaign for the mayoralty in New York City was reaching a climax, and Senator Copeland took full advantage of the opportunity. He told a Carnegie Hall audience: "I never expected to see the day when a member of that organization, sworn to bigotry and intolerance, should become a member of the court. Shame upon him that he did not have the courage and decency to tell his colleagues in the Senate that the suspicion of his affiliation was a reality." Copeland accused his rival, Jeremiah T. Mahoney, of approving Roosevelt's action in the "placing upon the court of a Klansman who wears a black robe of court by day and a white robe of the Klan by night." "Imagine a man named Mahoney being mixed up with the Klan," his opponent spluttered. "Show me a Ku Klux Klanner and I promise he won't be alive a minute after I see him!"

Negro spokesmen joined in the hue and cry. The National Association for the Advancement of Colored People urged the President to call upon Black "to resign his post in the absence of repudiation and disproof of charges" that he held life membership in the KKK. Robert L. Vann, who was the Negro editor of the *Pittsburgh Courier*, a special assistant United States attorney general, and also credited with playing the largest role in swinging Pennsylvania Negroes to the Democratic Party, wired Roosevelt to remove Black. "Your friends are on the spot," Vann said. "You must save your friends or you must release them."

Despite this widespread feeling, even Roosevelt's conservative critics in the Senate conceded that nothing could be done if Black decided to stick it out. The President could not oust a Justice, and since he had been lambasted month after month for trying to tamper with the Court, Roosevelt and his supporters surmised that any attempt to coerce Black into resigning would not be well received. People would be led to conclude "that, if the President should request Justice Black's resignation, he might also attempt to drive Justice McReynolds, Sutherland and Butler from the bench." Nor did there appear to be grounds for impeachment. The civil liberties attorney Osmond K. Fraenkel observed, "I don't believe a judge can be impeached for something that happened before his appointment, but even if that were so, I do not see how he could be impeached for membership in an organization. Membership in the Klan, however politically inadvisable, is not a crime."

The electrifying disclosures exasperated the President. Washington, which so recently had been the self-confident capital of the New Deal, was now jeered at as "Ku-Kluxville-on-the-Potomac." The situation was especially embarrassing to the New Dealers because Roosevelt had taken a firm stand for religious liberty in 1928 while campaigning for Al Smith, a Catholic, and had been severely criticized for having too many Jews in his administration and for giving too many benefits to Negroes. Despite this record the President now bore the onus of having brought the main battle of his second term to a climax by naming a Klansman to the Supreme Court.

In an editorial in the *Emporia Gazette* William Allen White wrote:

> When Franklin Roosevelt is dead and buried and all his bones are rotted, the fact that he played around with Black and appointed to the highest honorable office in American life a man who was a member of the Ku Klux Klan, as Black was charged when Roosevelt named him, well, as we started to say, when Roosevelt is dead and gone he will be remembered in the history of this day and time by the fact that he was not above dishonoring the Supreme Court by putting a Klansman there.
> Why could not a man as smart as Franklin Roosevelt, as brave and as benevolent, also be wise in a day of crisis?

IV.   "I DID JOIN THE KLAN"

While Roosevelt's prospects were imperiled by the unexpected turn of events, Black's life had become all but unendurable. The clamor followed the new Justice to Europe, where he was still vacationing when the Sprigle series broke. Journalists hounded him, first in Paris, then in London. "A dreadfully worried United States judge hid himself away in a palatial hotel suite in London yesterday while all his fellow countrymen were asking for a straight answer to a straight ques-

tion," reported the British *Daily Herald*. One newspaperman jumped
out of a darkened corridor scaring Black's wife, and another seized his
arm as he emerged from a London theater. "I don't see you; I don't
know you; I don't answer you," Black told him. The columnist Dorothy Thompson wrote, "In London tonight a Justice of the United
States Supreme Court is barricaded behind locked doors. His telephone
rings but he does not answer it. Reporters try to interview him but in
vain. This man . . . sees only the waiters who bring him food, the
maids who tidy his rooms and the traffic of London moving in the
streets below. . . . He is front page news in England, where the
British are taking revenge for the Simpson case." After letting it be
known that he would sail back to America on a large transatlantic
liner, on which one of his fellow passengers would have been Mr.
Justice McReynolds, Black escaped from his hotel by a service entrance
and drove to Southampton where he boarded a small mail steamer,
The City of Norfolk. He left England, said the *Sun*, "Klandestinely."

No longer would Black be permitted to remain silent. Senator
Walsh said that he had to speak out to be fair to the Catholic senators,
and to those with Catholic and Jewish constituents, who had voted for
his confirmation and who might suffer the consequences in the next
election. Democratic Senator Bennett Champ Clark of Missouri commented, "I do not wish to be in the position of concluding as to the
authenticity of the charges contained in the newspapers against Justice
Black, but it does seem to me that he has had ample opportunity to
answer a simple statement of fact." As Black's vessel headed westward
across the Atlantic toward Norfolk, a Gallup Poll revealed that 59
percent of those interviewed believed that he should resign if he were
proven to have been a member of the Klan. At Felix Frankfurter's
suggestion, the young *Nation* editor Max Lerner flew to Norfolk, made
his way through throngs of newspapermen, and at breakfast with Black
aboard ship argued that he should issue an explanation. That night,
Lerner spent four more hours with Black in Alexandria. Under all of
this pressure, Black finally decided to accept an invitation to speak
over the radio on October 1, but he now had less than two days to
draft his speech.

The address, carried over three national networks with three hundred stations, attracted the largest American audience of the decade,

except for that tuned in to the abdication of Edward VIII. (The huge audience, however, did lack one prominent listener—Franklin Roosevelt contrived to be in the Pacific Northwest in an automobile without a radio as Black spoke.) The fact of Black's speech was a sensation because of the cardinal rule that Justices do not make statements on public matters, and the dramatic nature of the occasion was enhanced when fiery crosses lit the hillsides in different parts of the country.

In his talk, Black admitted having belonged to the Klan—he could hardly do anything else—but said that he had resigned before entering the Senate and never rejoined. He minimized the grand passport as an "unsolicited card" which he did not view as membership in the Klan, had never used, and had not kept. He also voiced his disdain, without naming the KKK, for "any organization or group which, anywhere or at any time, arrogates to itself the un-American power to interfere in the slightest degree with complete religious freedom."

Black's speech is remembered today as a courageous denunciation of the Klan that foreshadowed his future character as a Justice, but in truth it was not. Black neither explained his past Klan membership nor offered any apology for signing up with the KKK; nor did he account for why he had sat through the Senate discussion of his alleged Klan connections without a word to anyone either in the Senate or, apparently, in the administration. He repudiated none of the atrocities perpetrated by the Klan in Alabama while he was in the secret order. In all, he used only eleven of the thirty minutes allotted to him. The most unfortunate aspect of his talk, however, was not what he failed to say but what he did say. He spent the first third of his remarks cautioning against the possibility of a revival of racial and religious hatred, but he warned that this might be brought about not by groups like the Klan but by those who questioned his right to be on the Supreme Court. He went on to affirm that some of his best friends were Jews and Catholics, told the national audience about his longtime Jewish chum in Birmingham, and mentioned that he numbered among his friends "many members of the colored race."

Rarely in the twentieth century has any statement by an American public figure brought down such abuse on him in the press as Black's brief address called forth. The *New York Herald Tribune* branded him a humbug and a coward: "The effort of Senator Black to suggest that he is the real protagonist of tolerance and that his enemies are intolerant is perhaps the greatest item of effrontery in a uniquely brazen utterance. Only a man heedless of the truth and a man afraid of his official skin could fall so low." The *Boston Post* called on him to resign, for "one who associates with bigots, bids for their support, takes the bigots' oath and then is so craven that he allows his friends in a crisis to deny it all, can't clear himself by asserting it was all contrary to his real character." About Black's references to Catholic, Jewish, and Negro friends, the *New York Post* said, "We might reply in kind that one of our best liberal friends was a Klansman but we still don't think he ought to be on the Supreme Court." The *Newark Ledger* added that Black had "resigned from the Klan to maintain an appearance of decency. He should resign from the Supreme Court to attain the substance of decency." Catholic outrage ranged across the political spectrum from the liberal *Commonweal* to periodicals and spokesmen on the right. "Since there was no sign of his being ashamed for himself," wrote the editor of *The Catholic World*, "I was ashamed for him; ashamed too for the Supreme Court, ashamed for the President of the United States."

Roosevelt, however, had no doubt that Black's performance had carried the day. When Jim Farley telephoned him a few days later the President asked, "What d'you think of Hugo's speech of the other night?" "He did the best he could under the circumstances, but I think he should have hit the Klan," Farley answered. "It was a grand job," Roosevelt returned. "It did the trick; you just wait and see."

The President was absolutely right. The address was inevitably applauded, if not altogether convincingly, by Black's supporters in the New Deal. "If you listened to Mr. Justice Black's radio talk," said Senator Green of Rhode Island, "I am sure that you must have felt as I did that he admirably expressed the principles on which Roger Williams founded this State." Elements of Roosevelt's urban coalition also remained loyal. Labor leaders praised Black's speech, and Rabbi Herbert S. Goldstein of Yeshiva College spoke for others in saying, "As a citizen, I do not seek 'the pound of flesh' and as a Jew, I do not seek retaliation." Most important, Black's discourse won the majority of his listeners, albeit not a substantial majority. After the broadcast 56 percent of the people polled by Gallup responded that Black should stay on the bench, which was precisely what he had intended to do all along.

V.   MR. JUSTICE BLACK

On the morning of October 4, three days after Black's radio talk, the
Supreme Court opened its fall term, and huge crowds gathered to see
the former Klansman take his seat. Long lines extended for hundreds
of feet in the corridor, and much of the throng was unable to enter
the courtroom. When the Justices filed in, it was noted pointedly that
Black sat to the "extreme left" of the Chief Justice. For the first time
in public, Black wore the silk robes of a Justice, but the occasion was
not the hour of triumph the man from Clay County, Alabama, might
have hoped for. To the dismay of his supporters, two petitions were
filed to challenge his right to be a Justice. For all Black's efforts and
those of Roosevelt, the controversy continued to simmer.

The President quickly remedied the situation. The next day in
Chicago, he delivered his historic "quarantine" address, and by night-
fall the country had turned its attention from Black to foreign affairs
and the prospect of a second world war. A distinguished authority on
international law, John Bassett Moore, wrote, "The President never
was more adroit than in his Chicago speech. All the talk about Black,
balancing the budget, the C.I.O., the 'dictatorial drift,' etc. etc., . . .
suddenly ceased when the war cry was raised." Critics charged that
FDR had deliberately seized the headlines in order to distract attention from the Black furor. "The speech would never have been made
if there had been no Black case," Hiram Johnson protested. Actually,
the situation was more complex than such conspiracy notions suggested. From Washington, His Majesty's Chargé D'Affaires sent the
British Foreign Secretary Anthony Eden a more balanced report:

> I have every reason to believe that the speech had long been
> contemplated, but the President was prepared to await the psy-
> chological moment for its delivery. He had returned from his
> Western tour fully convinced that, however lukewarm the feel-
> ing regarding the Supreme Court might be in those parts, the
> electors as a whole had not lost confidence in his personal leader-
> ship. On the other hand the regrettable "Black and Klan" inci-
> dent was still front page news and required something more
> important to remove it to the back page. In fact unkind Wall
> Street wits are talking of "a red herring drawn across the Black
> trail." The President's arrival at Chicago coincided with the

decision at Geneva to refer the Far Eastern crisis to the signa-
tories of the Nine-Power Treaty. Here was a good opportunity
for Mr. Roosevelt to make his appeal to the nation to abandon
a policy of complete isolation.

Although the quarantine address was followed by reduced attention
to Black in the press, lawyers and Washington correspondents continued to scrutinize him closely. Even after the Court summarily dismissed the petitions to deny Black a seat, every eye seemed to be in-
specting the new Justice. "I went to the Court last week and had the
opportunity to see Mr. Justice Black on the bench," Newton D. Baker
wrote to the former Supreme Court Justice John H. Clarke. "He is
young enough to make a good judge but he has a wavering expression
of the eyes which he will have great trouble in straightening out if he
wants to be like the judges on that Court usually are—impervious to
all considerations except their view of the public good." The veteran
New York Times columnist Arthur Krock had a different perspective;
he observed:

> Mr. Justice Black's court-room demeanor provided material for
> interesting study. His face had gained color. His manner had
> acquired content. He looked benign instead of harried. But now
> and then, as the Chief Justice read the orders and Mr. Justice
> Black looked out upon the lawyers and spectators from his im-
> pregnable fortress of life tenure, an expression touched his face
> which is common to certain types of martyrs. It was a mixture of
> forgiveness and satisfaction, of pity for unreconstructed dissent-
> ers and sympathy for himself who had borne so much in com-
> parative silence. Charles Dickens, who gave many passages to the
> description of Mr. Christopher Catesby, would have recognized
> it at once.

Black might well have nourished such sentiments in his first year on
the bench, for he was permitted to forget neither his Klan past nor his
limited judicial background. In his first month, Black drew scathing
criticism when the conviction of one of the Scottsboro boys came up
on appeal and Black disqualified himself. The treatment accorded
him by liberal Justices Louis Brandeis and, more particularly, Harlan
Fiske Stone caused greater distress. In strolls through Washington with
the newspaperman Marquis Childs, Stone abandoned discretion and
vented his distress over Black's inexpertise. Childs later said that Stone

was "like an old New England wood-carver, and here they suddenly brought someone in the shop who doesn't know a knife from a hoe. This really upset him very greatly." In an article inspired by his chats with Stone, Childs created a hullabaloo by stating that Black's opinions frequently had to be rewritten by his colleagues in order to bring them up to the standards of the Court and that Black's incompetence had caused the other Justices "acute discomfort and embarrassment." Yet even in these early days Black won admirers for his courage and skill. Rather than meekly accommodating himself as might be expected of a newcomer tarred by scandal, he boldly advanced iconoclastic notions. "Mr. Justice Black, dissenting" became a familiar phrase; indeed, he was said to have set a record for lone dissents. Walton Hamilton expressed his esteem for Black's cleanly written opinions and the independence of a man who "regards the sacred cows as ordinary heifers." By 1939 Erwin D. Canham was observing that "Mr. Justice Black . . . has climbed out of the pit into which the circumstances of his appointment had hurled him, and is on the way to being regarded as another Brandeis."

The allusion to Brandeis suggested both a craftsmanship that demeaning references to the police court judgeship had not prepared critics for and a solicitude for civil liberties that many people had not expected of an ex-Klansman. In 1940 Black was spokesman for the Court in two notable decisions. In *Chambers v. Florida,* generally thought to be his ablest opinion, he spoke for a unanimous Court in holding that the convictions of four Negroes for murder, obtained by using coerced confessions, violated the due process clause of the fourteenth amendment. In *Smith v. Texas,* he again spoke for all nine Justices in setting aside the rape conviction of a Negro based on an indictment handed down by a grand jury from which Negroes were excluded. Black became best known, however, not as the eloquent voice of a unanimous Court, but as a dissenter urging the Court to break new ground on civil liberties, particularly as an advocate of uninhibited application of the first amendment. Justice William O. Douglas observed in 1956, "I dare say that when the critical account is written, none will be rated higher than Justice Black for consistency in construing the laws and the Constitution so as to protect the civil rights of citizens and aliens, whatever the form of repression may be." A decade later Alexander Bickel wrote of "a Hugo Black majority" on the Court, "for in this second half of Justice Black's third decade of service, the Court was overturning many a precedent that had entered the books over his dissent." When he finally left the bench in 1971, Justice Black, who had once been jeered at for his alleged lack of expertise, was praised for his "extraordinary capacity to clarify and make vivid the issues in a case" through "seemingly impregnable logic," and as one of "the court's intellectual pillars" with a reputation for "judicial integrity, dignity and tight reasoning."

Black's subsequent career made the widespread alarm expressed at his appointment seem badly misdirected and gave Roosevelt a sense of vindication. The President had remained rather touchy about the Black affair. In February, 1938, Raymond Clapper related in his diary an episode that took place in the Gridiron Club, the organization of Washington correspondents: "President Geo Holmes told about visit he and Gould Lincoln made to Rvt on Monday after dinner. Rvt said like dinner except thought one skit in bad taste. Said that was Klan skit on Black. . . . Said Harding had an illegitimate child but Gridiron club never use anything on that. . . . Said matter was dying out skit by being printed in newspapers tended to reopen whole thing keep it agitated. Holmes told us he couldn't see analogy of Rvt's unless he meant that Black was like Nan Britton." When the *Chambers* decision was handed down, Roosevelt seized the opportunity at his press conference the next day to tell reporters, "I would put in a general dig that some of the Press should not only give a little praise but also a modicum of apology for things they have said in the last two years. Is that fair?"

VI. "A WONDERFULLY GOOD APPOINTMENT"

Black's emergence as a champion of civil liberties has been offered as proof that Roosevelt knew what he was doing all along, that he perceived potential in Black that others did not. Perhaps he did; it is hard to determine, particularly this long after the fact, what one man sensed in another. It is highly improbable, though, that FDR foresaw Black's ultimate accomplishments, even if he may have supposed that Black, like other men, might show new qualities when given the independence of life tenure.

Other commentators have said that Black's post-1937 conduct accorded with his pre-1937 career, for he had come out of a populist
tradition in Alabama and had long been an exponent of civil liberties
and individualism and a friend of labor and the Negro. This view
acknowledges that he had been a Klansman, but contends that the
KKK was a populist, prolabor movement that sponsored liberal, hu-
manitarian measures, such as aid for underprivileged children. Some
have also claimed that he joined at the urging of a Jewish friend in
order to exercise his benign influence within the Klan.

The evidence for these familiar arguments is, at best, ambiguous.
It is true that Black appears never to have been associated with Klan
violence, that he was an attorney for unions, and that he was responsible for reforms in court procedure in Alabama. Nevertheless, the
link of Black to populism has been too easily assumed, quite apart
from the difficulty of showing the connection between populism and
modern civil libertarianism. Black did have Negro clients, but he was
also reproached for making a blatant appeal to race prejudice while
defending the accused murderer of a priest. The strongest statement
that Daniel M. Berman could make in his informative article in the
Catholic University Law Review was that "there is no evidence that
Judge Black treated Negroes any more harshly than whites." As late
as 1932, Black had opposed a government relief bill because it would,
in code language, interfere with "social habits and social customs."
Correspondent Paul Y. Anderson reported that Black "became hysterical over the prospect of a federal relief plan which might feed Negroes
as well as whites, and gave an exhibition which brought a blush to
the face of Tom Heflin, lurking in the rear of the chamber." The one
thing known for certain about Black's attitude toward the Negro was
that, in the very month Roosevelt appointed him to the Supreme
Court, Black was planning to speak in the Senate against the anti-
lynching bill.

At a press conference in September Roosevelt responded "No" to
the question: "Prior to the appointment of former Senator Black, had
you received any information from any source as to his Klan membership?" The President may not have known about "membership," but
it is inconceivable that he had no awareness of a Klan connection. It
was widely recognized, at the very least, that the Alabama senator had
Klan backing when he was first elected to the U.S. Senate. In fact, as

a writer in the *Washington Post* noted, "It is difficult to find a sketch of Senator Black which does not contain some reference to the Ku Klux Klan." In addition, because of his association with the polio center at Warm Springs, Roosevelt regarded himself as much a son of Georgia as of New York, and in his many sojourns in Georgia he would have been likely to have acquired good intelligence about the politics of neighboring Alabama.

It is more likely that civil liberties considerations did not loom large in Roosevelt's mind in choosing a nominee. The central issue in the Court crisis had been the fate of New Deal economic legislation, and the President was looking for someone to legitimate the growth of the State. Concentration on such matters, rather than civil liberties and civil rights, reflected the basic attitudes of 1930s liberalism. It is true that interest in civil liberties and civil rights grew during the Depression, fostered by New Deal activities, particularly in the Justice Department, the inclinations of New Deal administrators like Harold Ickes, the example set by Eleanor Roosevelt, and the spirit of concern that the New Deal conveyed. Not until the 1940s, however, did civil liberties and civil rights come to have a truly prominent place on the agenda of American liberalism.

For many New Deal supporters, Black's Klan affiliation was distressing, but it was not thought to be central, as it would be today. Klan membership was regarded as the entry fee Black had to pay for political advancement in Alabama, nothing more. Senator George Norris, the most respected of all the progressives and father of the TVA, who had fought the Klan and been fought by it, called the naming of Black "a wonderfully good appointment." He added, "Even if he was a member of the Klan, there's no legal objection to that. I've an idea many members of the House and the Senate belong to the Klan also but that is their privilege."

Progressives characterized the outcry against Black as a conservative scheme to discredit the Roosevelt administration and thereby scuttle the New Deal and prospects for reform. They did not attack what was said about Black, but rather who said it; when Sprigle's series appeared, Black's supporters concentrated their fire on his publisher, Paul Block, and other hostile newspaper titans like William Randolph Hearst. They offered the defense, in Heywood Broun's words, that "few justices of the Supreme Court swim up to the high bench as immaculate as Little Eva on the way to Heaven" and contended that the elements opposed to Black would not have shown the same intense concern about the past of a reactionary nominee. The liberal columnist Jay Franklin wrote, "One point only should be made in relation to these charges: If Hugo L. Black had been a labor-baiter, a trust corporation attorney, a man who had amassed a fortune and achieved political prominence as a result of helping the banks, utilities and corporations to loot the State of Alabama and stifle competition by strong-arm monopolies, he could have engaged in devil-worship, he could have practiced polygamy, he could have hunted down run-away share-croppers with blood-hounds, and eaten babies for breakfast, for all that his conservative Northern critics would care."

The New Dealers insisted that Black should be measured by the yardstick of twentieth century social reform and by the imperatives of the Great Depression. *The Progressive,* the organ of the La Follette dynasty in Wisconsin, noting Black's "excellent and long standing record of liberalism," pointed out that Black had fought the big-navy lobby and the power trust. Congressman David Lewis, a Maryland Democrat who had cosponsored the social security bill, asserted, "The real issue is not Black's qualifications, but whether the court is going to keep out of the 'nullification business'—that is quit vetoing acts of Congress." A Providence newspaper observed, "We don't like the idea of a Supreme Court Judge having been at any time or for whatever purpose associated with the Ku Klux Klan, but the issue is not religion, it is not race or creed; the issue is economics."

In its "Topics of The Times" column, the *New York Times* satirized this sentiment in *Alice in Wonderland* style:

> After a while the White Rabbit summed up the debate, nobody dissenting.
> "You see, Alice," he said, "it's all because we have recently discovered that all life is functional. Once upon a time people thought there were definite things like truth, justice, honor, mercy, courage, and so forth. But now we know these things are only functions of the economic system. . . . That is why Liberals in the United States feel it does not matter if a member of the Supreme Court used to belong to the KKK. The only important thing is how does he stand on the question of 1½ cents per kilowatt hour f.o.b. Norris Dam."

This preoccupation with economic and social policy had led the President to choose Black, but it was not the only consideration. Roosevelt certainly sought an enthusiastic New Dealer, but he also wanted someone who was young, came from a section that did not have a Supreme Court Justice, and could readily be confirmed. He and Cummings had reduced a list of sixty names to seven, four of whom were federal judges. None of the judges, however, including the highly touted Bratton, had sufficient liberal ardor to suit the President. "Bratton belongs to a judicial school of thought that ought not to be represented on the bench," he later told Farley. So the candidates were reduced to three: Solicitor General Stanley Reed, Black, and Senator Sherman Minton of Indiana.

Reed was crossed off as "middle-of-the-road . . . a good man but without much force or color," and attention focused on the choice of a senator. Roosevelt found that solution particularly beguiling, especially after the Robinson episode in May, in which the Senate in effect made its own nomination of a Justice. If he named a senator, even one regarded as a radical, the Senate would be trapped into going along, a circumstance that appealed to FDR's love of surprise and of turning the tables on his opponents with a clever move. He was initially inclined toward the fiery Shay Minton, but the Hoosier senator recognized that during the recent struggle over the Court bill he had made too many harsh comments about the Justices who would be his colleagues. Moreover, he was needed in the Senate. The President therefore settled on Black, who was young enough at 51, from a large unrepresented circuit in the Deep South, and, most important, a true believer in expanding governmental power.

Far from seeking to placate Congress by picking a moderate like Bratton, Roosevelt wanted to make clear that he was as committed to the New Deal as ever, and his selection of Black was a symbolic and defiant act. FDR's original plan seems to have been motivated by a desire not only to reform the Court, but also to punish the Justices for wronging him in the past. The appointment afforded Roosevelt another opportunity to express his contempt for the illusion that the Court was a body that lived on Mt. Olympus and his conviction that it was essentially a political agency. The Senate was even more of a target for revenge, for it had just humiliated him in the Court-packing battle. Donald Richberg, a prominent New Dealer, confided, as Clapper noted, that "Roosevelt was mad and was determined to give the Senate the name which would be most disagreeable to it yet which it could not reject."

The President's faith in Black's liberal proclivities proved well founded. "Although Black's appointment did not mark the precise chronological point from which the Court's philosophy began its deviation from its previous path," Charlotte Williams has written, "it was this event which made it plain beyond all doubt that the Court was about to be reconstituted in the image of the New Deal." Black immediately gave the Administration a 6-3 majority on the Court, and his lone dissents indicated that he favored even more advanced stands than Justices like Brandeis, Cardozo, and Stone. Wallace Mendelson has calculated that in sixty cases involving the Federal Employer's Liability Act from 1938 through 1958, Black sustained workingmen's claims in every case but one, and that in the decade beginning 1949, in nineteen Sherman Act conflicts between business and consumer interests, "only Mr. Justice Black found a violation of the law in every instance."

In nominating Black, the President set the pattern that most of the other selections for "the Roosevelt Court" would follow. To the Supreme Court would go progressives, like Frank Murphy and William O. Douglas, who shared Black's zeal for the New Deal. The typical appointee would, like Black, be several years younger than William Howard Taft's representative choice. Only once would FDR pick a man with prior experience in the federal judiciary; indeed, Black was exceptional in that, except for Wiley Rutledge, the former police court magistrate was the only Roosevelt appointee who had ever served as a judge prior to joining the Court.

Black's appointment turned out to be only the first of many for the President. Roosevelt, who was unable to designate anyone for the Supreme Court in his first term, named eight Justices, including the Chief Justice, in the six years from 1937 to 1943. So rapidly did the composition of the Court change under Roosevelt and Truman that by the late 1940s Black, whose tenure seemed so precarious in 1937, was the senior member. Black remained on the bench through the thirties, forties, fifties, sixties and into the seventies, and would fall only months short of establishing a new record for length of service as a Justice.

The Black controversy is rich in paradox and irony—a former Klansman becoming one of the century's leading exponents of civil liberties, a Justice chosen for one set of reasons winning fame for accomplishments that had hardly been anticipated, an Alabaman who created alarm among Negro groups when he was nominated but who lived to be denounced as a foe of the white South—but not least of the many ironies is the fact that the President's bitterly fought campaign to rejuvenate the Court by terminating tenure at the age of seventy would end in his naming, as his first appointment, a man who would still be on the bench on his eighty-fifth birthday and whose lengthy and brilliant career would be seen as a testament to Roosevelt's perspicacity.

12

The Detroit Race Riot of 1943

HARVARD SITKOFF

• Of all the sources of civil disorder in American history, none has been more persistent than race relationships. Whether in the North or South, whether before or after the Civil War, whether in city or small town, this question has been at the root of more physical violence than any other. But because most forms of prejudice were more blatant and more virulent in the South than in the North, blacks sought for generations to cross the Mason-Dixon Line in search of a new land of equality and opportunity. Unfortunately, the big cities of the East and Middle West provided a fresh set of problems, and the continuing migration away from farm tenancy and share-cropping did not immediately improve the quality of Afro-American life. The pattern of the ghetto—residential segregation, underemployment, substandard housing, disrupted family life, inferior education, filth, and disease—was set even before 1920. Neither was violence left behind in the land of the plantation. In the "red summer of 1919," white-black rioting claimed more than one hundred lives and demonstrated again that the most striking feature of black life was not the existence of slum conditions, but the barriers to residential and occupational mobility.

Following closely upon earlier conflicts in Mobile, Los Angeles, and Beaumont, the Detroit riot of 1943 illustrates the range of racial disorders that broke out sporadically during World War II. The Negro population of the city had risen sharply from 40,000 to 120,000 in the single decade between 1920 and 1930, and had jumped again by 50,000 in the fifteen months before the riot. Sparked by scattered gang fighting on a hot summer day, the riot ended by taking thirty-four lives. It was particularly notable for its ferocity and duration and for the fact that it began on a recreational spot—Belle Isle—

Michigan History, Bureau of History, Michigan Department of State.

that had previously been used by both races. Professor Harvard Sitkoff's article recreates that tragic event and urges us to question whether the United States has moved very far along the path of racial justice in the last third of a century.

For the American Negro, World War II began a quarter of a century of increasing hope and frustration. After a long decade of depression, the war promised a better deal. Negroes confidently expected a crusade against Nazi racism and for the Four Freedoms, a battle requiring the loyalty and manpower of all Americans, to be the turning point for their race. This war would be "Civil War II," a "Double V" campaign. No Negro leader urged his people to suspend grievances until victory was won, as most did during World War I. Rather, the government's need for full cooperation from the total population, the ideological character of the war, the constant preaching to square American practices with the American Creed, and the beginning of the end of the era of white supremacy in the world intensified Negro demands for equality *now*.

Never before in American history had Negroes been so united and militant. Led by the *Baltimore Afro-American, Chicago Defender, Pittsburgh Courier,* and Adam Clayton Powell's *People's Voice* ("The New Paper for the New Negro"), the Negro press urged civil rights leaders to be more aggressive. It publicized protest movements, headlined atrocity stories of lynched and assaulted Negroes, and developed race solidarity. Every major civil rights organization subscribed to the "Double V" campaign, demanding an end to discrimination in industry and the armed forces. The National Association for the Advancement of Colored People, National Urban League, National Negro Congress, A. Philip Randolph's March-on-Washington Movement, and the newly organized Congress of Racial Equality joined with Negro professional and fraternal organizations, labor unions, and church leaders to insist on "Democracy in Our Time!" These groups organized rallies, formed committees, supported letter and telegram mail-ins, began picketing and boycotting, and threatened unruly demonstrations. This as well as collaboration with sympathetic whites helped exert pressure on government officials.

The combined effects of exhortation and organization made the Negro man-in-the-street increasingly militant. After years of futility, there was now bitter hope. As he slowly gained economic and political power, won victories in the courts, heard his aspirations legitimized by respected whites, and identified his cause with the two-thirds of the world's colored people, the Negro became more impatient with any impediment to first-class citizenship and more determined to assert his new status. Each gain increased his expectations; each improvement in the conditions of whites increased his dissatisfaction. Still forced to fight in a segregated army supplied by a Jim Crow industrial force, still denied his basic rights in the South and imprisoned in rat-and-vermin-infested ghettos in the North, he rejected all pleas to "go slow." At the same time many whites renewed their efforts to keep the Negro in an inferior economic and social position regardless of the changes wrought by the war. Frightened by his new militancy and wartime gains, resenting his competition for jobs, housing, and power, whites sought to retain their cherished status and keep "the nigger in his place." The more Negroes demanded their due, the more white resistance stiffened.

American engagement in a world war, as well as the lack of government action to relieve racial anxiety or even enforce "neutral" police control, made it likely that racial antagonism would erupt into violence. President Roosevelt, preoccupied with international diplomacy and military strategy, and still dependent on Southern support in Congress, ignored the deteriorating domestic situation. Participation in the war increased the prestige of violence and its use as an effective way to accomplish specific aims. The psychological effects of war, the new strains and uncertainty, multiplied hatred and insecurity. Many petty irritations—the rationing, shortages, overcrowding, and high prices—engendered short tempers; the fatigue of long work weeks, little opportunity for recreation, the anxious scanning of casualty lists, the new job and strange city, and the need for the noncombatant to prove his masculinity led to heightened tension and the desire to express it violently.

For three years public officials throughout the nation watched the growth of racial strife. Fights between Negroes and whites became a daily occurrence on public vehicles. Nearly every issue of the Negro press reported clashes between Negro soldiers and white military or civilian police. At least seventeen Negroes were lynched between 1940 and 1943. The accumulation of agitation and violence then burst into an epidemic of race riots in June, 1943. Racial gang fights, or "zoot-suit riots," broke out in several non-Southern cities. The worst of these hit Los Angeles. While the city fathers wrung their hands, white sailors and their civilian allies attacked scores of Negroes and Mexican-Americans. The only action taken by the Los Angeles City Council was to declare the wearing of a zoot suit a misdemeanor. In mid-June, a rumor of rape touched off a twenty-hour riot in Beaumont, Texas. White mobs burned and pillaged the Negro ghetto. War production stopped, businesses closed, thousands of dollars of property were damaged, two persons were killed, and more than seventy were injured. In Mobile, the attempt to upgrade some Negro workers as welders in the yards of the Alabama Dry Dock and Shipbuilders Company caused twenty thousand white workers to walk off their jobs and riot for four days. Only the intervention of federal troops stopped the riot. The President's Committee on Fair Employment Practices then backed down and agreed to let segregation continue in the shipyards.

Nowhere was trouble more expected than in Detroit. In the three years after 1940, more than fifty thousand Southern Negroes and half a million Southern whites migrated to the "Arsenal of Democracy" seeking employment. Negroes were forced to crowd into the already teeming thirty-block ghetto of Paradise Valley and some fifty registered "neighborhood improvement associations" and the Detroit Housing Commission kept them confined there. Although ten percent of the population, Negroes comprised less than 1 percent of the city teachers and police. Over half the workers on relief in 1942 were Negro, and most of those with jobs did menial work. Only three percent of the women employed in defense work were Negro, and these were mainly in custodial positions. The Negro demand for adequate housing, jobs, recreation, and transportation facilities, and the white refusal to give anything up, led to violence. Early in 1942, over a thousand whites armed with clubs, knives, and rifles rioted to stop Negroes from moving into the Sojourner Truth Housing Project. Fiery crosses burned throughout the city. More than a thousand state troopers had to escort two hundred Negro families into the project. Federal investigators warned Washington officials of that city's inability to keep racial peace, and the Office of Facts and Figures warned that "unless strong and quick intervention by some high official, preferably the President, is . . . taken at once, hell is going to be let loose." Nothing was done in Detroit or Washington. Throughout that year Negro and white students clashed in the city's high schools, and the number of outbreaks in factories multiplied.

In 1943, racial violence in Detroit increased in frequency and boldness. The forced close mingling of Negroes with Southern whites on buses and trolleys, crowded with nearly forty percent more passengers than at the start of the war, led to fights and stabbings. White soldiers battled Negroes in suburban Inkster. In April, a racial brawl in a city playground involved more than a hundred teenagers. Early in June, twenty-five thousand Packard employees struck in protest against the upgrading of three Negro workers. More than five hundred Negroes and whites fought at parks in different parts of the city. Negro leaders openly predicted greater violence unless something was done quickly to provide jobs and housing. Walter White of the NAACP told a packed rally in Cadillac Square: "Let us drag out into the open what has been whispered throughout Detroit for months—that a race riot may break out here at any time." Detroit newspaper and national magazines described the city as "a keg of powder with a short fuse." But no one in the city, state, or federal government dared to act. Everyone watched and waited. When the riot exploded, Mayor Edward Jeffries told reporters: "I was taken by surprise only by the day it happened."

The riot began, like those in 1919, with direct clashes between groups of Negroes and whites. Over 100,000 Detroiters crowded onto Belle Isle on Sunday, June 20, 1943, to seek relief from the hot, humid city streets. The temperature was over ninety. Long lines of Negroes and whites pushed and jostled to get into the bath house, rent canoes, and buy refreshments. Police continuously received reports of minor fights. Charles (Little Willie) Lyon, who had been attacked a few days earlier for trying to enter the all-white Eastwood Amusement Park, gathered a group of Negro teenagers to "take care of the Hunkies." They broke up picnics, forced whites to leave the park, beat up some boys, and started a melee on the bridge connecting Belle Isle with the city. Brawls broke out at the park's casino, ferry dock, playground, and bus stops. By evening rumors of a race riot swept the island. Sailors from a nearby armory, angered by a Negro assault on two sailors the previous day, hurried to the bridge to join the fray. Shortly after 11:00 P.M. more than five thousand people were fighting on the bridge. By 2:00 A.M. the police had arrested twenty-eight Negroes and nineteen whites, quelling the melee without a single gunshot.

As the thousands of rioters and onlookers returned home, stories of racial violence spread to every section of Detroit. In Paradise Valley, Leo Tipton jumped on the stage of the Forrest Club, grabbed the microphone and shouted: "There's a riot at Belle Isle! The whites have killed a colored lady and her baby. Thrown them over a bridge. Everybody come on! There's free transportation outside!" Hundreds rushed out of the nightclub, only to find the bridge barricaded and all traffic approaches to the Isle blocked. Sullen, the mob returned to the ghetto, stoning passing white motorists, hurling rocks and bottles at the police, and stopping streetcars to beat up unsuspecting whites. The frustrations bottled up by the war burst. Negroes—tired of moving to find the promised land, tired of finding the North too much like the South, tired of being Jim-Crowed, scorned, despised, spat upon, tired of being called "boy"—struck out in blind fury against the white-owned ghetto. Unlike the riots of 1919, Negroes now began to destroy the hated white property and symbols of authority. By early morning every white-owned store window on Hastings Avenue in the ghetto had been smashed. There was little looting at first, but the temptation of an open store soon turned Paradise Valley into an open-air market: liquor bottles, quarters of beef, and whole sides of bacon were freely carried about, sold, and bartered.

As the police hesitatingly struggled to end the rioting in the ghetto, rumors of white women being raped at Belle Isle enraged white crowds forming along Woodward Avenue. Unhampered by the police, the mobs attacked all Negroes caught outside the ghetto. They stopped, overturned, and burned cars driven by Negroes. The mob dragged off and beat Negroes in the all-night movies along the "strip" and those riding trolleys. When a white instructor at Wayne University asked the police to help a Negro caught by a white gang, they taunted him as a "nigger lover." The police would do nothing to help. Throughout the morning fresh rumors kept refueling the frenzy, and rioting grew. The excitement of a car burning in the night, the screeching wail of a police siren, plenty of free liquor, and a feeling of being free to do whatever one wished without fear of police retaliation, all fed the appetite of a riot-ready city.

At 4:00 A.M. Detroit Mayor Edward Jeffries met with the Police

Commissioner, the FBI, State Police, and Colonel August Krech, the highest-ranking Army officer stationed in Detroit. With hysteria growing, and the ability of the police to control violence diminishing, most of the meeting involved a discussion of the procedure to be used to obtain federal troops. They agreed that the Mayor should ask the Governor for troops; the Governor would telephone his request to General Henry Aurand, Commander of the Sixth Service in Chicago; and Aurand would call Krech in Detroit to order the troops into the city. Colonel Krech then alerted the 728th Military Police Battalion at River Rouge, and assured the Mayor that the military police would be patrolling Detroit within forty-nine minutes after receiving their orders. Nothing was done to check the plan for acquiring federal troops, and no mention was made of the need for martial law or a presidential proclamation.

When the meeting ended at 7:00 A.M. the Police Commissioner prematurely declared that the situation was now under control, and federal troops would not be needed. The opposite was true. Negro looting became widespread, and white mobs on Woodward Avenue swelled. Two hours later Negro leaders begged the Mayor to get federal troops to stop the riot. Jeffries refused, promising only to talk with them again at a noon meeting of the Detroit Citizens Committee. The Mayor would discuss neither the grievances of the Negro community nor how Negroes could help contain the destruction in the ghetto. A half hour later Jeffries changed his mind, telling those in his City Hall office that only federal troops could restore peace to Detroit.

Harry F. Kelly, the newly elected Republican Governor of Michigan, was enjoying his first session of the Conference of Governors in Ohio when shortly before 10:00 A.M. he was called to the telephone. Mayor Jeffries described the riot situation to the Governor, asserted that the city was out of control, and insisted that he needed more manpower. Kelly responded by ordering the Michigan state police and state troops on alert. An hour later he telephoned Sixth Service Command Headquarters in Chicago. Believing he had done all that was necessary to get federal troops into the city, Kelly hurriedly left for Detroit. But according to the Sixth Service Command, the Governor's call was only about a *possible* request for troops. Thus, the twelve-hour burlesque of deploying federal troops in Detroit began. The War Department and the White House flatly refused to take the initiative.

Army officials in Chicago and Washington kept passing the buck back and forth. And both Kelly and Jeffries feared doing anything that might indicate to the voters their inability to cope with the disorder. After Kelly's call to Chicago, Aurand dispatched his director of internal security, Brigadier General William Guthner, to Detroit to command federal troops "in the event" the Governor formally requested them. Military police units surrounding Detroit were put on alert but forbidden to enter the city. In Washington the top brass remained busy with conferences on the use of the Army taking over mines in the threatened coal strike. No advice or instructions were given to Aurand. The Washington generals privately agreed that Aurand could send troops into Detroit without involving the President, or waiting for a formal request by the Governor, by acting on the principle of protecting defense production. But the War Department refused to give any orders to Aurand because it might "furnish him with a first class alibi if things go wrong."

While the generals and politicians fiddled, the riot raged. With most of the Detroit police cordoning off the ghetto, white mobs freely roamed the city attacking Negroes. At noon, three police cars escorted the Mayor into Paradise Valley to attend a Detroit Citizens Committee meeting. The interracial committee roundly denounced the Mayor for doing too little but could not agree on what should be done. Some argued for federal troops and others for Negro auxiliary police. Exasperated, Jeffries finally agreed to appoint two hundred Negro auxiliaries. But with no power and little cooperation from the police, the auxiliaries accomplished nothing. Rioters on the streets continued to do as they pleased. At 1:30 P.M. high schools were closed, and many students joined the riot.

Shortly after three, General Guthner arrived in Detroit to tell Kelly and Jeffries that federal martial law, which could only be proclaimed by the President, was necessary before federal troops could be called in. Dumbfounded by this new procedure, the Governor telephoned Aurand for an explanation. Aurand, more determined than ever to escape the responsibility for calling the troops, confirmed Guthner's statement. Despite Jeffries's frantic plea for more men, Kelly refused to ask for martial law: such a request would be taken as an admission of his failure.

Not knowing what else to do, after almost twenty hours of rioting,

Jeffries and Kelly made their first radio appeal to the people of Detroit. The Governor proclaimed a state of emergency, banning the sale of alcoholic beverages, closing amusement places, asking persons not going to or from work to stay home, prohibiting the carrying of weapons, and refusing permission for crowds to assemble. The proclamation cleared the way for the use of state troops but still did not comply with Aurand's prerequisites for the use of federal troops. Mayor Jeffries pleaded for an end to hysteria, arguing that only the Axis benefited from the strife in Detroit.

On the streets neither the proclamation nor the plea had any effect. Negro and white mobs continued their assaults and destruction. The weary police were barely able to restrain whites from entering Paradise Valley or to check the extent of Negro looting. Just as the Mayor finished pleading for sanity, four teen-agers shot an elderly Negro because they "didn't have anything to do." Tired of milling about, they agreed to "go out and kill us a nigger. . . . We didn't know him. He wasn't bothering us. But other people were fighting and killing and we felt like it too." As the city darkened, the violence increased. At 8:00 P.M. Jeffries called for the state troops. The Governor had ordered the force of two thousand mobilized earlier, but now the Mayor learned that only thirty-two men were available. At the same time the Mayor was informed that a direct clash between whites and Negroes was imminent. At Cadillac Square, the police were losing their struggle to hold back a white mob heading for the ghetto. Nineteen different police precincts reported riot activity. Seventy-five percent of the Detroit area was affected. Sixteen transportation lines had to suspend operation. The Detroit Fire Department could no longer control the more than one hundred fires. Detroiters entered Receiving Hospital at the rate of one every other minute.

In Washington, Lieutenant General Brehon Somervell, Commander of all Army Service Forces, directed the Army's Provost Marshal, Major General Allen Guillon, to prepare a Presidential Proclamation. At 8:00 P.M. Guillon and Somervell took the proclamation to the home of Secretary of War Henry Stimson. Sitting in the Secretary's library, the three men laid plans for the use of federal troops; as they discussed the situation they kept in telephone contact with the President at Hyde Park, the Governor in Detroit, and General Aurand in Chicago. Stimson instructed Aurand not to issue the text of the proclamation until the President signed it. Shortly after nine, Kelly telephoned Colonel Krech to request federal troops. At 9:20, the Governor repeated his appeal to General Aurand. Aurand immediately ordered the military police units into Detroit, although federal martial law had not been declared and the President had not signed the proclamation.

As the politicians and generals wrangled over the legality of Aurand's order, three hundred and fifty men of the 701st Military Police Battalion raced into Cadillac Square to disperse a white mob of over ten thousand. In full battle gear, bayonets fixed at high port, the federal troops swept the mob away from Woodward Avenue without firing a shot. The 701st then linked up with the 728th Battalion, which had been on the alert since 4:00 A.M., to clear rioters out of the ghetto. Using tear gas grenades and rifle butts, the military police forced all Negroes and whites off the streets. At 11:30 the riot was over, but the Presidential Proclamation was still to be signed.

After Aurand had transmitted his orders to Guthner, he had called Somervell to get permission to issue the proclamation. Somervell demanded that Aurand follow Stimson's instructions to wait until Governor Kelly contacted the President and Roosevelt signed the official order. Aurand relayed this message to Guthner, but the Governor could not be located until the riot had been quelled. Not until shortly before midnight did Kelly call Hyde Park to request the troops already deployed in the city. President Roosevelt signed the proclamation at 11:55 P.M. The Detroit rioters, now pacified, were commanded "to disperse and retire peaceably to their respective abodes." Twenty-one hours had passed since Army officials in Detroit first planned to use federal troops to end the riot. More than fifteen hours had been wasted since the Mayor first asked for Army manpower. Half a day had been lost between the Governor's first call to Sixth Service Command and Aurand's decision to send the military police into Detroit. General Guthner sat in Detroit for six hours before deploying the troops he had been sent to command. And it was during that time that most of Detroit's riot toll was recorded: thirty-four killed, more than seven hundred injured, over two million dollars in property losses, and a million man-hours lost in war production.

The armed peace in Detroit continued into Tuesday morning. Five thousand soldiers patrolled the streets, and military vehicles escorted buses and trolleys on their usual runs. Although racial tension remained high, firm and impartial action by the federal troops kept the city calm. Following Aurand's recommendations, Guthner instructed his troops to act with extreme restraint. Each field order ended with the admonition: "Under no circumstances will the use of firearms be resorted to unless all other measures fail to control the situation, bearing in mind that the suppression of violence, when accomplished without bloodshed, is a worthy achievement."

Continued hysteria in the city caused most of Guthner's difficulties. Rumors of new violence and repeated instances of police brutality kept the Negro ghetto seething. Most Negroes feared to leave their homes to go to work or buy food. Guthner persistently urged the Commissioner to order the police to ease off in their treatment of Negroes, but Witherspoon refused. Tales of the riot inflamed Negroes in surrounding communities. A group of soldiers at Fort Custer, 140 miles west of Detroit, tried to seize arms and a truck to help their families in the city. In Toledo, police turned back 1,500 Negroes trying to get rail transportation to Detroit. Muskegon, Indiana Harbor, Springfield, East St. Louis, and Chicago reported racial disturbances. Aurand changed his mind about leaving Chicago for Detroit and ordered Sixth Service Command troops in Illinois on the alert.

Unrest and ill-feeling continued throughout the week. The city courts, disregarding the depths of racial hostility in Detroit, employed separate and unequal standards in sentencing Negroes and whites arrested in the riot. With little regard for due process of law, the police carried out systematic raids on Negro rooming houses and apartments. Anxiety increased, isolated racial fights continued, repeated rumors of a new riot on July Fourth poisoned the tense atmosphere. Negroes and whites prepared for "the next one." Workmen in defense plants made knives out of flat files and hacksaw blades. Kelly and Jeffries urged the President to keep the federal troops in Detroit.

While the troops patrolled the streets, the search for answers and scapegoats to give some meaning to the outburst began. Adamant that it really "can't happen here," the same liberals and Negro leaders who had warned that white racism made Detroit ripe for a riot now attributed the violence to Axis agents. Telegrams poured into the White House asking for an FBI investigation of German agents in Detroit who aimed to disrupt war production. When the myth of an organized fifth column behind the riot was quickly shattered, liberals accused domestic reactionaries. The KKK, Gerald L. K. Smith, Father Charles Coughlin, Reverend J. Frank Norris, Southern congressmen, and anti-union demagogues were all singled out for blame. The NAACP aimed its sights at reactionary Poles who led the battle against decent Negro housing. Conservatives were just as anxious to hold liberals and Japanese agents responsible for race conflict. Martin Dies, Chairman of the House Un-American Activities Committee, saw the Japanese-Americans released from internment camps behind the riot. Congressman John Rankin of Mississippi taunted his colleagues in the House who supported the antipoll tax bill by saying "their chickens are coming home to roost" and asserted that the Detroit violence had been caused by the "crazy policies of the so-called fair employment practices committee in attempting to mix the races in all kinds of employment." Many Southerners blamed Negro agitators. Some talked of "Eleanor Clubs" as the source of the riot. "It is blood on your hands, Mrs. Roosevelt," claimed the *Jackson Daily News.* "You have been personally proclaiming and practicing social equality at the White House and wherever you go, Mrs. Roosevelt. In Detroit, a city noted for the growing impudence and insolence of its Negro population, an attempt was made to put your preachments into practice, Mrs. Roosevelt. What followed is now history." A Gallup Poll revealed that most Northerners believed Axis propaganda and sabotage were responsible for the violence, while most Southerners attributed it to lack of segregation in the North. An analysis of two hundred newspapers indicated that Southern editors stressed Negro militancy as the primary cause, while Northern editors accused fifth column subversives and Southern migrants new to city ways.

In Detroit the causes and handling of the riot quickly became the central issue of city politics. The Congress of Industrial Organizations, Negro organizations, and many civil liberties groups formed an alliance to defeat Mayor Edward Jeffries in November, to get rid of Commissioner Witherspoon, and to demand additional housing and jobs for Negroes. Led by United Auto Worker President R. J. Thomas and City Councilman George Edwards, a former UAW organizer, the coalition gained the backing of most CIO locals, the NAACP and Urban League, International Labor Defense, National Lawyers Guild, National Negro Congress, National Federation for Constitutional

Liberties, Catholic Trade Unionists, Socialist Party of Michigan, Inter-
Racial Fellowship, Negro Council for Victory and Democracy, Metropolitan Detroit Youth Council, Union for Democratic Action, and
March-on-Washington Movement. They were supported editorially
by the *Detroit Free Press*, the *Detroit Tribune*, and the Negro *Michigan Chronicle*. Throughout the summer the coalition clamored for a
special grand jury to investigate the causes of the riot and the unsolved
riot deaths.

Michigan's leading Republicans, the Hearst press, and most real estate and antiunion groups opposed any change in the Negro's status.
The Governor, Mayor, and Police Commissioner, abetted by the oblig-
ing Common Council, squelched the pleas for better housing and jobs
and a grand jury investigation. Unwilling to make any changes in the
conditions underlying the riot, the Republicans made meaningless ges-
tures. The Mayor established an interracial committee with no power.
After a few sleepy sessions, it adjourned for a long summer vacation.
Commissioner Witherspoon refused to allow changes in the regulations to make possible the hiring of more Negro policemen. Instead of
a grand jury investigation, the Governor appointed his own Fact-
Finding Committee of four Republican law officers involved in the
handling of the riot. And the Detroit Council of Churches, nonparti-
san but similarly reluctant to face the issue of white racism, called
upon the city to observe the following Sunday as a day of humility
and penitence.

A week after the riot, Witherspoon appeared before the Common
Council to report on his department's actions. He blamed Negroes for
starting the riot and Army authorities for prolonging it. The Commissioner pictured white mob violence as only "retaliatory action" and
police behavior as a model of "rare courage and efficiency." In fact,
Witherspoon concluded, the police had been so fair that "some have
accused the Department of having a kid glove policy toward the Negro." No one on the Council bothered to ask the Commissioner why
the police failed to give Negroes the adequate protection required by
law, or how this policy accounted for seventeen of the twenty-five Negroes killed in the riot having been shot by the police. Two days later,
Mayor Jeffries presented his "white paper" to the Common Council.
He reiterated the Commissioner's criticism of the Army and praise for
the police and added an attack on "those Negro leaders who insist

that their people do not and will not trust policemen and the Police Department. After what happened I am certain that some of these leaders are more vocal in their caustic criticism of the Police Department than they are in educating their own people to their responsibilities as citizens." The Common Council heartily approved the two reports. Gus Dorias and William (Billy) Rogell, two Detroit athletic heroes on the Council, advocated a bigger ghetto to solve the racial crisis. Councilman Comstock did not think this or anything should be done. "The racial conflict has been going on in this country since our ancestors made the first mistake of bringing the Negro to the country." The conflict would go on regardless of what was done, added Comstock, so why do anything?

Throughout July the accusations and recriminations intensified. Then, as the city began to tire of the familiar arguments, a fresh controversy erupted. When three Negro leaders asked William Dowling, the Wayne County Prosecutor, to investigate the unsolved riot deaths, Dowling berated them for turning information over to the NAACP that they withheld from him. He charged the NAACP with being "the biggest instigators of the race riot. If a grand jury were called, they would be the first indicted." The NAACP threatened to sue Dowling for libel, and the county prosecutor quickly denied making the charge. "Why, I like Negroes," he said. "I know what it is to be a member of a minority group. I am an Irish Catholic myself." The next day Dowling again charged an "unnamed civil rights group" with causing the riot. Witherspoon endorsed Dowling's allegation, and the battle flared. "It was as if a bomb had been dropped," said one Negro church leader. "The situation is what it was just before June 21."

In the midst of this tense situation, the Governor released the report of his Fact-Finding Committee. Parts I and II, a detailed chronology of the riot and supporting exhibits, placed the blame for the violence squarely on Negroes who had started fights at Belle Isle and spread riot rumors. Content to fix liability on the initial aggressors, the report did not connect the Sunday fights with any of the scores of incidents of violence by whites against Negroes which preceded the fights at Belle Isle. Nor did the report mention any of the elements which permitted some fights to lead to such extensive hysteria and violence, or which allowed rumors to be so instantly efficacious. No whites were accused of contributing to the riot's causes. The sailors responsible for much of the fighting on the bridge, and the nineteen other whites arrested by the police Sunday night, escaped blame. The report emphasized the culpability of the Negro-instigated rumors, especially Leo Tipton's, but let the other rumors remain "lily-white." Although many instances of police brutality were attested and documented, the committee failed to mention them. And while only a court or grand jury in Michigan had the right to classify a homicide as legally "justifiable," the committee, hearing only police testimony, took it upon itself to "justify" all police killings of Negroes.

Part III, an analysis of Detroit's racial problems, completely departed from the committee's aim of avoiding "conclusions of a controversial or conjectural nature." The section on those responsible for racial tensions omitted any mention of the KKK, Black Legion, National Workers League, and the scores of anti-Negro demagogues and organizations openly preaching race hatred in Detroit. Racial tension was totally attributed to Negro agitators who "constantly beat the drums of: 'Racial prejudice, inequality, intolerance, discrimination.' " Repeatedly, the report referred to the Negro's "presumed grievances" and complaints of "alleged Jim Crowism." In the world of the Fact-Finding Committee no real Negro problems existed, or if they did, they were to be endured in silence. Publication of the obviously prejudiced report proved an immediate embarrassment to the Governor. Most newspapers and journals denounced it as a "whitewash," and Kelly's friends wisely buried it. The Common Council then declared the riot a "closed incident."

In Washington, too, politics went on as usual. The administration did nothing to prevent future riots or attempt to solve the American dilemma. The problem of responding to the riots became compounded when the same combination of underlying grievances and war-bred tensions which triggered the Detroit riot led to an orgy of looting and destruction in Harlem. Henry Wallace and Wendell Willkie delivered progressive speeches; leading radio commentators called for a new approach to racial problems; and many prominent Americans signed newspaper advertisements urging the President to condemn segregation and racial violence. But the White House remained silent.

In much the same way it had handled the question of segregation in the armed forces and discrimination in defense production, the Roosevelt administration muddled its way through a summer of violence. The four presidential aides handling race relations problems, all Southerners, determined to go slow, protect the "boss," and keep the shaky Democratic coalition together, fought all proposals for White House action. They politely buried pleas for the President to give a fireside chat on the riots and brushed aside recommendations that would force Roosevelt to acknowledge the gravity of the race problem. The Interior Department's plans for a national race relations commission, and those of Attorney General Francis Biddle for an interdepartmental committee were shelved in favor of Jonathan Daniels' inoffensive suggestion to correlate personally all information on racial problems. Even Marshall Field's proposal to circulate pledges asking people not to spread rumors and to help "win the war at home by combating racial discrimination wherever I meet it," which appealed to Roosevelt, went ignored. The federal government took only two actions: clarification of the procedure by which federal troops could be called, and approval of J. Edgar Hoover's recommendation to defer from the draft members of city police forces. Like the Republicans in Michigan, the Democrats in the capital occupied themselves with the efficient handling of a future riot rather than its prevention.

With a war to win, Detroit and the nation resumed "business as usual." Negroes continued to be brutalized by the police and the "first fired, last hired." In the Senate, the administration killed a proposal to have Congress investigate the riots, and Michigan's Homer Ferguson and Arthur Vandenberg stymied every proposal for Negro housing in Detroit's suburbs. Their constituents continued boasting "the sun never sets on a nigger in Dearborn." Governor Kelly appropriated a million dollars to equip and train special riot troops. Mayor Jeffries, running as a defender of "white supremacy," easily won re-election in 1943 and 1945. The lesson learned from the riot? In the Mayor's words: "We'll know what to do next time." Yet Southern Negroes continued to pour into Detroit looking for the promised land—only to find discrimination, hatred, a world of little opportunity and less dignity. The dream deferred waited to explode. "There ain't no North any more," sighed an old Negro woman. "Everything now is South."

13

Returning Heroes: The Obligations
of Women to Veterans in 1945

SUSAN M. HARTMANN

• At 7:00 P.M. (eastern standard time) on August 14, 1945,
radio stations across the nation interrupted normal program-
ming for President Harry S. Truman's announcement of the
surrender of Japan. It was a moment in time that those who
experienced it will never forget. World War II was over.
Across the length and breadth of the land, Americans gathered to celebrate their victory. In New York City two million
people converged on Times Square as though it were New
Year's Eve. In smaller cities and towns, the response was no
less tumultuous, as spontaneous cheers, horns, sirens, and
church bells telegraphed the news to every household and
hamlet, convincing even small children that it was a very
special day. To the average person, the most important consequence of victory was not the end of shortages, not the re-
structuring of international boundaries or reparations payments or big power politics, but the survival of husbands and
sons. They felt a collective sigh of relief. Normal family life
could resume. The long vigil was over. Their men would be
coming home.

But what of the women whose first decent-paying, responsible jobs would be taken away by returning veterans? How
would wives accustomed to wartime independence deal with
the division of power and responsibility within marriage?
How would war brides, many of whom had known their husbands for only a few days or weeks before they shipped out,
react to their returning heroes? Many of the suggestions of
those who wrote on the subject in the 1940s will be shocking

Reprinted by permission of the editor from Women's Studies, 5 (1978),
223-268.

to readers in the 1980s, but we might ask whether society's expectations that women should be the responders and the adapters have changed all that much in the past half-century.

Recent scholarship in the history of women has presented a serious challenge to the conventional wisdom that war produces positive changes in the status of women. Analyzing the major changes in women's labor force participation since 1940, Valerie Kincade Oppenheimer concludes that the interaction of demographic and socioeconomic factors—factors not directly related to World War II—most significantly contributed to the documented changes in women's work roles. Although William H. Chafe considers World War II "a watershed event," "a milestone for women in America," he also demonstrates the persistence of economic inequality and the endurance of traditional values concerning women's place. Examining the wartime experience much more closely, Eleanor Straub emphasizes the inadequacies of government policy and the lack of a cohesive women's movement, concluding that the war did not significantly alter women's status.

The analyses by Chafe and Straub rightly begin with the assumption that the wartime emergency generated unprecedented needs for the services of women, and thus created the potential for substantial changes in sex roles. In seeking to understand why this potential remained unrealized, Chafe and Straub emphasize negative phenomena—the resistance to equality among large segments of business and labor, the half-hearted efforts by government to facilitate women's integration into the labor force on an equal basis, the inability of women leaders to form a unified movement and program. It is my argument, however, that although the war crisis presented opportunities for redefining sex roles, those possibilities were not realized because at the same time the war generated needs whose fulfillment strengthened traditional sex roles.

The vast social change and insecurity accompanying the war put a high premium on the preservation of social order. And, typically, the family seemed the one institution which most effectively could provide a rudder for this rapidly changing society. Concern over the increased incidence of juvenile delinquency prompted serious questions about the effects of mothers' employment outside the home. Since men played the most direct part in defeating the enemy, the war enhanced the significance of male contributions and reminded women of their inability to fulfill the most critical defense need. In addition, military service promoted male bonding, encouraged male exclusiveness (since women could neither share nor fully understand the experience of war), and thus strengthened sexual polarization.

Perhaps more than the war itself, its aftermath—the demobilization period—contributed to the reinforcement of traditional sex roles for American women and men. By 1944, as public attention began to focus on the postwar period, large numbers of writers and speakers defined the readjustment of 16 million veterans as the major domestic problem. Although their primary concern centered on the economy and employment opportunities, they also addressed the social aspects of demobilization. Opinions expressed about the problems of veterans were by no means unanimous; yet in the period, 1944–1946, a substantial body of literature appeared which awakened readers to the social problems of demobilization, described the specific adjustments facing ex-servicemen, and prescribed appropriate behavior and attitudes for civilians. The literature took various forms—books, articles, novels, short stories and movies; found expression in various kinds of media—government pamphlets, newspapers, professional journals, popular magazines and women's magazines; and was produced by psychiatrists, military doctors, sociologists, fiction writers, and ex-servicemen themselves.

Common to much of the literature were the themes of the critical nature of the veteran's readjustment, the enormity of his sacrifice, and the crucial role for women in the social aspects of demobilization. Willard Waller, sociologist at Barnard and prolific writer on the subject, considered the veteran to be the "major social problem of the next few years." Another sociologist, Ernest R. Groves, regarded problems of reunion "one of the greatest of all the ills that accompany warfare . . . one of the major hazards of war." To John Mariano the veteran's marriage problems were "our number-one family problem today," to Grace Sloan Overton the crisis was "the most desperately serious one the American family has ever felt." A former foot soldier in the Tunisian campaign predicted that ex-GI's would have more difficulty adjusting to home than they had in adapting to the military.

"We're a strange, temperamental lot," he warned. While other writers refrained from alarmist tones, they did counsel against stressing economic problems to the neglect of the social and psychological difficulties of demobilization.

Several writers decried all the attention given to the potential emotional crises facing veterans. In a *Harper's* article summarizing the lectures he gave to returnees, Christopher LaFarge stressed the veterans' responsibility for their own adjustment and warned them not to expect too much from civilians. Others charged that all the advice showered upon civilians was encouraging them to treat veterans as if they were not normal human beings and pointed out that servicemen were disgusted with all the publicity about their presumed maladjustment. These writers nonetheless went on to offer their own advice. The strongest objections to this emphasis on veterans' social and psychological adjustment came from a few men who themselves had returned from combat. Lt. William Best denounced the portrayals of soldiers as "tamed dogs gone wild," and insisted that most returnees would need only "normal considerate treatment." Marine Sergeant David Dempsey believed that the advice literature to wives and mothers was "in danger of turning them into kitchen psychologists determined to 'cure' the veteran—even at the cost of his sanity"; he suggested that most returnees needed only "some guidance" and "a little pre-Freudian love and understanding" from their wives. The political cartoonist Bill Mauldin, too, insisted that only a few would have real problems; he pointed out that while veterans had been "inconvenienced" by the war and had done a "great and hard job," only a relative few had actually "lived through misery."

Statistics on the experiences of military personnel support Mauldin's generalizations. Of the 16 millions who served between 1940 and 1946, a little less than one-half were in battle zones, and only one in eight actually saw combat. Yet, according to one man who had been there, service at a domestic base—a "brick foxhole"—was equally hazardous to the psyche: "if war is hell, then a brick foxhole is damnation." Usually the writers did not distinguish between the various experiences and levels of adversity endured by men in service; instead there was a strong tendency to dwell on the enormity of their sacrifice. Medical reporter Maxine Davis recognized the hardships endured by the women at home, but concluded, "compared to what he's been through, that wasn't much." Others stressed the "grim military existence," the "hazardous and tormenting environments," in which men served, the "monotony, uncertainty, loneliness, privation, exhaustion and horrific dangers and experiences." Willard Waller put this theme most dramatically:

> We have used them for war and war has put its curse on them; they are our boys whom we delivered to Moloch; our finest and bravest, a whole generation of our men-children. We must somehow find the way to win them back.

Civilians could never compensate veterans for their sacrifice. They could however discharge a portion of the debt by easing the veterans' return to peacetime life. Psychiatric consultant to the Association of Family Living in Chicago, Edwin O. Krause believed that it was only natural for veterans to expect "increased consideration, social standing and significance," in return for their sacrifice. Edward A. Strecker and Kenneth E. Appel, psychiatric consultants to the armed services, told civilians that despite the "loneliness, privation, and frustration" experienced by civilians, servicemen had "endured more deeply, more acutely, and more constantly"; the Army psychiatrists urged civilians to " 'even' your share of the burden by accepting more than half the load of adjustment." An ex-serviceman informed *Saturday Evening Post* readers that veterans were counting on civilians to develop great understanding and patience, to give us the benefit of the doubt. . . . You can't do less. . . ."

While Willard Waller encouraged every teacher, employer, wife and mother to become an expert on veteran psychology, he did not contradict the general consensus that the home—and the veteran's relationships with women—were at the core of satisfactory social adjustment. Coleman R. Griffith, professor of education and consultant to the War Manpower Commission, insisted that the home would be the peacetime focal point and that families "may have to do more adjusting to the veteran than the veteran to the family." Eleanor Roosevelt criticized the lack of understanding, imagination and patience in some American families and urged veterans' relatives to try to get "some conception of the type of life the boys in service had to endure." Other writers told women that they had "the biggest morale job in history"; that veterans expected "special consideration from their wives"; that "the personal side of reconstruction is women's work"; and that the wife of the ex-GI was the "indispensable person" in his adaption to civilian life. An army lieutenant who had interviewed returning servicemen reported that "nothing affects the returnee's behavior and morale so much as the reception he gets from his girl," and another veteran attributed his own "pretty wonderful" homecoming to his tolerant and understanding wife.

As women were handed a primary role in the social aspects of demobilization, they were also inundated by suggestions for discharging this responsibility. They were, above all, to be sensitive and responsive, to adjust their interests, needs and desires to those of their men—at least temporarily. *House Beautiful* instructed wives to make the veteran realize that "he's head man again. . . . Your part in the remaking of this man is to fit his home to him, understanding why he wants it this way, forgetting your own preferences." Writing in the *Ladies Home Journal*, Waller recognized the individual needs of the wife, but maintained that she must accept "more than the wife's usual responsibility for her marriage," until she could get her husband to take on his share. A practicing psychiatrist prescribed a light touch: "Any suggestions from you should be made subtly and only after you sense that he is ready to hear them." Role models in fiction reinforced these prescriptions. One heroine declared, "I'll simply and purely walk on eggshells when he comes home. If he wants me to be pale and grave and silent, I'll be it if it kills me. It's not my way, but I'll do it." Another fictional character endured her veteran husband's bossiness and criticism, remaining patient and quiet, "resolved not to quarrel with him." When one wife wrote complaining that her husband had come back "expecting to be treated like a conquering hero," and refusing to recognize her own hardships and sacrifices, Army base physician Frank Howard Richardson prompted her to give him time and not to jeopardize her marriage "by demanding your rights at once, *even though they are your rights.*"

Women's magazines were not alone in counseling self-abnegation on the parts of wives. A psychiatrist with experience in treating veterans, Alexander G. Dumas, emphasized that wives would need great "understanding and patience." A flight surgeon predicted that combat pilots "will demand, with some grounds, all the pampering and petting that is characteristic of the female species." In a March of Time film, *The Returning Veteran*, a female counsellor at a veterans' service center advised a war bride to cater to her husband's interests and pointed out, "There's nothing a man likes so much as to be listened to." Waller advised wives and mothers to try to understand what the veteran felt, to "make him feel secure . . . tolerate his outbursts," to refrain from nagging about new habits. "Above all, she must give him lavish—and undemanding—affection," and expect "no immediate return." A book, whose title *Readjustment or Revolution* expressed the author's anxieties, cautioned veterans' relatives not to question their decisions and actions. Another praised the wife who dealt effectively with her husband's moodiness and outbursts of anger: "Since she was persistent and feminine, she instinctively felt that just as he had changed, so must she. . . . Being a clever wife, *she* adjusted."

Illustrating various ways in which women should adapt to their husbands' needs, Herpert I. Kupper, staff psychiatrist at a marine hospital, expressed both anxiety about female assertiveness and ambiguity concerning what men really wanted in women. His advice that a woman should "submerge her (sexual) feelings and drives," and "attempt to conform to his," reflected a recognition of female sexuality as well as a perception of the threat it held for men. Kupper expressed additional concern about female assertiveness in pointing out that a romantic courtship would renew war-broken relationships. He urged women to behave as they had during the courting period, to be submissive, to "subordinate their real desires to those of the suitor." Although he assumed that women did this instinctively, he believed they needed the reminder "to use these charms again." Elsewhere, however, he wrote of the veterans' need for "mothering," thereby suggesting a role for women quite different from that of the submissive girl being courted. By asserting that, "it is best for the woman to be guided by the attitude of the returning veteran," Kupper found a solution both to the contradictions in what roles men desired in women and to the anxiety over female assertiveness.

Fear that the war had generated more independence in women was also reflected in the insistence by several writers that returning veterans both needed and desired "feminine" women. Reporter Ernie Pyle pointed out that men had become "rougher" and needed "the gentling effect of femininity." Henry Elkin, a social scientist and second lieutenant, explained that the war had separated men from domestic institutions, "from feminine influence and surroundings," and thereby diminished the effect of "previous social controls." While returnees may have been unaware of the family's importance as a social control mechanism and of women's traditional role in that function, they nonetheless *wanted* femininity in their women. A book addressed to veterans as well as to those who would welcome them home stated that the normal man would want, besides physical relief, "something else from a woman, like tenderness, or admiration, or at least submissiveness." According to Amran Scheinfeld, writing in the *Ladies Home Journal*, most GI's wanted to settle down . . . with a womanly woman and to have a houseful of kids." In a fictionalized account of one veteran's homecoming, an ex-lieutenant, remarked on women in slacks "telling loud jokes at bars," and reflected that servicemen would not like "some of these fads, like long pants on girls. I believe they'll want womanliness, at least in the girls they came back to." Another fictional veteran could accept his girl's new competence as a bus driver only when he saw her burst into tears because her special dress was not back from the cleaners for his homecoming. Reassured, he thought: "Let them wear overalls, let them work a riveting machine, let them drive a bus. They're still women." Finally, Clifford R. Adams, Director of the Marriage Counselling Service at Pennsylvania State College, reported that prospective husbands above all wanted their wives to be "utterly feminine." An accompanying quiz listed as unfeminine such characteristics as preference for colorless nails, slacks, and economic independence; an aptitude for medicine, law, engineering or science; enjoyment of basketball, softball, hunting or fishing; and ease in discussing business and world affairs with men.

If women were to cultivate feminine traits, they were also to recognize and accept the fact that the military experience sharpened masculine modes of behavior, especially male bonding. They were reminded of their exclusion from those military experiences "that only a soldier can understand, that only a comrade can share or even truly appraise." Ex-lieutenant Frederick Robin warned women that they could provide the "special sort of comradeship which cannot be found outside the society of fighting men." Thus, two officers of the Rehabilitation Division of the National Committee for the Mental Health, in a pamphlet which generally placed most of the responsibility for adjustment on the veteran himself, nevertheless counseled wives to accept their husbands' need to be with military pals, "with good grace and show wifely attentiveness when he is at home. . . ." And George Pratt, a psychiatric examiner for the Armed Forces, recommended that wives encourage husbands to escape "domestic cares as well as joys" by taking "an evening or so in a wholly masculine environment."

Women also received advice on the question of sexual morality. Although writers unanimously argued that the war had dealt a sharp blow to traditional morality they continued to insist on the double standard. While no one explicitly condoned extra-marital sex, writers stressed that wartime circumstances had made servicemen's infidelity understandable and forgivable. A veteran wrote to wives that it was natural for their husbands to be with other women. The wife was to realize that such liaisons were unsatisfactory substitutes, to try to live up to her husband's image of her, and to yield "nothing by way of allure to those other women he has known." Psychiatrist Howard Kitching insisted that one could not send men into combat and expect them at the same time all to be honest, chaste. . . ." Fidelity was an admirable goal, but wives must not "be too intolerant of an occasional infidelity." The novel *Shore Leave* portrayed a group of Navy fliers on an unremitting quest for women and alcoholic oblivion. Thinking about his own infidelity one character reflected that although he preferred the sexual attentions of his wife, "war took his right of choice away from him," and in war he owed fidelity only to his comrades in battle. Another anticipated the tolerance of veterans' wives: "Today we were all out of our cages, we animals . . . and no one knew it any better than our women. And no one would forgive us sooner, when we came back. . . ." Although initially repelled by the knowledge that the hardships of military duty at a domestic base had driven her husband to a prostitute, the heroine in *The Brick Foxhole* discovered her own forgiving and redemptive capacity and determined "to prove she was the better woman. . . ."

The continuing strength of the double standard was evident as writers repeatedly stressed the crucial role of woman's fidelity in bolstering the morale of retired soldiers. "If she is true, all other adjustments of homecoming matter little to him." Kitching recognized that women too had sexual needs but unlike men, theirs were more emotional than physical and reflected the need for "love, affection and surrender." Nonetheless, while he judged the double standard unfair to women, he urged that since it existed it must be accepted.

The most critical problem for wives, however, was the necessity of balancing their recently discovered competence and newly enjoyed independence with the needs of their returning husbands. All writers spoke to this point, and a later survey of veterans' adjustments confirmed that re-establishing this balance was "perhaps the chief source of the average veterans' marital difficulties." Women were warned that their husbands might return with "diminished ego capacity." A wife should help her husband regain his self-confidence: "Let him know you are tired of living alone, that you want him now to take charge." A wife accustomed to managing family affairs would "have to be tactful and wise to avoid the danger of ignoring your husband on the one hand and of controlling or regulating him on the other." She should "give him a sense of importance in the family . . . and plenty of opportunity to participate with you to regain his position as head of the house." Grace Sloan Overton commended women for their competence in the absence of men, but reminded those whose husbands were returning: "*he comes first. . . . Marriage for a woman must always be primary if it is to succeed.*" A National Research Council publication attempted to promote greater self-actualization for women, yet in its contradictory prescriptions reflected an underlying anxiety that women might have become too independent. *Psychology for the Returning Veteran* counseled veterans to allow their wives to continue to run the home if they did it well and liked it, and warned men that women had become more independent, that "caveman tactics would not work." But at the same time it insisted that women remained feminine: "A woman likes manliness, virility and courage in a man. She wants him to be aggressive and to take the lead."

The economic independence gained by women during the war was the most troublesome problem facing these writers as they sought to offer guidelines for re-establishing a division of power and responsibility in the veteran's marriage. A large amount of literature dealt with the question of wives' employment outside the home in the context of general economic stability and much of it either assumed that women would retire from their jobs in favor of veterans or urged them to do so. The writers analyzed in this paper, however, focused on the effect of women's employment on the marital relationship. In an essay addressed to veterans Margaret Mead recognized their anxiety concerning women's employment and sought to reassure them by minimizing the amount of change. She pointed to the long-term trend of women's employment outside the home and argued that "the war has speeded the process up a little, that's all." She predicted that after the war, as before, most women would work between completing school and marriage or the appearance of the first child; some would go back to work after their children were grown, and an increasing number would work in the absence of husbands or others to support them. Mead concluded that "far from wanting to get out of the home, during the years they are needed in it, more women will want, if possible, to devote themselves to their homes and children."

Other writers seemed less certain about women's own plans and offered suggestions for dealing with the possibility that women would want to continue in their jobs. Underlying such advice was the assumption that masculine status deriving from productivity was critical to family stability and took precedence over women's needs for self-expression. John Mariano believed that an employed wife was only a little better than divorce: "A wife should be kept at home, but if she has (worked) . . . this counsel might prove unpalatable to the point even where it threatens to disrupt marriage if enforced." On the other hand, Pratt emphasized that many women needed outlets for creativity, competence, interesting work and new friendships; such women would be better wives and mothers if they could fulfill these needs through a job. Most writers fell between these two extremes and tended to treat the subject gingerly. Two authors suggested that when wives' jobs threatened husbands, it was wise for women to concede for the time being: the husband might change later "if you yield now gracefully and lovingly. . . ." Others recognized the importance of employment to women, but emphasized their primary duty to the family. Dumas and Keen insisted that while a woman may prefer to go on with her career, she had accepted responsibility for "making a home . . . and her personal problems must be solved with full consideration for this obligation to the comfort and happiness of . . . others." Approving the work of women during the war, Kitching also warned that women's economic competence was likely "to raise problems in the future," and that women should realize that "reunion means relinquishing it—to some extent at any rate." Even a writer who considered "as remote as the bustle" the attitude that women's place was limited to the home, when discussing the attempt of a wife to decide whether to work after the war, loaded the question: "Should Jenny try to get a suitable job or should she prepare to become a good wife and mother?"

The appropriate position for a wife to take, according to most of these writers, was portrayed in a popular book (later, a movie), *Since You Went Away*. Describing her new job on a newspaper, the heroine wrote to her husband:

> I'll try never to sound like a lady executive or be anything but helpless. . . . Because if I did you might stop loving me—and that . . . is more important than all the papers in the world.

The advice to women was not without its contradictions, and women were also cautioned about attempting to relinquish their responsibility for family management too quickly. Several writers predicted that some veterans would be unable to deal with domestic problems right away. Often a veteran was not "ready emotionally to become the family man"; these burdens were "the last thing the returning GI wants right away." Men frequently returned unable to endure the "demands of domestic and civilian life," and a woman should not "burden a harrassed man . . . with her anxieties and insecurities."

Nonetheless, most of the advice literature disclosed a fear that women had changed, had matured and grown in ways that posed a threat to family stability. Thus the writers asked women to conceal or to reverse those changes; or they assumed that those changes could not be permanent because they conflicted with the "female nature." Only a few wrote encouragingly about women's self-development. These commentators noted that war matured men and suggested that reunion would be more satisfactory if women too attained greater maturity and intellectual growth. In the Federation of Business and Professional Women's *Independent Woman*, Sylvia Hahn wrote that servicemen had grown more knowledgeable and had higher standards and expectations. Women should try to live up to them by learning more about the world and current events, keeping up with new literary and cultural trends, developing fitness and athletic abilities, and contributing as much as possible to the war effort. Then, you will be "so nice to come home to." Here too however, the emphasis was on the returning veterans' needs and interests and on the responsibility of women for making the accommodations to them.

Before forming conclusions about the literature on the role of women in veterans' readjustment, it is useful to look at the possibilities and limitations of prescriptive literature as a means of understanding the historical development of sex roles. As Carl Degler has pointed out in a different context, historians must be cautious about depending upon advice literature for describing either generally held attitudes or actual behavior. At the very least, we can say that the attitudes reported here represent the views of one significant group of opinion leaders. They revealed above all anxiety and uncertainty about sex roles. If they presented images of women which were less than flattering and sometimes contradictory, these writers also viewed men with some ambivalence—on the one hand as heroic, and, on the other as childlike and dependent. A sense of guilt over their own failure to make the sacrifices required of servicemen may account for the tendency of these predominantly male writers to emphasize the severity of the veterans' burdens. In displacing such guilt on women, these writers were part of a larger trend in the popular psychology and sociology of the period which saw women as the cause and/or potential redeemers of a deteriorating society.

In addition, the advice literature suggests some speculations about women's experiences. If women did not in fact conform to these prescriptions, they were likely to suffer some anxiety over failing to live up to the standards of experts, and, according to these experts, the expectations of their returning men. On the other hand, since many of the prescriptions would come naturally to women conditioned to traditional sex roles, now welcoming back loved ones who had endured at least interruptions of career and family life, and at worst the horrors of combat, such advice could only reinforce those roles. Finally, it should be noted that a portion of this literature was in fact descriptive. Since many of the writers were veterans themselves, or clinicians dealing directly with military personnel, their words did to some extent reflect veterans' expectations as well as the proclivities of their wives to live up to them.

Whether greeted approvingly, or noted anxiously—as was more often the case—the potential for wartime crisis to equalize sex roles formed an overwhelming consensus among opinion leaders during World War II. Only a few dissented. Psychiatrist Edwin Krause, noting that war put a premium on men's lives, increased their prestige and cast them in heroic roles, believed that war represented a "disturbance of the peacetime trend toward an equalization on the sexes." Pearl Buck insisted even more strongly on war's detrimental effects upon women's status, arguing that "every war sets women back a generation. . . ."

When peace came women would have to relinquish most of their economic gains or "they would be called ungrateful. . . ." Moreover,

> Psychologically and emotionally, war sets women back both in man's mind and their own. For man comes home from war a spoiled creature, and one too often weakened by self-pity and conceit. He has to be pampered and praised into considering himself a hero . . . and everyday life is flat after the war, and his wife must go on with the pampering and praising or he will feel her unappreciative.

It is not necessary to accept Buck's stereotypical portrayal of the veteran to recognize in retrospect the validity of the dissenting view on war and women's status. Although writers of advice literature expressed anxiety that women had changed significantly (an unrealistic fear, I think), their counsel promoted traditional sex role behavior. They advocated attention to the male ego, the necessity for rebuilding it, and the importance of women conceding some of their newly found competence and economic independence. Sexual polarization, diminished during the war to the extent that women took on more historically male responsibilities, was in other ways strengthened. Male exclusiveness was promoted by the military experience, male bonding was accepted and even encouraged in its aftermath. The sexual double standard was reinforced on the grounds that the horrors of war both excused male infidelity and required female faithfulness. Finally, a premium was placed on women's femininity. While many of the prescribed characteristics of femininity were then and are still vitally important to society and worthy in themselves, their ascription to a single sex reinforced sexual polarization and its inherent inequality.

Whatever the specific problems in reunion and regardless of the specific suggestions for resolving them, the advice literature above all portrayed women as the responders and adapters. While women were assigned the crucial responsibility for solving this major postwar problem, they were to do in terms of traditional female roles. Through self-abnegation, by putting the needs of the veteran first, women might successfully renew their war-broken relationships, but they would do so at the price of their own autonomy.

14

The Atomic Bomb and the Origins of the Cold War

MARTIN J. SHERWIN

• In early August 1945, Japan was prostrate before the economic and military power of the United States. Its once proud Imperial Fleet and great battleships were at the bottom of the Pacific, its best-trained pilots were dead, its army was decimated by hopeless defenses of isolated islands, its skies were violated with impunity by the bombers of the American army and navy, and its population was practically starving. If that was not enough, the Soviet Union was already shifting its armies from Germany and Europe to the Far East, where they would attack Japanese forces on the Asian mainland.

In such circumstances, was the United States justified in dropping atomic bombs on Hiroshima and Nagasaki? Would the Japanese have realized the hopelessness of their position even without the introduction of nuclear weapons? Could the bombs have had an equivalent psychological impact if they had been dropped in rural areas rather than in the midst of crowded cities? Was the atomic bomb the last shot of World War II or the first shot of the Cold War?

Although such questions have inspired a large and diversified literature, perhaps no one has approached the subject with more care and clarity than Martin J. Sherwin of Tufts University. As you read his article, and especially as you reflect upon the statement by University of Chicago scientists in the final paragraph, you might attempt to imagine yourself as the diplomatic representative of another nation—perhaps France or Russia or Japan. What reasons would they have had for assuming that the ultimate weapon was anything more or less than an instrument for advancing American foreign policy? Do you think that the United States was then,

From the *American Historical Review*, 78 (October 1973). Reprinted by permission of the author. Martin J. Sherwin, Walter S. Dickson Professor of History at Tufts University, is author of *A World Destroyed: The Atomic Bomb and The Grand Alliance* (1975).

or is now, willing to share its military secrets for the benefit
of mankind?

During the second World War the atomic bomb was seen and valued
as a potential rather than an actual instrument of policy. Responsible
officials believed that its impact on diplomacy had to await its development and, perhaps, even a demonstration of its power. As Henry L.
Stimson, the secretary of war, observed in his memoirs: "The bomb as
a merely probable weapon had seemed a weak reed on which to rely,
but the bomb as a colossal reality was very different." That policymakers considered this difference before Hiroshima has been well documented, but whether they based wartime diplomatic policies upon an
anticipated successful demonstration of the bomb's power remains a
source of controversy. Two questions delineate the issues in this debate. First, did the development of the atomic bomb affect the way
American policymakers conducted diplomacy with the Soviet Union?
Second, did diplomatic considerations related to the Soviet Union
influence the decision to use the atomic bomb against Japan?

These important questions relating the atomic bomb to American
diplomacy, and ultimately to the origins of the cold war, have been
addressed almost exclusively to the formulation of policy during the
early months of the Truman administration. As a result, two anterior
questions of equal importance, questions with implications for those
already posed, have been overlooked. Did diplomatic considerations
related to Soviet postwar behavior influence the formulation of Roosevelt's atomic-energy policies? What effect did the atomic legacy Truman inherited have on the diplomatic and atomic-energy policies of
his administration?

To comprehend the nature of the relationship between atomic-
energy and diplomatic policies that developed during the war, the
bomb must be seen as policymakers saw it before Hiroshima, as a
weapon that might be used to control postwar diplomacy. For this task
our present view is conceptually inadequate. After more than a quarter century of experience we understand, as wartime policy makers did
not, the bomb's limitations as a diplomatic instrument. To appreciate
the profound influence of the unchallenged wartime assumption about
the bomb's impact on diplomacy we must recognize the postwar purposes for which policymakers and their advisers believed the bomb

could be used. In this effort Churchill's expectations must be scruti-
nized as carefully as Roosevelt's, and scientists' ideas must be considered along with those of politicians. Truman's decision to use the
atomic bomb against Japan must be evaluated in the light of Roosevelt's atomic legacy, and the problems of impending peace must be
considered along with the exigencies of war. To isolate the basic
atomic-energy policy alternatives that emerged during the war requires that we first ask whether alternatives were, in fact, recognized.

What emerges most clearly from a close examination of wartime formulation of atomic-energy policy is the conclusion that policy makers
never seriously questioned the assumption that the atomic bomb
should be used against Germany or Japan. From October 9, 1941, the
time of the first meeting to organize the atomic-energy project, Stimson, Roosevelt, and other members of the "top policy group" conceived of the development of the atomic bomb as an essential part of
the total war effort. Though the suggestion to build the bomb was
initially made by scientists who feared that Germany might develop
the weapon first, those with political responsibility for prosecuting the
war accepted the circumstances of the bomb's creation as sufficient
justification for its use against any enemy.

Having nurtured this point of view during the war, Stimson charged
those who later criticized the use of the bomb with two errors. First,
these critics asked the wrong question: it was not whether surrender
could have been obtained without using the bomb, but whether a different diplomatic and military course from that followed by the Truman administration would have achieved an earlier surrender. Second,
the basic assumption of these critics was false: the idea that American
policy should have been based primarily on a desire not to employ
the bomb seemed as "irresponsible" as a policy controlled by a positive desire to use it. The war, not the bomb, Stimson argued, had been
the primary focus of his attention; as secretary of war his responsibilities permitted no alternative.

Stimson's own wartime diary nevertheless indicates that from 1941
on, the problems associated with the atomic bomb moved steadily
closer to the center of his own and Roosevelt's concerns. As the war
progressed, the implications of the weapon's development became
diplomatic as well as military, postwar as well as wartime. Recognizing
that a monopoly of the atomic bomb gave the United States a pow-

erful new military advantage, Roosevelt and Stimson became increasingly anxious to convert it to diplomatic advantage. In December 1944 they spoke of using the "secret" of the atomic bomb as a means of obtaining a *quid pro quo* from the Soviet Union. But viewing the bomb as a potential instrument of diplomacy, they were not moved to formulate a concrete plan for carrying out this exchange before the bomb was used. The bomb had "this unique peculiarity," Stimson noted several months later in his diary; "Success is 99% assured, yet only by the first actual war trial of the weapon can the actual certainty be fixed." Whether or not the specter of postwar Soviet ambitions created "a positive desire" to ascertain the bomb's power, until that decision was executed "atomic diplomacy" remained an idea that never crystallized into policy.

Although Roosevelt left no definitive statement assigning a postwar role to the atomic bomb, his expectations for its potential diplomatic value can be recalled from the existing record. An analysis of the policies he chose from among the alternatives he faced suggests that the potential diplomatic value of the bomb began to shape his atomic-energy policies as early as 1943. He may have been cautious about counting on the bomb as a reality during the war, but he nevertheless consistently chose policy alternatives that would promote the postwar diplomatic potential of the bomb if the predictions of scientists proved true. These policies were based on the assumption that the bomb could be used effectively to secure postwar diplomatic aims; and this assumption was carried over from the Roosevelt to the Truman administration.

Despite general agreement that the bomb would be an extraordinarily important diplomatic factor after the war, those closely associated with its development did not agree on how to use it most effectively as an instrument of diplomacy. Convinced that wartime atomic-energy policies would have postwar diplomatic consequences, several scientists advised Roosevelt to adopt policies aimed at achieving a postwar international control system. Churchill, on the other hand, urged the president to maintain the Anglo-American atomic monopoly as a diplomatic counter against the postwar ambitions of other nations—particularly against the Soviet Union. Roosevelt fashioned his atomic-energy policies from the choices he made between these conflicting recommendations. In 1943 he rejected the counsel

of his science advisers and began to consider the diplomatic component of atomic-energy policy in consultation with Churchill alone.
This decision-making procedure and Roosevelt's untimely death have
left his motives ambiguous. Nevertheless it is clear that he pursued
policies consistent with Churchill's monopolistic, anti-Soviet views.

The findings of this study thus raise serious questions concerning
generalizations historians have commonly made about Roosevelt's diplomacy: that it was consistent with his public reputation for cooperation and conciliation; that he was naive with respect to postwar Soviet
behavior; that, like Wilson, he believed in collective security as an
effective guarantor of national safety; and that he made every possible
effort to assure that the Soviet Union and its allies would continue to
function as postwar partners. Although this article does not dispute
the view that Roosevelt desired amicable postwar relations with the
Soviet Union, or even that he worked hard to achieve them, it does
suggest that historians have exaggerated his confidence in (and perhaps his commitment to) such an outcome. His most secret and
among his most important long-range decisions—those responsible for
prescribing a diplomatic role for the atomic bomb—reflected his lack
of confidence. Finally, in light of this study's conclusions, the widely
held assumption that Truman's attitude toward the atomic bomb was
substantially different from Roosevelt's must also be revised.

Like the grand alliance itself, the Anglo-American atomic-energy partnership was forged by the war and its exigencies. The threat of a German atomic bomb precipitated a hasty marriage of convenience between British research and American resources. When scientists in
Britain proposed a theory that explained how an atomic bomb might
quickly be built, policy makers had to assume that German scientists
were building one. "If such an explosive were made," Vannevar Bush,
the director of the Office of Scientific Research and Development,
told Roosevelt in July 1941, "it would be thousands of times more
powerful than existing explosives, and its use might be determining."
Roosevelt assumed nothing less. Even before the atomic-energy project was fully organized he assigned it the highest priority. He wanted
the program "pushed not only in regard to development, but also
with due regard to time. This is very much of the essence," he told
Bush in March 1942. "We both felt painfully the dangers of doing

nothing," Churchill recalled, referring to an early wartime discussion with Roosevelt about the bomb.

The high stakes at issue during the war did not prevent officials in Great Britain or the United States from considering the postwar implications of their atomic-energy decisions. As early as 1941, during the debate over whether to join the United States in an atomic-energy partnership, members of the British government's atomic-energy committee argued that the matter "was so important for the future that work should proceed in Britain." Weighing the obvious difficulties of proceeding alone against the possible advantages of working with the United States, Sir John Anderson, then lord president of the council and the minister responsible for atomic-energy research, advocated the partnership. As he explained to Churchill, by working closely with the Americans British scientists would be able "to take up the work again [after the war], not where we left off, but where the combined effort had by then brought it."

As early as October 1942 Roosevelt's science advisers exhibited a similar concern with the potential postwar value of atomic energy. After conducting a full-scale review of the atomic-energy project, James B. Conant, the president of Harvard University and Bush's deputy, recommended discontinuing the Anglo-American partnership "as far as development and manufacture is concerned." Conant had in mind three considerations when he suggested a more limited arrangement with the British: first, the project had been transferred from scientific to military control; second, the United States was doing almost all the developmental work; and third, security dictated "moving in a direction of holding much more closely the information about the development of this program." Under these conditions it was difficult, Conant observed, "to see how a joint British-American project could be sponsored in this country." What prompted Conant's recommendations, however, was his suspicion—soon to be shared by other senior atomic-energy administrators—that the British were rather more concerned with information for postwar industrial purposes than for wartime use. What right did the British have to the fruits of American labor? "We were doing nine-tenths of the work," Stimson told Roosevelt in October. By December 1942 there was general agreement among the president's atomic-energy advisers that the British no longer had a valid claim to all atomic-energy information.

Conant's arguments and suggestions for a more limited partnership were incorporated into a "Report to the President by the Military Policy Committee." Roosevelt approved the recommendations on December 28. Early in January the British were officially informed that the rules governing the Anglo-American atomic-energy partnership had been altered on "orders from the top."

By approving the policy of "restricted interchange" Roosevelt undermined a major incentive for British cooperation. It is not surprising, therefore, that Churchill took up the matter directly with the president and with Harry Hopkins, "Roosevelt's own, personal Foreign Office." The prime minister's initial response to the new policy reflected his determination to have it reversed: "That we should each work separately," he threatened, "would be a sombre decision."

Conant and Bush understood the implications of Churchill's intervention and sought to counter its effect. "It is our duty," Conant wrote Bush, "to see to it that the President of the United States, in writing, is informed of what is involved in these decisions." Their memorandums no longer concentrated on tortuous discussions differentiating between the scientific research and the manufacturing stages of the bomb's development but focused on what to Conant was "the major consideration . . . that of *national security and postwar strategic significance.*" Information on manufacturing an atomic bomb, Conant noted, was a "military secret which is in a totally different class from anything the world has ever seen if the potentialities of this project are realized." To provide the British with detailed knowledge about the construction of a bomb "might be the equivalent to joint occupation of a fortress or strategic harbor in perpetuity." Though British and American atomic-energy policies might coincide during the war, Conant and Bush expected them to conflict afterward.

The controversy over the policy of "restricted interchange" of atomic-energy information shifted attention to postwar diplomatic considerations. As Bush wrote to Hopkins, "We can hardly give away the fruits of our developments as a part of postwar planning except on the basis of some overall agreement on that subject, which agreement does not now exist." The central issue was clearly drawn. The atomic-energy policy of the United States was related to the very fabric of Anglo-American postwar relations and, as Churchill would insist, to postwar relations between each of them and the Soviet Union. Just as the possibility of British postwar commercial competition had played a major role in shaping the U.S. policy of restricted interchange, the specter of Soviet postwar military power played a major role in shaping the prime minister's attitude toward atomic-energy policies in 1943.

"We cannot," Sir John Anderson wrote Churchill, "afford after the war to face the future without this weapon and rely entirely on America should Russia or some other power develop it." The prime minister agreed. The atomic bomb was an instrument of postwar diplomacy that Britain had to have. He could cite numerous reasons for his determination to acquire an independent atomic arsenal after the war, but Great Britain's postwar military-diplomatic position with respect to the Soviet Union invariably led the list. When Bush and Stimson visited London in July, Churchill told them quite frankly that he was "vitally interested in the possession of all [atomic-energy] information because this will be necessary for Britain's independence in the future as well as for success during the war." Nor was Churchill evasive about his reasoning: "It would never do to have Germany or Russia win the race for something which might be used for international blackmail," he stated bluntly and then pointed out that "Russia might be in a position to accomplish this result unless we worked together." In Washington, two months earlier, Churchill's science adviser Lord Cherwell had told Bush and Hopkins virtually the same thing. The British government, Cherwell stated, was considering "the whole [atomic-energy] affair on an after-the-war military basis." It intended, he said, "to manufacture and produce the weapon." Prior to the convening of the Quebec Conference, Anderson explained his own and Churchill's view of the bomb to the Canadian prime minister, MacKenzie King. The British knew, Anderson said, "that both Germany and Russia were working on the same thing," which, he noted, "would be a terrific factor in the postwar world as giving an absolute control to whatever country possessed the secret." Convinced that the British attitude toward the bomb would undermine any possibility of postwar cooperation with the Soviet Union, Bush and Conant vigorously continued to oppose any revival of the Anglo-American atomic-energy partnership.

On July 20, however, Roosevelt chose to accept a recommendation from Hopkins to restore full partnership, and he ordered Bush to "renew, in an inclusive manner, the full exchange of information with the British." A garbled trans-Atlantic cable to Bush reading "review" rather than "renew" gave him the opportunity to continue his negotiations in London with Churchill and thereby to modify the president's order. But Bush could not alter Roosevelt's intentions. On August 19, at the Quebec Conference, the president and the prime minister agreed that the British would share the atomic bomb. Despite Bush's negotiations with Churchill, the Quebec Agreement revived the principle of an Anglo-American atomic-energy partnership, albeit the British were reinstated as junior rather than equal partners.

The president's decision was not a casual one taken in ignorance. As the official history of the Atomic Energy Commission notes: "Both Roosevelt and Churchill knew that the stake of their diplomacy was a technological breakthrough so revolutionary that it transcended in importance even the bloody work of carrying the war to the heartland of the Nazi foe." The president had been informed of Churchill's position as well as of Bush's and Conant's. But how much closer Roosevelt was to Churchill than to his own advisers at this time is suggested by a report written after the war by General Leslie R. Groves, military director of the atomic-energy project. "It is not known what if any Americans President Roosevelt consulted at Quebec," Groves wrote. "It is doubtful if there were any. All that is known is that the Quebec Agreement was signed by President Roosevelt and that, as finally signed, it agreed practically in toto with the version presented by Sir John Anderson to Dr. Bush in Washington a few weeks earlier."

The debate that preceded the Quebec Agreement is noteworthy for yet another reason: it led to a new relationship between Roosevelt and his atomic-energy advisers. After August 1943 the president did not consult with them about the diplomatic aspects of atomic-energy policy. Though he responded politely when they offered their views, he acted decisively only in consultation with Churchill. Bush and Conant appear to have lost a large measure of their influence because they had used it to oppose Churchill's position. What they did not suspect was the extent to which the president had come to share the prime minister's view.

It can be argued that Roosevelt, the political pragmatist, renewed the wartime atomic-energy partnership to keep relations with the British harmonious rather than disrupt them on the basis of a postwar issue. Indeed it seems logical that the president took this consideration into account. But it must also be recognized that he was perfectly comfortable with the concept Churchill advocated—that military power was a prerequisite to successful postwar diplomacy. As early as August 1941, during the Atlantic Conference, Roosevelt had rejected the idea that an "effective international organization" could be relied upon to keep the peace; an Anglo-American international police force would be far more effective, he told Churchill. By the spring of 1942 the concept had broadened: the two "policemen" became four, and the idea was added that every other nation would be totally disarmed. "The Four Policemen" would have "to build up a reservoir of force so powerful that no aggressor would dare to challenge it," Roosevelt told Arthur Sweetser, an ardent internationalist. Violators first would be quarantined, and, if they persisted in their disruptive activities, bombed at the rate of a city a day until they agreed to behave. The president told Molotov about this idea in May, and in November he repeated it to Clark Eichelberger, who was coordinating the activities of the American internationalists. A year later, at the Teheran Conference, Roosevelt again discussed his idea, this time with Stalin. As Robert A. Divine has noted: "Roosevelt's concept of big power domination remained the central idea in his approach to international organization throughout World War II."

Precisely how Roosevelt expected to integrate the atomic bomb into his plans for keeping the peace in the postwar world is not clear. However, against the background of his atomic-energy policy decisions of 1943 and his peace-keeping concepts, his actions in 1944 suggest that he intended to take full advantage of the bomb's potential as a postwar instrument of Anglo-American diplomacy. If Roosevelt thought the bomb could be used to create a more peaceful world order, he seems to have considered the threat of its power more effective than any opportunities it offered for international cooperation. If Roosevelt was less worried than Churchill about Soviet postwar ambitions, he was no less determined than the prime minister to avoid any commitments to the Soviets for the international control of atomic energy. There could still be four policemen, but only two of them would have the bomb.

The atomic-energy policies Roosevelt pursued during the remainder of his life reinforce this interpretation of his ideas for the postwar period. The following three questions offer a useful framework for analyzing his intentions. Did Roosevelt make any additional agreements with Churchill that would further support the view that he intended to maintain an Anglo-American monopoly after the war? Did Roosevelt demonstrate any interest in the international control of atomic energy? Was Roosevelt aware that an effort to maintain an Anglo-American monopoly of the atomic bomb might lead to a postwar atomic arms race with the Soviet Union?

An examination of the wartime activities of the eminent Danish physicist, Niels Bohr, who arrived in America early in 1944 as a consultant to the atomic-bomb project, will help answer these questions. "Officially and secretly he came to help the technical enterprise," noted J. Robert Oppenheimer, the director of the Los Alamos atomic-bomb laboratory, but "most secretly of all . . . he came to advance his case and his cause." Bohr was convinced that a postwar atomic armaments race with the Soviet Union was inevitable unless Roosevelt and Churchill initiated efforts during the war to establish the international control of atomic energy. Bohr's attempts to promote this idea in the United States were aided by Justice Felix Frankfurter.

Bohr and Frankfurter were old acquaintances. They had first met in 1933 at Oxford and then in 1939 on several occasions in London and the United States. At these meetings Bohr had been impressed by the breadth of Frankfurter's interests and, perhaps, overimpressed with his influence on Roosevelt. In 1944 the Danish minister to the United States brought them together, once again, at his home in Washington. Frankfurter, who appears to have suspected why Bohr had come to America and why this meeting had been arranged, had learned about the atomic-bomb project earlier in the war when, as he told the story, several troubled scientists had sought his advice on a matter of "greatest importance." He therefore invited Bohr to lunch in his chambers and, by dropping hints about his knowledge, encouraged Bohr to discuss the issue.

After listening to Bohr's analysis of the postwar alternatives—an atomic armaments race or some form of international control—Frankfurter saw Roosevelt. Bohr had persuaded him, Frankfurter reported, that disastrous consequences would result if Russia learned on her own about the atomic-bomb project. Frankfurter suggested that it was a matter of great importance that the president explore the possibility of seeking an effective arrangement with the Soviets for controlling the bomb. He also noted that Bohr, whose knowledge of Soviet science was extensive, believed that the Russians had the capability to build their own atomic weapons. If the international control of atomic energy was not discussed among the Allies during the war, an atomic arms race between the Allies would almost certainly develop after the war. It seemed imperative, therefore, that Roosevelt consider approaching Stalin with a proposal as soon as possible.

Frankfurter discussed these points with the president for an hour and a half, and he left feeling that Roosevelt was "plainly impressed by my account of the matter." When Frankfurter had suggested that the solution of this problem might be more important than all the plans for a world organization, Roosevelt had agreed. Moreover he had authorized Frankfurter to tell Bohr, who was scheduled to return to England, that he might inform "our friends in London that the President was most eager to explore the proper safeguards in relation to X [the atomic bomb]." Roosevelt also told Frankfurter that the problem of the atomic bomb "worried him to death" and that he was very eager for all the help he could have in dealing with it.

The alternatives placed before Roosevelt posed a difficult dilemma. On the one hand, he could continue to exclude the Soviet government from any official information about the development of the bomb, a policy that would probably strengthen America's postwar military-diplomatic position. But such a policy would also encourage Soviet mistrust of Anglo-American intentions and was bound to make postwar cooperation more difficult. On the other hand, Roosevelt could use the atomic-bomb project as an instrument of cooperation by informing Stalin of the American government's intention of cooperating in the development of a plan for the international control of atomic weapons, an objective that might never be achieved.

Either choice involved serious risks. Roosevelt had to balance the diplomatic advantages of being well ahead of the Soviet Union in atomic-energy production after the war against the advantages of initiating wartime negotiations for postwar cooperation. The issue here, it must be emphasized, is not whether the initiative Bohr suggested would have led to successful international control, but rather whether

Roosevelt demonstrated any serious interest in laying the groundwork for such a policy.

Several considerations indicate that Roosevelt was already committed to a course of action that precluded Bohr's internationalist approach. First, Frankfurter appears to have been misled. Though Roosevelt's response had been characteristically agreeable, he did not mention Bohr's ideas to his atomic-energy advisers until September 1944, when he told Bush that he was very disturbed that Frankfurter had learned about the project. Roosevelt knew at this time, moreover, that the Soviets were finding out on their own about the development of the atomic bomb. Security personnel had reported an active Communist cell in the Radiation Laboratory at the University of California. Their reports indicated that at least one scientist at Berkeley was selling information to Russian agents. "They [Soviet agents] are already getting information about vital secrets and sending them to Russia," Stimson told the president on September 9, 1943. If Roosevelt was indeed worried to death about the effect the atomic bomb could have on Soviet-American postwar relations, he took no action to remove the potential danger, nor did he make any effort to explore the possibility of encouraging Soviet postwar cooperation on this problem. The available evidence indicates that he never discussed the merits of the international control of atomic energy with his advisers after this first or any subsequent meeting with Frankfurter.

How is the president's policy, of neither discussing international control nor promoting the idea, to be explained if not by an intention to use the bomb as an instrument of Anglo-American postwar diplomacy? Perhaps his concern for maintaining the tightest possible secrecy against German espionage led him to oppose any discussion about the project. Or he may have concluded, after considering Bohr's analysis, that Soviet suspicion and mistrust would be further aroused if Stalin were informed of the existence of the project without receiving detailed information about the bomb's construction. The possibility also exists that Roosevelt believed that neither Congress nor the American public would approve of a policy giving the Soviet Union any measure of control over the new weapon. Finally Roosevelt might have thought that the spring of 1944 was not the proper moment for such an initiative.

Though it would be unreasonable to state categorically that these considerations did not contribute to his decision, they appear to have been secondary. Roosevelt was clearly, and properly, concerned about secrecy, but the most important secret with respect to Soviet-American relations was that the United States was developing an atomic bomb. And that secret, he was aware, already had been passed on to Moscow. Soviet mistrust of Anglo-American postwar intentions could only be exacerbated by continuing the existing policy. Moreover an attempt to initiate planning for international control of atomic energy would not have required the revelation of technical secrets. Nor is it sufficient to cite Roosevelt's well-known sensitivity to domestic politics as an explanation for his atomic-energy policies. He was willing to take enormous political risks, as he did at Yalta, to support his diplomatic objectives.

Had Roosevelt avoided all postwar atomic-energy commitments, his lack of support for international control could have been interpreted as an attempt to reserve his opinion on the best course to follow. But he had made commitments in 1943 supporting Churchill's monopolistic, anti-Soviet position, and he continued to make others in 1944. On June 13, for example, Roosevelt and Churchill signed an Agreement and Declaration of Trust, specifying that the United States and Great Britain would cooperate in seeking to control available supplies of uranium and thorium ore both during and after the war. This commitment, taken against the background of Roosevelt's peace-keeping ideas and his other commitments, suggests that the president's attitude toward the international control of atomic energy was similar to the prime minister's.

Churchill had dismissed out of hand the concept of international control when Bohr talked with him about it in May 1944. Their meeting was not long under way before Churchill lost interest and became involved in an argument with Lord Cherwell, who was also present. Bohr, left out of the discussion, was frustrated and depressed; he was unable to return the conversation to what he considered the most important diplomatic problem of the war. When the allotted half hour elapsed, Bohr asked if he might send the prime minister a memorandum on the subject. A letter from Niels Bohr, Churchill bitingly replied, was always welcome, but he hoped it would deal with a subject other than politics. As Bohr described their meeting: "We did not even speak the same language."

Churchill rejected the assumption upon which Bohr's views were founded—that international control of atomic energy could be used as a cornerstone for constructing a peaceful world order. An atomic monopoly would be a significant diplomatic advantage in postwar diplomacy, and Churchill did not believe that anything useful could be gained by surrendering this advantage. The argument that a new weapon created a unique opportunity to refashion international affairs ignored every lesson Churchill read into history. "You can be quite sure," he would write in a memorandum less than a year later, "that any power that gets hold of the secret will try to make the article, and this touches the existence of human society. This matter is out of all relation to anything else that exists in the world, and I could not think of participating in any disclosure to third or fourth parties at the present time."

Several months after Bohr met Churchill, Frankfurter arranged a meeting between Bohr and Roosevelt. Their discussion lasted an hour and a half. Roosevelt told Bohr that contact with the Soviet Union along the lines he suggested had to be tried. The president also said he was optimistic that such an initiative would have a "good result." In his opinion Stalin was enough of a realist to understand the revolutionary importance of this development and its consequences. The president also expressed confidence that the prime minister would eventually share these views. They had disagreed in the past, he told Bohr, but they had always succeeded in resolving their differences.

Roosevelt's enthusiasm for Bohr's ideas was more apparent than real. The president did not mention them to anyone until he met with Churchill at Hyde Park on September 18, following the second wartime conference at Quebec. The decisions reached on atomic energy at Hyde Park were summarized and documented in an *aide-mémoire* signed by Roosevelt and Churchill on September 19, 1944. The agreement bears the markings of Churchill's attitude toward the atomic bomb and his poor opinion of Bohr. "Enquiries should be made," the last paragraph reads, "regarding the activities of Professor Bohr and steps taken to ensure that he is responsible for no leakage of information particularly to the Russians." If Bohr's activities prompted Roosevelt to suspect his loyalty, there can be no doubt that Churchill encouraged the president's suspicions. Atomic energy and Britain's future position as a world power had become part of a single equation for the prime minister. Bohr's ideas, like the earlier idea of restricted interchange, threatened the continuation of the Anglo-American atomic-energy partnership. With such great stakes at issue Churchill did not hesitate to discredit Bohr along with his ideas. "It seems to me," Churchill wrote to Cherwell soon after Hyde Park, "Bohr ought to be confined or at any rate made to see that he is very near the edge of mortal crimes."

The *aide-mémoire* also contained an explicit rejection of any war-time efforts toward international control: "The suggestion that the world should be informed regarding tube alloys [the atomic bomb], with a view to an international agreement regarding its control and use, is not accepted. The matter should continue to be regarded as of the utmost secrecy." But Bohr had never suggested that the world be informed about the atomic bomb. He had argued in memorandums and in person that peace was not possible unless the Soviet government—not the world—was officially notified only about the project's existence before the time when any discussion would appear coercive rather than friendly.

It was the second paragraph, however, that revealed the full extent of Roosevelt's agreement with Churchill's point of view. "Full collaboration between the United States and the British Government in developing tube alloys for military and commercial purposes," it noted, "should continue after the defeat of Japan unless and until terminated by joint agreement." Finally the *aide-mémoire* offers some insight into Roosevelt's intentions for the military use of the weapon in the war: "When a bomb is finally available, it might perhaps, after mature consideration, be used against the Japanese, who should be warned that this bombardment will be repeated until they surrender."

Within the context of the complex problem of the origins of the cold war the Hyde Park meeting is far more important than historians of the war generally have recognized. Overshadowed by the Second Quebec Conference on one side and by the drama of Yalta on the other, its significance often has been overlooked. But the agreements reached in September 1944 reflect a set of attitudes, aims, and assumptions that guided the relationship between the atomic bomb and American diplomacy during the Roosevelt administration and, through the transfer of its atomic legacy, during the Truman administration as well. Two alternatives had been recognized long before Roosevelt and

Churchill met in 1944 at Hyde Park: the bomb could have been used to initiate a diplomatic effort to work out a system for its international control, or it could remain isolated during the war from any cooperative initiatives and held in reserve should cooperation fail. Roosevelt consistently favored the latter alternative. An insight into his reasoning is found in a memorandum Bush wrote following a conversation with Roosevelt several days after the Hyde Park meeting: "The President evidently thought he could join with Churchill in bringing about a US-UK postwar agreement on this subject [the atomic bomb] by which it would be held closely and presumably to control the peace of the world." By 1944 Roosevelt's earlier musings about the four policemen had faded into the background. But the idea behind it, the concept of controlling the peace of the world by amassing overwhelming military power, appears to have remained a prominent feature of his postwar plans.

In the seven months between his meeting with Churchill in September and his death the following April Roosevelt did not alter his atomic-energy policies. Nor did he reverse his earlier decision not to take his advisers into his confidence about diplomatic issues related to the new weapon. They were never told about the Hyde Park agreements, nor were they able to discuss with him their ideas for the postwar handling of atomic-energy affairs. Though officially uninformed, Bush suspected that Roosevelt had made a commitment to continue the atomic-energy partnership exclusively with the British after the war, and he, as well as Conant, opposed the idea. They believed such a policy "might well lead to extraordinary efforts on the part of Russia to establish its own position in the field secretly, and might lead to a clash, say 20 years from now." Unable to reach the president directly, they sought to influence his policies through Stimson, whose access to Roosevelt's office (though not to his thoughts on atomic energy) was better than their own.

Summarizing their views on September 30 for the secretary of war, Bush and Conant predicted that an atomic bomb equivalent to from one to ten thousand tons of high explosive could be "demonstrated" before August 1, 1945. They doubted that the present American and British monopoly could be maintained for more than three or four years, and they pointed out that any nation with good technical and scientific resources could catch up; accidents of research, moreover, might even put some other nation ahead. In addition atomic bombs were only the first step along the road of nuclear weapons technology. In the not-too-distant future loomed the awesome prospect of a weapon perhaps a thousand times more destructive—the hydrogen bomb. Every major center of population in the world would then lie at the mercy of a nation that struck first in war. Security therefore could be found neither in secrecy nor even in the control of raw materials, for the supply of heavy hydrogen was practically unlimited.

These predictions by Bush and Conant were more specific than Bohr's, but not dissimilar. They, too, believed that a nuclear arms race could be prevented only through international control. Their efforts were directed, however, toward abrogating existing agreements with the British rather than toward initiating new agreements with the Soviets. Like Bohr they based their hope for Stalin's eventual cooperation on his desire to avoid the circumstances that could lead to a nuclear war. But while Bohr urged Roosevelt to approach Stalin with the carrot of international control before the bomb became a reality, Bush and Conant were inclined to delay such an approach until the bomb was demonstrated, until it was clear that without international control the new weapon could be used as a terribly effective stick.

In their attempt to persuade Roosevelt to their point of view Bush and Conant failed. But their efforts were not in vain. By March 1945 Stimson shared their concerns, and he agreed that peace without international control was a forlorn hope. Postwar problems relating to the atomic bomb "went right down to the bottom facts of human nature, morals and government, and it is by far the most searching and important thing that I have had to do since I have been here in the office of Secretary of War," Stimson wrote on March 5. Ten days later he presented his views on postwar atomic-energy policy to Roosevelt. This was their last meeting. In less than a month a new president took the oath of office.

Harry S. Truman inherited a set of military and diplomatic atomic-energy policies that included partially formulated intentions, several commitments to Churchill, and the assumption that the bomb would be a legitimate weapon to be used against Japan. But no policy was definitely settled. According to the Quebec Agreement the president had the option of deciding the future of the commercial aspects of the atomic-energy partnership according to his own estimate of what was fair. Although the policy of "utmost secrecy" had been confirmed at Hyde Park the previous September, Roosevelt had not informed his atomic-energy advisers about the *aide-mémoire* he and Churchill signed. Although the assumption that the bomb would be used in the war was shared by those privy to its development, assumptions formulated early in the war were not necessarily valid at its conclusion. Yet Truman was bound to the past by his own uncertain position and by the prestige of his predecessor. Since Roosevelt had refused to open negotiations with the Soviet government for the international control of atomic energy, and since he had never expressed any objection to the wartime use of the bomb, it would have required considerable political courage and confidence for Truman to alter those policies. Moreover it would have required the encouragement of his advisers, for under the circumstances the most serious constraint on the new president's choices was his dependence upon advice. So Truman's atomic legacy, while it included several options, did not necessarily entail complete freedom to choose from among all the possible alternatives.

"I think it is very important that I should have a talk with you as soon as possible on a highly secret matter," Stimson wrote to Truman on April 24. It has "such a bearing on our present foreign relations and has such an important effect upon all my thinking in this field that I think you ought to know about it without further delay." Stimson had been preparing to brief Truman on the atomic bomb for almost ten days, but in the preceding twenty-four hours he had been seized by a sense of urgency. Relations with the Soviet Union had declined precipitously during the past week, the result, he thought, of the failure of the State Department to settle the major problems between the Allies before going ahead with the San Francisco Conference on the United Nations Organization. The secretary of state, Edward R. Stettinius, Jr., along with the department's Soviet specialists, now felt "compelled to bull the thing through." To get out of the "mess" they had created, Stimson wrote in his diary, they were urging Truman to get tough with the Russians. He had. Twenty-four hours earlier the president met with the Soviet foreign minister, V. M. Molotov, and "with rather brutal frankness" accused his government of breaking the Yalta Agreement. Molotov was furious. "I have never been talked to like that in my life," he told the president before leaving.

With a memorandum on the "political aspects of the S-1 [atomic bomb's] performance" in hand and General Groves in reserve, Stimson went to the White House on April 25. The document he carried was the distillation of numerous decisions already taken, each one the product of attitudes that developed along with the new weapon. The secretary himself was not entirely aware of how various forces had shaped these decisions: the recommendations of Bush and Conant, the policies Roosevelt had followed, the uncertainties inherent in the wartime alliance, the oppressive concern for secrecy, and his own inclination to consider long-range implications. It was a curious document. Though its language revealed Stimson's sensitivity to the historic significance of the atomic bomb, he did not question the wisdom of using it against Japan. Nor did he suggest any concrete steps for developing a postwar policy. His objective was to inform Truman of the salient problems: the possibility of an atomic arms race, the danger of atomic war, and the necessity for international control if the United Nations Organization was to work. "If the problem of the proper use of this weapon can be solved," he wrote, "we would have the opportunity to bring the world into a pattern in which the peace of the world and our civilizations can be saved." To cope with this difficult challenge Stimson suggested the "establishment of a select committee" to consider the postwar problems inherent in the development of the bomb. If his presentation was the "forceful statement" of the problem that historians of the Atomic Energy Commission have described it as being, its force inhered in the problem itself, not in any bold formulations or initiatives he offered toward a solution. If, as another historian has claimed, this meeting led to a "strategy of delayed showdown," requiring "the delay of all disputes with Russia until the atomic bomb had been demonstrated," there is no evidence in the extant records of the meeting that Stimson had such a strategy in mind or that Truman misunderstood the secretary's views.

What emerges from a careful reading of Stimson's diary, his memorandum of April 25 to Truman, a summary by Groves of the meeting, and Truman's recollections is an argument for overall caution in American diplomatic relations with the Soviet Union: it was an argument against any showdown. Since the atomic bomb was potentially the most dangerous issue facing the postwar world and since the most desirable resolution of the problem was some form of international control, Soviet cooperation had to be secured. It was imprudent, Stimson suggested, to pursue a policy that would preclude the possibility of international cooperation on atomic-energy matters after the war ended. Truman's overall impression of Stimson's argument was that the secretary of war was "at least as much concerned with the role of the atomic bomb in the shaping of history as in its capacity to shorten the war." These were indeed Stimson's dual concerns on April 25, and he could see no conflict between them.

Despite the profound consequences Stimson attributed to the development of the new weapon, he had not suggested that Truman reconsider its use against Japan. Nor had he thought to mention the possibility that chances of securing Soviet postwar cooperation might be diminished if Stalin did not receive a commitment to international control prior to an attack. The question of why these alternatives were overlooked naturally arises. Perhaps what Frankfurter once referred to as Stimson's habit of setting "his mind at one thing like the needle of an old victrola caught in a single groove" may help to explain his not mentioning these possibilities. Yet Bush and Conant never raised them either. Even Niels Bohr had made a clear distinction between the bomb's wartime use and its postwar impact on diplomacy. "What role it [the atomic bomb] may play in the present war," Bohr had written to Roosevelt in July 1944, was a question "quite apart" from the overriding concern: the need to avoid an atomic arms race.

The preoccupation with winning the war obviously helped to create this seeming dichotomy between the wartime use of the bomb and the potential postwar diplomatic problems with the Soviet Union raised by its development. But a closer look at how Bohr and Stimson each defined the nature of the diplomatic problem created by the bomb suggests that for the secretary of war and his advisers (and ultimately for the president they advised) there was no dichotomy at all. Bohr apprehended the meaning of the new weapon even before it was developed, and he had no doubt that scientists in the Soviet Union would also understand its profound implications for the postwar world. He was also certain that they would interpret the meaning of the development to Stalin just as scientists in the United States and Great Britain had explained it to Roosevelt and Churchill. Thus the diplomatic problem, as Bohr analyzed it, was not the need to convince Stalin that the atomic bomb was an unprecedented weapon that threatened the life of the world but the need to assure the Soviet leader that he had nothing to fear from the circumstances of its development. By informing Stalin during the war that the United States intended to cooperate with him in neutralizing the bomb through international control, Bohr reasoned that its wartime use could be considered apart from postwar problems.

Stimson approached the problem rather differently. Although he believed that the bomb "might even mean the doom of civilization or it might mean the perfection of civilization" he was less confident than Bohr that the weapon in an undeveloped state could be used as an effective instrument of diplomacy. Until its "actual certainty [was] fixed," Stimson considered any prior approach to Stalin as premature. But as the uncertainties of impending peace became more apparent and worrisome, Stimson, Truman, and the secretary of state-designate, James F. Byrnes, began to think of the bomb as something of a diplomatic panacea for their postwar problems. Byrnes had told Truman in April that the bomb "might well put us in a position to dictate our own terms at the end of the war." By June, Truman and Stimson were discussing "further *quid pro quos* which should be established in consideration for our taking them [the Soviet Union] into [atomic-energy] partnership." Assuming that the bomb's impact on diplomacy would be immediate and extraordinary, they agreed on no less than "the settlement of the Polish, Rumanian, Yugoslavian, and Manchurian problems." But they also concluded that no revelation would be made "to Russia or anyone else until the first bomb had been successfully laid on Japan." Truman and Stimson based their expectations on how they saw and valued the bomb; its use against Japan, they reasoned, would transfer this view to the Soviet Union.

Was an implicit warning to Moscow, then, the principal reason for deciding to use the atomic bomb against Japan? In light of the ambiguity of the available evidence the question defies an unequivocal answer. What can be said with certainty is that Truman, Stimson, Byrnes, and several others involved in the decision consciously considered two effects of a combat demonstration of the bomb's power: first, the impact of the atomic attack on Japan's leaders, who might be persuaded thereby to end the war; and second, the impact of that attack on the Soviet Union's leaders, who might then prove to be more cooperative. But if the assumption that the bomb might bring the war to a rapid conclusion was the principal motive for using the atomic bomb, the expectation that its use would also inhibit Soviet diplomatic ambitions clearly discouraged any inclination to question that assumption.

Policymakers were not alone in expecting a military demonstration of the bomb to have a salubrious effect on international affairs. James Conant, for example, believed that such a demonstration would further the prospects for international control. "President Conant has written me," Stimson informed the news commentator Raymond Swing in February 1947, "that one of the principal reasons he had for advising me that the bomb must be used was that that was the only way to awaken the world to the necessity of abolishing war altogether." And the director of the atomic-energy laboratory at the University of Chicago made the same point to Stimson in June 1945: "If the bomb were not used in the present war," Arthur Compton noted, "the world would have no adequate warning as to what was to be expected if war should break out again." Even Edward Teller who has publicly decried the attack on Hiroshima and declared his early opposition to it, adopted a similar position in July 1945. "Our only hope is in getting the facts of our results before the people," he wrote to his colleague, Leo Szilard, who was circulating a petition among scientists opposing the bomb's use. "This might help to convince everybody that the next war would be fatal," Teller noted. "For this purpose actual combat use might even be the best thing."

Thus by the end of the war the most influential and widely accepted attitude toward the bomb was a logical extension of how the weapon was seen and valued earlier—as a potential instrument of diplomacy. Caught between the remnants of war and the uncertainties of peace, scientists as well as policy makers were trapped by the logic of their own unquestioned assumptions. By the summer of 1945 not only the conclusion of the war but the organization of an acceptable peace seemed to depend upon the success of the atomic attacks against Japan. When news of the successful atomic test of July 16 reached the president at the Potsdam Conference, he was visibly elated. Stimson noted that Truman "was tremendously pepped up by it and spoke to me of it again and again when I saw him. He said it gave him an entirely new feeling of confidence." The day after receiving the complete report of the test Truman altered his negotiating style. According to Churchill the president "got to the meeting after having read this report [and] he was a changed man. He told the Russians just where they got on and off and generally bossed the whole meeting." After the plenary session on July 24 Truman "casually mentioned to Stalin" that the United States had "a new weapon of unusual destructive force." Truman took this step in response to a recommendation by the Interim Committee, a group of political and scientific advisers organized by Stimson in May 1945 to advise the president on atomic-energy policy. But it is an unavoidable conclusion that what the president told the premier followed the letter of the recommendation rather than its spirit, which embodied the hope that an overture to Stalin would initiate the process toward international control. In less than three weeks the new weapon's destructive potential would be demonstrated to the world. Stalin would then be forced to reconsider his diplomatic goals. It is no wonder that upon learning of the raid against Hiroshima Truman exclaimed: "This is the greatest thing in history."

As Stimson had expected, as a colossal reality the bomb was very different. But had American diplomacy been altered by it? Those who conducted diplomacy became more confident, more certain that through the accomplishments of American science, technology and industry the "new world" could be made into one better than the old. But just how the atomic bomb would be used to help accomplish this ideal remained unclear. Three months and one day after Hiroshima was bombed Bush wrote that the whole matter of international relations on atomic energy "is in a thoroughly chaotic condition." The wartime relationship between atomic-energy policy and diplomacy had been based upon the simple assumption that the Soviet government would surrender important geographical, political, and ideological objectives in exchange for the neutralization of the new weapon. As a result of policies based on this assumption American diplomacy and prestige suffered grievously: an opportunity to gauge the Soviet Union's response during the war to the international control of atomic energy was missed, and an atomic-energy policy for dealing with the Soviet government after the war was ignored. Instead of promoting American postwar aims, wartime atomic-energy policies made them more difficult to achieve. As a group of scientists at the University of Chicago's atomic-energy laboratory presciently warned the government in June 1945: "It may be difficult to persuade the world that a nation which was capable of secretly preparing and suddenly releasing a weapon as indiscriminate as the [German] rocket bomb and a million times more destructive, is to be trusted in its proclaimed desire of having such weapons abolished by international agreement." This reasoning, however, flowed from alternative assumptions formulated during the closing months of the war by scientists far removed from the wartime policy-making process. Hiroshima and Nagasaki, the culmination of that process, became the symbols of a new American barbarism, reinforcing charges, with dramatic circumstantial evidence, that the policies of the United States contributed to the origins of the cold war.

15

Truman vs. MacArthur:
The Last Battle of the American Caesar

WALTER KARP

• *Few American traditions are as sacred and as important as that of civilian control of the nation's armed forces. Generals and admirals, no matter how many stars or ribbons they wear, serve at the pleasure of the president. Under the terms of the United States Constitution, the President is the commander in chief of every military unit, and it is he who appoints even the lowliest second lieutenant to his or her office.*

In 1951, soon after the Chinese People's Liberation Army intervened in the Korean War, General of the Army Douglas MacArthur publicly disagreed with the policy of President Harry S. Truman not to allow American forces north of the Yalu River. MacArthur thus challenged one of the fundamental precepts of American government. And MacArthur was not just any officer. He was a five-star general and a bemedaled hero of two world wars. When he spoke, the nation listened.

Truman, who earlier had admonished the general to make no further public statements without clearing them in Washington, was furious with this latest outburst and removed MacArthur from his command. This action resulted in a public outcry in support of the general and outrage that Truman had replaced a great soldier who apparently wanted victory, not stalemate, in Korea.

MacArthur returned home to a hero's welcome and joyous ovations but after an initial flurry of excitement and publicity, including triumphal ticker tape parades in New York and other cities and a special address to a joint session of Con-

© American Heritage Publishing Co., Inc. Reprinted by permission from *American Heritage*, April/May 1984.

gress, the general drifted into obscurity and lived out his remaining years in the tower of the Waldorf-Astoria Hotel.
Ultimately, MacArthur lost more than the struggle about
military policy in limited wars. As historians began to look
more closely at his World War II record, they learned that
he had bungled the defense of the Philippines and very much
exaggerated his role in the conquest of Japan. He was disagreeable with his superiors and unpopular with his troops,
who called him "Dugout Doug" because of his ability to
avoid danger and to surround himself with photographers
and newsmen. Walter Karp's essay can thus be read as part
of the reevaluation of the man who was once called "the
American Caesar."

At 1:00 A.M. on the morning of April 11, 1951, a tense band of Washington reporters filed into the White House newsroom for an emergency press conference. Hastily summoned by the White House
switchboard, they had no idea of what was to come. The Truman administration, detested by millions, had grown hesitant, timid, and unpredictable. The Korean War, so boldly begun ten months before, had
degenerated into a "limited war" with no discernible limit, a bloody
stalemate. Some reporters, guessing, thought they were going to hear
about a declaration of war, that the administration was ready to carry
the fighting into China and bring it to a swift and victorious end.
That was what General Douglas MacArthur, supreme commander of
U.S. and United Nations forces in the Far East, had passionately been
urging for months, ever since Chinese communist troops had sent his
armies reeling in retreat from the Yalu River.

President Truman did not appear in the newsroom. His press secretary merely handed out copies of three terse presidential statements.
At 1:03 A.M. the great wire-service networks were carrying the news to
the ends of the earth. The President had not adopted the victory plans
of America's greatest living general. Instead he had relieved him of all
his commands, "effective at once." The President had acted because
"General of the Army Douglas MacArthur is unable to give his whole-
hearted support to the policies of the United States and the United
Nations."

With that announcement President Truman precipitated perhaps the most convulsive popular outburst in American history and the severest test which civilian control of the military has ever had to face in this republic. On April 11 there was little reason to believe that the faltering President would triumph over his vaunting general in the clash that must ensue.

Even before the news broke, the American people were upset. "A vast impatience, a turbulent bitterness, a rancor akin to revolt" coursed through the body politic, a contemporary historian observed. Dislike of communism, once a matter of course in America, had boiled into a national frenzy, devouring common prudence, common sense, and common decency. It was a time when school textbooks urged children to report suspicious neighbors to the FBI "in line with American tradition," a time when an entire city flew into a rage on learning that the geography lesson printed on children's candy wrappers dared to describe Russia as the "largest country in the world." Americans saw conspiracy in every untoward event: abroad, "Kremlin plots to conquer the world"; at home, communist plots to "take over the government." In April 1951 a substantial part of the citizenry believed that the secretary of state, Dean Acheson, was a "dupe" of the Kremlin, that the secretary of defense, George C. Marshall, a five-star general, was a "front man" for traitors in government. And now it seemed that a great general, World War II's most glamorous hero, had been mercilessly broken for daring to call for victory in Korea.

On the morning of April 11 only Western Union's rules of propriety kept Congress from being deluged with furious obscenity. "Impeach the B who calls himself President," read one telegram typical of those pouring into Washington at an unprecedented rate—125,000 within forty-eight hours. "Impeach the little ward politician stupidity from Kansas City," read another, voicing the contempt millions now felt for the "plucky Harry" of just a few years before. The letters and telegrams, the White House admitted, were running 20 to 1 against the President. So were the telephone calls that jangled in every newsroom and radio studio. In countless towns the President was hanged in effigy. Across the country flags flew at half-mast or upside down. Angry signs blossomed on houses: "To hell with the Reds and Harry Truman."

Wherever politicians met that day, the anger in the streets was echoed and amplified. In Los Angeles the city council adjourned for the day "in sorrowful contemplation of the political assassination of General MacArthur." In Michigan the state legislature solemnly noted that "at 1:00 A.M. of this day, World Communism achieved its greatest victory of a decade in the dismissal of General MacArthur." On the Senate floor in Washington, Republicans took turns denouncing the President: "I charge that this country today is in the hands of a secret inner coterie which is directed by agents of the Soviet Union. We must cut this whole cancerous conspiracy out of our Government at once," said William Jenner of Indiana. Truman had given "the Communists and their stooges . . . what they always wanted—MacArthur's scalp." So spoke the country's fastest-rising politician, Richard Nixon. Only four senators—two Democrats and two Republicans—dared defend the President.

For most Republican leaders in Congress the popular hysteria was manna in the political desert. Their best men—Ohio's Robert Taft most conspicuously—had felt doomed to perpetual impotence, spurned by an electorate that still revered the memory, and supported the policies, of the late Franklin Roosevelt. Now they saw their chance. They were determined to discredit the Democratic party and its stumbling President. At a hasty meeting on the morning of MacArthur's dismissal, Republican congressional leaders came to a decision. They intended to use every political resource at their disposal to channel popular anger over MacArthur's recall into a mass revolt against "limited war," against President Truman and the ghost of the Roosevelt New Deal.

It was a reckless decision; exalting MacArthur over the President, as Harold Ickes, the old Bull Moose Republican, was to warn a few days later, would set a "precedent" that would "develop into a monstrosity"—an uncontrollable military.

Such, in truth, were the stakes now at hazard. In the four months preceding his dismissal, General MacArthur had transgressed the fundamental rule of civilian supremacy, a rule given its classic formulation in Lincoln's stern instructions to Grant: "You are not to decide, discuss or confer with anyone or ask political questions; such questions the President holds in his own hands, and will submit them to no military conferences or conventions." What MacArthur had done was to carry out a public political campaign designed to discredit the President's policies and compel the White House to follow his own. For that the President had ordered his recall. If that recall were to end by destroying the President, if MacArthur, backed by a wave of popular support, were to force his policies on the civil authority, then for all practical purposes civilian supremacy over the military would become a dead letter. Given such a precedent, what future President would dare dismiss a popular general in wartime for publicly challenging his authority?

When the Republican meeting broke up at 10:00 A.M., the press was informed of the plan to exalt the general over the President. Republicans intended to demand a full-dress investigation of the President's war policies. That was remarkable enough considering that it was wartime. The second element in their plan, however, was more than remarkable. It had no precedent in our history. Republicans intended (if Democratic votes were forthcoming) to invite General MacArthur to address a joint session of Congress, the most august assembly the United States can provide. In the well of the House of Representatives, where only a handful of foreign statesmen and homecoming heroes had ever been allowed to speak, a rebellious, contumacious general was to be given his chance to defend his cause against the President of the United States.

What would MacArthur do? In Germany, General Eisenhower, supreme commander of Allied forces in Europe, expressed the sentiments of a good many Americans. He hoped the seventy-one-year-old general, his onetime superior, would drift quietly into retirement. "I would not like to see acrimony," Eisenhower remarked somewhat wistfully to a reporter. In fact, there was no chance that MacArthur would not carry his fight to the country.

By any standard General MacArthur was an awesome and prodigious figure. He possessed an uncommonly powerful intellect, one sharpened by vast erudition, intense meditation, and an extraordinary facility with words. He was utterly fearless, unshakably self-possessed, and relentlessly willful. At the White House the President had shrunk from confronting him for months. Moreover, MacArthur's strengths were magnified by the aura surrounding him. He was dramatic, compelling, aloof, and imperious, qualities he himself had cultivated with all the theatrical arts at his command. What was to govern his conduct in the ensuing months, however, were not his great gifts but a bitter flaw in his character—a blind, all consuming vanity. The general was vain in small ways; the famous MacArthur sunglasses, for example, disguised the prosaic fact of myopia. He was vain in his choice of associates; his entourage consisted of toadies and idolators. Vanity even colored his conceptions of grand strategy; the center of the world for MacArthur was always the military theater under his command. During World War II his military colleagues used to say the general had a bad case of "localitis." Vanity sometimes drove him to the borders of paranoia: a lifetime of triumphs could not efface his belief that homefront "cabals" were plotting his ruin, that "insidious forces" were stabbing him in the back. His worst enemies, MacArthur often said, had "always been behind me." Vanity led him, too, to that most perilous of convictions—an absolute faith in his own infallibility. Therein lay the crux of the matter, for that faith had been brutally assaulted five months earlier when Mac-Arthur's armies, poised for victory near the Yalu River, had fallen into a colossal Chinese trap. On November 24, 1950, America's greatest military strategist had presided over one of the worst defeats in the history of American arms. From that day forward General MacArthur was a man thirsting for vindication and vengeance. To drive the Chinese out of North Korea had become a fixed and obsessive goal. To break the administration that stood in his way had now become, of necessity, his political object. "He did not want facts or logic," as a longtime admirer, Carlos Romulo of the Philippines, was to put it after an interview with the general. "He wanted salve for his wounded pride." That was a dangerous motive, indeed, for a general who had become, overnight, the second most powerful man in America.

In the last years of the Roman Republic, people had watched with mounting tension as Pompey the Great made his triumphal return home from the East. So it was in America in mid-April of 1951 as MacArthur prepared to depart from Tokyo on his personal plane, the *Bataan*.

On April 13 Americans learned that the general, hastening his return, intended to reach America within a few days, destroying the hopes of the President's supporters that the popular fury would abate before MacArthur set foot on native soil. That day, too, Democratic leaders, under popular pressure, gave up their struggle to prevent Congress from inviting MacArthur to address a joint session. One slightly comical concession was all they would wrest from the onrushing Republican minority: officially the general would be addressing not a "joint session" but a "joint meeting."

On Sunday, April 15, newspaper headlines told of MacArthur's "triumphant goodby" from Japan, of the crowds lining the streets, of the Japanese dignitaries on hand for the departure. The triumphal progress had now begun, its ultimate destination the nation's capital, where, at exactly 12:30 P.M. on the nineteenth, it was now announced, the general would enter the House of Representatives and throw down his gauntlet to the President. Bulletins flashing over the nation's radios marked the progress of the general's plane. At 1:00 A.M. Eastern time on Monday, the *Bataan* passed over Wake Island; first stop, Honolulu. If the general was in official disgrace, there was no sign of it: at the Hawaiian capital MacArthur and his wife and thirteen-year-old son stopped over for twenty-four hours as the guest of Admiral Arthur W. Radford, commander in chief of America's naval forces in the Pacific. At Honolulu University the general received an honorary degree in civil law, an ironic honor considering that its recipient had by now convinced himself—as he was soon to say—that American generals had the constitutional right to say whatever they pleased in public regardless of the orders of their commander in chief. Far away in New York, the city fathers announced plans to greet the general with the biggest parade in the history of that city of ticker-tape acclamations.

On the evening of April 17 General MacArthur's plane touched down at San Francisco's airport, ending the general's fourteen-year absence from his country. At the airport ten thousand people, desperate for a glimpse of their hero, surged past police barricades, mobbing the general and his entourage. It was "an indescribable scene of pandemonium," one of MacArthur's aides recalled. Tens of thousands of automobiles jammed the roads for miles around, creating the worst traffic snarl in San Francisco's history. A half-million people lined the route from the airport to MacArthur's hotel, where a powerful police cordon alone kept the general from being trampled by his admirers. Twenty-eight hours later, at Washington's National Airport, pandemonium broke loose again with surging mobs, tumultuous cheers, and a battered police cordon trying to clear a space around the general, who remained, as always, calm and unruffled, the eye of the hurricane he had created.

At the White House the President took cold comfort from his professed belief that Americans were *not* hailing an insubordinate general nor embracing his "victory" policy but merely giving a belated welcome to the last World War II hero to return to America. Like the "joint meeting" of Congress, now just hours away, it was a distinction apparent to few.

At 12:31 P.M. on April 19 a record thirty million people tuned in their radios to hear General MacArthur address Congress, his countrymen, and the world. This was the moment every supporter of the President had dreaded. Truman's case for a limited war of attrition had not yet been effectively made. Half the country was not even aware that attrition was the chosen policy of the government. Even well-informed supporters of the President were not sure what the policy meant or why it was necessary. Now General MacArthur, backed by an adoring nation and armed with high gifts of intellect and eloquence, was about to speak against it.

"I address you with neither rancor nor bitterness in the fading twilight of life," the general began in his vibrant, well-modulated voice after the wild initial ovation had subsided. MacArthur devoted the first half of his speech to a lofty and lucid disquisition on the politics and destiny of the Orient. His object, he said, was to dispel the prevailing "unreality" of American thinking on the subject. His authority established, MacArthur proceeded to praise the administration for intervening in Korea—the only time that Democrats in the audience had a chance to applaud—and for attempting to drive the communists out of North Korea. That objective had lain in his grasp when the Chinese communists intervened in the struggle. "This created a new war and an entirely new situation." Yet the administration was not fighting that new war to win. It was not attempting to "defeat this new enemy as we had defeated the old." By confining the war against Chinese aggression to Korea, it was condemning the country to "prolonged indecision."

Yet the means to achieve victory were swift and sure. Three quite moderate military measures would drive the Chinese from the Korean peninsula: bombing China's "sanctuaries" in Manchuria; blockading the Chinese coast; unleashing Chiang Kai-shek's army, holed up in Formosa, for diversionary raids on the Chinese mainland. Such was MacArthur's plan "to bring hostilities to a close with the least possible delay." What was there to be said against it? "In war, indeed, there is no substitute for victory," said MacArthur, providing his supporters with their most potent slogan. " 'Why,' my soldiers asked of me, 'surrender military advantages to a enemy in the field?' " MacArthur's voice fell to a whisper: "I could not answer." Why fight Red China without attempting to drive her from Korea? This was a policy of "appeasement," said the general, hurling the deadliest epithet of the day at the Truman administration. Moreover, said MacArthur, his plan to carry the war to the Chinese mainland had been supported by "our own Joint Chiefs of Staff." With that assertion Republicans in the House gave the speaker a thunderous standing ovation, for, in fact, it was the most devastating remark in MacArthur's entire speech. In the prevailing atmosphere of derangement and conspiracy it implied that victory in Korea had been snatched from America's grasp not by the military judgment of the Pentagon but by a mere, meddlesome civilian, the President of the United States. MacArthur's assertion also posed a challenge to the Joint Chiefs themselves: he was daring them to side with the President when, as he fully believed, their purely military judgment agreed with his own.

For close observers that was the real news of the hour, the story that made the headlines. What stirred the rest of the country, however, was MacArthur's lush, emotional peroration. He recalled the old barracks ballad that "proclaimed, most proudly, that 'Old soldiers never die. They just fade away.' And like the soldier of the ballad, I now close my military career and just fade away—an old soldier who tried to do his duty as God gave him the light to see that duty." And then in a hushed voice: "Good-bye."

Generals in the audience openly wept. Legislators hurled themselves at the departing general, virtually prostrating themselves at his feet. "It's disloyal not to agree with General MacArthur!" one senator shouted from the floor. "We have heard God speak today. God in the flesh, the voice of God," shouted Representative Dewey Short of Missouri, who had been educated at Harvard, Oxford, and Heidelberg. The normally level-headed former President Herbert Hoover hailed MacArthur as the "reincarnation of St. Paul." Fury over his dismissal boiled up anew and newspaper offices again were besieged with vehement calls condemning the "traitorous" State Department and the "bankrupt haberdasher" who was "appeasing Red China." It boiled up, too, on the floor of the House. As one senator confided to a reporter later that day: "I have never feared more for the institutions of the country. I honestly felt that if the speech had gone on much longer there might have been a march on the White House."

MacArthur's powerful speech, a magniloquent contrast to the President's pawky little lectures, "visibly and profoundly shook" the President's supporters in Congress, as *The New York Times* reported. The President's cabinet, after watching MacArthur on a White House television set, sank into gloom, convinced that the general, in a single blow, had put a finish to the Truman administration. The welcoming parade for the general in New York City confirmed their worst fears.

MacArthur flew to the city on the evening of the nineteenth, settling into what was to be his home for the remaining thirteen years of his life: a palatial ten-room suite on the thirty-seventh floor of the Waldorf-Astoria. The hotel was to be the parade's point of departure. The general would be driven in an open car—the same that had carried General Eisenhower six years before—through Central Park, down to the Battery, up through the canyons of Wall Street, and homeward along Fifth Avenue—over nineteen miles in all. The triumphal progress was to begin at 11:00 A.M., but by dawn hundreds of thousands of people had already begun pouring into the city. By the time the general's motorcade had reached the financial district, some six million flag-waving enthusiasts were jamming the sidewalks, dwarfing Eisenhower's postwar parade and Lindbergh's almost legendary reception. Overhead in the bright, cloudless sky, airplanes spelled out "Welcome Home" in mile-long streamers. Shreds of paper fell in dense blizzards, covering people's feet to the ankles and darkening television screens for minutes at a time. As the general's car approached, the crowds craned hungrily forward, then burst into cheers, deafening in their volume, startling in their intensity. Not everyone shouted his acclaim. There were people who watched the general pass by in silence, faces rapt and grim, marking a cross on their breasts. New York, as MacArthur's bodyguard was to put it, had been turned into "a band of hysterical sheep"—hard-bitten, cynical New York, stronghold of the Democratic party.

Late that afternoon, while the general was passing up howling Fifth Avenue, a popular demonstration of a different sort took place at a baseball park in the nation's capital. As the President and his entourage were about to leave Griffith Stadium—Truman had thrown out the traditional first ball of the year—he was met with a storm of boos. Republicans were now saying the choice before the country was "Truman or MacArthur"; on April 20, Americans seemed already to have made it.

In his struggle with MacArthur, the President faced severe handicaps, most of them self-inflicted. The political derangement of the country was to a large extent his own doing. Determined to arouse the nation to the menace of Soviet expansion, yet convinced that he governed an obstinately "isolationist" people, Truman had never scrupled to exaggerate every danger, to sound alarms, to decry in any communist move he opposed another step in the "Kremlin plot for world conquest." Moreover, he had constantly used the great World War II generals—MacArthur included—to defend his policies and shield him from criticism. The results were inevitable. Because Truman had glorified the wisdom of the generals, he had weakened the civilian authority he was now forced to defend. Because he justified even prudent deeds with inflammatory words, it had become difficult to justify prudent deeds with prudent arguments—the sort of argument he was now forced to make.

The President's inept handling of the Korean War was the severest handicap of all. In June 1950 Truman had intervened to repel the North Korean invasion of South Korea, an essentially defensive objective. When North Korean armies began fleeing back beyond the thirty-eighth parallel, however, Truman made a momentous and disastrous decision. He directed General MacArthur to cross the parallel and liberate North Korea from communist control too. Thus it was Truman, not MacArthur, who had first defined victory in Korea as the extirpation of communism from the entire Korean peninsula. When four hundred thousand Chinese entered the fray, however, the administration changed its mind again. Without informing the electorate, Truman decided that liberating North Korea—victory—was a prize not worth the terrible risks involved. He was now content to confine the fighting to Korea until exhausted Chinese armies eventually decided to call it a day at the thirty-eighth parallel. The administration, in short, was fighting to restore Korea to the situation it had been in on the eve of the North Korean invasion—at the cost of sixty thousand American casualties by mid-April and with no truce in sight.

Such was the policy the administration now had to defend in the court of inflamed public opinion against the clarity and emotional force of MacArthur's crisp plan for "victory." In two major radio addresses, the President's first attempts to make a case for his policy proved ineffective. His two chief arguments simply lacked conviction. First, the bombing of Chinese supply lines would, he said, lead to a general war in Asia and possibly to World War III. Here a large majority of Americans simply preferred MacArthur's military judgment to the President's. Moreover, in citing the risks involved, Truman was compelled to argue that Korea was not all that important compared with the defense of Europe. The President, in effect, was belittling his own war, which did nothing to strengthen popular confidence in his judgment.

Truman's second argument was even less convincing. The stalemated war, he insisted, was already a resounding success. It had stopped in its tracks, said the President, the Kremlin's "carefully prepared plot for conquering all of Asia." It had "slowed down the timetable of conquest," he assured the country, invoking memories of Hitler's step-by-step conquest of Europe. Since the Kremlin "timetable" was entirely suppositious, the President could offer no evidence whatever of its alleged slowdown.

Republicans had no trouble tearing the President's speeches to shreds. They simply turned Truman's own Cold War propaganda against him. Time and again the administration had argued that "punishing aggression" in Korea was preventing World War III—more echoes of the Hitler years. If so, Republicans now argued, then why was the President unwilling to punish the Chinese aggressors. It was the President's "half-war" against Red China, not MacArthur's plan for victory, that was inviting World War III. As for the President's apparent willingness to settle for a truce at the thirty-eighth parallel, it would be a "sellout," a "super-Munich."

Most of all, Republicans struck at the very notion of fighting a "limited war." It was, wrote *Time*, "an idea unique in world history, that it is wrong and dangerous to fight the enemy in any place not of the enemy's choosing." It meant sacrificing American lives on "an altar of futility." It meant giving the enemy "privileged sanctuaries" outside

Korea from which to kill American boys more effectively. It "shocks our national sense of decency," said Senator Henry Cabot Lodge, himself no friend of MacArthur's. "Psychologically, no one will stand for it," said Seantor Taft, sadly abandoning his lifelong opposition to excessive overseas commitments.

Keenly aware of his fading powers of persuasion, Truman countered with dubious blows of his own. He "leaked" to *The New York Times* the secret White House notes of his October 15, 1950, meeting with MacArthur at Wake Island, a meeting in which, said the notes, MacArthur had confidently assured the President that there was "very little" chance of Chinese intervention in Korea. Stung for the first time, MacArthur retorted from the Waldorf that the administration, too, had misread Chinese intentions, although it had far greater intelligence resources than a mere theater commander possessed. This was quite true. Blaming MacArthur for disastrously misleading the President was grossly unfair, but "politics isn't beanbag," as Mr. Dooley had long before observed. A few days after the "leak," MacArthur once again demonstrated his extraordinary hold on his countrymen. A flying trip to the Midwest on April 26 brought in the latest returns from the grass roots: three million acclaimed him in Chicago, one million in Milwaukee. The general had not "faded away," but five different versions of "Old Soldiers Never Die" were now blaring from America's jukeboxes.

The stage was now set for the second half of the Republican campaign to exalt the general over the President. This was the forthcoming congressional investigation of the administration's Far Eastern policies, with the general as star witness for the Republican prosecution. Nobody knew at the time that the hearings would mark the beginning of the end for MacArthur. The confident Republicans demanded public, televised hearings, the largest possible audience for their hero and their weapon. Equally convinced of the President's weakness and none too sure of the Joint Chiefs of Staff, the Democrats fought desperately to keep the hearings secret, piously citing the need to prevent high matters of state from reaching enemy ears. It took several days of bitter parliamentary strife before the ground rules of the hearings were finally laid down. They were to be conducted jointly by the Senate Armed Services and Foreign Relations Committees—fourteen Democrats and twelve Republicans in all. Press, public, and even the House of Representatives were to be strictly excluded, but censored transcripts of the testimony would be released every hour to an avid public. In the very midst of war the military policies of the United States were to be subjected to intense and critical scrutiny as the struggle between President and general moved into the arena of a Senate caucus room. It was, as *The New York Times* put it, a "debate unprecedented in American and probably world history."

On the morning of May 3 the huge wooden doors of the caucus room banged shut on a horde of newsmen as General of the Army Douglas MacArthur took his seat as the hearing's first witness. Every major newspaper in the country planned to print his entire testimony. In the witness chair, *Time* noted, the general's "self-confidence was monumental." He carried no notes, consulted no aides, and answered every question without the slightest hesitation. While Democratic senators fumbled with their queries, he calmly puffed on a briar pipe.

As expected, he hit the administration hard. What was unexpected were his passionate outbursts. In a voice charged with emotion he accused the government again and again of wantonly squandering American lives. "I shrink—shrink with a horror that I cannot express in words—at this continuous slaughter of men. . . . Are you going to let that go by any sophistry of reasoning?" Administration arguments he dealt with skillfully. Its contention that a win-the-war policy would cost us our European allies he termed a mere pretext; the United States was already doing most of the fighting in Korea. Its contention that Russia, not China, was America's main enemy he adroitly denied by using the Truman Doctrine against Truman: the enemy was not Russia but "communism all over the world." He belittled the danger of Soviet intervention on Red China's behalf. It was the administration's policy of "appeasement" that invited aggression.

Once again MacArthur insisted that the Joint Chiefs had agreed with his plan. Their views and his were "practically identical." He even cited an official document that seemed to prove it: a January 12 memorandum from the Chiefs "tentatively" agreeing to some of the measures against China that the general was advocating. To MacArthur the document was conclusive. On January 12, 1951, the Joint Chiefs of Staff had not been persuaded by the "sophistry of reasoning" now being woven by the "politicians," MacArthur's contemptuous—and revealing—term for the civil government of the United States.

As propaganda in a war of headlines, MacArthur's three days of testimony proved powerful indeed. Nonetheless it revealed much that would soon prove detrimental to the general and his cause. Americans acclaimed him as a great military strategist, yet as a witness he sounded like a man so obsessed with striking back at China that he seemed deliberately blind to the risks. Americans saw him as an honest soldier, yet he often sounded like a demagogue. In the Senate caucus room it was already becoming clear, like a photograph slowly developing, that MacArthur was no martyred hero but an extraordinarily ambitious and self-willed general. Whether the bulk of the electorate would come to see this was anybody's guess.

Everything depended on the next series of Senate witnesses, namely the President's principal military advisers: General George C. Marshall, secretary of defense; General Omar Bradley, chairman of the Joint Chiefs of Staff; and the three service chiefs composing that body. This was the supreme irony of the political crisis. In the spring of 1951 the fate of civilian control of the military was absolutely dependent on the military's unswerving fidelity to that principle. It was not merely a matter of swearing fealty to the rule at the hearings. It was not even enough to endorse in a general way the President's policy of limited war. MacArthur's challenge to the President was too powerful for half-measures. The military chiefs would have to do what MacArthur was certain they would never do, what he believed them too "professional" to do. They would have to appear in the caucus room, before hostile senators, and concede absolutely nothing to General MacArthur. If they harbored doubts about limited war, they would have to keep such sentiments to themselves. If they saw merit in any of MacArthur's arguments, they would have to refuse, nonetheless, to acknowledge it. To the intense relief of the President's supporters, that is exactly what they proceeded to do.

Truman's five military spokesmen spent nineteen days in the witness chair, nineteen days in which MacArthur's conduct, MacArthur's victory plan, and even MacArthur's military reputation were ceaselessly battered. Was MacArthur's dismissal warranted? It was more than warranted; it was absolutely necessary. "General MacArthur's actions were continuing to jeopardize civilian control over military affairs." His public campaign to discredit the President's policies "was against all custom and tradition for a military man." What was wrong with MacArthur's victory plan? It would not bring victory "but a larger deadlock at greater expense." Would bombing Chinese "sanctuaries" help decisively in Korea? No, but it would leave America's home air defenses "naked." What of the Joint Chiefs' now-celebrated January 12 memorandum? The military chiefs brushed it aside. It was contingent on imminent defeat in Korea, and that contingency had long since passed. Never for a single moment had the Joint Chiefs of Staff subscribed to MacArthur's plan for victory. What about "the deification of this infallible leader," asked Senator William Fulbright. Had he not blundered at the Yalu when he walked into a Chinese trap? Apparently he had—a stunning accusation. As James Reston of *The New York Times* observed: "MacArthur started as the prosecutor and is now the defendant."

It was General Bradley, a genuine World War II hero and a man untainted by political controversy, who delivered the heaviest blows and the only quotable remark the administration managed to coin. MacArthur's plan, said Bradley, would involve the United States in "the wrong war at the wrong time with the wrong enemy." That was on May 15, Bradley's first day of testimony, with more of the same to come. Republican senators were stunned. Blindly trusting MacArthur, they simply had not expected the Pentagon to line up behind Truman's policies with such uncompromising zeal. Still less had they expected the Joint Chiefs to belittle their great colleague's military reputation or to accuse him, as General Marshall did, of undermining the morale of American combat troops by his condemnation of the war they were fighting. Republican leaders had underestimated not only the military's fidelity to "custom and tradition" but also the intense personal dislike that the imperious MacArthur had inspired in his World War II colleagues.

The testimony of the military chiefs was by no means unimpeachable. It was often glib and evasive. It was certainly no model of candor. Yet it was quite obvious to contemporaries that Republican committee members did little to discredit their testimony. Exalting MacArthur had been reckless enough. Blackening the Joint Chiefs of Staff in wartime was more than most Republicans had the heart to attempt. Already there were mutterings from the party professionals—national committeemen meeting in Tulsa—that the MacArthur affair might "boomerang" and leave Republicans looking like the "war party" for the 1952 elections. When General Bradley completed his testimony,

Republicans lamely proposed that no more generals be called. The Democratic majority was not about to oblige them. Following Bradley the three service chiefs—Army, Navy, and Air Force—duly took the witness chair to hammer away in turn at MacArthur and his plan.

The testimony of the President's generals had a curious effect on public opinion. It brought no rush of support for the President—far from it. It did not personally discredit the general. It accomplished something far more significant than either: it put an end to hysteria. It compelled an inflamed citizenry to stop and think for themselves. It is to the credit of the American people that they did so and still more to their credit that they proved so open-minded, too much so for some of the President's warmer partisans—*The New York Times*, for example.

While Bradley was still offering his testimony, the *Times* canvassed newspapers around the country to determine the hearings' effect on popular opinion. Virtually every newspaper reported the same general result. Their readers were "baffled." With some consternation the *Times* reported on May 20 that "the powerful argumentation by the two sides in the dispute appears to have confused the issues instead of clarifying them." A Gallup poll taken a few days later confirmed the *Times*'s informal soundings. A mere 19 percent of the electorate explicitly supported the President's position. Thirty percent still supported the general's. Half the people polled professed themselves utterly undecided. That indecision was entirely reasonable. The President called for a war of attrition leading merely to the status quo ante. MacArthur called for a victory that could conceivably embroil the world. There was precious little to choose between the two. The two sets of arguments canceled each other out.

What the "powerful argumentation by the two sides" had really proved was that Korea was an even worse situation than most Americans had hitherto suspected. Both sides, in effect, had belittled the war. MacArthur insisted that it was "slaughter" unless crowned with "victory." The administration insisted it was too unimportant to risk a try for victory. Then why on earth were we in Korea at all? Beneath the indecision and bafflement, the great majority of Americans were coming to a conclusion more prudent than MacArthur's and more honest than the administration's. There simply was not enough merit in the Korean War to justify anything but an end to hostilities. For

bringing America into the fighting, Americans were not about to forgive President Truman. The tide was turning, nonetheless, against
"victory," against "liberation," against any concern whatever for the
future form of government in communist North Korea—in a word,
against MacArthur.

Republicans began calling the hearings an administration "filibus-
ter." On Memorial Day, Truman took his first holiday in months. Yet,
despite the signs of returning reason, the President seemed hesitant
and timid. As James Reston of the *Times* observed on June 3, limited
war meant a negotiated settlement, but the administration was doing
nothing to encourage negotiations. It continued to denounce Red
China. It continued to speak vaguely about the ultimate "unification"
of Korea. Despite the millions of words expended in defense of its
limited war, the President still seemed to fear the general.

It was left to MacArthur himself to deliver the final blow to his
cause. Never far from egomania, the general had by now convinced
himself that opposition to his "victory" plan could not possibly be due
to an honest difference of opinion. It was due, he believed, to corruption so deep and so sinister it was imperiling the nation itself. There
is a hint of madness in such a conclusion, but MacArthur had nobody
to gainsay him. The flunkies surrounding the general believed whatever he said. "He realized," explained General Courtney Whitney,
MacArthur's factotum and spokesman, "that the dry rot that in-
fected U.S.-Korea policy was eating away at our conduct of affairs at
home. . . . He felt the compelling need to warn of the dangers he
saw menacing the land and the people he loves." He would not let his
countrymen down—"not to warn them was to betray them." In this
dark, messianic mood MacArthur decided to launch himself on a nationwide speaking tour. He called it his "crusade" for "the spiritual
recrudescence" of America.

It began on June 13 with a five-city tour of Texas. The tour, like the
larger crusade, revealed few of the general's virtues and all his flaws:
his vanity, his vindictiveness, his utter want of humility. He lashed out
savagely against the Truman administration, condemning its "moral
weakness," its disgraceful willingness to "cower before the Kremlin,"
its betrayal of the "Alamo spirit." He spoke darkly of the efforts being
made through "propaganda to sow the seeds of fear and timidity" in
America. He could be referring to nothing else but the testimony of

the Joint Chiefs of Staff. He warned of "insidious forces working from within" to destroy traditional "moral precepts" and to turn the government itself into "an instrument of despotism." These same sinister forces, he hinted, had engineered his dismissal and were even using the taxing power to destroy the American soul. They "seek to make the burden of taxation so great and its progressive increases so alarming that the spirit of adventure, tireless energy and masterful initiative . . . shall become stultified and inert."

The general insisted that he harbored no presidential ambitions. Nobody believed him. He had harbored such ambitions in 1948 and he sounded like a presidential aspirant now. The electorate judged him accordingly, which is to say, with the skepticism they habitually reserve for office seekers. By wearing his uniform on the tour, MacArthur hoped to remain what he had always seemed to his countrymen—a soldier devoted to duty and country. The bemedaled uniform merely made his political ambition seem vaguely improper. By linking "victory" in Korea to the "spiritual recrudescence" of the American republic, he hoped to strengthen his cause. It merely made the electorate that much more skeptical of "victory." Overseas wars had never seemed to most Americans the true glory of their republic. Between the general and the American people lay a political chasm, and it was MacArthur's crusade, more than anything else, that revealed it to the people.

The Texas tour was only the crusade's beginning but it marked the end of MacArthur's influence over the country at large. That the general was cutting his own throat was by no means lost on the White House. On June 25, nine days after MacArthur returned from Texas to the Waldorf, President Truman finally announced his willingness to do what MacArthur and his supporters had done their utmost to prevent him from doing. He was ready, he said, to negotiate a settlement of the war at the thirty-eighth parallel. This was the "appeasement peace" against which MacArthur had hurled his thunderbolts, against which he had pitted his enormous prestige, his lofty reputation, and, so it had seemed back in April, the entire body of the American people. He had failed to block it, and because he did, the "precedent" that would "grow into a monstrosity" had been forestalled. Civilian supremacy had beaten back its severest challenge. On July 10 American and Chinese delegates met at a Korean town named Kaesŏng to discuss terms for a truce. The crisis was over. In the end the great majority of Americans had decided against MacArthur, and though the talks would grow bitter and frustrating, that decision, once made, was never revoked.

The defeat took its toll on the general. In public his superb self-possession slowly began draining away. In speeches his beautifully modulated voice often became strident and squeaky. The polished performer developed odd mannerisms, such as jumping up and down as he spoke. His keynote address to the 1952 Republican Convention was so dull and ill-delivered that halfway through it the delegates' private chatter virtually drowned him out. Fourteen months after holding the entire nation in his thrall, General MacArthur could not even hold the attention of a Republican audience. In a mood of deep self-disgust MacArthur flew home that day to the Waldorf and out of the public life of the country.

It was the general, nonetheless, who supplied the final grace note to the great crisis of 1951. It was to come eleven years later before the corps of cadets at West Point. The general was eighty-two years old by then and he had come to his beloved military academy to deliver a last farewell. In the course of an eloquent and emotional speech, he had a word of stern advice for the future officers arrayed before him. In the high political affairs of the country, they were duty-bound not to meddle. "These great national problems," said the frail old man, "are not for your professional or military solution." An errant son of the republic had at last returned to the fold.

16

"Our Needs Know No Laws": The Issue of Illegal Mexican Immigration Since 1941

JUAN RAMON GARCIA

• The United States has always had a peculiar relationship with Mexico. Since it first emerged as an independent nation in the first quarter of the nineteenth century, Mexico has had to contend with the policies and ambitions of a northern neighbor that was richer, stronger, more populous, and more advanced. Consequently, every Mexican government has had to adjust its plans and goals to the colossus of the North.

American policies have often been ambivalent, however. In the 1920s and 1930s presidents Calvin Coolidge, Herbert Hoover, and Franklin D. Roosevelt withstood right-wing pressure and allowed Mexico to proceed with social and economic reforms. This "Good Neighbor Policy" was designed to prove that the United States would not intervene in the domestic affairs of a nearby nation even when Washington disapproved of the direction of government policy. Thus it was hoped that the traditional mistrust of a rich and powerful Uncle Sam would be alleviated.

Unfortunately, the rhetoric of American tolerance sometimes exceeded the reality of actual policy. In the early 1980s, when Mexican peasants in the northern parts of that country seized the lands on which they worked, President Luis Escheverría legalized their occupation by supporting genuine land reform. But the resulting shock waves in the American business community that was and is dependent on lucrative winter crops from Mexico were felt in Washington. Partly because of pressure from the United States, Escheverría's successor, Lopez Portillo, backed away from the previously strong governmental support for land seizures by peasants.

The inability of most Mexican peasants to achieve a decent

living standard has had an important impact on immigration
into the United States. As Professor Juan Ramon Garcia of
the University of Arizona argues in the following essay, successive American attempts to control illegal entrants from
south of the border have failed because they deal only with
symptoms rather than with causes. Mass deportations and
contract labor programs, he writes, will not work because the
border is so long as to be virtually unpatrollable. The real
solution lies in improving the economic position of Mexican
nationals, who will otherwise try to improve their lives by
crossing over, legally or illegally, into the easily accessible
United States.

In 1951 an undocumented worker stood before a judge during his
deportation hearing. As the weary judge examined the file, he noted
that the man had been charged several times with entering this country illegally. Looking up at him, the judge asked testily, "Don't you
respect the laws of this country?" The worker replied, "Our necessi-
ties know no laws." Ten years later another undocumented worker,
awaiting transportation back to Mexico in a detention center, told
an interviewer, "Many people condemn us for trying to make a living.
They are so busy in attacking us that they too often forget that we
are human beings." In 1978, police in the Chicago area stopped a
U-Haul truck carrying eighteen undocumented workers. The men had
been locked in the back of the truck for forty-eight hours with no
food, little water, and only two slop buckets for their personal needs.
They had boarded the truck in Phoenix, where the temperature had
been one hundred twelve degrees. It was at least twenty degrees hotter
inside the truck. Even the case-hardened cops were moved to compas-
sion by the suffering which these men, most of them less than twenty
years of age, had endured. As one of the policemen put it, "I thought
I had seen just about everything in twenty-five years on the job. But
this is about the worst I've seen done to human beings by other
human beings."

The question of illegal immigration from Mexico to this country
has been, and continues to be, both vexing and controversial. It is

vexing because it has led to abuse, exploitation, and suffering for the people who enter illegally. It is controversial because the problem is rooted in a quagmire of emotional, moral, social, political, economic, and international issues which at times defy description or solution. Throughout this protracted controversy, which dates back in terms of intensity to the early 1940s, a number of remedies have been proposed. To date the majority have either failed to be enacted or have been too limited to resolve a complex and worrisome problem.

The issue of illegal immigration from Mexico has once again generated national concern and interest. In part this is due to increased coverage of the subject by the mass media and to the fact that Americans are in the midst of an economic crisis which affects their jobs, earnings, and livelihoods. As has been the case historically, Americans in economically hard-pressed times are usually more sensitive to those factors which they perceive as responsible for their problems. In their eyes the presence of large numbers of undocumented workers in this country is part of the problem. To critics and opponents of this "uncontrolled influx," undocumented workers deprive American citizens of jobs, overtax social service agencies, increase the tax burden, and contribute to a myriad of social problems which affect the overall quality of life in the United States.

There is of course another side to the argument. Those sympathetic to the plight of undocumented workers argue that they contribute a great deal to the American economy, while deriving few benefits from it. According to them, a large percentage of undocumented workers who are employed in the United States pay a variety of taxes. Yet these people seldom take advantage of the services available to them because of fear of detection and deportation. Moreover, the majority of "illegals" are honest, hard-working, law-abiding people who, under different circumstances, would be considered model citizens. To date neither side in the controversy has been able to fully substantiate its viewpoint.

Groups on both sides of the controversy have made their views clear, and they have increasingly exerted pressure on policymakers. Yet the steps taken by national leaders have been both halting and of necessity limited, for they recognize the issue is explosive and emotional. They realize that no solution will please everyone. Further complicating matters is the fact that the great majority of illegal immigrants are Mexican citizens. In the past this was not a matter of great concern, but the recent discovery of vast oil reserves in Mexico, when coupled with the energy needs of this country, now requires American officials to take greater cognizance of this fact. They cannot afford to alienate an oil-rich Mexico by mishandling a tremendously delicate issue.

The problems confronting the United States in terms of illegal immigration and most of the proposals set forth to resolve them date back to the World War II period. United States entry into the war in 1941 created a tremendous labor shortage, particularly in the agricultural sector. Growers found that they could not compete with the wages paid by industrial employers. Those who had traditionally performed farm work either joined the military or flocked to the urban centers in search of better pay. As a result of intense lobbying pressure and the importance of agriculture to the war effort, the federal government negotiated a contract labor program with Mexico in 1941. Under this treaty Mexico agreed to provide its own nationals to perform work in agriculture and a few other designated areas for specified periods. In return the United States assumed responsibility for placing these individuals on jobs and providing food, shelter, and transportation back to Mexico once the contract period had ended. Braceros, as the temporary workers were called, would be given contracts guaranteeing them fair treatment and clearly spelling out the terms of their employment. Although the bracero program was enacted as a temporary wartime measure, it was continually renewed from 1942 to 1964. During this twenty-two-year period, some 4.5 million migrant workers came to the United States.

From the outset the program was plagued by exploitation, misunderstandings, confusion, and conflicting interests. Furthermore, it did not end the growing influx of illegal entrants from Mexico, as its proponents had predicted. Instead, the bracero program acted as one more catalyst to northern migration. The promise of a contract drew thousands of hopeful applicants to border recruiting stations. As a result there were usually more applicants than there were jobs. Those who failed to obtain a contract were loath to return home emptyhanded, for many of them had either borrowed money or invested what little they had to reach the border contracting stations. They therefore opted to cross the border illegally. Thus the guest worker program only served to increase the entry of undocumented workers. The inconsistent immigration policy followed by the United States also contributed to increased illegal entry after World War II. Then, as now, the United States implemented "special" policies with regard to Mexican immigration whenever the government deemed them necessary and beneficial to groups who held vested interests in the acquisition of cheap labor. For this reason the United States has on several occasions undertaken policies which are contrary to its own immigration laws. More often than not, this special policy has been in the form of ad hoc exemptions and administrative adjustment to those laws. A case in point was the bracero program. Another example can be found in the unilateral recruitment of Mexican workers in 1948 and in 1954.

Because of the failure of the United States to institute penalties against those who hired illegals, the Mexican government decided to terminate the bracero agreement in 1948. But it did not produce the anticipated response. Instead, the United States viewed the ploy as both arbitrary and unjustified, and it threatened to open the border if Mexico did not reinstate the program immediately. When Mexico refused, United States officials ordered the border opened to any bracero seeking employment. Word spread quickly among Mexicans who had anxiously been awaiting contracts. At first only a few bold individuals risked crossing the border in full view of American immigration authorities. When the rest realized that American officials were not going to prevent their entry, a wholesale rush occurred.

As hundreds of Mexicans crossed the river into El Paso, immigration officials placed them under technical arrest and then immediately paroled them to members of the Texas Employment Commission. As a result of the El Paso Incident of October 1948, some five thousand braceros were allowed to enter the United States illegally at the behest of immigration officials, whose job it was to enforce the laws against illegal entry. Although Mexico and the United States worked out their differences shortly thereafter, the lesson of the El Paso Incident was not lost on many. It was obvious that the United States would undertake legal and extralegal measures to acquire laborers whenever the need arose.

This was again clearly demonstrated in 1954 when negotiations over the renewal of the bracero program reached an impasse. As in

1948, American officials threatened that if Mexico terminated the agreement, they would resort to the unilateral recruitment of Mexican workers. To prove its point, the United States announced that contracting would resume on January 2, 1954, in El Centro, California, with or without an international agreement. Mexican officials responded that they were not prepared to negotiate under duress. At the same time Mexico attempted through threats and pleas to deter its people from going to the California border, but to no avail. When negotiations broke off, the United States opened the border at El Centro and seven hundred Mexicans were allowed to enter illegally. Mexico responded by posting armed guards on its side of the border. The presence of troops caused a tense situation, which was exacerbated by United States officials who resorted to a process of instant legalization of anyone who managed to cross the border. The legalization process was accomplished by having Mexicans who entered illegally run back to the official border crossing-point, put one foot on Mexican soil, and then dart back so that they could be legally processed. At times this practice approached the absurd, as depicted in a photograph showing a hapless Mexican being pulled south by a Mexican border official and north by an official of the United States. The look, a combination of fear, confusion, and chagrin, on this man's face, told the whole story.

Between January 23 and February 5, 1954, a series of bloody clashes erupted between Mexican troops and desperate, hungry braceros. According to the New York Times, Mexican officials were dismayed and angered at the sight of thousands of their countrymen jammed like "sardines" and gasping for air in the crunch to cross the border for a handful of harvest jobs. Tulio Lopez-Lira, who was in charge of emigration at the Mexican border port, blamed the Americans for the riots. "My countrymen," he said, "have been trapped here by American lies and propaganda that the border would be open to them." Another outspoken critic of the unilateral recruitment policy which instantly accorded legal status to illegal entrants was Congressman John F. Shelley of California. In condemning the recent events in his home state, Shelley leveled a broadside at the myopic view of the federal government on the issue of illegal immigration. "Apparently the government's reasoning is that if we simply remove all restrictions on border crossing, as we have done since expiration of the bracero agreement, all crossings will be legal and we will, therefore, wipe out the wetback problem."

Shelley's observation was essentially correct. Not only had the United States violated its own immigration laws by resorting to unilateral recruitment, but it had also implemented other questionable procedures which further encouraged illegal immigration from Mexico. One such procedure involved the legalization of wetbacks, a practice which was implemented by the Immigration and Naturalization Service (INS) in 1947 in an attempt to reduce the number of illegals in this country by "regularizing" their presence. This program was undertaken with the full consent and approval of Mexican officials, who were ostensibly opposed to any measures which would further encourage illegal emigration. The legalization process was formalized through clauses in the bracero agreements of 1947, 1949, and 1950. By 1951, the program had so proved its merits in the eyes of Mexico and the United States that it was incorporated into Public Law 78 (the official title of the bracero agreement) under Section 501. Under this clause the secretary of labor was authorized "to recruit Mexican workers, including illegal entrants who had resided in the United States for the preceding five years, or who had entered originally under legal contract and remained after it expired." Those who supported the legalization program claimed that it helped reduce the number of illegals in the country by making them legalized braceros. Thus the majority of braceros contracted after 1951 were in reality legalized undocumented workers.

This practice seriously undermined the enforcement of immigration laws. One of the strongest condemnations of the policy came from the President's Commission on Migratory Labor, which was appointed in June 1950. In its final report, the commission accused the federal government of having condoned the wetback traffic during the harvest season:

> Wetbacks who were apprehended were given identification slips in the United States by the Immigration and Naturalization Service, which entitled them, within a few minutes, to step back across the border and become contract workers. There was no other way to obtain the indispensable slip of paper except to be found illegally in the United States. Thus violators of the law were rewarded by receiving legal contracts while the same oppor-

tunities were denied law-abiding citizens of Mexico. The United
States, having engaged in a program giving preference in contracting to those who had broken the law, had encouraged violation of immigration laws. Our government thus had become
a contributor to the growth of an illegal traffic which it has the
responsibility to prevent.

While it is evident that the United States exacerbated the problem of
illegal entry, Mexico must also share in the blame, for it condoned
these practices because of the benefits derived from illegal emigration.
For example, the money sent back by illegals to friends, family, and
creditors helped Mexico's ailing economy. More importantly, the legal
and illegal emigration of Mexicans served as a safety valve, drawing
out potentially explosive elements who were unemployed and dis-
gruntled. Finally, the Mexican government netted political gains on
the home front by attacking the United States for its failure to end
illegal entry and to protect the rights of Mexican nationals within its
boundaries. Thus the United States became a convenient and easily
assailable scapegoat for Mexico. It should be noted that the above
views and circumstances still apply today.

In spite of the intensity and the importance of immigration from
Mexico after 1941, the American people considered the wetback
influx as largely a local problem confined to the border regions. This
lack of concern and interest was mirrored by newspapers, weekly news
magazines, and the popular pictorial magazines. But beginning in
1951, media attitudes began to change. Seemingly overnight, the
public was inundated with articles and feature stories about undocumented workers. Most of the stories emphasized the ill effects which
the "silent invasion" of "aliens" had on American society. These
stories charged that illegals were responsible for increased disease rates,
crime, narcotics traffic, and welfare costs, and that they served as a
cover for subversive elements who were infiltrating the country. Thus
what became embedded in the public mind was a negative view about
illegal immigration, a view which was reinforced by the widespread
use of terms such as "horde," "tide," "invasion," "wetback," "illegal,"
and "alien" to describe undocumented persons. To most Americans
these terms conjured up images of faceless, shadowy, and sinister beings who skulked across the border in the dead of night in order to
deprive American citizens of their jobs and livelihood.

Of course not all Americans opposed the entry of undocumented workers. The illegal was the very backbone of economic survival for a number of southwestern communities, and the widespread use and exploitation of illegal labor from Mexico had become a long-accepted norm. Many people in these communities had developed entrenched moral, ethical, and social justifications which supported the hiring and the abuse of undocumented workers. For the most part, those who employed wetbacks were scornful of interlopers who threatened to undercut their labor supply either through legislation penalizing employers or through stepped-up enforcement measures. They believed that the "handling of wetbacks" should be left to them, for they "knew and understood" these people best. Unfortunately for undocumented workers, such understanding was grounded in deeply embedded and negative stereotypes about Mexicans. This was especially true in the Rio Grande Valley of Texas, an area where most of the Mexicans hired were illegals. To employers the Mexicans were childlike, undisciplined, and lazy. Mexicans were also perceived as subhumans who were of little value except in performing hard work. As one valley resident put it, Mexicans did not really mind the hard work, the long hours, and the low pay. They were used to this. After all, he concluded, they "have behind them five hundred years of burden-bearing and animal-like living and just can't adjust to civilization in the way a white man does." Other long-time employers of illegals agreed. In their view Mexicans had enough bad attributes, and efforts to improve their way of life only added to the problem of dealing with them. To their way of thinking, they were doing illegals a favor by hiring them. After all, if things were really that bad in the United States, why did they make such determined efforts to come here?

In 1954 rising unemployment, the continued interest of the mass media, a growing public outcry against the "illegal influx," and the expression by immigration officials that they had begun to lose control of the border all forced the Eisenhower administration to deal with the problem. Attorney General Herbert Brownell adopted a two-pronged approach. The first was the implementation of a massive program to regain control of the border and reduce illegal entry. The program, code-named "Operation Wetback," began in June 1954. It was a large-scale, paramilitary program undertaken by the INS involving concentrated strike forces and raids in areas which had heavy concentrations of illegals. Focusing on the states of California, Texas, Arizona and New Mexico, the raids lasted throughout the summer and resulted in the deportation and repatriation of more than one million undocumented workers. Although recent research has found that the success of Operation Wetback was greatly exaggerated, it nonetheless represented a major effort by the federal government and the INS to enforce the immigration laws and to restore a semblance of control along the United States–Mexican border. Since 1954 the INS has sporadically conducted similar drives. These drives have usually followed hard on the heels of intense and protracted media attention upon the influx of illegals, rising unemployment, a noticeable downswing in the economy, and public outcry fostered by these conditions. Like Operation Wetback, the ensuing roundups merely represented a stopgap measure designed to placate an aroused public. While such drives do serve limited purposes, they do not address the major causes of illegal entry from Mexico.

While Operation Wetback was being planned and implemented, Herbert Brownell undertook the second part of his program. This was the introduction of legislation to impose penalties against those who "knowingly" employed illegals or were captured in the act of smuggling or harboring them. The legislation was introduced in Congress in 1954 by Republican Senator Arthur Watkins of Utah and Democratic Representative Louis E. Graham of Pennsylvania.

Attempts to introduce penalty legislation against employers during President Harry Truman's tenure had met with resounding defeat, and from the outset it was apparent that Brownell's proposals would also face an uphill battle. Opposing the penalty legislation was a powerful and well-organized group in Congress which was determined to protect the interests of those whose economic survival depended upon a cheap source of labor. As a result of this strong opposition, Brownell's proposals were never enacted. After Operation Wetback, interest in reintroducing penalty legislation quickly faded. The much-publicized "success" of the deportation drives of 1954 lulled many proponents of such legislation into believing that the influx of illegals was at last under control, and that perhaps penalty legislation, which would always encounter tremendous opposition, was not the solution after all.

They were of course mistaken. Operation Wetback did not signal the end of illegal immigration from Mexico although it presented that impression to many. After 1954, agricultural employers contracted with individual Mexicans. Thus between 1954 and 1960, there occurred a dramatic increase in the number of braceros hired (see Table 1). During this same period INS figures reflected a dramatic decrease in the numbers of undocumented workers apprehended. This tended to support the claims of the INS that the problem of illegal entry was now under control. At the same time these figures bolstered the arguments of those who favored the continuation of a bracero program. Proponents argued that it served as a deterrent to illegal entry, and they warned federal officials that termination of the program

TABLE 1

Number of Braceros Contracted 1951–1964		Number of Undocumented Persons 1951–1964	
Year	Contracted	Year	Contracted
1951	190,745[a]	1951	500,628
1952	197,100	1952	543,538
1953	201,380	1953	875,318
1954	309,033	1954	1,075,168
1955	398,650	1955	242,608
1956	445,197	1956	72,442
1957	436,049	1957	44,451
1958	432,857	1958	37,242
1959	437,643	1959	30,196
1960	315,846	1960	29,651
1961	291,420	1961	29,877
1962	194,978	1962	30,272
1963	186,865	1963	39,124
1964	177,736	1964	43,844
Total	4,215,499		

[a] Includes 46,076 contracted under 1948 agreement prior to July 15.
SOURCE: U.S. Department of Labor, "Summary of Migratory Station Activities."

SOURCE: U.S. Immigration and Naturalization Service.

would only reopen the floodgates to illegal entry. These arguments and the power of probracero groups proved effective and resulted in the continuation of the program until 1964.

As if to underscore the warnings of probracero groups, apprehension of illegals began to increase in 1963 and 1964. On the surface it seemed that the program had in fact been a deterrent to illegal entry. Yet appearances were deceiving, as other critical factors had been responsible for the apparent decline of illegal immigration from Mexico. One factor was that after 1954 the Border Patrol returned to routine operations, largely abandoning the concentrated approach as implemented in 1954. The Border Patrol also continued the legalization of apprehended wetbacks, which meant that a good proportion of the braceros contracted were in reality illegals whose presence in this country had been regularized. Another reason for the "decline" of illegal immigration was the introduction of increased labor-saving technology, which reduced needs in the unskilled agricultural labor market.

After 1959 there was a rapid decline in the number of braceros contracted, in part because of labor-saving technology and the more rigid enforcement of wage guarantees. The government also began to tighten certification requirements for establishing the need to import and hire braceros. Thus prior to the end of the bracero program in 1964, many employers had again begun to resort to an increased use of undocumented workers. Among those employed were large numbers of commuters who had entered the United States by using a border-crossing permit. The permits, which were fairly easy to acquire, permitted the holder to enter the United States for the purposes of entertainment, shopping, visiting, or business. Holders of this permit were prohibited from working while in this country or from traveling more than twenty-five miles from the border. Those holding the permit were allowed to enter the United States for periods not to exceed seventy-two hours.

Obviously, the temptation proved too great for many. Once here they mailed the cards back to Mexico to avoid having them confiscated in case of apprehension by INS authorities. As no records were kept of the number of people entering or leaving the United States on a daily basis, it proved almost impossible to determine how many had entered legally and remained illegally. The unavailability of records in this area added to the numerical illusion that illegal entry, as shown by apprehensions, had declined.

Further adding to the incentive to enter illegally was the enactment of more stringent immigration restrictions by the United States in 1965 and 1968. Under the new regulations, applicants were given preference if they were blood relatives of citizens or legal residents already in the United States. Members of preferred professions such as engineering and medicine were also given higher priority. Preference was also shown to applicants who had employers who would sponsor them. People who did not fall into any of these categories were free to apply as well, although their chances for legal admission, given the long waiting lists, were almost nil. Many were unwilling to make application upon such slim chances, especially given the high cost and the complicated procedures.

Factors in Mexico also served to spur illegal emigration. The growth in Mexico's economy between 1950 and 1960 was not sufficient to keep up with its population growth, which had more than doubled between 1940 and 1963, rising from twenty-two to forty-five million. Therefore, the lack of employment opportunities, a rapidly expanding population, and Mexico's economic overdependence on the United States, when coupled with the availability of work in the United States and a largely unpatrolled border, all served once again to attract Mexican nationals in increasing numbers.

By the late 1960s, illegal immigration had increased significantly. Labor organizations and social reform groups once again called for measures to deal with what they saw as a problem of major proportions. Yet their concern was not shared by important government officials or the general public. The boom economy of the 1960s appeared capable of absorbing and utilizing an enlarged labor force, regardless of its source. Furthermore, the hostile environment toward undocumented persons had for the moment dissipated. Americans were more concerned with the domestic and foreign issues raised by the Vietnam War.

As the war ground to an end, as some semblance of domestic tranquility returned, and as the nation began to experience the economic problems inherent in adjusting to a peacetime economy, illegal immigration once again became an issue of major public and governmental concern. Newspaper stories and government reports reflected a steady increase in the number of undocumented persons apprehended each year. According to INS estimates, the number of illegal aliens apprehended increased from about two hundred thousand in 1968 to five hundred thousand in 1972. Accompanying these reports were renewed attacks from various groups. As in the past, undocumented workers were accused of overburdening social and welfare agencies, of depriving Americans of jobs, and of driving up rates of crime and disease. Some claimed that if this large-scale influx continued unchecked, it would lead to the formation of "welfare reservations" and "wetback subcultures" which would be breeding grounds for discontent, alienation, and potential revolution. Adding to the "alien scare" were the statements of high-ranking immigration officials who sought additional funding for their programs. One of the more vociferous was Leonard Chapman, the head of the INS. In 1972 he warned that the United States was undergoing a "growing, silent invasion of illegals" and called upon Americans to demand swift action to halt it, for there "was no time to lose."

The scare tactics and warnings had their desired effects. Stepped-up INS campaigns against undocumented workers followed, studies were commissioned, various state and federal subcommittees held hearings, and some states enacted legislation against those who "knowingly" employed illegals. For the most part, the reports and the hearings stirred a great deal of interest, debate, and controversy but did little to resolve the problem. The penalty legislation enacted at the state level also did little to discourage employment of illegals because it contained vague language and numerous loopholes which made prosecution and conviction very difficult. Instead, a number of these state laws were used by unscrupulous employers to intensify their discrimination against Hispanic people. According to one observer, some employers used the laws as a pretext for refusing to hire minorities, claiming that applicants had failed to prove beyond a shadow of a doubt that they were indeed legal residents or citizens of the United States.

At the federal level, Congressman Peter Rodino and Senator Edward F. Kennedy introduced bills in 1972 and 1974 respectively designed to regularize the status of aliens already in the United States and to impose sanctions against employers who hired illegals. Neither of the proposals won wide support in Congress. Although they continued to stir interest and controversy, repeated efforts to have the bills enacted failed. By mid-1975 the question of illegal immigration from Mexico had once again become a major issue both here and in Mexico. Deadlocked over what path to follow, Congress deferred any action. It instead adopted a wait-and-see posture.

In 1977 President Jimmy Carter introduced a series of measures which he hoped would prove acceptable to a majority of people. Similar to those proposed under Truman and Eisenhower, they called for increased personnel to patrol the border, legislation to penalize those who employed illegals, and closer cooperation with those countries from which undocumented persons came. A fourth measure entailed granting "amnesty" to illegal aliens. Under this provision, undocumented persons who entered before 1970 and who had resided in the United States continually since their arrival would be permitted to remain. They could also begin the process of becoming naturalized citizens. The plan also proposed that aliens who entered between 1970 and 1977 would be permitted to remain in the United States, but only on a temporary basis. A more definite ruling on their future status would come after the federal government "had studied the matter further." Finally, under Carter's plan, those who entered illegally after 1977 would be subject to immediate deportation.

President Carter's plan was vigorously discussed and received widespread criticism from a variety of groups and organizations. Critics of the plan assailed it as either too amorphous, too lenient, or too stringent. As debate raged around the proposals, the Carter administration came under attack from other sectors. When economic conditions in the country deteriorated further, the energy problem deepened, and affairs in the Middle East worsened, Carter's proposal on illegal immigration fell by the wayside. There was little that the beleaguered president could do to gain support for any of his proposals, and thus no legislative action was taken on them.

Yet even if Carter's proposals had been enacted, it is doubtful that they would have had any significant impact on the problem of illegal immigration. For example, it is unlikely that Congress would have enacted a stringent and effective law against employers of illegals. It is also doubtful that a large number of undocumented persons would have taken advantage of the amnesty provisions. First of all, applying

for amnesty would have meant exposure to INS officials. To a group
of people long conditioned to remaining invisible, such a step would
have been threatening and dangerous. Furthermore, the burden of
proof in terms of continuous residency before 1970 would have fallen
totally on those seeking citizenship status. There was always the chance
that such proof would not be accepted by immigration officials, in
which case applicants would be subject to deportation. To many the
process involved appeared complicated, the risks great, and the benefits
minimal and uncertain. For those who had entered after 1970 the
assignment of a temporary resident status was not worth the risk of
identifying themselves, especially since there was little or no indication
of what might happen to them after the government "had studied the
matter." For obvious reasons, Carter's plan was even less appealing to
those who entered after 1977.

The proposal for increasing border patrol personnel also had its
weaknesses. For example, increasing personnel and equipping them
with sophisticated hardware would have no impact whatsoever in controlling those who entered the United States legally by using their
temporary tourist or student cards, and then overstayed, thus becoming illegals. Critics also pointed out that although this proposal would
make it more difficult for those without cards to enter illegally, it
would not deter them. If anything, the program would only increase
the profits of "coyotes" (commercial smugglers), who already operated lucrative businesses assisting undocumented persons in crossing
the border. Finally, Carter's plan contained little that would have attacked the problem at its roots. His plan did not sufficiently address
itself to reducing the major push factors extant in Mexico which contribute to illegal emigration.

President Ronald Reagan's proposal also fails to address the basic
causes of the problem. There is little or no discussion of helping
Mexico battle its economic underdevelopment, or of alleviating the
large trade imbalance which exists between it and the United States.
There is also little indication that Mexico will receive increased capital from the World Bank to invest in projects such as its integrated
rural development program, which thus far appears to be helping its
economically depressed rural sectors. Reagan's proposals place emphasis on the unilateral approach to reducing the problem—an approach which has met with little success in the past.

In addition, Reagan's plans contain serious flaws which will exacerbate the problem. Because of the "serious dimensions" of the situation, he has requested that the government be given wide-ranging emergency powers. Among them is the authority to establish detention centers for illegals without requiring environmental studies in advance. This proposal, if enacted, might not bode well for those illegals unfortunate enough to be captured and detained. Without proper safeguards, these places might lapse into pestilential and poorly maintained camps. Reagan's program also calls for stiff fines against those who employ illegals. Yet he has provided a palatable alternative in an effort to gain the support of powerful interest groups who would vehemently resist sanctions against employers. Reagan has proposed a two-year experimental guest worker program that would bring in fifty thousand braceros to the United States each year. If successful, the program would then be expanded to bring in between five hundred thousand and one million guest workers annually. Thus the program would substitute one source of cheap labor for another.

The Reagan administration claims the guest worker program would help reduce illegal entry. Yet it might serve to encourage illegal entry, much as the bracero program of 1942 to 1964 did. In essence, there are likely to be more applicants than jobs. For those who fail to obtain a contract, the tendency will be to enter illegally. Moreover, guest workers may opt to remain illegally after their contract term has expired. Finally, the program would create a class of highly exploited laborers since extensive contract guarantees might not be included in the agreement or, if included, might not be strictly enforced given Reagan's emphasis on deregulation of the private sector. It is interesting to note that the president's proposal of a guest worker program comes at a time when the United States is experiencing high employment.

In conclusion, past experience has adequately demonstrated the ineffectiveness of mass deportations, restrictive measures, contract labor programs, and a unilateral approach in providing long-term solutions to the problem of illegal immigration. Undocumented persons will continue to seek better opportunities in the United States so long as those opportunities are lacking or denied them at home. That is one of the consequences of a contiguous and negotiable border separating a rich nation from a poor one.

17

The Last War, the Next War, and the New Revisionists

WALTER LA FEBER

• During the 1960 presidential campaign, John F. Kennedy repeatedly criticized the Eisenhower administration for too great a reliance on nuclear weapons. After his election, the new president implemented a policy of flexible response to so-called wars of national liberation. When guerrilla conflict began in Vietnam, President Kennedy sent airplanes, artillery, and 16,000 "advisers" to bolster Premier Diem's regime.

The war continued to widen, and in 1963 Lyndon B. Johnson inherited a shaky Saigon regime dependent upon American support. Rather than face charges of appeasement in world affairs, President Johnson increased the Southeast Asian involvement. In August 1964, in response to an alleged attack on an American destroyer, President Johnson ordered the bombing of North Vietnam. This prompted the Senate to pass—with only two dissenting votes—the Gulf of Tonkin Resolution, which granted the chief executive extraordinary powers to protect the national interest. By 1967, more than a half-million United States servicemen were trying to prevent a Communist takeover, "contain" China, and convince other governments of America's resolve to defend its friends.

As everyone now realizes, this huge effort was unsuccessful, and the cost in the lives of young men and in more than a decade of runaway inflation was enormous. But there has been less agreement as to why the rich and powerful United States, with its technologically sophisticated weaponry and its absolute command of the air and the sea, could not bring

Reprinted by permission of *democracy*. Copyright 1980. Walter LaFeber is Professor of History at Cornell and author of *America, Russia and the Cold War, 1945–1980* (Alfred A. Knopf, 1985), among other works.

to heel a small, poor, and backward nation that was divided against itself. The following essay by Cornell University historian Walter LaFeber is perhaps the finest piece yet written about this unfortunate episode.

As if to prove Lord Acton's dictum that "the strong man with the dagger is followed by the weak man with the sponge," a remarkable rewriting of the Vietnam war's history is under way. It is especially remarkable because the new revisionists are either ignorant of American policy in the conflict or have chosen to forget past policies in order to mold present opinion. More generally, they are rewriting the record of failed military interventionism in the 1950 to 1975 era in order to build support for interventionism in the 1980s. More specifically, the new revisionists are attempting to shift historical guilt from those who instigated and ran the war to those who opposed it.

Immediately after South Vietnam fell in 1975, Secretary of State Henry Kissinger urged Americans to forget the quarter-century-long war. That advice was no doubt related to his other concern at the time: committing U.S. military power to Angola and the Horn of Africa. Congress had fortunately learned from experience and stopped Kissinger from involving the country in an African Vietnam. The next year, however, influential authors began to discover that Vietnam's history was more usable than Kissinger had imagined. General William Westmoreland, who commanded U.S. forces during the worst months of fighting in the 1960s, set the line when he argued in his memoirs and public speeches that the conflict was not lost on the battlefield, but at home where overly sensitive politicians followed a "no-win policy" to accommodate "a misguided minority opposition . . . masterfully manipulated by Hanoi and Moscow." The enemy, Westmoreland claimed, finally won "the war politically in Washington."

Part of Westmoreland's thesis was developed with more scholarship and cooler prose by Leslie H. Gelb and Richard K. Betts in *The Irony of Vietnam: The System Worked.* It was not the "system"—that is, the Cold War national security establishment—that failed, the authors argued. Failure was to be blamed on the American people, who never understood the war and finally tired of it, and on the Presidents who supinely followed the people. Thus the "system" worked doubly well: the professional bureaucrats gave the correct advice, as they were paid to do, and the Presidents followed the public's wishes, as democratic theory provides that they should.

Westmoreland's argument that the antiwar groups wrongly labeled Vietnam an illegal and immoral conflict was developed by Guenter Lewy's *America in Vietnam*. Lewy, however, was so honest that his own evidence destroyed the thesis. Although he wrote that U.S. soldiers followed civilized modes of war even though this sometimes meant virtual suicide, Lewy also gave striking examples of how the troops ruthlessly destroyed villages and civilians. "It is well to remember," he wrote, "that revulsion at the fate of thousands of hapless civilians killed and maimed" because of American reliance upon high-technology weapons "may undercut the willingness of a democratic nation to fight communist insurgents." That becomes a fair judgment when "thousands" is changed to "hundreds of thousands." Lewy nevertheless held grimly to his thesis about the war's morality and legality, even as he reached his closing pages: "the simplistic slogan 'No more Vietnams' not only may encourage international disorder, but could mean abandoning basic American values." It apparently made little difference to Lewy that those basic American values had been ravaged at My Lai, or at Cam Ne, where a Marine commander burned down a village and then observed in his after-action report that "it is extremely difficult for a ground commander to reconcile his tactical mission and a people-to-people program." Lewy's conclusions, not his evidence, set a tone that was widely echoed, particularly after the foreign policy crises of late 1979.

The Soviet invasion of Afghanistan was seized upon with almost audible sighs of relief in some quarters. *Commentary*, which had publicly introduced Lewy's argument in 1978, published a series of essays in early 1980 that developed some of his conclusions, especially the view that if the Vietnam experience inhibited future U.S. interventions, it "could mean abandoning basic American values." In an essay that thoughtfully explored the meaning of his own antiwar protests in the 1960s, Peter Berger nevertheless drew the conclusion that the American defeat in Vietnam "greatly altered" the world balance of power, and that "American power has dramatically declined, politi-

cally as well as militarily." Charles Horner condemned President
Jimmy Carter's early belief that Vietnam taught us the limits of U.S.
power. "That view," Horner claimed, "is the single greatest restraint
on our capacity to deal with the world, and that capacity will not
much increase unless the view behind it is changed, thoroughly and
profoundly." Horner did his best to reinterpret the meaning of Vietnam, but it was *Commentary*'s editor, Norman Podhoretz, who best
demonstrated how history could be rewritten to obtain desired conclusions.

"Now that Vietnam is coming to be seen by more and more people
as an imprudent effort to save Indochina from the horrors of Communist rule rather than an immoral intervention or a crime," Podhoretz
wrote in the March 1980 issue, "the policy out of which it grew is
also coming to be seen in a new light." He believed that the "policy—
of defending democracy [*sic*] wherever it existed, or of holding the
line against the advance of Communist totalitarianism by political
means where possible and by military means when necessary," was
based on the Wilsonian idea that "in the long run," U.S. interests depended on " 'the survival and the success of liberty' in the world as a
whole." This revisionist view of Vietnam, Podhoretz argued, is helping to create a "new nationalism"—the kind of outlook that "Woodrow
Wilson appealed to in seeking to 'make the world safe for democracy'
and that John F. Kennedy echoed.

Podhoretz's grasp of historical facts is not reassuring; the essay has
three major errors in its first three pages. George A. Carver, Jr.'s essay
subtitled "The Teachings of Vietnam," in the July 1980 issue of
Harper's, only adds to that problem. An old C.I.A. hand who was
deeply involved in Vietnam policy planning, Carver is identified in
Harper's only as "a senior fellow" at Georgetown University's Center
for Strategic and International Studies. That identification is nevertheless of note, for the Center serves as an important source of personnel and ideas for what passes as Ronald Reagan's foreign policy
program. In the article, Carver set out to "dispel Vietnam's shadows"
so the United States could again exercise great power and influence.
When he mentioned earlier policy, Carver simply postulated that
South Vietnam fell to North Vietnamese conventional forces, not to
"any popular southern rebellion," and that "the press and media, and
their internal competitive imperatives" misrepresented the real prog-

ress the U.S. forces were making in the war. Beyond that, the analysis consists of empty generalizations (Americans are encumbered in their foreign policy by "theological intensity" and "childlike innocence"), and it climaxes with the insight that "the world is cruel."

Read closely, Carver's warning about the dangers of "theological intensity" contradicts Podhoretz's call for a new Wilsonianism. But in the wake of the Iranian and Afghanistan crises, few read these calls to the ramparts of freedom very closely. The essays were more valuable for their feelings than for their historical accuracy. The new revisionists wanted to create a mood, not recall an actual past, and their success became dramatically apparent when that highly sensitive barometer of popular feelings, commercial television, quickly put together a new sitcom on the war, "The Six O'Clock Follies." One reviewer labeled it a "gutlessly cynical comedy," signaling that "suddenly we are supposed to be able to laugh at Vietnam." As the *Washington Post*'s critic observed, however, since the conflict has "been deemed a safe zone . . . all three networks have Vietnam sitcoms in the works" for 1980–1981. Television was placing its seal of approval on a revisionism that promised to be commercially as well as ideologically satisfying.

Given this new mood, it was natural that those who wielded, or planned to wield, power were also prepared to help wring the sponge. In 1978 Zbigniew Brzezinski had lamented privately to Senate staff members that the floundering administration needed a *Mayagüez* incident so Carter, as Ford had in 1975, could get tough with Communists (preferably, apparently, from a small country), and rally Americans behind a battle flag. By the end of 1979, Carter had not one but two such opportunities with the Iranian hostage issue and the Soviet invasion of Afghanistan, and as usual Americans indeed closed ranks behind the President. In mid-December, Brzezinski observed that the country was finally getting over its post-Vietnam opposition to military spending and overseas intervention.

Three months later, Ronald Reagan, in his only major foreign policy speech prior to the Republican Convention, urged a return to Wilsonianism—what one reporter characterized as a belief that Americans have "an inescapable duty to act as the tutor and protector of the free world in confronting . . . alien ideologies." To carry out this mission, Reagan proclaimed, "we must rid ourselves of the 'Vietnam syndrome.' " He of course meant the old "syndrome," not the new syndrome of the revisionists that the war was to be admired for its intent if not its outcome. A frustrated job seeker at the Republican Convention best captured the effects of the new revisionism. A reporter teased Henry Kissinger about his prediction in the early 1970s that if the war did not end well for Americans there would be a fierce right-wing reaction. "It turned out just about the way I predicted it would," Kissinger replied. The former Secretary of State, however, contributed to the mood that threatened to confine him to academia. In recent writings and speeches, Kissinger has argued that if the Watergate scandal had not driven Nixon from office, South Vietnam would not have been allowed to fall. His claim cannot, of course, be completely disproved, but it is totally unsupported by either the post-1973 military and political situation in Vietnam, or the antiwar course of American policies, including Nixon's, that appeared long before the Watergate scandal paralyzed the administration.

The arguments of the new revisionists—or the new nationalists, as some prefer to be called (in perhaps unconscious reference to the New Nationalism of Theodore Roosevelt and Herbert Croly that pledged an imperial "Big Stick" foerign policy)—dominated the foreign policy debates and, indeed, the Carter-Brzezinski foreign policies in early 1980. Because those arguments rest heavily on interpretations of the Vietnam conflict, their use of the war's history deserves analysis. This can be done on two levels: the new revisionists' explicit claims, and the events they choose to ignore.

The most notable explicit theme is captured by Westmoreland's assertion that the war was lost because of pressure from a "misguided minority opposition" at home, or by Peter Berger's more careful statement that "the anti-war movement was a primary causal factor in the American withdrawal from Indochina." Since at least the mid-1960s, detailed public opinion polls have existed that show that Americans supported a tough policy in Vietnam. In this, as in nearly all foreign policies, the public followed the President. As Herbert Y. Schandler concluded after his careful study of public opinion between 1964 and 1969, "If the administration is using increasing force, the public will respond like hawks; if it is seeking peace, the public responds like doves." When Lyndon Johnson tried to convince doubters by whipping out the latest opinion polls showing support for the war, he did not have to make up the figures. George Ball has testified that the antiwar protests only "dug us in more deeply" and intensified the administration's determination to win. Ball, who served as Under Secretary of State under Johnson, rightly calculated that "only late in the day did widespread discontent . . . appreciably slow the escalation of the war." Even those who dissented in the 1960s were more hawk than dove. Richard Scammon and Ben Wattenberg's analysis of the 1968 election concluded that a plurality of the Democrats who voted for Eugene McCarthy in the primaries supported George Wallace in November, and that finding is corroborated by polls revealing that a majority of those who opposed the conduct of the war also opposed protests against the war. Westmoreland's "misguided minority opposition" was of significantly less importance than a much larger group that wanted him to have whatever he needed to end the war. It simply is not true, as Barry Goldwater claimed at the 1980 Republican Convention, that the "will" to win the war was missing in the 1960s.

By 1970–1971, antiwar opposition had increased, but it did not stop Nixon from expanding the conflict into Cambodia and Laos. One statistic stands out: before Nixon sent in the troops, 56 percent of college-educated Americans wanted to "stay out" of Cambodia, and after he committed the forces, 50 percent of the same group supported the Cambodian invasion. When Nixon carpet-bombed North Vietnam two years later and for the first time mined the North's ports, 59 percent of those polled supported the President, and only 24 percent opposed him, even though it was clear that the mining could lead to a confrontation with the Russians and Chinese, whose ships used the harbors.

The effectiveness of the antiwar movement has been greatly overrated by the new revisionists, and the movement has consquently served as the scapegoat for them as well as for the national security managers whose policies failed in Vietnam. Given the new revisionist arguments, it needs to be emphasized that the United States lost in Vietnam because it was defeated militarily, and that that defeat occurred because Americans could not win the war without destroying what they were fighting to save—or, alternatively, without fighting for decades while surrendering those values at home and in the Western alliance for which the cold war was supposedly being waged. The anti-war protesters only pointed up these contradictions; they did not create them.

The new revisionists argue that the nation has largely recovered from the disaster. Carl Gershman writes that "as the polls reveal, the American people have now overwhelmingly rejected the ideas of the new [Carter-Vance-Young] establishment." The strategy of the post-Vietnam "establishment" is to contain communism only in selected areas, and by using nonmilitary means if possible. The polls actually reveal considerable support for this strategy. In January 1980, after the invasion of Afghanistan, a CBS/*New York Times* survey showed that about two-fifths of those polled wanted to respond with non-military tactics, two-fifths wanted to "hold off for now," and less than one-fifth favored a military response. Lou Harris discovered that within six weeks after the seizure of the hostages in Iran, support for military retaliation dropped off sharply. Quite clearly, if the new nationalists hope to whip up public sentiment for using military force wherever they perceive "democracy" to be threatened, they have much work yet to do. Most Americans have not overwhelmingly rejected nonmilitary responses, even after being shaken by the diplomatic earthquakes of 1979–1980. And they appear too sophisticated to agree with Podhoretz's Wilsonian assumption that "American interests in the long run [depend] on the survival and the success of liberty in the world as a whole." A majority of Americans seem to agree with that part of the post-Vietnam "establishment" represented by Vance and Young that it is wiser to trust nationalisms in the Third World than to undertake a Wilsonian crusade to rescue those nationalisms for an American-defined "liberty."

There is a reason for this confusion among new revisionist writers. They focus almost entirely on the Soviet Union instead of on the in-stability in Third World areas that the Soviets have at times turned to their own advantage. Such an approach allows the new revisionists to stress military power rather than the political or economic strategies that are most appropriate for dealing with Third World problems. The new nationalists, like the old, pride themselves on being realists in regard to power, but their concept of power is one-dimensional. Once this military dimension becomes unusable, nothing is left. A direct military strategy is appropriate for dealing with the Soviets in certain cases—for example, if the Red Army invaded Western Europe or Middle East oil fields. That strategy, however, has existed since the days of Harry Truman; the Vietnam war, regardless of how it is reinterpreted, has nothing new to teach us about that kind of massive response. A quarter-century ago, when the United States took its first military steps into Vietnam, Reinhold Niebuhr warned that the policy placed "undue reliance on purely military power" and therefore missed the fundamental political point: a U.S. military response was incapable of ending "the injustices of [Asia's] decaying feudalism and the inequalities of its recent colonialism." Niebuhr's advice was of course ignored. The supposed realists of the day proceeded to commit military power in Vietnam—to *contain China*. For, in the mid-1960s, China was the villain for the national security managers, as the Soviets are now for the new revisionists.

The reason for the failure of U.S. military power was not that it was severely limited. Lyndon Johnson bragged that he put 100,000 men into Vietnam in just one hundred and twenty days. Those troops were supported by the most powerful naval and air force ever used in Asia. Laos became the most heavily bombed country in history, North Vietnam's ports and cities were bombed and mined almost yard by yard, and Nixon dropped a ton of bombs on Indochina for every minute of his first term in the White House. Neither the will nor the power was missing. As Michael Herr wrote in *Dispatches*, "There was such a dense concentration of American energy there, American and essentially adolescent, if that energy could have been channeled into anything more than noise, waste and pain, it would have lighted up Indochina for a thousand years." Vietnam provides a classic lesson in the misuse of military power, but that lesson is being overlooked by the new revisionists.

And if they have misunderstood the conflict's central political and military features, so have the new revisionists lost sight of the historical context. They stress that Vietnam caused the decline of American power. It is quite probable, however, that when historians look back with proper perspective on the last half of the twentieth century, they will conclude that U.S. foreign policy problems in the 1970s and 1980s resulted not from the Vietnam experience, but more generally from political misperception and from an overestimation of American power. The *hubris* produced by the American triumph in the Cuban missile crisis contributed to such misestimation, but the problems also resulted from the failure to understand that U.S. power began a relative decline in the late 1950s and early 1960s. It was during those earlier years that the American economy and international trade began a decline that only accelerated—not started—in the 1970s; that such important allies as Japan and West Germany directly attacked American markets and helped to undermine the dollar; that the Western alliance displayed its first signs of slipping out of Washington's control; and that the Third World rapidly multiplied its numbers and decided—as the creation of OPEC in 1969 demonstrated—that it no longer had to join either one of the superpower camps. Future historians will consequently see the Vietnam war as one result, not a cause, of the relative decline of American power that began in the late 1950s. They will also probably conclude that space ventures, and the achievement of independence by nearly one hundred nations in the Third World, were of greater historical significance than the Vietnam conflict or the U.S.-USSR rivalry that obsesses the new revisionists.

Even with their narrow focus on the lessons of Vietnam, it is striking how much the new revisionists omit from their accounts of the war. They say relatively little about the South Vietnamese. The war is viewed as an eyeball-to-eyeball confrontation between Americans and Communists, and the turn comes when the Americans, undone by what Carver calls their "childlike innocence," blink. This approach resembles watching two football teams but not noticing the ball that is being kicked and passed around. The new revisionists have downplayed the inability of the South Vietnamese to establish a stable and effective government amid a massive U.S. buildup, the Vietnamese hatred for the growing American domination, and the massive desertions from the South's army in 1966–1967, even when the U.S. forces arrived to help. As early as 1966, non-Communist student leaders accurately called the country's presidential elections "a farce directed by foreigners." By 1971, a Saigon newspaper ran a daily contest in which readers submitted stories of rape or homicide committed by

Americans. As Woodrow Wilson learned in 1919, some people just do not want to be saved—at least by outsiders with whom they have little in common.

The new revisionists also overlook the role the allies played in Vietnam. There is a good reason for this ommission: of the forty nations tied to the United States by treaties, only four—Australia, New Zealand, South Korea, and Thailand—committed any combat troops. The major European and Latin American allies refused to send such forces. We later discovered that the South Koreans, whom Americans had saved at tremendous cost in 1950, agreed to help only after Washington bribed them with one billion dollars of aid. The key Asian ally, Japan, carefully distanced itself from the U.S. effort. This was especially bitter for American officials, for Truman and Eisenhower had made the original commitment to Vietnam in part to keep the area's raw materials and markets open for the Japanese. Relations between Tokyo and Washington deteriorated rapidly. When Lyndon Johnson asked whether he could visit Japan in 1966, the answer came back, "inconceivable." An article in the authoritative *Japan Quarterly* stated that if the United States became involved in another war with China, divisions in Japanese public opinion "would split the nation in two" and lead to "disturbances approaching a civil war in scale."

As Jimmy Carter admitted in early 1980, the United States needs strong support from allies if it hopes to contain the Soviets in the Middle East. It would be well, therefore, to note carefully the allied view of U.S. policy in Vietnam and elsewhere before embarking on a Wilsonian crusade to make "democracy" safe everywhere. Having chosen to ignore the lesson that Vietnam teaches about the allies, the new revisionists resemble traditional isolationists, who, as scholars have agreed, were characterized by a desire for maximum freedom of action, minimum commitment to other nations ("no entangling alliances"), and a primary reliance on military force rather than on the compromises of political negotiations.

Finally, these recent accounts neglect the war's domestic costs. The new revisionists stress the decline of the American "will" to win, but they say little about how the economic disasters and a corrupted presidency produced by the war influenced that "will." As early as January 1966, Lyndon Johnson admitted that "because of Vietnam we cannot do all that we should, or all that we would like to do" in building a more just society at home. As the phrase went at the time, Americans—those "people of plenty"—suddenly discovered they could not have both guns and butter. The butter, or, more generally, the Great Society program, was sacrificed. A Pentagon analysis drawn up under the direction of Secretary of Defense Clark Clifford after the 1968 Tet offensive faced the problem squarely. It concluded that militarily the war could not be won, "even with the 200,000 additional troops" requested by Westmoreland. A drastic escalation, moreover, would result not only in "increased defiance of the draft," but in "growing unrest in the cities because of the belief that we are ignoring domestic problems." A "domestic crisis of unprecedented proportions" threatened. If the new revisionists and Reagan Republicans plan to manipulate the war's history to obtain higher defense budgets and unilateral commitments overseas, they should discuss this crucial characteristic of the war's course: it was determined less by campus protesters than by the growing realization that the costs worsened the conditions of the poorest and most discriminated against in American society until an "unprecedented" crisis loomed. Clifford turned against the war after businessmen he respected suddenly became scared and dovish. Clifford learned, but there is little evidence that the new revisionists understand the choices that were embedded in what they dismiss as the "Vietnam syndrome."

As persons who attack centralized power in the federal government, the new revisionists and the Reagan Republicans should at least discuss the effect of Vietnam on the imperial presidency. They could note, for example, that nothing centralizes power more rapidly than waging the cold war militarily, unless it is waging hot war in Korea and Vietnam. In 1967, Under Secretary of State Nicholas Katzenbach told the Senate that the power given by the Constitution to Congress to declare war was "an outmoded phraseology." In 1969–1972, Nixon used "national security" as the rationale for ordering a series of acts that resulted in nearly forty criminal indictments. Vietnam raised the central question in American foreign policy: How can the nation's interests be defended without destroying the economic and political principles that make it worth defending? In their extensive study of Vietnam, the new revisionists have chosen to ignore that question.

They have instead concentrated on an objective that is as simple as it is potentially catastrophic; the removal of the restraints of history, so that the next war can be waged from the start with fewer limitations. They are offering a particular interpretation of the last war, so the next war can be fought differently. This purpose helps explain why these writers stress the narrow military aspects of the war and ignore the larger problems of historical context, the Western allies, economic costs, and political corruption. Westmoreland again set the tone with his remark that "if we go to war . . . we need heed the old Oriental saying, 'It takes the full strength of a tiger to kill a rabbit' and use appropriate force to bring the war to a timely end." In his reassessment of the tragedy, Ambassador Robert Komer condemned the "institutional factors—bureaucratic restraints" that made success impossible. Lewy argued that the struggle was considered a mistake at the time because of "the conviction that the war was not being won and apparently showed little prospect of coming to a successful conclusion." If only the restraints had been lifted, the new revisionists imply, the war—which they consider morally and politically justified—could have been fought to a successful conclusion. This inference is drawn with little attention to either the inherent contradictions in Vietnam military strategy (for example, that villages had to be destroyed to be saved) or the nonmilitary aspects of the conflict. It comes perilously close to an end-justifies-the-means argument.

By trying to make the last war more acceptable, the new revisionists are asking us to make the next war legitimate, even before we know where it will be or what it will be fought for. A Chinese official once told Henry Kissinger that "one should not lose the whole world just to gain South Vietnam." Nor, it might be added, should men with sponges try to legitimize their global cold-war policies by whitewashing the history of the war in South Vietnam.

18

Up From Segregation: The American South and the Promise of Racial Justice

JOHN SHELTON REED

• No history of the United States since World War II could possibly be complete without an account of the black struggle for equality. In 1954, the United States Supreme Court ruled unconstitutional the "separate but equal" schools that had typified the nation officially since 1898 and in fact throughout its history. In 1956, the Montgomery bus boycott in Alabama brought national attention to segregated facilities in public conveyances, and soon thereafter sit-ins and "freedom rides" kept up a constant pressure for integration in the South. And in 1963, at the giant March on Washington, Dr. Martin Luther King, Jr., spoke from the steps of the Lincoln Memorial to proclaim the goal: "Free at Last."

The March on Washington was followed by the Civil Rights Act of 1964, the Voting Registration Act of 1965, the explosive riots in Los Angeles, Detroit, and Newark in the mid-1960s, and the rise of a militant black nationalist movement that signaled political and social changes between blacks and whites in the United States. Southern blacks, protected by federal marshals, registered to vote and in succeeding years put into office hundreds of black officials and whites responsive to their black constituents.

In the following essay, John Shelton Reed argues that the momentous changes in the South in the last quarter-century have made that section the most promising in terms of the ultimate goal of racial justice. After so much pain and violence, there is at last the hope that the old Confederacy will "give the world its first grand example of two races living together in equality and with mutual respect."

Around 1970, a number of Southerners began to say something rather odd. Independently, they had concluded that the South might be coming out of a tense and turbulent era in black-white relations in better condition than the rest of the country. Some even ventured to hope that the South could show other Americans, and the world, what an equitable biracial society looks like. The then-governor of Virginia, Linwood Holton, for instance, told a Rotary convention in St. Augustine that "we in the South have a better opportunity than any area of America to resolve the American dilemma, to become a model for race relations." Other observers—journalists and scholars as well as politicians—were starting to express similar opinions. It was about that time that I wrote an article with the self-explanatory title, "Can the South Show the Way?"

As the seventies began, black Southerners were worse off than non-Southern blacks by nearly every measure one might examine—the standard of living they were able to achieve, their influence in politics, the white attitudes they confronted. But, I argued, their circumstances were improving faster in all of these respects. This had two important implications. In the first place, it helped to explain the otherwise puzzling fact that one opinion poll after another, throughout the 1960s, had shown "that Southern blacks [were] less resentful, more hopeful, and less alienated than other black Americans." People evaluate their situation not only in terms of how good or bad it is, but in light of how it is changing, and how rapidly. Things were clearly getting better for Southern blacks, and the polls showed that they recognized this. In consequence, they showed a degree of satisfaction to which many non-Southern blacks (for whom things were not improving as fast, if at all) were not disposed. This translated into a degree of patience, I wrote, that gave Southern whites the chance to make change "gracefully, in an atmosphere relatively free of urgency and acrimony."

The other implication, by simple arithmetic, was that the condition of black Southerners would soon be better than that of non-Southern blacks *in absolute terms.* I hedged: "The question is what the limits of these changes are to be. Straightforward extrapolation suggests that Southern blacks will soon be better off . . . than Northern black people; cynicism suggests that this is too much to hope for, and that [white Southerners] should be content with a pattern of race relations and racial inequalities no worse than that found elsewhere."

I don't know what Governor Holton's audience made of his speech, but the response to my article was . . . mixed. Some conservatives liked its insistence that the North was far from perfection in racial matters, because it supported their view that Northerners ought to leave the South alone and put their own house in order. But others didn't care for the assumption that white supremacy was doomed; they were not hog-wild about biracial societies in the first place and equitable ones least of all. A few liberals seemed to like the article because it could be used to shame Northerners ("If even the South can have good race relations, surely we can do better"), but others disliked what they saw as my complacence; they pointed out that the trends I was so coldbloodedly examining didn't just *happen* but were the product of human struggle and sacrifice. Other liberals apparently didn't feel the South *deserved* good race relations. And still others were damned if they were going to agree with any article published in *National Review*, as mine was.

All in all, however, the world little noted nor long remembered that article. I am still fond of it, though, not just because it was my first effort at political journalism but because its predictions increasingly look to be right.

Even at the time, although nobody knew it, black Americans were beginning to vote with their feet. In the early seventies, for the first time since the end of the slave trade, more blacks moved to the South than left it—a pattern that continues. As an expanding economy and the death of Jim Crow have created a black middle class in the South alongside the old segregated triad of preacher, teacher, and undertaker, black managers and professionals have been moving to the South's cities and suburbs. The in-gathering has been taking place at the bottom of the economic ladder, too, although there it is often not a matter of Southern promise but of crushed hopes in the North: poverty in rural Mississippi is at least safer and warmer than poverty in a Northern ghetto.

The pattern I noted of greater satisfaction and less impatience among Southern blacks has continued. A University of Michigan survey in 1978, for instance, found blacks in the South more likely than those elsewhere to say they were "completely satisfied with life": one non-Southern black in five said that, but one out of every three black Southerners did. In part this simply indicates that Southern blacks are good Southerners, since the same regional difference exists among whites. But the difference was greater among blacks than among whites; Southern blacks were more likely to express satisfaction than whites from any region; and the difference between Southern and non-Southern blacks was greater in 1978 than it had been seven years earlier. Those data suggest that conditions were still improving faster for Southern blacks than for non-Southern blacks, or at least that black Southerners were more likely to believe their conditions were improving.

If that is what they thought, they were correct. We can look in more detail at three ways that their situation was changing, corresponding roughly to what Max Weber identified as the three ways someone's situation *can* improve or deteriorate: one can have more or less *money, power,* and *respect.*

Money is the easiest to deal with, since it lends itself best to counting. In 1970 Southern blacks were (as they always had been) poorer, on the average, than blacks in any other part of the country. Black Southern families were nearly twice as likely to be poor as black families in every other region of the U.S. The gap was closing, but one could not expect it to close immediately. Part of the problem had to do with the South's economy: white incomes were lower in the South, too. And black Southerners of the older generation carried the burden of *past* discrimination: they had, on the average, poorer education and less of it than blacks elsewhere in the country; they were already in worse-paying jobs, with little likelihood that would change anytime soon.

Despite all of the built-in inertia, though, the gap has been closing, and in 1982, for the first time, the poverty rate for black families in the South was no longer the highest in the country. It was still higher than that for black families in the Northeast or the West, but it was lower than in the North Central states, and that is something truly unprecedented. Figures for family income show the same convergence. In 1982, black family income in the South averaged about $13,000—some 5 percent higher than the figure for the North Central states.

Obviously many Southern blacks still have economic problems, but their problems are now no worse than those of black families everywhere else in the nation. In part, unfortunately, this is because the situation of blacks elsewhere has been deteriorating. During the 12 years from 1970 to 1982 the percentage of black families living in poverty decreased by five points in the South, while it was increasing everywhere else: by 14 points in the North Central states, by 12 points in the Northeast, and by two and a half points in the West. Currently 38 percent of black families in the South are poor—a disgraceful figure, but that percentage is decreasing and is already lower than the figure for one other major American region. Black poverty is a serious problem, but my point here is that it is no longer a peculiarly *Southern* problem.

Moreover, the South may be better-equipped than some other parts of the country to deal with that problem; if so, the trend of the past 15 years or so should continue. The "Sunbelt" is not wholly a fiction, and the economic prospects for the South are certainly rosier than those for the cities of the Northeast and North Central states, where most blacks outside the South live. It has often been observed that a no-growth economy means one group can improve its condition only at the expense of another, which quite naturally resents and resists that improvement; in an expanding economy, though, one group can improve faster than another without anyone's particularly noticing. If the South's economy continues to generate new jobs, some at least will go to black Southerners, and some benefits will trickle down (probably an accurate phrase) to those who are now the poorest—the economically marginal rural black population of the Deep South. Finally, it is ironic that the weakness of labor unions in the South, which some see as an unmistakable mark of Southern backwardness, may work to at least the short-run advantage of Southern blacks. Elsewhere, unions may have kept up the wages of those who had jobs, but it seems likely that they have reduced the total number of jobs available and they have often operated, one way or another, to exclude blacks from employment.

When we turn from economics to politics, we see the same pattern, but even more dramatic: faster improvement, and in some respects a better situation, for blacks in the South. Here one finds an especially

striking discontinuity, and it can be dated precisely: 1965. The Voting
Rights Act of that year is arguably the single most important accomplishment of the entire civil rights movement.

Only 25 years ago, a mere quarter of the eligible black voters in the
eleven formerly Confederate states were registered to vote. The poll
taxes, literacy tests, and other devices that kept that figure low are a
matter of public record; the economic and sometimes physical intimi-
dation used for the same purpose usually operated less conspicuously.
In 1964, well into the era of the civil rights movement, that figure had
increased from 25 percent or so to only 38 percent, and in some states,
of course, it was much lower. In Mississippi only 6 percent of eligible
blacks were registered in 1965. By 1968, three years after the passage
of the Voting Rights Act, the black registration percentage had increased from 38 percent to 62 percent in the South as a whole, and
from 6 percent to nearly 60 percent in Mississippi. That percentage
has not changed greatly since—it went up a little more by 1970 and
subsequently decreased a bit—but it is almost as high as the percentage
of whites registered to vote; it is about the same as the figure for black
registration in the rest of the country; and it is high enough to have
transformed Southern politics.

The most conspicuous change has probably been the election of
blacks to public office in the South. There are tens of thousands of
elected officials in the South, serving in the U.S. Congress and state
legislatures, in city and county offices and in law enforcement, on
state and local school boards. Of these tens of thousands, in 1965,
precisely 78 were black. By 1970, when Governor Holton made his
speech and I wrote that article, there had been a ninefold increase, to
711. By 1981, *that* figure had more than trebled: more than 2,500
blacks held elective office in the eleven ex-Confederate states, and
Mississippi had more black elected officials than any other state in
the Union.

Between 1970 and the presidential campaign of Jesse Jackson,
there was no increase in the percentage of Southern blacks registered
to vote, so the growing number of black politicians in the South
clearly indicates the growing political sophistication of the region's
black voters. (Still, registration does no good without voter turnout.
Here, too, though, there are encouraging portents for those who believe that black political participation indicates a healthy body politic.

In the Democratic primaries on "Super Tuesday," March 13, 1984, black Southern Democrats were half again as likely as white ones to vote; and their votes delivered Georgia and Alabama to Walter Mondale and kept Jesse Jackson's candidacy alive.)

While the number and percentage of black elected officials in the South continues to grow, there remains a disparity between the percentage of black population and the percentage of black elected officials. Although blacks are about 19 percent of the South's population, only 3 percent or so of the South's elected officials are black. But in the Northeast only 1/2 of 1 percent of elected officials are black; in the North Central states and in the West, 4/10 of 1 percent. Put another way: 22 of every hundred thousand black Southerners are elected public officials. In the North Central states, the figure is 19 per hundred thousand; in the West, 15; in the Northeast, 12.

Here again, there is little cause for Southern self-congratulation. Whites are much more likely than blacks to hold public office in the South, and the number and variety of ingenious schemes to keep it that way may well merit the attention of the Justice Department. But blacks are now less underrepresented in the South than in other parts of the country; that is a remarkable change; and that is my point.

This is not because Southern whites are more willing than non-Southern whites to vote for black politicians. Public opinion polls and election results reveal no such difference. In the South, like everywhere else in the country, most elected black politicians represent constituencies with black majorities or close to it. But there are many more such constituencies in the South. The same concentration of black voting strength has drastically affected the behavior of white elected officials, even when it has not produced black office-holders. Southern white politicians are much more likely now to respond to the interests of their black constituents. Black enfranchisement has produced new faces: Jimmy Carter is probably the epitome, but there are many others. In other cases, the new faces have been affixed to old heads. Think only of George Wallace's last gubernatorial race or Strom Thurmond's recent sponsorship of National Historically Black Colleges Week. (It is probably unkind to point out that the senator has always been in favor of black colleges.)

Political predictions are even riskier than economic ones, but there are some reasons to expect these trends to continue. In the Every-

Cloud-Has-a-Silver-Lining Department, the increasing segregation of the South's cities means that more and more of them, like more and more cities elsewhere, will find themselves with black mayors and city councils (although a variety of redistricting and municipal reorganization schemes—all under intense judicial scrutiny—could affect this one way or the other). Less troublesome is what may be the increasing willingness of *some* white voters to support *some* black candidates. Charlotte is only the latest in a long string of Southern communities where black officeholders have been elected by biracial majorities. For the time being, at least, these majorities seem to result from the so-called "Atlanta coalition" between blacks and middle-class whites, rather than the populist coalition of have-nots that Chandler Davidson claims in his book, *Bi-racial Politics*, to have spied once in Houston.

When we turn from considerations of money and power to matters of *respect*, the problem of measuring well-being gets even trickier, but what we are talking about here is essentially the attitudes of white Southerners toward their black fellow citizens, and we can turn to attitude surveys, with all their problems, for at least a first approximation. Here again, there is the familiar pattern of faster change in the South than elsewhere, leading to regional convergence.

Consider where we started. In 1942, public opinion polls showed that 98 percent of white Southerners favored absolute segregation of the public schools. *Ninety-eight percent.* That's everybody. (Two percent probably misunderstood the question.) By 1956, two years after the *Brown* decision, there had been only a little change in white Southern opinion: 14 percent of whites from the Southern and border states thought black and white children should attend the same schools. But by 1970, only 16 percent of white Southern parents—one in six—objected to having their children in school with "a few" black children, and this trend, too, has continued. By 1980, only 5 percent of white Southern parents said they didn't want their children in school with *any* black children. Again, that's practically unanimous, but it's on the other side, and that number—5 percent—is no different from the figure for the country as a whole.

Imagine: a regional difference of great—indeed, calamitous—importance 30 years ago has simply evaporated, or so it appears. Of course, some of these people are lying: it is not entirely respectable in the 1980s to express segregationist views to a stranger who turns up on your doorstep. But in 1942, and 1956, it was not respectable *not* to express such views. And that, too, is a change of great importance.

There are still some regional differences in other measures of racial attitudes. White Southern parents are more likely than white parents elsewhere to say they don't want their children in schools with a black majority, for instance. But the regional difference is small, and most white parents everywhere say they would object to that. White Southerners are somewhat less likely than other whites to say they would vote for a qualified black presidential candidate, but most say they would. Most white Southerners say they do not approve of racial inter-marriage, but almost as large a majority of non-Southern whites say that. All in all, the differences in racial attitudes between white Southerners and other white Americans are now differences only of degree, and of relatively small degree at that. Those differences are smaller than they have been at any time in the recent past, and they are getting smaller still with each year.

In practice I doubt that these remaining differences mean much. In the first place, what matters to non-Southern black people, day to day, is less the attitudes of all non-Southern whites than those of whites in the large cities of the Northeast and Midwest, where most blacks outside the South actually live. What whites in Vermont or Oregon think about race relations is of some academic interest, and occasionally of political importance, but it has little to do with the everyday experience of black Americans. I have not seen the attitudes of whites in Chicago, say, or Boston broken out separately in attitude surveys, but surely few would care to argue that they are good examples for white Southerners to emulate.

In the second place, and more important, the attitudes someone expresses to a survey researcher are only part of the story and often not the most important part. The norms, the customs, that govern interaction can be as important as your attitudes in determining how you treat somebody. We saw how this worked under Jim Crow: how a white person felt about black people (or vice versa) had little to do with how they interacted. That was prescribed in detail by an "etiquette of race relations" (to borrow the title of Bertram Doyle's 1937 book on the subject); individuals could only embroider the basic pattern a bit to suit their attitudes.

Perhaps I should say that *some* of us saw how it worked under Jim Crow. It bears emphasizing that upward of 60 percent of Southerners, black and white, are too young to remember *Brown v. Board of Education*. Those Southerners who did not live through the last 30 years—my students, for example, who have a way of being born a bit later each year—find it hard to believe what most of us took for granted as just *the way things were* in the 1940s and 50s. My students find it hilarious when I tell them that the *Brown* decision apparently produced a measurable deflection in the white Southern birthrate, or when they read in Howard Odum's *Race and Rumors of Race* about the "Eleanor [Roosevelt] Clubs" that many Southern whites believed their black maids belonged to. The splendid anthropological studies of the Jim Crow South have about as much immediacy for them, I would guess, as Malinowsky on the Trobrianders. When I describe the segregated bathrooms and water fountains and dry cleaners and basketball teams of my youth, they appear to believe me—just as one would believe a Martian's description of his home planet. I gather that their parents, as a rule, don't talk about it.

It gives me some sympathy for immigrant parents who have to deal with American children. Southerners in their forties and older have "immigrated," in effect, just by staying put. The South we grew up in is as different from our children's as the Polish shtetl from Manhattan's Lower East Side, or Naples from Boston's North End.

Even those who remember sometimes find it hard to believe. At least I do. Last year I saw a couple of etched glass doors in a small South Carolina town: one said WHITE, the other COLORED. I was almost literally stunned—stunned to realize that signs like that had once been an ordinary part of my life and stunned to realize that it had been nearly 20 years since I had last seen any. Like so much that was once thought to be terribly important, they had disappeared, largely without my noticing. It is a nice touch, I think, that these doors last year were in an antique shop—and if the dealer hadn't wanted 50 dollars for the pair I would have bought them. God only knows what for—maybe I'd have used them in my teaching and taken an income-tax deduction.

Obviously things have changed. Laws have changed, and attitudes have changed, and (to return to the point) *etiquette* has changed. Not long ago, I had to do business in the courthouse of one of the poorest and blackest of North Carolina's counties. Ahead of me in line for the tax clerk was an elderly black man. Thirty years ago, he would have automatically effaced himself and I would just as automatically have gone ahead of him. I cannot say what he would have been thinking, but I probably would not have noticed. When his turn came, the young white woman at the counter would have addressed him as "James" or maybe, in that part of North Carolina, as "Uncle." She would not have meant to demean him, and, like me, she would not have been thinking about the implications of her behavior. Indeed, she would probably have denied that her behavior *had* any implications. She and I—and he, for that matter—would just have been doing what we were supposed to do, and our attitudes would have been neither here nor there.

That is not, obviously, what happened in 1984. I dare say that if Gallup ever came to that county, he would not find it a hotbed of racial liberalism. If he interviewed the young woman at the counter, I doubt that her attitudes would satisfy the members of the old Civil Rights Commission. But in 1984 she waited on the man in his turn, exchanged some routine pleasantries with him about the unpleasant weather, called him "sir" at first and "Mr. Jones" after that—she treated him, in other words, like any other presumptively decent citizen of that county. And she was just doing what she was supposed to do.

Argument from anecdote is bad form in my trade, and I won't let my students do it, but I do believe that episode is increasingly typical. Manners *have* changed. More and more, in places like courthouses and stores and schools, Southern whites seem disposed to treat black Southerners as sort of honorary white folks—and by and large, whatever their private opinions of one another, white Southerners treat each other with courtesy and at least the appearance of good-natured respect. Southern blacks, for their part, seem willing to return the favor. The upshot is that on a day to-day basis (which is how most of us lead our lives, after all) black-white relations in the South seem more cordial, less prickly, than black-white relations in the cities of the North. There is even some survey evidence to support this (again,

from the University of Michigan): overall, 44 percent of non-Southerners described their lives as "very friendly"; 54 percent of all Southerners—and 58 percent of black Southerners—did so.

There is an irony here. William Chafe, in his study of the civil
rights movement in Greensboro, *Civilities and Civil Rights*, argues
that the value Southerners place on civility worked against the movement to oversimplify his point, that even blacks' potential allies in the
white community saw sit-ins and other forms of black protest and self-
assertion as a violation of the norms of civility, as *bad manners*. If I
am right, those same norms may contribute to amicable race relations
today and in the future. Walker Percy has written somewhere that
Southerners know the point of manners: they exist so no one will not
know what to do. A great many Southerners are apparently willing to
do what they are supposed to do—whatever that may be—and that can
contribute to good race relations as easily as to bad.

No doubt some would argue that the value of civility still keeps
many unresolved issues from being addressed squarely, and they may
be right. One should recognize, though, that it is not just *white* Southerners who value civility. That black Southerners for a time were not
willing to do what they were "supposed to do" does not indicate that
they do not share that value: instead, their actions were dramatic evidence of the extent of their frustration and exasperation.

One more story: After Chicago disgraced itself [in 1983] with a
bitter black-against-white mayoralty campaign, Harvey Gantt, who
was running for mayor of Charlotte, said that race would not be the
same sort of issue there. "We're much politer here," he told the
North Carolina Independent. "We're not going to see that kind of
down-in-the-gutter fight." He was right: Charlotte didn't, and he is
now Charlotte's first black mayor.

Gantt's choice of pronouns points to another change that anyone who
wishes the South well must welcome. Notice who is more polite: it is
we (Southerners), not *they* (whites). When William Ferris, director
of the Center for the Study of Southern Culture, was on William
Buckley's "Firing Line" a couple of years ago, he said something fas-
cinating: "In the decade of the 80s what we're seeing is an interesting
kind of evolution from the 60s and 70s to a sense of Southerners as
Southerners as opposed to black versus white." Well, some days I am

more ready to believe that than others, but there are signs of the growth of a sense of regional identification that transcends racial differences, if one wants to look for them, and that would be something new, and wholly delightful, in my view.

There have always been similarities of style and culture between black and white Southerners. How could it be otherwise? One frivolous example: On television [in 1983] I saw the Mighty Reverend Al Greene lead the Soul Train Dancers in a remarkable rendition of "Amazing Grace." The very next day (I swear it), on the radio, I heard Jerry Lee Lewis swing directly from "Great Balls of Fire" to "If We Could Spend Our Vacation in Heaven." Which better illustrates W. J. Cash's observation about the mixture of hedonism and piety in the Southern mind?

The great cultural similarity between black and white Southerners seems especially evident to those who have come to know one another outside the South. That experience is increasingly common, and it may have something to do with what Bill Ferris told Bill Buckley: Ferris came back to Mississippi from the Ivy League. Anyone who needs convincing really should read Albert Murray's *South to a Very Old Place*, a remarkable book with the bad luck to be published at least ten years before its time. It is certainly no accident that Murray was returning to Alabama from New York.

Despite the cultural similarity, though, Southern blacks have not generally been inclined or encouraged in the past to think of themselves as black *Southerners*, and there is survey evidence to show that as late as the 1960s most probably did not. As Merle Black and I showed in an article in the *Journal of Politics*, though, that has changed dramatically since then. (Unfortunately we had no data on how Southern whites construe the word *Southerner* and whether that has changed.) We will know the process of identification is complete when more black Southerners, like Harvey Gantt, talk, of the South's superiority—and when they habitually complain that non-Southerners do not understand the South, that they are tired of hearing the South put down, and so forth. Examples are still rare enough to be collectible, but they are starting to turn up here and there. When Robert Botsch, a political scientist, asked a black North Carolina furniture worker why he was planning to vote for Jimmy Carter, for instance, the man told him he was getting "tired of listening to all these slick

Yankees who think they know everything and have all the answers."
It is hard to sound more Southern than *that*.

To repeat the question some of us were asking *circa* 1970: Can the
South show the way? Can the South, I wondered then, "do more
than catch up with the Northern pattern of race relations?" Can it
"break through to an accommodation qualitatively different from and
superior to that displayed in, say, Philadelphia or Cicero?" Well, perhaps it is beginning to. It is not really for me or for any other white
Southerner to say whether the South has already become a better
place than the Northeast or Midwest for black Americans to live, but
it is certainly a better place now than it was 30 years ago, or 15—and
that may not be true of other parts of the United States. The South
has not shown the way yet. Black Southerners still have many legitimate grievances. They still do not have their share of money, power,
and respect. But at least there is no reason for Southerners to apologize
to *Yankees* anymore.

There is, to repeat, no reason to be smug about it. Catching up with
the rest of the country is not an especially impressive achievement, and
only a few white Southerners can take much credit even for that. But
black Southerners can be proud of their accomplishment, and they
have served their region—our region—well. The South is now more
worthy than ever of Southerners' affection for it.

Those of us who predicted that 12 or 15 years ago have no reason
to be smug either. A remarkable article in *The Virginia Quarterly
Review* predicted the same thing a decade earlier, in 1961, at a time
when it sounded not just unlikely but downright *crazy*. Leslie W.
Dunbar, then executive director of the Southern Regional Council
(the South's oldest biracial organization), had no illusions about his
fellow white Southerners. He knew that white supremacy would not
be given up without a fight, less because white profited from it than
because many Southern whites would feel it a duty to defend their
past and their society. But Dunbar wrote:

> Once the fight is decisively lost (the verdict has to be decisive),
> once the Negro has secured the right to vote, has gained admit-
> tance to the public library, has fought his way into a desegrated
> public school, has been permitted to sup at a lunch counter, the
> typical white Southerner will shrug his shoulder, resume his

stride, and go on. He has, after all, shared a land with his black neighbors for a long while; he can manage well enough even if the patterns change. There is now one fewer fight which history requires of him. He has done his ancestral duty. He . . . can relax a bit more.

And so, surprisingly enough, it has come to pass. The South has taken on a new character, as Dunbar said it would. Despite the conflict and turmoil since he wrote—indeed, largely because of it—the South still has the opportunity he saw a generation ago, one "it can fulfill better than any place or people anywhere." The South may yet "give the world its first grand example of two races of men living together in equality and with mutual respect."

19

The Soviet-American Conflict:

A Strange Phenomenon

NORMAN A. GRAEBNER

• In April 1945, the armies of the United States and the Soviet Union met at the Elbe River in Germany. The once invincible Wehrmacht had at last been crushed, and the threat of a Hitler-dominated Europe had finally been put to rest. The greatest war in history was about to come to a successful conclusion (the Japanese would hold out for four more months), and the victors had already agreed to organize the United Nations to help future generations avoid the terrible horrors of armed conflict.

On one level, the promise of the United Nations has been kept. While there have been dozens of little wars in the last forty years, the superpowers have somehow kept the peace between themselves, and the world as we know it has somehow endured. But on another level the United States and the Soviet Union have not moved at all toward peaceful coexistence, instead stockpiling ever more powerful weapons and confronting each other in every part of the globe. The origins of the Cold War have long been in dispute, but no scholar has achieved more prominence in dealing with the history of modern international relations than Professor Norman A. Graebner of the University of Virginia. The following essay suggests that Americans must recognize the peculiar history of the Soviet people and admit that the United States lacks the ability to bring about fundamental change in Russian society.

From its beginnings in the late 1940s America's Cold War rivalry with the Soviet Union has rested on images of danger—what Walter Lippmann once described as "pictures in our heads." Animated generally by feelings of hostility, U.S. officials have at times exaggerated the perils to this country's security in events which implicated the Kremlin. It was this tendency in official perception that permitted the Soviet invasion of Afghanistan, a region of no historic American concern, to inaugurate a conflict over beliefs and intentions so intense that it soon threatened the whole international order with catastrophe. Marshall Shulman, director of Columbia University's W. Averell Harriman Institute for Advanced Study of the Soviet Union, has likened the post-Afghan international climate to that produced by the Cuban missile crisis of October 1962. Former Ambassador to Russia Malcolm Toon has called relations with Soviets worse than at any time since World War II. Reports from Moscow reveal that the Russians view the present state of Soviet-American relations with equal anxiety. Perhaps the grimmest assessment comes from Soviet expert George F. Kennan. Writing in the October 3, 1983, issue of *The New Yorker*, Kennan observed that public discussion of Russian-American relations had created the impression that a military showdown remains the only means of settling differences worth considering. "Can anyone mistake, or doubt," he asked, "the ominous meaning of such a state of affairs? The phenomena just described . . . are the familiar characteristics, the unfailing characteristics, of a march toward war—that, and nothing else."

What measures the magnitude of the Soviet-American rivalry most visibly is the nuclear arms race. During the past quarter century, the United States has spent several trillion dollars for defense. The Stockholm International Peace Research Institute estimated that global military spending in 1982 alone reached no less than $700 billion, an acceleration over previous years caused largely by new levels in U.S. military expenditures. Nuclear weapons had acquired a momentum of their own, backed by the imperative that a nuclear power must exploit the scientific knowledge and technological capabilities at its command. Washington officials assumed, moreover, that the buildup of the American military establishment would contain Soviet expansionism and compel the Russians ultimately to accept some resolution of the Soviet-American conflict largely on Western terms.

Strangely American weapons, however numerous and destructive, have revealed no capacity to stabilize the Soviet-American relationship or to curtail those modes of Russian behavior that have sustained this nation's fears and insecurity. Indeed, unclear arsenals have proved to be quite irrelevant to the task of creating a stable international order. No one can predict with any accuracy what impact several thousand nuclear explosions would have on human society. Nuclear weapons might comprise a significant element in international life; yet governments must conduct their external relations with the realization that a nuclear war, even a limited one, would be so appalling in its consequences that no political or ideological objective could justify it. "Nuclear weapons," Robert McNamara wrote in September 1983, "serve no military purpose whatsoever. They are totally useless—except to deter one's opponent from using them." Although instrumental in discouraging direct aggression against the status quo, America's conventional power, like its nuclear armaments, has not been very effective in managing international affairs.

In large measure the current fascination with the arms race assumes that weapons comprise the chief danger to civilization. Yet negotiations for weapons reduction are as unrelated to the essential purpose of reducing the danger of armed conflict as is the continued building of the American military establishment itself. Novelists, scientists, and scholars who describe the horrors of nuclear war seldom bother to explain its coming, and with good reason. Weapons may be troublesome, even dangerous, but they are not central to the status of war and peace. Weapons do not cause war; they determine only its nature. Despite their extensive preparations for war, the U.S. and the U.S.S.R., through 35 years of high tension and mutual recrimination, did not confront one another with force. Indeed, the two superpowers did not even approach such a decision, and the Cuban missile crisis of October 1962 was no clear exception. Historically nations have engaged in war not over competition for military supremacy but over conflicting purposes that engaged their perceived interests and transcended the possibilities of negotiated settlements. Overwhelmingly the wars of modern Europe involved contests over territory—the lands along the Rhine and the Baltic, the principalities of Germany, northern Italy, and the Balkans, or the strategic entrances to the Mediterranean. National ambitions were sufficiently specific to render most wars predictable.

It is true that the tragic confrontation between Europe's two alli-

ance systems in the summer of 1914 raised questions of national prestige far more than specific economic or security interests. Even then a
generation of American and European analysts had predicted accurately that war would come to Europe over the clash of Austrian and
Russian ambitions in the Balkans. At Versailles in 1919 British Prime
Minister David Lloyd George observed that Germany's predictable determination to recover the Germanic territories of East-Central Europe would set off another war. In February 1925, Sir James Headlam-
Morley, historical adviser to the British Foreign Office, warned his
government that the Vistula, not the Rhine, was the real danger point
in Europe. In a prophetic memorandum to the foreign minister, Sir
Austen Chamberlain, he posed a critical question:

> Has anyone attempted to realize what would happen if there
> were to be a new partition of Poland, or if the Czechoslovak
> state were to be so curtailed and dismembered that in fact it
> disappeared from the map of Europe? The whole of Europe
> would at once be in chaos. There would no longer be any prin-
> ciple, meaning, or sense in the territorial arrangements of the
> continent. Imagine, for instance, that under some improbable
> condition, Austria joined Germany; that Germany, using the
> discontented minority in Bohemia, demanded a new frontier far
> over the Mountains, including Carlsbad and Pilsen. . . . This
> would be catastrophic. . . .

Hitler's quarrel with Europe after 1937 always focused on specific territories where German ambitions were historic and predictable. America's burgeoning conflict with Japan in the western Pacific over the future of East Asia was no less specific. Every contest in Europe and
Asia was over ends, not means.

Unlike the major international conflicts of the past, that between
the U.S. and the U.S.S.R. suggests no areas where the two powers are
clearly and unmistakably in opposition. Through more than 30 years
of Cold War, Washington officials have insisted that the Soviet-
American rivalry flows from the nature of the Russian regime and its
global ambitions. Yet never have they framed a rational explanation
of the presumed determination of Soviet leaders to extend their power
across the world. Nor have they explained away the responsibility
which Soviet leaders carry for the welfare of the Russian masses whose
lives would be shattered by a general war. Despite the global fears that

sustain the Cold War, the Soviet danger has remained so imprecise that no one has managed to define it. Nowhere—not in Europe, the Middle East, Asia, Africa, or Latin America—have the Russians revealed any ambition or interest of sufficient importance to merit military aggression or a showdown with the United States. What brought war to the world between 1939 and 1941 was a series of thoroughly predictable assaults on the treaty structures of Europe and Asia. Unlike Hitler's Germany, the Soviet Union has not threatened to launch a direct military assault against any region regarded vital to the security of the United States and its Western allies. Kennan reminded a Washington audience in November 1983 of the absence of specific dangers in the Soviet-American conflict. "There are no considerations of policy—no aspirations, no ambitions, no anxieties, no defensive impulses," he said, "that could justify the continuation of this dreadful situation."

After mid-century, much of the Soviet-American rivalry invaded the Third World, where subversion and revolution seemed to offer the Kremlin untold opportunities to extend its influence at the expense of the West. Yet nowhere outside Europe did Soviet behavior in support of revolution create dangers precise enough to invite even one threat of military retaliation. Revolutions, invariably indigenous and historic, permit little gain to those who support them. The very nationalistic impulses and objectives that unleashed the postwar upheavals across the Afro-Asian world erected formidable barriers against external influences, whether they emanated from the U.S. or the U.S.S.R. Washington's counterrevolutionary efforts, designed to contain perceived Soviet expansionism, never engaged the U.S.S.R. directly simply because the success or failure of Third World revolutions never delineated any interests, either Russian or American, whose defense was worth the risk of a direct military confrontation. The Kremlin's reluctance to expose its troops to death and destruction in regions beyond Russia's periphery measured its limited interests in the Third World. The Soviet challenge to American will in Asia, Africa, and the Caribbean had little relevance to Russia's strategic capabilities; the Kremlin, in practice, limited its ambitions to what its comparatively modest exports of weapons and advisers could achieve. Such aid might sustain unwanted revolutionary activity and create perceptions of acute danger among

Washington officials; in the absence of any Russian military presence it could hardly comprise a reason for war.

History reminds us that the causes of war can be trivial. The Great War of 1914 revealed a horrifying disparity between the causes of war and the war itself. That war bled a generation of Europeans white, destroyed three venerated European dynasties, produced a vindictive peace, and set the stage for another giant war. Nothing at stake in 1914 could justify a war with such endless and exorbitant consequences. Unfortunately, the issues that sustain the Soviet-American rivalry lend themselves to no better definition than did those which divided Europe in 1914. None of them have any significance comparable to the cost of the war that the United States is preparing to fight. Thus in many respects the world of the 1980s is perilously similar to that of 1914, with the leading powers arming for a war that nobody wants and over issues that few consider critical. "We are trapped," wrote Thomas Powers in the January 1984, issue of *The Atlantic Monthly*, "in a tightening spiral of fear and hostility. We don't know why we have got into this situation, we don't know how to get out of it, and we have not found the humility to admit we don't know. In desperation, we simply try to manage our enmity from day to day."

To understand the many peculiarities in the Soviet-American conflict, most of them quite unprecedented in modern times, requires an examination of the conflict at its source. What dangers, first perceived in the late 1940s, compelled the U.S. to spend trillions of dollars for defense without apparently acquiring any real sense of security? The remarkably successful Truman Doctrine and Marshall Plan stabilized the periphery of Soviet power from Western Europe to Iran and established the foundations of Europe's astonishing recovery. Still the world of 1948 did not conform to this nation's postwar vision at all. The United States had not achieved peace on Western terms. Whether contained or not, the U.S.S.R. continued to loom as a mighty barrier to the fulfillment of the American century—a world organized at last in accordance with Western liberal-democratic ideals. Not only did the Soviet Union defy American principles of self-determination in Eastern Europe, but also it proclaimed an ideology that challenged totally the American quest for a single world community of trade, investment, and political cooperation. When Soviet ideologue Andrei

Zhdanov, in the summer of 1947, divided the world into two competing ideological camps, some American officials no longer viewed the struggle with the U.S.S.R. as one of keeping the Russians out of Western Europe and the eastern Mediterranean; that struggle had now become a global confrontation between communism and freedom, one unlimited in scope and magnitude.

Essentially this broader, less precise, definition of the Soviet danger attributed the Kremlin's expansionary power less to Russian armies than to Russia's control of international communism and its devotion to the Marxist-Leninist advocacy of world revolution. Thus the immediate threat to Eurasia did not lie in Russia's military capabilities but in the chaotic economic and political conditions that prevailed through much of Europe and Asia. The political and social turmoil in India, China, Indochina, and the Dutch East Indies, the economic paralysis of Germany and Japan, the Communist movements in France and Italy, and the collapse of most traditional sources of international stability seemed to present the Kremlin unprecedented opportunities for ideological exploitation. The doubtful viability of liberal ideas and capitalist institutions in a revolutionary world suggested that much of Eurasia and its resources might still escape the West and fall into the clutches of the Kremlin. President Harry S. Truman furthered the tendency to view the Soviet challenge as primarily one of ideology when he failed to distinguish between the generally abstentionist policy of the U.S.S.R. and the Communist-led assault on the Greek government. Washington's central Cold War assumption attributed to Russia the unprecedented capacity to expand without direct armed aggression and to advance its power and influence in regions far beyond the reach of Russian armies. Thereafter it mattered little whether Soviet forces or even Soviet officials were present at all.

By 1948 U.S. officials could detect no visible limit to Soviet power and ambition. The National Security Council's study, NSC 7, dated March 30, 1948, emphasized the Soviet challenge's global dimensions. Declared NSC 7:

> The ultimate objective of Soviet-directed world communism is the domination of the world. To this end, Soviet-directed world communism employs against its victims in opportunistic coordination the complementary instruments of Soviet aggressive pres-

sure from without and militant revolutionary subversion from within. . . . The Soviet Union is the source of power from which international communism chiefly derives its capability to threaten the existence of free nations. The United States is the only source of power capable of mobilizing successful opposition to the communist goal of world conquest.

With its control of international communism, the U.S.S.R. had engaged the U.S. in a struggle for power "in which our national security is at stake and from which we cannot withdraw short of national suicide." The Soviet world, ran the document's catalog of Russia's recent gains, "extends from the Elbe River and the Adriatic Sea on the west to Manchuria on the east, and embraces one-fifth of the land surface of the world." The supposition of NSC 7—and subsequent national security documents culminating in NSC 68 of April 1950—that the U.S.S.R. could gain control of vast areas of the globe without resort to direct armed aggression accounts for the burgeoning dichotomy between the gigantic fears of Russian expansionism, shared by countless Americans, for which no defense seems adequate, and the absence of any discernible Soviet military threat, reminiscent of Hitler's Germany, outside the Russian periphery.

That dichotomy became more pronounced with the passage of time. President Dwight D. Eisenhower accepted the basic assumptions of NSC 68 when he warned the nation early in 1953 that it stood in greater peril than at any time in its history. Again the danger lay in the proposition that all Communist-led governments of the world were under the direct control of the Kremlin. On January 27, six days after he assumed his new office, Secretary of State John Foster Dulles informed a national radio and television audience: "Already our proclaimed enemies control one-third of all the people of the world. . . . At the end of the Second World War, only a little over seven years ago, [the Soviets] only controlled about 200 million people. Today, they control 800 million people and they're hard at work to get control of other parts of the world." Even as the Eisenhower administration mounted a defense based on massive retaliation and thousands of nuclear warheads, the fears continued to mount. In June 1957, Walter S. Robertson, assistant secretary of state for Far Eastern Affairs, could tell the nation: "Starting from zero in our generation, the international Communists now hold in a grip of ruthless power 16 nations, 900 million people—a circumstance recently described by the Secretary of State as 'the most frightening fact history records.' "

What lay behind the global fears of Russian expansionism during the Eisenhower years was the assumption that the U.S.S.R., by perfecting its international party organization and saturating the world with its appealing propaganda, had attained a totally unprecedented ability to conduct indirect aggression against the non-Soviet world. To check this strangulation of the West, the U.S. had no choice but to meet the Communist danger wherever it existed and prepare to roll it back. To accept the apparent Russian gains in Eastern Europe and Asia would merely broaden the base of Soviet authority and assure its further expansion. Secretary Dulles established the requirements of U.S. policy in Europe when he reminded the American Society of Newspaper Editors in April 1953 that Western security demanded clear assurances to the captive peoples of Eastern Europe that the U.S. did not accept their captivity as a permanent fact of history. "If they thought otherwise and became hopeless," he said, "we would unwittingly have become partners to the forging of a hostile power so vast that it could encompass our destruction." Elsewhere—wherever alleged Soviet control of Communist regimes appeared especially dangerous—the administration embarked on programs designed to eliminate the threats to global security. Toward China no less than toward Eastern Europe Dulles pursued the popular and promising crusade of liberation based essentially on the doctrine of nonrecognition. In Indochina the Eisenhower administration assumed after 1954 that the Saigon regime, with ample American support and encouragement, would eliminate the Communist threat of Ho Chi Minh. Clearly there was no room in a secure, stable international order for a Kremlin-dominated monolith with the unalterable will to dominate much of the world. For both the Truman and Eisenhower administrations the choices posed by Soviet expansionism appeared to be narrow indeed.

Actually neither administration believed the Soviet-American conflict beyond the capacity of the U.S. to resolve on Western terms. Both Democratic and Republican leaders assumed that the U.S.S.R. could not, in the long run, survive the pressures exerted by the successful containment of Soviet expansionism. Kennan made this comfortable prediction in his noted "X" article, "The Sources of Soviet Conduct," which appeared in the July 1947, issue of *Foreign Affairs*. After delineating the unprecedented dangers which the United States faced in Soviet power and paranoia, Kennan added his own rejoinder:

> It is curious to note that the ideological power of Soviet authority is strongest today in areas beyond the frontiers of Russia, beyond the reach of its police power. . . . [W]ho can say with assurance that the strong light still cast by the Kremlin on the dissatisfied peoples of the Western world is not the powerful afterglow of a constellation which is in actuality on the wane? This cannot be proved. And it cannot be disproved. But the possibility remains . . . that Soviet power, like the capitalist world of its conception, bears within it the seeds of its own decay, and that the sprouting of these seeds is well advanced.

Thereafter the assumptions of underlying Soviet weakness continued to determine the outlook—and ultimately the behavior—of American officials. So vulnerable appeared the Soviet satellite empire to overextension and fragmentation that even the goal of liberating that region seemed well within the reach of a countering strategy. Secretary of State Dean Acheson and other Truman officials believed that Western power had eliminated the need for negotiation with the U.S.S.R. Confronted with inflexible will over West Berlin, the Soviets had retreated. Following the show of Western unity at the Paris Foreign Ministers Conference in May 1949, Acheson announced that the West had gained the initiative in Europe and could thereafter anticipate Russia's eventual capitulation. "[T]hese conferences from now on," Acheson informed the press on June 23, "seem to me to be like the steam gauge on a boiler. . . . They indicate the pressure which has been built up. They indicate the various gains and losses in positions which have taken place between the meetings, and I think that the recording of this conference is that the position of the West has grown greatly in strength, and that the position of the Soviet Union in regard to the struggle for the soul of Europe has changed from the offensive to the defensive." Settlements, when they came, would simply record the corroding effect of Western power on the ambitions and designs of the Kremlin.

However grave the danger described by NSC 68, that document, like its predecessors, assumed that the U.S., with "calculated and gradual coercion," could unleash the forces of destruction within the Soviet empire. Even in war the country had no reason to curtail its overall objective of eliminating the Russian problem. Rather than pursue unconditional surrender in peacetime, however, the United States would seek Soviet acceptance of "the specific and limited conditions requisite to an international environment in which free institutions can flourish, and in which the Russian people will have a new chance of working out their own destiny." In this purpose of trimming Soviet ambitions to the needs of Soviet citizens, the U.S. could anticipate support even within the U.S.S.R. "If we can make the Russian people our allies in this enterprise," NSC 68 predicted, "we will obviously have made our task easier and victory more certain." In the process of inducing change the U.S. would avoid, as far as possible, any direct challenge to Soviet prestige and "keep open the possibility for the U.S.S.R. to retreat before pressure with a minimum loss of face. . . ."

Dulles, like Acheson, assumed that the U.S.S.R. could not survive the pressures exerted by Western containment. Upon taking office in January 1953, Dulles proclaimed American purpose toward the Soviet bloc as that of creating "in other peoples such a love of freedom that they can never really be absorbed by the despotism, the totalitarian dictatorships, of the Communist world." Upon Stalin's death Dulles responded to Georgy Malenkov's appeal for peaceful coexistence in the summer of 1953 not by encouraging the president to seek a more cordial, promising relationship with the U.S.S.R. but rather with assertions that the occasion had come for breaking Soviet control of Eastern Europe completely. He informed the Cabinet on July 10: "This is the kind of time when we ought to be *doubling* our bets, not reducing them—as all the Western parliaments want to do. This is the time to *crowd* the enemy—and maybe *finish* him, once and for all." At the same time Dulles assured the nation: "[T]he Communist structure is over-extended, over-rigid and ill-founded." As oppressed populations demonstrated their spirit of independence, the secretary continued, the Kremlin "would come to recognize the futility of trying to hold captive so many peoples who, by their faith and their patriotism, can never really be consolidated into a Soviet Communist world."

Dulles' strategy of massive retaliation, he informed the nation in January 1954, would permit time and the human desire for freedom to work their destruction on the Communist enemy. "If we persist in the course I outline," he promised, "we shall confront dictatorship with a task that is, in the long run, beyond its strength. . . . If the dictators persist in their present course, then it is they who will be limited to superficial successes, while their foundations crumble under the treads of their iron boots. . . ." The secretary interpreted the Soviet agreement on the neutralization of Austria in 1955 as evidence of Soviet weakness. Indeed, Dulles' assumption that all acceptable Russian behavior reflected political necessity permitted him to maintain his posture of unrelenting hostility toward the Soviets as well as his predictions of an eventual Soviet collapse.

No less reassuring were the Eisenhower administration's claims of impending success for its anti-Communist policies in China and Indochina. For State Department officials, nonrecognition alone carried the assurance of China's liberation. As Dulles himself declared in June 1957: "We can confidently assume that international communism's rule of strict conformity is, in China as elsewhere, a passing and not a perpetual phase. We owe it to ourselves, our allies, and the Chinese people to do all we can to contribute to that passing." Repeatedly, administration spokesmen assured the American people of Ho Chi Minh's coming demise in Indochina. In May 1957, President Eisenhower greeted South Vietnamese President Ngo Dinh Diem at the Washington airport. There he lauded the Vietnamese leader publicly for bringing to his task of organizing his country "the greatest of courage, the greatest of statesmanship. . . ." When Diem departed Washington on May 11, the two presidents issued a joint communiqué which "looked forward to an end of the unhappy division of the Vietnamese people and confirmed the determination of the two Governments to work together to seek suitable means to bring about the peaceful unification of Viet-Nam in freedom." Such statements—and countless others like them—suggested that successful containment would in time undermine the Communist positions in Eastern Europe, China, and Indochina, enabling the West to dispose of the Russian challenge on its own terms.

That dichotomy of the Truman-Eisenhower years, between the assumptions of unprecedented danger and the promise of easy success, continues to govern the American approach to the Russian chal-

lenge in the 1980s. President Ronald Reagan entered the White
House in January 1981 committed to the reassertion of the country's
global leadership in response to the post-Afghan perceptions of an expanding Soviet threat. The new president defined the Russian danger
at a White House news conference in late January 1981:

> From the time of the Russian revolution until the present, So-
> viet leaders have reiterated their determination that their goal
> must be the promotion of world revolution and a one world so-
> cialist or communist state. . . . They have openly and publicly
> declared that the only morality they recognize is what will fur-
> ther their cause; meaning they reserve unto themselves the right
> to commit any crime; to lie; to cheat in order to obtain that. . . .

Reagan's views of the Soviet enemy contained no ambiguities which
might demand further study or reflection. The Soviet Union, he
charged, "underlies all the unrest that is going on . . . in the world."
Alexander M. Haig, Jr., the new secretary of state, shared the president's somber view of the Soviet danger. At his confirmation hearings
in early January 1981, he reminded members of the Senate Foreign
Relations Committee that "the years immediately ahead will be unusually dangerous. Evidence of that danger is everywhere." The nation
had no choice but to marshal its resources to shape the future. "Unchecked," he warned, "the growth of Soviet military power must eventually paralyze Western policy altogether." Again many in Washington attributed the unfortunate state of Soviet-American relations to
the nature of the Soviet system and therefore unavoidable.

Under the assumption that Soviet expansionism was the single
source of unwanted turmoil everywhere, Reagan was prepared to meet
the challenge of Soviet-backed radicalism wherever it might appear. He
decided early to convert tiny El Salvador into a major arena of Soviet-
American confrontation. Reagan's team knew long before inauguration
day that Cuba and other Soviet bloc nations had shipped arms to Salvadorian guerrillas through Nicaragua. By launching a counteroffensive
in El Salvador the administration could not only reassert American responsibility for hemispheric defense but also do so under conditions
that would eliminate the danger of a direct American involvement.
Haig met the challenge of El Salvador by quickly elevating that country to a symbol of world crisis. To Haig, Cuba and Nicaragua, as well

as the Salvadorian rebels, were tools of the Soviet Union; he expected the Kremlin to control its clients or take responsibility for their behavior. Testifying before the House Foreign Affairs Committee in mid-March 1981, the secretary declared that El Salvador was one entry on "a priority target list—a hit list, if you will, for the ultimate takeover of Central America." Unless the United States stopped the spread of Soviet-sponsored terrorism, he warned, "we will find it within our own borders tomorrow. . . . When you get to the bottom of the question, it is the Soviet Union which bears responsibility today for the proliferation and hemorrhaging of international terrorism as we have come to know it." Nicaragua had already fallen under Soviet domination; El Salvador, Guatemala, and Honduras were destined to follow.

As the strife in Central America continued into 1983 with no resolution of the alleged Soviet challenge in sight, the Reagan administration continued to remind Americans of the consequences of Russian success in building a bridgehead in the center of the hemisphere. "Our credibility," the president warned, "would collapse, our alliances would crumble, and the safety of our homeland would be in jeopardy." That spring Secretary of Defense Caspar W. Weinberger declared that the administration was determined to confront the Soviets in any part of the world it considered important. Failure to stop the insurgency in Central America, he said, would compel the U.S. to withdraw its forces from Europe, Japan, and Korea, leaving the entire Eastern Hemisphere to Soviet purposes. Time brought no respite. In mid-April 1984, President Reagan accused Nicaragua of joining the Soviet Union and Cuba in trying "to install communism by force throughout this hemisphere. . . . We cannot turn our backs on this crisis at our doorstep." Later that month the president warned a group of Hispanic Americans at the White House: "If Central America is lost, then our borders will be threatened. . . . A faraway totalitarian power is committing enormous resources to change the strategic balance of the world by turning Central America into a string of anti-American, Soviet-styled dictatorships." That Russia was committing "enormous resources" to either the government of Nicaragua or the rebels of El Salvador was doubtful. War in Central America could involve the U.S.; it would not involve the U.S.S.R.

Even as the Reagan administration detected a Soviet danger wherever instability reigned, it shared the earlier assumption that economic weakness assured Russia's demise as a global threat. Time seemed to demonstrate that the Soviet Union could not afford both guns and butter; thus the Kremlin's decision to produce guns in profusion limited the growth of the civilian economy. Russia's economic progress, if substantial, had simply failed to match the far more impressive gains of the Western nations and Japan. Much of Russia's nonmilitary industry was decades behind that of the other industrialized countries. Russia's economic deficiencies were reflected in the bleak life style of the average Soviet consumer. Only in the military, where the Soviets spent some $200 billion a year, did the Soviet system work with some efficiency. Without its arsenal of nuclear weapons Russia would scarcely have the appearance of a superpower at all.

Russia had gained little in territory and international standing from its vast postwar military effort. It had no allies of importance; it could hardly trust its Eastern European satellites. Outside the Soviet sphere even small countries continued to stand up to the U.S.S.R. with surprising boldness. The concept of Finlandization assumed that the Russians could acquire dangerous influence over bordering states through the sheer magnitude of their military power, forcing those states to defer to Soviet wishes in a variety of ways. Actually Finlandization turned out to be an empty myth. The Soviets had almost no influence on the politics of Western Europe and Japan. They failed to establish the credibility of their power simply because neighboring countries doubted that the U.S.S.R. had sufficient interest in exerting such influence to threaten the use of force. So meager were the Soviet gains from the vast investment in military power that Kremlin leaders at times felt defrauded by their lack of success in achieving the prestige and influence that they believed would flow from their great power and wartime victories. Kremlin watchers saw danger not in the successes of Soviet expansionism but in its failure.

Russia's internal weaknesses sustained the Truman-Eisenhower predictions that, in the long run, Russia could not survive the combined political, economic, and military pressures of the Western World. William Clark, formerly Reagan's national security adviser, once termed the Soviet regime merely an evil episode in human history. Some Americans long regarded the notion of Russia's superpower status a myth sustained by Soviet propaganda. How could a country be a superpower, they wondered, if it could not feed and satisfy the basic needs of its own people? It was not strange that some American officials, journalists, and academicians argued that the United States could shape Russia's international behavior most assuredly by accelerating the demise of the Soviet system. As one American naval officer phrased it, "We must pursue policies which aggravate its condition until it bleeds to death from within."

President Reagan and his advisers shared such convictions. The higher levels of American preparedness, the president promised, would produce long-desired changes in Soviet policy. The "astonishing" failure of the Russian economy, he said, presaged "the march of freedom and democracy which [would] leave Marxism-Leninism on the ash heap of history." Haig would employ the issue of nuclear arms control, which touched Soviet interests directly, to modify the Kremlin's ambitions in the Third World and terminate its support for wars of national liberation. To speed the Russian collapse, the Reagan team would supplement the buildup of American power with a program to deny Russia the benefits of Western trade, credits, and technology. Convinced that the U.S. possessed the power to undermine the Soviet economy, White House adviser Richard Pipes of Harvard University, in opposing economic cooperation with the U.S.S.R., asserted that Washington should compel the Soviet Union "to bear the consequences of its own priorities. We should not make it easier for the [ruling apparatus] to have its cake and eat it; to maintain an inefficient system . . . and build up an aggressive military force and expand globally." More impatient Americans advocated a massive showdown to demonstrate Russian weakness and failure so dramatically that even the Kremlin leaders would have no choice but to acknowledge it. Such a crisis would compel the needed changes in Russia's outlook, ambition, and behavior, and at last resolve the Cold War on Western terms. That course of action, if successful, would indeed offer the most appealing solution for the Russian problem—its total elimination without war.

Such attitudes were not lost on Soviet leaders. "The Russians I spoke to," Thomas Powers reported after a trip to Moscow, "feel pushed and crowded." Russians argued that the Soviet Union had "proven it is a power in the world; why can't America accept this, and deal with it as an equal?" One Kremlin official reacted to the president's anti-Soviet rhetoric: "He offends our national pride. How can we deal with a man who calls us outlaws, criminals, and the source of evil in the world?" Soviet spokesmen complained that the U.S. had never accepted Russia's status as a great power with legitimate global interests of its own, never accorded the Soviet view of the world any genuine or consistent attention, never recognized Russia's strategic parity with the U.S. or acted on the proposition that the two powers would live together or die together on this planet. Russians pointed to the endless ring of military bases surrounding the U.S.S.R. from Japan to Norway. What troubled the Russians above all was the widespread American assumption that in time the U.S. could eliminate the U.S.S.R. from world politics without war. Critics wondered how there could be genuine, long-term coexistence without some acceptance of Soviet legitimacy. Yet that acceptance, complained former Senator J. William Fulbright in October 1983, the U.S. refused to grant. "We seem unable," he said, "to understand their history and culture. We have this tremendous lack of knowledge about them, and why they're so sensitive about their borders, so difficult to deal with. We refuse to accept the idea that we can't dominate them." Kenneth Dam, Reagan's deputy secretary of state, admitted that Washington, despite 35 years of Cold War, still knew and understood far too little about the Soviet Union.

In the long run, the U.S. faces the simple choice of eliminating the Soviet problem or coming to terms with it. The first alternative must lead to war because the West has no capacity to effect change in the Soviet system peacefully. If the U.S., despite successive and costly efforts, could not influence domestic conditions effectively in Vietnam, Iran, Lebanon, or El Salvador, it cannot do so in the Soviet Union. External economic pressure, however extreme, would demolish neither the Russian economy nor the Soviet political structure. The Moscow Politburo could experience an absolute economic decline over a period of years without collapsing. Whatever the cost of an arms race, Soviet leaders have the power to redeploy their country's economic resources, restrict civilian consumption, enforce internal discipline, and create the necessary external dangers to mount whatever arms program they might favor. Throughout history the Russian people have demonstrated an amazing capacity for patience and endurance.

This country possesses no coercive options to compel changes in Kremlin behavior. Economic sanctions extreme enough to produce some discomfiture in Russian society would meet strenuous opposition in both the United States and Western Europe among influential elements who would reject any infringements on their economic well-being, whether the issue be grain sales or the construction of the Russian-based natural-gas pipeline. Both the U.S. and its European allies face too many economic problems of their own, including massive deficits, to carry the burden of sanctions aimed at the U.S.S.R. The U.S. no longer possesses the industrial and technological predominance that once permitted it to promote and manage the affairs of the non-Soviet world with astonishing success. Three decades of obsessive concern with the Soviet Union distorted the American economy and caused the country to lose much of its industrial lead—the true foundation of its economic greatness—to others. What challenges American primacy in world affairs is less the power of the U.S.S.R. than the capacity of Western Europe and Japan to outstrip the U.S. in major areas of industrial efficiency.

This country's military establishment—the greatest in human history—is no more effective than its economy in coercing other nations. Largely unusable in the pursuit of day-to-day national objectives, American armaments could not remove the Russians from Afghanistan, the Cubans from Angola, or the Syrians from Lebanon. The price of attempting to do so would challenge the country's rationality. American power has failed to prevent a myriad of Soviet actions, many condemned as dangerous and unacceptable, which fell below the threshold of a credible counterstrategy. Even great powers dare not squander their energies and prestige or act militarily where the requirements of success are questionable. Ronald Steele has warned: "We can dissipate our power by expending it on unattainable ends, demean it by using it unjustly, and trivialize it by applying it capriciously."

If the U.S. cannot eliminate the Soviet system or determine the objectives that Russian leaders pursue, it must seek some accommodation. The improvement in Soviet-American relations, and with it the continued avoidance of war, demands above all the recognition of Russia's existence as a great power and the need to come to terms with it. When Washington took the Soviet Union seriously, Nikita Khrushchev once admonished the Senate Foreign Relations Committee, the two countries would get along. Perennial images of the Kremlin's global ambitions, mixed with images of Russian weakness and decay, have rendered negotiations either too dangerous or too inconsequential. To view Russia as an "evil empire" and to combine disapproval of specific Soviet behavior that touches no vital Western interest with public condemnation serves no recognizable national purpose. The hurling of international insults may please some Americans; it does not impress Europeans or Asians, perhaps not even a majority of this nation's citizens. It serves no greater national interest to transform animosity into closed communications bordering on nonrecognition. The nature of the Soviet power structure is irrelevant to the requirement of dealing openly and frankly with the Kremlin. "Like Mount Everest," wrote Meg Greenfield in September 1983, "the Russians are there. And, like Mount Everest, their features are not exactly a mystery. We need to stop gasping and sighing and exclaiming and nearly dying of shock every time something truly disagreeable happens. We have to grow up and confront them—as they are."

Negotiations between strong, determined powers are never easy. Accumulated fears and animosities render the task even more difficult. Yet, to avoid disaster, Soviet and American leaders must arrange some form of modus vivendi in the most literal sense. This might comprise explicit and verifiable treaties and agreements; it might entail written or unwritten understandings that define the limits of acceptable international behavior. We can only hope that in time the great powers can move beyond mere cohabitation of the planet toward more promising forms of cooperation, enabling the world to extend the possibilities of what has been one of the golden ages of history. The notion that the U.S. cannot and need not pursue such understandings reduces American foreign policy to the necessity of preparing the nation to fight the inevitable war under optimum conditions. Facing the narrow choice between accommodation and catastrophe, the government of the U.S. must travel the path to successful coexistence—not for a decade or even a century but for as long as human extinction is the possible price of war.